Performance as Research

UNIVERSITY OF
WINC~

Performance as Research (PAR) is characterised by an extraordinary elasticity and interdisciplinary drive. *Performance as Research: Knowledge, Methods, Impact* celebrates this energy, bringing together chapters from a wide range of disciplines and eight different countries. This volume focuses explicitly on three critical, often contentious themes that run through much discussion of PAR as a discipline:

- Knowledge – the areas and manners in which performance can generate knowledge;
- Methods – methods and methodologies for approaching performance as research;
- Impact – a broad understanding of the impact of this form of research.

These themes are framed by four essays from the book's editors, contextualising their interrelated conversations, teasing out common threads, and exploring the new questions that the contributions pose to the field of performance. As both an intervention into and extension of current debates, this is a vital collection for any reader concerned with the value and legitimacy of performance as research.

Annette Arlander is an artist, researcher, and pedagogue. She is currently principal investigator of the research project How to Do Things with Performance? and engaged in the project Performing with Plants.

Bruce Barton is a creator/scholar, Artistic Director of the interdisciplinary performance hub Vertical City, and Director of the School of Creative and Performing Arts, University of Calgary.

Melanie Dreyer-Lude is a director, actor, producer, and teacher. She is a resident producing artist at Civic Ensemble, Ithaca, and an Assistant Professor in the Department of Theatre and Dance, Missouri University.

Ben Spatz is author of *What a Body Can Do: Technique as Knowledge, Practice as Research* and editor of the videographic *Journal of Embodied Research*. They are currently Senio
Huddersfield.

Performance as Research

Knowledge, Methods, Impact

Edited by Annette Arlander, Bruce Barton, Melanie Dreyer-Lude, and Ben Spatz

Routledge
Taylor & Francis Group
LONDON AND NEW YORK

First edition published 2018
by Routledge
2 Park Square, Milton Park, Abingdon, Oxon, OX14 4RN

and by Routledge
711 Third Avenue, New York, NY 10017

Routledge is an imprint of the Taylor & Francis Group, an informa business

British Library Cataloguing-in-Publication Data
A catalogue record for this book is available from the British Library

Library of Congress Cataloging-in-Publication Data
Names: Arlander, Annette, 1956– editor. | Barton, Bruce, 1958– editor. | Dreyer-Lude, Melanie, editor. | Spatz, Ben, editor.
Title: Performance as research : knowledge, methods, impact / edited by Annette Arlander, Bruce Barton, Melanie Dreyer-Lude, and Ben Spatz.
Description: First edition. | New York : Routledge, 2017. | Includes bibliographical references.
Identifiers: LCCN 2017020995 | ISBN 9781138068704 (hardback) | ISBN 9781138068711 (pbk.) | ISBN 9781315157672 (ebook)
Subjects: LCSH: Performing arts—Research—Methodology.
Classification: LCC PN1576 .P43 2017 | DDC 790.2—dc23
LC record available at https://lccn.loc.gov/2017020995

ISBN: 978-1-138-06870-4 (hbk)
ISBN: 978-1-138-06871-1 (pbk)
ISBN: 978-1-315-15767-2 (ebk)

Typeset in Bembo
by Apex CoVantage, LLC

Contents

Figures

Contributors

Annette Arlander is an artist, researcher, and a pedagogue based in Helsinki. She received a diploma in theatre directing (1981), MA (philosophy) and DA (theatre and drama, 1999). She was professor of performance art and theory at Theatre Academy, Helsinki (2001–2013), head of the Performing Arts Research Centre (2007–2009), professor of artistic research and vice dean for research at University of the Arts Helsinki Theatre Academy (2015–2016), visiting professor at Stockholm University of the Arts (2015–2016), and professor of artistic research at Academy of Fine Arts, University of the Arts Helsinki (2016). At present she is engaged in the project Performing with Plants at the Helsinki Collegium for Advanced Studies. Arlander is a member of the editorial board of *JAR* (*Journal for Artistic Research*) and co-convener of the Artistic Research Working Group of Performance Studies International. She is the PI of the Academy of Finland-funded research project How to Do Things with Performance. Her research interests include artistic research, performance as research, performance studies, site-specificity, and the environment. Her artwork involves performing landscape by means of video or recorded voice, moving between performance art, video, and environmental art. For a full biography see https://annettearlander.com.

Bruce Barton is a creator/scholar whose practice-based research and teaching focus on physical dramaturgies in devised, immersive, and intermedial performance. He has published in a wide range of scholarly and practical periodicals, including *Performance Research*, *TDR*, *Theatre Journal*, *Theatre Topics*, *Canadian Theatre Review*, and *Theatre Research in Canada*, as well as numerous national and international essay collections. His book publications include *At the Intersection Between Art and Research* (2010), and *Collective Creation, Collaboration and Devising* (2008). Bruce is a co-convenor of the Performance as Research Working Group of the International Federation for Theatre Research, a co-convenor of the Artistic Research Working Group at Performance Studies international, and the artist relations officer on the PSi Board. Bruce is also an award-winning playmaker who works extensively as a director, writer, and dramaturg with many of Canada's most accomplished physical performance companies. He is the artistic director of Vertical City, an interdisciplinary performance hub located in Calgary. In January 2015, Bruce became the first director of the new School of Creative and Performing Arts at the University of Calgary. For a full biography see http://brucew barton.com/about-3/.

Yvon Bonenfant likes voices that do what voices don't usually do, and bodies that make technical virtuosities out of their 'flaws'. In 2012, his work took an interactive turn, investigating how we entice audiences to explore their own extra-normal voicings. His art, presentations, and publications have been supported by the AHRC, the British Academy, Arts Council England, EMPAC, and others; he has been Laureate of a Wellcome Trust Large Arts Award. His works have appeared in ten countries and he has published widely. Recently, he has begun experimenting with how we might render the aesthetic experience of queered vocal identity tactile; he co-developed Tract and Touch's voice-styling/hair-styling/touch-styling console *Curious Replicas* with vibration engineer Peter Glynne-Jones and coder Kingsley Ash. He is a professor of artistic process, voice and extended practices at the University of Winchester and artistic director of Tract and Touch.

Joanna Bucknall is a practitioner-scholar who has been making theatre, live art, performance art, durational works, and immersive performance since 2004. Her research interests include PBR methodologies, lively approaches to performance documentation, immersive/interactive dramaturgies, and embodied approaches to reception studies. She makes work that is audience-centric; immediate, intimate, and interactive. She currently works with two performance companies: KeepHouse Performance and Vertical Exchange Performance Collective. She is an associate artist at the New Theatre Royal (NTR) in Portsmouth. In the past she has worked with Fierce, The Barbican in Plymouth, Camden People's Theatre, The Basement in Brighton, Performing Arts Centre Lincoln, Brighton Fringe Festival, and Battersea Arts Centre. She is the creator of Talking About Immersive Theatre (TAIT). TAIT is a podcast series that hosts interviews with immersive and interactive theatre makers, producers, and performers working mostly in the UK.

Melanie Dreyer-Lude currently serves as Associate Professor and Coordinator of Theatre Studies in the Department of Theatre and Dance at Missouri State University. She is the former co-artistic director of ShatterMask Theatre (St. Louis) and International Culture Lab (New York City), and has been directing professionally for 25 years in many venues both domestic and abroad. She recently returned from Berlin, Germany, on a Fulbright Fellowship, where she investigated Germany's response to the current refugee crisis. Fluent in German, Dreyer-Lude translates and directs contemporary German plays that have been produced in the United States and Canada. She has been a passionate advocate and participant in PAR practice since 2007. Currently, she is exploring collaborative projects with artists in Kampala, Uganda.

Carla Fernandes holds a PhD in cognitive linguistics. She was an Assistant Professor at IPLeiria until 2007, and is currently working as Principal Investigator and Invited Professor at FCSH – Universidade Nova de Lisboa. She was awarded a European Research Council grant for her interdisciplinary project BlackBox, a collaborative platform to document performance composition from conceptual structures in the backstage to customizable visualizations in the front-end, running under her direction at FCSH-UNL from 2014 to 2019. At present her research focus is in the intersection of arts and cognition, multimodal communication, new media, and the performing arts (from cognitive and ethnographic perspectives). Particular interests include the analysis of multimodal corpora and their relevance for the creation of digital "archives of processes," as alternative ways to document ephemeral art forms, such as contemporary dance. She is the author of book chapters and papers in international journals and conferences in the fields of multimodal communication, performance studies, digital media, and intangible heritage.

Manola K. Gayatri is a praxis-oriented writer, researcher, artist, and teacher. She is currently Postdoctoral Fellow in the Drama Department of University of Pretoria and Visiting Faculty at Ambedkar University, Delhi, at Centre for Development Practice. She received her doctorate in theatre and performance studies at the School of Arts and Aesthetics, Jawaharlal Nehru University, where she traced a feminist genealogy of women's poetic utterance. She was a postdoctoral project partner in the UGC-UKIERI project "Gendered Citizenship: Manifestations and Performance" (University of Warwick and JNU). She is co-founder of TILT, The Institute of Leadership and Transformation, based in Pretoria, and will be convener of the Performance-as-Research Working Group of the International Federation for Theatre Research from July 2017. As an artistic researcher she has presented work at national and international conferences in India, the UK, Italy, Germany, South Africa, Sweden, and other places.

Yelena Gluzman is a theatre and film director, scholar, and editor. Since 1999, she has made numerous "science projects" – performances that experimentally explore the conditions of encounter in theatre. Her recent work on academic methods of knowledge production includes a collaborative reading project called *Feminist Theory Theatre* (In *Imagined Theatres*, ed. Daniel Sack, 2017). Yelena is a founding editor at Ugly Duckling Presse, and edits both *Emergency INDEX* and the *Emergency Playscripts* series (*Emergency INDEX Vol. 6* and Annie Dorsen's *A Piece of Work* are forthcoming in 2017). She holds an MFA in theatre directing from Columbia University and is currently working towards a PhD in communication and science studies at UC San Diego. She is the recipient of a Making & Doing Award (with Sarah

Klein) from the Society for Social Studies of Science (2015), an Interdisciplinary Award from the UCSD Graduate Students Association (2016), and a Frontiers of Innovation Scholars Program (FISP) award.

Pil Hansen is an Assistant Professor of Dance and Drama at the University of Calgary, a founding member of Vertical City Performance, and a dance/devising dramaturg. Her empirical and PAR experiments examine cognitive dynamics of memory and perception in creative processes. She developed the tool-set "Perceptual Dramaturgy" and, with Bruce Barton, the interdisciplinary research model "Research-Based Practice." Hansen has dramaturged 26 works and her scholarly research is published in *TDR: The Drama Review, Performance Research, Journal of Dramatic Theory and Criticism, Connection Science, Theatre Topics, Canadian Theatre Review, Peripiti, Koreografisk Journal, MAPA D2*, and 11 essay collections. Hansen is primary editor of *Dance Dramaturgy: Modes of Agency, Awareness and Engagement* (2015) and *Performing the Remembered Present: The Cognition of Memory in Dance, Theatre and Music* (2017). Current and recent artistic collaborators are: Kaeja d'Dance, Theatre Junction Grand, Toronto Dance Theatre, and Public Recordings.

Jonathan Heron is IATL Deputy Director and a Principal Teaching Fellow at the University of Warwick, where he specialises in interdisciplinary practice. He was previously Research Associate at the CAPITAL Centre (a collaboration with the Royal Shakespeare Company) and Youth Arts Leader at Pegasus Oxford, during their fiftieth anniversary. He co-founded Fail Better Productions in 2001, the Student Ensemble in 2009, and the Samuel Beckett Laboratory (at Trinity College Dublin) in 2013. He co-convened the International Federation for Theatre Research 'Performance-as-Research' working group (2013–16) and co-established the 'Modernism, Medicine and Embodied Mind' AHRC-funded network (with Bristol University). His academic research has been published in the *Journal of Beckett Studies* (2014), *Shakespeare on the University Stage* (2015), *Medical Humanities* (British Medical Journals, 2016), and *Research in Drama Education: The Journal of Applied Theatre and Performance* (2017).

Stephan Jürgens holds a PhD in contemporary choreography and new media technologies. His research interests concentrate on designing creative strategies for live performance involving interactive systems. He has been teaching movement research, interdisciplinary choreography, and interactive system design. As a choreographer he has presented several works supported by the Portuguese Ministry of Culture. His collaborative digital performance work *.txt* won the national multimedia prize in 2010. He is the author of several peer-reviewed papers and book chapters. As a core researcher of the ERC-funded *BlackBox project*, Stephan is collaboratively exploring the intersection of the performing arts with the newest digital media technologies to support software development assisting creative processes and performance composition. More concretely, his focus is on the "translation" of artistic conceptual structures in the work of selected artists into the software architecture of a novel collaborative platform to be built during the course of the project.

Baz Kershaw is Emeritus Professor of Theatre and Performance at University of Warwick. An engineer before gaining English, philosophy, and drama degrees from Manchester, Hawaii, and Exeter Universities, he has been visiting researcher at several universities abroad and keynote speaker at many international conferences. He directed PARIP (Practice as Research in Performance, 2000–06), the first major research initiative/enquiry for performing arts as research. Projects as a practitioner in experimental, community, and radical theatre include shows at the legendary London Drury Lane Arts Lab, with Ann Jellicoe's Colway Theatre Trust and Welfare State International, plus since 2000 several eco-specific events in southwest England. His many publications include *The Politics of Performance* (1992), *The Radical in Performance* (1999), *Cambridge History of British Theatre Vol. 3 Since 1895, Theatre Ecology* (2007), and (with Helen Nicholson) *Research Methods in Theatre and Performance* (2011). In 2010 he set up an Earthrise Repair Shop that aims to mend broken imaginings of Earth.

Shana MacDonald is an Assistant Professor in the Department of Drama and Speech Communication at the University of Waterloo. Her research examines the intersections between cinema, performance, screen-based installation, and public art with a focus on historical and contemporary feminist experimental media. This work is closely aligned with her practice as an internationally screened filmmaker, curator, and installation artist. She is founder and director of the 'Mobile Art Studio' (MAS), a transitory creative lab space that brings art out of the gallery and into public participatory spaces. Her artistic research is committed to finding new aesthetic forms for abandoned and undervalued materials, experiences, and histories. She has recent publications in *Performance Research, Media Fields, Feminist Media Histories,* and the *Canadian Journal of Film Studies.*

Juan Manuel Aldape Muñoz is concerned about choreographic processes, latinidad, undocumented bodies, and sweat citizenships. He is a co-organizer of the Festival of Latin American Contemporary Choreographers, as well as the e-resource convener for the International Federation for Theatre Research's Performance as Research working group. He is the co-founder of A PerFarmance Project, site-specific collaborations between farmers and performers researching the concept of food security and labour. For ten years, he was a member of the improvisational dance company Movement Forum. He is a PhD student in the performance studies program at UC Berkeley (US) and he holds an MA in international performance research from the University of Warwick (UK).

Laurelann Porter is currently an Assistant Professor of Communication Arts at Benedictine University. She received her PhD in theatre and performance of the Americas from Arizona State University. She earned her BFA in independent theatre studies from Boston University and her MFA in playwriting from Arizona State University. Her current research project is a collaboration with Brazilian dancer and choreographer Mestre Monza Calabar. Their work together seeks to explore the possibilities of teaching Afro-Brazilian histories and epistemologies through dance, movement, crafts, and culinary arts. Porter is also a playwright and solo performer. "Sympathy for Exú" is the newest product of her creative practice. The solo piece incorporates elements of Afro-Brazilian mythologies, in particular stories of the trickster figure, Exú. Her current playwriting project is a collaboration with a nursing scholar and fellow ethnographer, Dr Amy Funk. The project, "27 listeners" is based on Funk's dissertation research on sibling grief.

Monica Sand is a Swedish artist and artistic researcher with a PhD in architecture from the School of Architecture, the Royal Institute of Technology in 2008. During 2009–11 she was a postdoc at the University College of Arts Crafts and Design (Konstfack). Since 2011 Sand has been employed as a researcher and research-coordinator at the Swedish Centre for Architecture and Design in Stockholm. In both artistic practice and research as well as through courses in art and architecture, Sand stages spatial and collective experiments as a method to form and perform artistic research. With the long-term research project *Playing the Space* her aim is to compose and recompose urban rhythms and resonances through playful events in collaboration with sound-artists, dancers, musicians, students, researchers, and urban planners. https://playingthespace.wordpress.com.

Göze Saner is an actor, a practitioner-researcher, and a lecturer at the Department of Theatre and Performance, Goldsmiths, University of London. She studied philosophy at Bryn Mawr College and completed a practice-based PhD on archetype and performance at Royal Holloway, University of London. She has trained and performed internationally, with Bilsak Tiyatro Atölyesi led by Nihal Koldaş, with the Quick and the Dead led by Alison Hodge, with the New Winds led by Iben Nagel Rasmussen, and with her own company, cafila aeterna. *Göçmen Adımlar/Migrant Steps*, a community theatre project where she worked with groups of Turkish-speaking migrant women in the UK and Europe, won a Walk21 Walking Visionaries Jury Prize and continues with workshops in different public contexts. Investigating how the actor's work can be disseminated remotely to non-actors, Göze is currently developing a DIY *Migrant Steps* toolkit.

Valentina Signore is a freelance architect and Research Fellow in the Faculty of Architecture at KU Leuven. She gained a PhD in urban studies from the Università degli Studi di Roma Tre with the dissertation *The Performative*

Project: How to Recognise and Interpret It (2013). As a postdoc researcher she participated in the EU-funded project ADAPT-r, where she studied more than 20 creative practices and their practice researches. Valentina investigates research as a creative practice, focusing on the design of its artefacts as research outputs. She has contributed a chapter to the volume *Performative Urbanism Generating and Designing Urban Space* (Munich: Jovis, 2014) and is professionally trained in shiatsu.

Ben Spatz is Senior Lecturer in Drama, Theatre and Performance at the University of Huddersfield; author of *What a Body Can Do: Technique as Knowledge, Practice as Research* (2015); convener of the Embodied Research Working Group within the International Federation for Theatre Research; editor of the *Journal of Embodied Research*, a peer-reviewed videographic journal launched in 2017; and Arts & Humanities Research Council Leadership Fellow (2016–2018) with the project 'Judaica: An Embodied Laboratory for Song-Action'. Recent talks and workshops include 'What Is a Song?' (The British Library), 'Beyond Performer Training' (University of Kent), 'An Epistemic Context for Martial Arts' (University of Cardiff), 'Decolonizing Song-Action: A Laboratory Report' (Maynooth University), 'Re-Reading Grotowski in the Anthropocene' (University of the Arts Helsinki), and 'Future Documents: Video Epistemology and Embodied Research' (University of Manchester).

Acknowledgements

The editors wish to acknowledge the core influence of the Performance as Research Working Group of the International Federation for Theatre Research (FIRT/IFTR) in the endeavour of creating this book. Many, but not all, contributions in this volume are made by members or visitors of the working group. After initial meetings at conferences in Amsterdam (2002) and St. Petersburg (2005), organised by the first convenors Baz Kershaw and Jacqueline Martin, the group had its first official meeting at the IFTR conference in Helsinki (2006) and has since met at every yearly conference. We want to thank the subsequent convenors of the working group, not contributing to this volume, Anna Birch, Mark Fleishman, Emma Meehan and Johnmichael Rossi, for developing the practices and discourses around performance as research and for supporting publication endeavours. We want to extend our gratitude to all presenters and participants over the years, some of whom joined the group for one conference, while others have participated in most of the meetings, here listed in alphabetical order (with apologies for any unintended omissions):

Cynthia Asperger, Jane Bacon, Paul Barker, Stefanie Bauerochse, Annouchka Bayley, Matteo Bonfitto, June Boyce-Tillman, Mari Boyd, Marie-Louise Crawley, Alison Curtis-Jones, Flavia D'Avila, Chloé Déchery, Maria Ni Dubhain, Natalia Duong, Natalia Esling, Rakel Ezpeleta, Robert Faguy, Angie Farrow, Anna Fenemore, Ciane Fernandes, Kristin Fredricksson, David Furnham, Bree Hadley, Kristina Hagström-Ståhl, Daniela Hahn, Dorita Hannah, Luciana Hartmann, I Lien Ho, Ali Hodge, Carolien Hermans, Pauliina Hulkko, Tomi Humalisto, Lynette Hunter, Mark Hunter, Kathleen Irwin, Ola Johansson, Esa Kirkkopelto, Anu Koskinen, May Agnes Krell, Annelis Kuhlmann, Soile Lahdenperä, Karen Lauke, Jean Lee, Peilin Liang, Alys Longley, Holly Maples, David Mason, Marina Marcondes Machado, Junghwa Mah, Jiao Yin Mei, Nando Messias, Roberta Mock, Tero Nauha, Tessa Needham, Ursula Neuerburger Denzer, Helen Newall, Ludimila Mota Nunes, Richard O'Brien, Dan Olsen, Elaine O'Sullivan, Kjell Yngve Petersen, Diego Pizarro, Pilvi Porkola, Stephen Purcell, Lucia Repasska, Walmeri Ribeiro, Alison Richards, Helen Richardsson, Elisabeth de Roza, Judith Rudakoff, Stefanie Sachsenmaier, Paula Salosaari, Cibele Sastre, Christina Schmutz, Marianne Sharp, Lena Simic, Jaqui Singer,

Karin Sondergaard, Zoe Svendsen, Mark Swetz, Mary Tarantino, Mark Tatlow, Myer Taub, Mariana Terra, Liz Tomlin, James Wilson, Harry Wilson, Viktoria Volkova, Martin Wylde, and Abd Latif Zaina.

The editors also wish to thank the contributors for their patience during the publication process; editorial assistant Natalia Esling and University of Calgary graduate research assistants, Sarah Bannister and Adrian Young, for their invaluable help in preparing the manuscript for submission; and our editors at Routledge, Kate Edwards and Ben Piggott, for their professionalism and skill in producing this volume.

Wherefore PAR?

Discussions on "a line of flight"

Bruce Barton

Perhaps it will come across as contrarian to begin the introduction to a volume of essays with the primary title *Performance as Research* with a refusal to attempt to define performance as research (PAR). However, PAR, in all its many permutations, has often been the domain of good-natured and well-intentioned contrarians, and in this regard the present volume continues a firmly established tradition. Certainly, in a number of ways this publication adopts structures and strategies that will be familiar for readers acquainted with previous essay collections on this and related topics. The voices gathered here are similarly (if not more so) diverse in terms of geography, culture, and artistic discipline, as well as in their relationship to embodied practice and institutional affiliation. However, this collection also attempts, both directly and through nuance, some distinct departures from earlier collections that we hope will be productively facilitative, rather than (merely) provocative. These include most explicitly the points of individual focus named in its subtitle, but also an attempt to both recognize and establish sites of connection, juxtaposition, and intersection between conspicuously diverse approaches to an undeniably diversified field of research.

It will be useful here to trace the trajectory of this volume back to its inception. Its birthplace was the Performance as Research Working Group of the International Federation for Theatre Research (IFTR), which has met annually since its first gathering in 2006, then under the stewardship of Baz Kershaw and Jacqueline Martin. In 2013 the Working Group (then convened by Annette Arlander along with Jonathan Heron and Emma Meehan) established a publications subcommittee made up of the other three editors of this volume (Barton, Dreyer-Lude, and Spatz). Thus, as editors we were gathered within the pre-established context of the Working Group's self-designation as a PAR organization, including that group's congregate, historically evolving understandings of what PAR is and can be. Seeking to both honor and exploit that context but also to push the discourse beyond prior publications on the topic, we drafted an uncommonly detailed, even prescriptive open call for proposals. The resulting collection thus includes entries by some of the Working Group's longstanding members as well as many new voices from around the globe. Further, in this CFP we aimed to both acknowledge existing perspectives and chart an extended trajectory through the distinct yet interrelated categories of *knowledge*, *methods*, and *impact*. As stated in the open call,

> In order to make meaningful contributions to an academic environment that increasingly prioritizes interdisciplinary social and political inquiry, does PAR need to demonstrate not only rigorous application of methodologies and documentation strategies, but also substantive results? What form might these results take? Beyond performative "symbolic data" – which only increases in artistic value through ambiguity and openness to interpretation – must PAR generate more conventionally accessible and less ambiguous results? Must these results satisfy the criteria more commonly associated with other forms of research activity, such as *outcomes, impact, utility, circulation, transmissibility*, and *transferability*? To what degree, and in what ways, should the established criteria of *knowledge production* determine and shape the potential of PAR activity, currently and in the coming decades? How might PAR practitioners advocate for expanded and refined engagement with a diverse range of fields of knowledge – somatic, kinesthetic, and phenomenological, in addition to more traditional analytical and empirical models – as a means of extending the potential of PAR validity and relevance?

These questions reflect a set of priorities shared by all of the volume's editors. Our common goal was to court both an expansive disciplinary range and a distinct degree of specificity in terms of critical articulation: "We welcome proposals addressing PAR processes and projects drawn from a broad, thoroughly interdisciplinary spectrum, and from both academic and non-institutional contexts. All proposals should be grounded in specific creative, artistic, and/ or embodied practices. Further, all proposals should reflect the authors' careful and explicit reflection on the key considerations detailed above: (1) *contextual disciplines or fields of knowledge*; (2) *methods and/or methodologies*; and (3) *results of the research*."

Despite this solidarity, however, and despite the real pleasure we take in working with one another, I think it is safe to say that the four of us have quite different relationships with PAR, both in terms of our own practices and in terms of the now extensive existing scholarship in this area. No doubt, then, both the preconceptions with which we entered this publication project and the explicit individual contributions we have made to its pages reflect this heterogeneity – as does the somewhat unorthodox decision to punctuate the volume with no fewer than four separate 'introductions,' each of which asserts a distinct and characteristic orientation on our shared topic. Even within the confines of a small sub-committee of a focused Working Group within a single scholarly association, PAR remains a conspicuously elusive idea – at precisely the same time that it is passionately advocated.

These same two characteristics of PAR as it relates to artistic practice – its elusive nature and its passionate pursuit – are in ample evidence throughout the essays contained in this volume. Arguably, a call for proposals organized under the rubric of practice as research, practice-based research, practice-led research, or any number of other affiliated designations would have attracted a similarly diverse set of submissions – possibly from many of the same authors. Despite the many concerted and worthy efforts by practitioners and scholars to stake claims, delimit territories, and define jurisdictions, the research conducted under the banner of performance as research is almost inevitably *congregate*, even aquisitory (as in "seeking to acquire and own, often greedily" [Dictionary.com]) in terms of its engagement with both methods and methodology. Thus, while attempts to distinguish between multiple categories of related activity (PAR, PaR, PBR, etc.) are often successful in differentiating *theoretically* between pre-liminary motivations, methodological priorities, institutional contexts, and geographic locations, the same designations are only occasionally respected neatly or simply by the research activity itself. This situation in no way diminishes the importance of these efforts towards definitions, which are critical acts that serve (at least) the twinned necessities of personal self-reflection and institutional self-validation. But these same circumstances assert additional obligations, within such a highly diversified and mutable field of activity, towards more locally oriented and specifically focused articulation.

This introductory essay – as noted, the first of four – is one attempt among several within this volume to imagine and perform strategies to fulfill this obligation of focused articulation. As also noted, our establishment of three key areas of emphasis was among our earliest and most explicit gestures in this regard. Co-editor Melanie Dreyer-Lude's astute and attentive cross-referencing of key tropes, preoccupations, and structural elements (Introduction II) across all the entries in the collection is another. Ben Spatz's intentionally (if benevolently) provocative querying of the very possibility of PAR (Introduction III), with its insistence on a much needed if uncommon precision of terminology, is another. And Annette Arlander's thoroughly informed and contextualized speculation on future developments (Introduction IV), which seeks to position PAR within a broader assessment of the "performative turn," is yet another. For my part, I propose that the path to higher levels of precision in articulation requires an initial, perhaps counter-intuitive concession to *generalization* as a process of *distillation*, and the use of a broader brush as a means towards a common basis from which key entry points and appropriate frames of reference for more narrowly defined specificity may be determined.

To this end, my strategy in this essay is to expand my focus by one full layer in the discourse, to leave the discussion of PAR's specificity to other voices in this collection and to open up the conversation more widely in an effort to enclose PAR within an embrace that also includes the many orientations towards knowledge discovery/creation with which it is often affiliated. This is certainly not to assert that there aren't significant distinctions at the level of methodological specificity between, for instance, performance as research and practice as research (an issue Spatz's contribution directly addresses), or between either of these approaches and practice-led research or research-led practice. Rather, my proposal is that, for the purposes of this introduction, they may be effectively carried forward as a congregate (rather than a collapsed or conflated) *field* of research activity.

The first challenge offered by this approach is determining how to refer to this meta-grouping of research orientations in a manner that is sufficiently both circumscribed *and* elastic. We could return to one of the earliest and most influential research projects in this field and use the designation practice as research in performance (see my discussion of the UK-based PARIP project, ahead). This gesture addresses, at least in part, the commonly perceived tension between 'performance' and 'practice' as the primary correlate to 'research,' and would certainly be adequate to describe the majority of the activity addressed within this volume. However, the much-discussed implications of placing "as" between performance or practice and research continue to evoke a binary relationship between these primary terms – one that is at times accurate and productive but as often imprecise and distracting. Therefore, for the purpose of this introduction I propose the blanket designation "artistic research in performance" (ARP). "Artistic research" as a pre-existing categorization is, of course, not free from associated preconceptions or regional specificity, but combined with an explicit reference to performance it would seem to offer the most effective combination of flexibility, inclusivity, and precision for what I am attempting in this writing.

The first step in this attempt towards articulation is to frame an understanding of artistic research (AR), generally. As Arlander suggests in her concluding introduction in this volume, AR is perhaps most effectively understood as a field comprising multiple more or less methodologically singular and/or stable subfields, an intentionally inclusive category that enfolds a diverse set of research activities that employ artistic or creative practice as an integrated aspect of the inquiry process. There is substantial and significant scholarship in this field; there is also increasing scholarly and professional activity on an international level that asserts AR's priorities and endeavors to advance its practices. However, the field remains a highly disparate one, both challenged and energized by a multiplicity of definitions, interpretations, and applications. This diversity is one of the field's explicit strengths, requiring a collective openness to alternative perspectives, development, and growth. The same diversity, however, is also the primary cause of the relatively ambiguous profile and at times tenuous status of AR within many institutional *and* professional artistic contexts.

Effectively, then, AR can be employed as an "umbrella concept" that captures "a landscape of various approaches to knowledge production in performing arts" (Arlander 2009, 77). Following this line of argument, AR can be understood as consisting of a diversity of more narrowly focused and defined methodological approaches, including but not limited to the following.

Performance as research (here referred to as PAR)
Practice as research (PaR)

Practice-based research (PBR)
Practice-led research (PLR)
Arts-based research (ABR)
Research-led practice (RLP)
Research-based practice (RBP)
Research practice (RP)
Research through practice (RtP)
Research creation (RC)
Creative research (CR)
Studio research (SR)

Some of these subcategories (a less than exhaustive list) reflect precise and strategic differentiations – between, for instance, *practice-led research*, the results of which can be fully communicated through written documentation, and *practice-based research*, the results of which cannot be fully comprehended without direct access to the creative products and processes of its incorporated practices (Candy 2006, 3). However, the distinctions between many of these approaches – between, for instance, research practice, research through practice, research creation, and creative research – are often elusive, nuanced, and context-specific, making confident and reliable communication and exchange difficult across (and, indeed, within) geographic, cultural, institutional, and disciplinary borders. Indeed, as noted earlier, 'PaR' is often used for both performance as research and practice as research – a practice evident within some of the entries in this volume. For clarity, I have here adopted the distinctions offered by Lynette Hunter – PAR for performance as research and PaR for practice as research – but for other writers the gesture of merging the two orientations within a single acronym ranges from unwitting to incidental to intentional. In contrast, my gesture here of resorting to "artistic research" is in no way meant to avoid or discount these important sites of precision (and equally significant sites of imprecision or conflation), but rather to identify a set of common attributes on a meta level across virtually all of these epistemological orientations.

One important criterion, however, is established by returning, full-circle, to the combination of AR with *performance* in our working concept of "artistic research in performance" (ARP). For instance: despite adopting a pronounced level of inclusivity, for the purposes of this introduction ARP here does not include arts-informed research – "a mode and form of qualitative research that is influenced by, but not based in, the arts" (MacCallum 2016). Similarly, while several of the sub-categories identified earlier have firmly established histories and profiles within a wide range of non-artistic disciplinary contexts – including social work, nursing/medicine, and design – my reflections in this essay focus predominantly on the application of AR to the performing arts (within the admittedly broad parameters of interdisciplinarity discussed ahead). Perhaps more controversially, I am also excluding personal artistic inquiry – a sub-category particularly susceptible to multiple interpretations but here understood as localized individual development conducted without the intention to communicate or share results beyond those individuals immediately participating. This extended gesture of transmission, effecting a transfer of utility, is here considered a baseline characteristic of ARP.

At the risk of overstatement: I offer ARP here as a congregate concept, one that focuses on global commonalities among its constituent practices while respecting the distinctiveness of each. None of the authors cited here use "artistic research in performance" in their discussions; as such, in each of the contexts to which I refer to ARP where a cited author originally focuses on one of these constituents – for example, PAR, PaR, and PBR – I specify that original research orientation in parentheses: for example, 'ARP (sp. performance as research)' or 'ARP (sp. practice-based research).' My intention here is not the erasure of differences but rather the identification of key shared characteristics.

I offer this gesture of generalization-amidst-difference as a cautious but direct reflection of the experience I have benefited from in multiple contexts where the elusive relationship between practice, performance, and research was/is being teased out and sorted. In addition to participating in the IFTR PAR Working Group, I had the privilege of working as a founding member of the Practice-Based Research Study Circle at the Nordic Summer University in Northern Europe, where I provided a modest editorial contribution to *At the Intersection Between Art and Research: Practice-Based Research in the Performing Arts* (Friberg, Parekh-Gaihede, and Barton 2010), the essay collection that emerged from the first three-year cycle of that group's collaboration. The section titles in Sidsel Pape's introduction to that volume make explicit the negotiations of terminology that characterized the Study Circle's deliberations: "Expanding the Field," "Our Linguistic Journey," and "Multiple Viewpoints" (2010, 9–12). I attended as a core member for nearly ten years the now-defunct Performance as Research Working Group at the American Society for Theatre Research (ASTR), an uncommonly and unfailingly heterogeneous gathering of kindred spirits from diverse locations, backgrounds, paradigms, and institutional contexts. I have participated in the Artistic Research Working Group of Performance Studies international (PSi), having recently become the group's co-convenor as well as the Artist Relations Officer on the PSi board, with responsibility for the AR component of that organization's annual conference programming. In Canada I am the founding convenor of the "Articulating Artistic Research" Seminar at the annual conference of the Canadian Association for Theatre Research (CATR), which marked its fifth gathering in 2017, and for a decade I was responsible for the core master's- and PhD-level courses in praxis (practice-based research) at the University of Toronto's Centre for Drama, Theatre and Performance Studies. These many sites of encounter have continually shaped my understanding(s) of the overlaps and divergences, intersections and inter-weavings, complementarities and antipathies that animate the global ARP conversation.

As also noted earlier, the available literature on PAR, PaR, and related research orientations here enfolded into ARP has burgeoned over the past two decades, a reflection of the increasing occurrence and diversity of approaches and priorities. Within this scholarship, articulating precisely what ARP, broadly defined, constitutes remains a topic of animated discussion. Is it a "methodology" (Hannula et al. 2014), a "discipline" or "species" (Barrett and Bolt 2007, 1), a "paradigm" (Jones 2009, 19; Bolt 2016) or "pre-paradigm" (or "non-paradigm") (Kjørup 2012, 36), an "anti-discipline" (Kershaw and Nicholson 2011, 3), or a colonization of traditional research practice by artistic priorities (Klein 2010)? Yet what unites virtually all variants of ARP is an explicit – if at times reluctant – investment in baseline criteria for defining research within institutionalized academic contexts. Foremost among these criteria are *documentation*, *dissemination*, and *utility* through *transferability*. While these criteria represent challenges within virtually all artistic disciplines, the performing arts, with their reliance on embodied practice, interpretive subjectivity, and immediate experience, are particularly vulnerable in this regard. Peggy Phelan's now-legendary assertion, almost a quarter century ago, that performance "becomes itself through disappearance" (Phelan 1993, 146) provided both an enduring conceptual pivot for artistic practice and a dogged impediment in the process of securing ARP's place in the academy. Phelan's highly influential prioritizing of the *ephemerality* of performance ensured that the status of ARP would be both fraught and complicated within conventional processes of institutional recognition, analysis, evaluation, and accreditation.

Not surprisingly, then, this anxiety about institutional validation has been a formative preoccupation within efforts to establish and articulate ARP as a legitimate field of activity. This process of self-justification – what Hawkins and Wilson (2016) term "special pleadings" – is at times interpreted as a galvanizing source of solidarity amid diversity; at others, however, it is experienced as an unresolvable if inevitable distraction, one which holds the potential to constrain and even distort ARP's potential for discovery. Shannon Jackson's carefully considered response to the question "when is art research?" is, in part, "to suggest that we need not be 'governed quite so much' or at least, 'not quite like that'" (2009, 163); however, such permissions are as rare as they are hard won. Within the performing arts, this tension is clearly evident in one of the earliest, most significant, and commonly recognized ARP-oriented initiatives, already referenced earlier: Practice as Research in Performance (PARIP), a five-year research project hosted by the University of Bristol from 2001 to 2006. Explicitly named in PARIP's key Aims and Objectives was the need to "develop knowledges about appropriate criteria for evaluation," as well as consultation "on a series of creative projects [. . .] to advance potential uses of new digital technologies for the documentation and dissemination of best practices" ("Overview"). While the emerging capacities of new media resulted in an impressive gallery of research "Artefacts," a dominant strain throughout much of the extant PARIP documentation relates to the "inherent paradox" (Rye 2003) offered by digital recording's deceiving efficiency. "How, then," queried PARIP participant Angela Piccini, is this type of research best identified, evidenced and disseminated, if we accept that the academy will continue to demand such activity? And when these research knowledges are translated into other media what are the best ways to indicate, in the translation, what knowledges are lost or gained?

(Piccini 2002)

Arguably, this ambivalence about the potential distortion of documentation in relation to the performing arts represents a central, complicating trope in any effort to articulate modes of ARP, one that endures in many contexts through to the present moment (e.g., considerable time at the 2015 gathering of the IFTR PAR Working Group was dedicated to the question "Why document?"). This is the case despite significant advances in complex understandings of liveness, particularly within intermedial performance contexts (see, e.g., Auslander 1999/2008; Barton 2008, 2009; Barton, Dreyer-Lude and Birch 2013; Birringer 2008, 2015; Dixon 2007, 2016; Scott 2016). However, much of the literature produced on approaches to ARP in the years following the PARIP initiative – such as the persuasive example offered by Stephan Jürgens and Carla Fernandes in this volume – engages with this perceived dilemma of articulation, reflecting significant advances in its framing, comprehension, and resolution.

Significant among early twentieth-century efforts to broker the apparently paradoxical demands discussed earlier was that offered by Henk Borgdorff, who positioned ARP (sp. artistic research) squarely between the priorities of academia on the one hand and those found within art professions on the other. At that intersection, he proposes, AR can address "questions that are pertinent in the research context and in the art world" (2006, 10). Thus, for Borgdorff, while AR attempts to "articulate the tacit knowledge that is situated and embodied in specific artworks and artistic processes," it nonetheless employs "experimental and hermeneutic methods" and its "processes and outcomes are documented and disseminated in an appropriate manner to the research community and the wider public" (2006, 18). In stark contrast, in the same publication year Brad Haseman asserted the need for ARP (sp. performance as research) to push past conventional interpretations of practice-led research to what he proposed as "performative research." Drawing on J.L. Austin's proposal of *performative utterances* (1962), Haseman advocates for research models that eschew problems or questions as starting points, substituting "an enthusiasm of practice" (Haseman 2006, 3) as both catalyst and motivation. Further, and most significantly, Haseman promotes research practices that insist "that their research outputs and claims to knowing must be made through the symbolic language and forms of their practice" (ibid., 4). (I will return to the 'performative turn' as a conceptual framework later in this introduction; the same topic is picked up again in detail in Arlander's concluding introduction.)

It could be argued that most attempts to explain ARP locate themselves, regardless of whether intentionally, along a continuum between Borgdorff's and Haseman's proposals, as both provide, explicitly and implicitly, three key points of entry into the discussion from which to frame a position: *knowledge*: ARP's distinct and potentially expansive epistemological horizons; *methods*: ARP's application of and status within the network of existing methodological orientations to research; and *impact*: ARP's conflicted and contentious relationship with outcomes, products, results, applications, and utility. Many of the essays in this collection also explicitly address these same porous categories, and certainly all engage with them, often no less thoroughly, on an implicit level. It is not my intention, therefore, to attempt some sort of exhaustive survey or authoritative assessment of the status of these elements within the many variants of ARP or its discourse, but rather to delineate what I see as some of the most pertinent of attributes across a wide spectrum of artistic research orientations.

Knowledge

Virtually all articulations of PAR and related approaches to ARP, not surprisingly, seek their co-ordinates through a relationship to the production of *knowledge*. Regularly referenced as a starting point in this process is the *OECD Glossary of Statistical Terms* (2008, qtd. in Klein 2010, 1), which defines research as "any creative systematic activity undertaken in order to increase the stock of knowledge, including knowledge of man, culture and society, and the use of this knowledge to devise new applications." Estelle Barrett and Barbara Bolt preface their exploration of the specifics of ARP (sp. artistic research) with the generalized proposal that "artistic practice be viewed as the production of knowledge or philosophy in action" with "the potential to extend the frontiers of research" (Barrett and Bolt 2007, 13). Extending this assertion through the lenses of Bergson and Deleuze, Mark Fleishman, in a discussion of PAR, asserts the "difference of performance as a mode of research" as "its refusal of binaries (body – mind, theory – practice, space – time, subject – object), its radical openness, its multiplicities, its unrepresentability, its destabilization of all pretentions to fixity and determination" (Fleishman 2012, 32). Here Fleishman would seem to share Borgdorff's assertion that the "primary importance [of ARP-aligned research] lies not in explicating the implicit or non-implicit knowledge enclosed in art. It is more directed at not-knowing, or not-yet-knowing. It creates room for that which is unthought, that which is unexpected" (Borgdorff 2010; see also Borgdorff's extended 2012 discussion on this topic).

Clearly, however, this championing of "unrepresentability" and "not-knowing" stands both as one of ARP's defining characteristics and as one of its primary obstacles in its ongoing quest for shared conceptual frameworks to facilitate exchange and collaboration. A central aspect of this paradox is the commonly held priority that, to a defining degree, both the processes and the knowledge generated within/through ARP are *fully embodied*. Julien Klein asserts that the knowledge accessed via ARP (sp. artistic research)

> has to be acquired through sensory and emotional perception, precisely through artistic experience, from which it can not [sic] be separated.

Whether silent or verbal, declarative or procedural, implicit or explicit – in any case, artistic knowledge is sensual and physical, 'embodied knowledge'. The knowledge that artistic research strives for, [sic] is a *felt* knowledge.

(Klein 2010, 6)

This echoes Haseman's dismissal of the obligation to translate findings into verbal or numerical registers, and his assertion that a 'performative research' understanding of ARP (sp. performance as research) "challenges traditional ways of representing knowledge claims." For Haseman, this leads to the insistence that "people who wish to evaluate the research outcomes also need to experience them in direct (co-presence) or indirect (asynchronous, recorded) form" (Haseman 2006, 3).

As Pil Hansen succinctly puts it in her contribution to this collection, "discussions of politics of knowledge are central to the evolving PAR-discourse."

Proposals are made for how the knowledge production of PAR approaches can be recognized independently of established knowledge criteria, in part by advancing what I read as an epistemology of enaction or interaction and a (n)ontology of emergence. With these terms I refer to the notion that phenomena are believed neither to exist ontologically in and of themselves nor to be accessible through objective methods of observation; they emerge relationally, through active and embodied engagement, which also is how they are accessed. In other words, the ontology is epistemological. Artist-researchers are, understandably, raising guards against more established knowledge paradigms in order to evolve research practices on these terms.

Yet however seductive the defensive maneuver, this need not necessarily be the hill on which ARP conquers or perishes. To attain acknowledgment and acceptance within contemporary 'knowledge economies,' some scholars and scholar-practitioners (including Hansen) have found themselves pursuing diversified registers within which significant aspects of ARP-aligned activity, and its value, can be widely recognized and readily utilized.

Conceding the powerfully affective and primarily embodied nature of much ARP-related activity, yet resisting the gravitational pull to sustained binaries cautioned by Fleishman,[1] Robin Nelson has advanced a hybrid model for PaR first introduced in 2006 and further developed in later essays and his influential 2013 volume *Practice as Research in the Arts*. As contrasted with the familiar "know-that" orientation of traditional research practices, Nelson's "modes of knowing" framework foregrounds the multiple knowledges accessed through PaR. He thus distinguishes between "know-how" ('insider' close-up knowing that is experiential, haptic, tacit, and embodied) and "know-what" (which is further divided into the "tacit made explicit through critical reflection" on the part of the artist and "'outsider' distant knowledge" available through observation and analysis) (Nelson 2006, 2009, 2013). Nelson asserts that, at least at present (and perhaps unavoidably), it is only through the combination of this full range of modes of knowing – including the "know-that" practices of "documentation and complementary writings" (Nelson 2013, 70) – that the full potential of PaR may be realized.

> Accordingly, my model for PaR, while fully recognizing the importance of close-up, tacit, haptic know-how, seeks a means to establish as fully as possible the articulation of 'liquid knowing,' and a shift through intersubjectivity into the know-what of shared and corroborated soft knowledge, in turn resonating with the harder know-that of established conceptual frameworks.
>
> (Ibid. 60)

Nelson's model shares multiple key priorities with "research-based practice" (RBP), a model that Hansen and I first introduced in 2008 and have continued to develop through successive ARP contexts. As Hansen's entry in this volume demonstrates, however, there are several defining differences, as well – distinctions that serve as a bridge to the second of this volume's subtitled areas of emphasis. A conspicuously mixed-method approach to ARP, RBP extends the recognition of multiple conceptual spaces utilized by Nelson to a process of literal 'space making.' Through efforts to clarify and prioritize methodological distinctions within a multistage framework, RBP attempts to defuse the epistemological and ideological tensions that can hobble ARP initiatives, particularly in interdisciplinary contexts.

Methods

Epistemology and methodology are, of course, inseparably interwoven, and it would be difficult here to effectively catalogue or chronicle the methodological diversity demonstrated within the full spectrum of ARP activities. Extending the possibilities (and exacerbating the challenges) associated with methodological diversity is the observation that ARP approaches, in both their processes and their resultant knowledge, are inherently *interdisciplinary* and *transdisciplinary*, qualities that Barrett and Bolt, discussing PAR, directly associate with its embodied, affective, and interactive nature. Specifically, they assert that PAR's "*relationality*" and its "capacity to reinvent social relations" dismantle disciplinary distinctions and create "conditions for the emergence of new analogies, metaphors and models for understanding objects of inquiry" (Barrett and Bolt 2007, 7). In a related gesture, Kershaw and Nicholson (following Dwight Conquergood) identify "creative inquiry through practical theatre and performance making" as an "anti-discipline [. . .] with a determination to explore productive instabilities between existing epistemological practices and ontological results" (Kershaw and Nicholson 2011, 2–3).

Perhaps the single most common methodological preoccupation among ARP-related researchers is the *emergent* nature of both its processes and its products. Foregrounding the intersection between subjectivity and interaction in which the researcher "is both the practitioner who makes things happen and the audience or respondent" (Hunter 2009, 151), Lynette Hunter anchors the emergent nature of ARP (sp. performance as research) within its production of *situated* knowledge: "In the arts, situated knowledge becomes a situated textuality, knowledge always in the making, focusing on the process but situated wherever it engages an audience" (ibid., 152). Generated within situated sites of interaction, then, ARP (sp. practice as research) emerges, for Barrett and Bolt, both spatially and, of particular significance, *temporally* "through material processes. Because such processes are (at least in part) predicated on the tacit and alternative logic of practice *in time*, their precise operations cannot be predetermined" (Barrett and Bolt 2007, 6). In this light, readers familiar with Baz Kershaw's extensive writing on the conditions of ARP-related approaches (both PAR and PaR) will find his contribution to this volume reaffirming when he describes one of his most recent and instructively titled projects, "Meadow Meanderings": "[T]he *meandering* of the path is at least as important as its ecological analogue, because its apparent aimlessness constitutes a lacuna or gap in experience for the meanderer that is potentially profound." Indeed, as Dieter Lesage has observed, "What all these different practices have in common is the need of time, time to think, time to see, time to waste." However, Lesage concedes, "As time is money, time is never given to anyone for free, and certainly not to the artist" (Lesage 2013, 150).

One strategy to purchase time for methodologies of emergence is, as with Nelson's model, to couple them with more familiar research activities and outputs – although, to a degree, this can also impose more regulated patterns of documentation and dissemination. Another, as with research-based practice (RBP), is to link emergence sequentially and causally with more traditional product and process orientations to both research *and* artistic practice, thereby earning allowance – spatial, temporal, and conceptual – for a "3rd Space" (Hansen and Barton 2009, 122) of autonomy through a guarantee of eventual relevance and utility. Still others, such as that proposed by Joanna Bucknall in her contribution to this collection, seek to explicitly "marshal, map, analyse and document the discourse that is produced in and by PBR, as well as the role of relational fields of discourse in the development of praxis." Bucknall's methodical reflection on the "relational heritage" of any one project through the excavation of the longer-term influences at play in its creation proposes the recognition of a significantly wider temporal horizon of gestation and realization, one that arguably respects few limitations.

Fleishman's treatise on "the difference" of ARP (sp. performance as research) offers yet another strategy that effectively emphasizes the field's interweaving of knowledge and methods, and in the process articulates an eloquent interpretation of its distinct relation to time. Beginning with the proposal that PAR "is a series of embodied repetitions [. . .] in time [. . .] in search of difference" (Fleishman 2012, 30), drawing upon Deleuze and Guattari, Fleishman then describes a series of case study performances produced over multiple years as essentially iterations (repetitions with difference) in a "process of creative evolution"[2]:

> [I]f there is difference arising from the successive iterations of each project, it is not occurring serially in the individual representations as a set of connectable points. Rather it is occurring in the 'middle' as a process of inventive becoming, and "becoming has neither beginning nor end, departure nor arrival, origin nor destination . . . [it] is neither one nor two nor the relation of the two; it is the in-between, the border or line of flight"[3] that runs perpendicular to both.
>
> (Ibid., 34)

This understanding of PAR's perpetual emergence is directly linked to Fleishman's assertion of its "unrepresentabilty," and he contends that we "need to find ways to 'feel and live the intervals'[4]" if we are to truly engage PAR's constitutive difference. Yet in the absence of such . . . grace, perhaps? . . . Fleishman concedes, however reluctantly, that the articulation of PAR is possible only through a resort to "a kind of perceptual still point, a slowing down or thickening of the ongoing, of the flow" (ibid., 35). This is, of course, the crux, the familiar image (bringing to mind the cliché of butterflies and straight pins), and the central methodological challenge – one that serves nicely as a segue into this volume's final subtitle area of emphasis.

Impact

It is the burden of impact that is most frequently understood not as an impetus to explore perceptual still points but rather as an imposed obligation that threatens to bring the flow of ARP activities to a grinding, economically motivated standstill. Impact is often perceived as the gateway to quantitative measurement and the instrumentalization of artistic processes, framed within statistical discourse and driven by monetary imperatives.

These are 'knee-jerk' responses, perhaps, but there are certainly grounds for such strongly negative expectations. This is particularly so within the PAR/PaR-dense UK context, which has only recently weathered the direct consequences of the 2014 Research Excellence Framework (REF) that officially established expectations of impact in its comprehensive assessment of the quality of research generated by 154 UK universities (in addition to "outputs" and "environment"). In this instance, impact was evaluated by means of submitted case studies demonstrating "any social, economic or cultural impact or benefit beyond academia that has taken place during the assessment period [. . .] underpinned by excellent research produced by the submitting institution within a given timeframe" ("REF2014"). Impact was further defined by means of the criteria of "'reach' (how widely the impact was felt) and 'significance' (how transformative it was)" ("Workshops" 2010, 3).

In theory, the inclusion of a category of research benefit that extends beyond a project's academic footprint is a worthy and welcome gesture. However, as Tom Cahill and Mark Bazzaco assert, multiple factors challenge the straight-forward assessment of academic research impact, including complications associated with *timing* (impacts are often delayed and/or long-term), *attribution* (determining responsibility within multiple, often isolated roles·and initiatives), *appropriability* (determining who benefits within diverse networks of impacts), and *inequality* (measurement across different types of research and impacts) (Cahill and Bazzaco 2015). With particular reference to this last factor, it is not difficult to see how much more complicated it is to assess social and cultural, as compared to economic, impact, a reality that almost inevitably makes systematic a privileging of certain types of research results – those accessible through concrete and empirical measurement strategies – over those that broker in more elusive modes of impact.

The clearly well-intentioned observations offered following a series of REF "Workshops on the impacts of research in the practice-based creative and performing arts, the humanities and social sciences" demonstrate how potentially ill-suited standard gauges of impact can be when applied to ARP activities:

> In relation to reach, it was felt that information such as audience sizes and viewing figures did not always provide sufficient information on the reach of the impact. It was also noted that reach should not be simply equated with geography. It was felt that international dissemination did not necessarily reflect an international impact.
>
> ("Workshops" 2010, 3)

The anticipation that audience statistics or touring schedules could possibly provide assessments of "reach" directly reflects the inadequacy of traditional modes of measurement when considering ARP, with assessments of 'significance' even more difficult to imagine through such criteria.

However, the reduction of impact to purely economic considerations is by no means the only option available to ARP. While there is certainly no shortage of impact measurement schema in terms of empirical scientific research, many research fields that are based in practice, including those in the social sciences, have developed or are developing robust systems for measuring their impact across a networked range of indicators (Harlock 2013; Werner 2012; Epstein and Yuthas 2014; *Framework* 2012). These efforts often involve an attempt to carefully distinguish between research *outputs* – essentially "countable units" – and research *outcomes*, such as "improved confidence" or "improved well-being" (Harlock 2013, 11), along with efforts to develop appropriately flexible and sensitive assessment instruments. The interdisciplinary nature of much ARP activity potentially opens itself to the transfer and adaptation of the best (i.e., most appropriate) of these strategies.

Arguably, however, even these nuances direct evaluating attention towards "end products" ("Glossary"), fixed (if not necessarily final) points of impact in pursuit of stable moments of measurement. Here, Fleishman's citation of Bergson is instructive:

> For, as Bergson makes clear, conventional scientific enquiry is "accustomed . . . to think the moving by means of the unmovable". It is always focused on "immobilities", on stable points or "points of rest" in the movement flow. The intervals between these stable points, "the movements constituting the action itself[,] either elude our consciousness or reach it only confusedly".
>
> (Fleishman 2012, 35)

The challenge for ARP (sp. performance as research), in this interpretation, is to articulate a mode of impact assessment that does indeed address the need to "feel and live the intervals." In what ways can ARP discourse divert attention from end products to the rhythms of in-process becoming, from final outputs to utility in iterative application? Indeed, to what degree can the formulation of an ARP-based understanding of impact have, as one of its measures of benefit, a productively contagious effect on impact recognition and assessment throughout other research paradigms?

To this end, multiple voices have proposed an understanding of the workings of ARP-related approaches as part of a larger 'performative turn.' Arlander unpacks this gesture in considerable detail within her concluding essay in this volume, so I will here only touch upon the possibilities in terms of research impact that it grasps towards. While we have endured a great deal of 'turning' in the study of performing arts in the last decade or two, an embrace of this particular gesture can be seen to be significant both literally and figuratively. As Barbara Bolt, championing AR as a paradigmatic shift, explains,

> [T]he performative needs to be understood in terms of the performative *force* of art, that is, its capacity to effect "movement" in thought, word and deed in the individual and social sensorium. These movements enable a reconfiguration of conventions from within rather than outside of convention. Seen in the context of other research paradigms – namely the qualitative and quantitative paradigms of research – I will argue that what is at stake are the possibilities that a performative paradigm offers a new perspective on research not just in the social sciences and humanities, but also in the sciences.
>
> (Bolt 2016, 130)

Embracing Haseman's defiant assertion of the transformative autonomy of "performative research" (referenced earlier in this introduction), Bolt builds her case on key points of contrast between what she presents (following Heidegger) as "science-as-research" as compared to "art-as-research." The former, she asserts is "constative," in that it "describes/models the world"; its methodology is based upon "repetition of the same," and its interpretation of the world relies upon "truth as correspondence" (facilitating confirmation or refutation). Conversely, Bolt contends, art-as-research is performative as it "does things in the world"; its methodology is based (concurring with Fleishman) upon "repetition with difference," and its interpretation of the world articulates "'truth' as force and effect" (ibid., 140).

The resort to binaries is both familiar and, by definition, reductive (something the latter part of Bolt's essay complicates effectively); more pertinent to this discussion is the explicit attempt to articulate impact as "the *movement* in concepts, understandings, methodologies, material practice, affect and sensorial experience that arises in and through the research experience" (Bolt 2016, 141, emphasis in original). Accordingly, the criteria of impact measurement that Bolt proposes are all articulated as indications of "shift," "work [. . .] do(ne), "a/effect," and "emerge(nce)" (ibid., 141). In this interpretation, how much and, even more important, *how* things have moved, rather than where they have landed, become the most meaningful measures of impact. Ultimately, extending the benefits of this reorientation beyond AR contexts, Bolt proposes that such a shift potentially holds the key to bypassing the "'flaw' in the very procedures through which science-as-research aims to establish its truth claims. In science, as in art, we might suggest that the paradigmatic shifts have occurred through this mutability rather than repetition of the same" (ibid., 138).

Stopping short of proposing a solution for the "flaw" in scientific research practices, and without asserting, with Bolt, a fundamental paradigmatic shift, the benefits of encircling the elusive concept of artistic research in performance from these three interrelated lenses of knowledge, methods, and impact are ample and highly instructive. The suggestion that ARP has the potential to enhance and expand the epistemological horizons of legitimate knowledge discovery/creation is, by now, a familiar one, yet also one that warrants both regular repeating and persuasive qualification. Such qualification is found, I believe, in the recognition that both the processes *and* the products of ARP are *animate*, their value located in, accomplished through, and measurable by qualities of *movement* (shift, emergence, effort, force, e/affect, etc.), rather than by the distance traveled or the destination reached. These observations do not, necessarily, in themselves solve the 'hard sell' of research validity, but they do offer a conceptual framework for the *kinds of specificity* to which ARP practitioners can productively attend in their efforts towards articulation.

Each of the essays in this collection is one such gesture. Each presents a 'study in motion' – a transition out of the generalized characteristics of what I have here been referring to as artistic research in performance into a detailed consideration of a distinct 'line of flight.' Each offers a unique attempt to trace a particular instance or aspect of emergence, to recognize its knowledge contribution and gauge its impact by attending with rigorous specificity in pursuit of a precision of articulation. The diversity of subject matter, point of departure, and approach is conspicuous, resulting in a shifting, continuously negotiated constellation of relationships between performance, practice, and research. The answer that they collectively offer to the question that provides the title to this introduction . . . remains a work-in-progress.

Notes

1 "Now, this particular contest narrative, while politically expedient at certain key moments in terms of certain immediate struggles within the academy, and while both complicating and clarifying an understanding of the workings of the binary described above, tends perversely to reinforce and propagate the very binaries and dualities that the political project is trying to do away with" (2012, 30).
2 "This idea of duration informs Bergson's notion of 'creative evolution'. In his book *Creative Evolution*, Bergson rejects both neo-Darwinian mechanism, in which evolution is driven by a pre-existent model or latent code that plays itself out mechanistically over time (a compulsion of the past), and neo-Lamarckian finalism, in which evolution works towards a perfect form achieved at the 'end' (the attraction of the future). Instead he suggests that evolution is a process of constant invention (a series of explosions) in which contingency plays a significant role. For evolution to take place requires only two things: an accumulation of energy and 'an elastic canalization of this energy in variable and indeterminable directions'" (Fleishman 2012, 33).
3 Deleuze and Guattari, *A Thousand Plateaus*, p. 293.
4 Bergson, *Creative Evolution*, p. 327.

References

Allengue, Ludivine, Simon Jones, Baz Kershaw and Angela Piccini, eds. *Practice-as-Research: In Performance and Screen*. Houndmills: Palgrave, 2009.

Arlander, Annette. "Artistic Research – From Apartness to the Umbrella Concept at the Theatre Academy, Finland." In Riley and Hunter, 2009. p. 77–83.

Auslander, Philip. *Liveness*. London: Routledge, 1999, 2008.

Austin, John Langshaw (JL). *How to Do Things With Words*. Cambridge, MA: Harvard University Press, 1962.

Barrett, Estelle and Barbara Bolt, eds. *Practice as Research: Approaches to Creative Arts Inquiry*. London: I.B. Tauris, 2007.

Barton, Bruce. "Paradox as Process: Intermedial Anxiety and the Betrayals of Intimacy." *Theatre Journal* 61.4 (2009): 575–601.

———. "Subjectivity<>Culture<>Communications<>Intermedia: A Meditation on the 'Impure Interactions' of Performance and the 'in-Between' Space of Intimacy in a Wired World." *Theatre Research in Canada* 29.1 (2008): 51–92.

Barton, Bruce, Melanie Dreyer-Lude and Anna Birch, eds. *Mediating Practice(s): Performance as Research and/in/Through Mediation*. Experiments and Intensities Series. Winchester: University of Winchester Press, 2013.

Bergson, Henri. *Creative Evolution*. Trans. Arthur Mitchell. New York: Random House, 1944.

Birringer, Johannes. "The New Digital Materialism." *PAJ: A Journal of Performance and Art* 37.3 (2015): 102–110.

———. *Performance, Science, and Technology*. Cambridge: PAJ, 2008.

Bolt, Barbara. "Artistic Research: A Performative Paradigm?" *Parse* 3 (July 2016). Web. http://parsejournal.com/article/artistic-research-a-performative-paradigm/

Borgdorff, Henk. *The Conflict of the Faculties: Perspectives on Artistic Research and Academia.* Leiden: Leiden University Press, 2012.

———. "The Debate on Research in the Arts." Bergen: Kunsthøgskolen i Bergen, 2006. Web. www.ips.gu.se/digitalAssets/1322/1322713_the_debate_on_research_in_the_arts.pdf

———. "The Production of Knowledge in Artistic Research." In *The Routledge Companion to Research in the Arts.* Michael Biggs and Henrik Karlsson, eds. London: Routledge, 2010. p. 44–63.

Cahill, Tom and Mark Bazzaco. "There Is No Easy Way to Measure the Impact of University Research on Society." *The Conversation* (December 2, 2015). Web. http://the conversation. com/there-is-no-easy-way-to-measure-the-impact-of-university-research-on-society-50856.

Candy, Linda. "Practice-based Research: A Guide." *Creativity and Cognitions Studio Report.* V1.0 (November 2006): 3. Web. https://www.creativityandcognition.com/resources/PBR%20Guide-1.1-2006.pdf

Deleuze, Gilles and Felix Guattari. *A Thousand Plateaus: Capitalism and Schizophrenia.* Trans. Brian Massumi. Minneapolis, MN and London: University of Minnesota Press, 1987.

Dixon, Steve. "Cybernetic-Existentialism." *International Journal of Performance Art and Digital Media* 12.1 (2016): 11–30.

———. *Digital Performance: A History of New Media in Theater, Dance, Performance Art, and Installation.* Cambridge, MA: MIT Press, 2007.

Epstein, Mark J. and Kristi Yuthas. *Measuring and Improving Social Impacts: A Guide for Non-profits, Companies, and Impact Investors.* Oakland, CA: Berrett-Koehler, 2014.

Fleishman, Mark. "The Difference of Performance as Research." *Theatre Research International* 37.1 (2012): 28–37.

Framework for Measuring Impact. University of Stirling, 2012. Web. http://measuringimpact. org.

Friberg, Carsten and Rose Parekh-Gaihede with Bruce Barton, eds. *At the Intersection Between Art and Research: Practice-Based Research in the Performing Arts.* Malmö, Sweden: NSUP, 2010.

"Glossary." *Framework for Measuring Impact.* University of Stirling. Web. http://measuring impact.org/glossary.

Hannula, Mikka, Juha Souoranta and Tere Vadén. *Artistic Research: Methodology.* Brussels: Peter Lang, 2014.

Hansen, Pil and Bruce Barton. "Research-Based Practice: Situating Vertical City Between Artistic Development and Applied Cognitive Science." *TDR: The Drama Review* 53.4 (2009): 120–136.

Harlock, Jenny. "Impact Measurement Practice in the UK Third Sector: A Review of Emerging Evidence." *Third Sector Research Centre.* Working Paper 106 (July, 2013).

Haseman, Brad. "A Manifesto for Performative Research." *Media International Australia Incorporating Culture and Policy: Quarterly Journal of Media Research and Resources* 118 (2006): 98–106.

Hawkins, Barbara and Brett Wilson. "A Fresh Theoretical Perspective on Practice-Led Research." *The International Journal of Art and Design Education* 36.1 (2016): 82–91.

Hunter, Lynette. "Situated Knowledge." In *Mapping Landscapes for Performance as Research: Scholarly Acts and Creative Cartographies.* Shannon Rose Riley and Lynette Hunter, eds. Houndsmills: Palgrave, 2009. p. 151–153.

Jackson, Shannon. "When Is Art Research?" In *Mapping Landscapes for Performance as Research: Scholarly Acts and Creative Cartographies.* Shannon Rose Riley and Lynette Hunter, eds. Houndsmills: Palgrave, 2009. p. 157–163.

Jones, Simon. "The Courage of Complementarity: Practice as Research as a Paradigm Shift in Performance Studies." In *Practice-as-Research: In Performance and Screen*. Ludvine Allengue Simon Jones, Baz Kershaw and Angela Piccini, eds. Houndsmills: Palgrave, 2009. p. 18–33.

Kershaw, Baz and Heather Nicholson. *Research Methods in Theatre and Performance*. Research Methods for the Arts and Humanities series. Edinburgh: Edinburgh University Press, 2011.

Kjørup, Søren. "Pleading for Plurality: Artistic and Other Kinds of Research." In *The Routledge Companion to Research in the Arts*. Michael Biggs and Henrik Karlsson, eds. London: Routledge, 2012. p. 24–43.

Klein, Julien. "What Is Artistic Research?" *Research Catalogue* (2010). p. 1–6. Web. https://media.researchcatalogue.net/rc/master/5785/5785bf295ddfff55902b08051f9c1143.pdf.

Lesage, Dieter. "PaR in Continental Europe: A Site of Many Contests." In *Practice as Research in the Arts*. Robin Nelson, Houndsmills: Palgrave, 2013. p. 142–51.

MacCallum, Lindsey. "Arts Informed Research." *Mount Saint Vincent University* (2016). Web. http://libguides.msvu.ca/arts-informed-research.

Nelson, Robin. "Modes of Practice-as-Research Knowledge and Their Place in the Academy." In *Practice-as-Research: In Performance and Screen*. Ludvine Allengue, Simon Jones, Baz Kershaw and Angela Piccini, eds. Houndsmills: Palgrave, 2009. p. 112–31.

———. *Practice as Research in the Arts*. Houndmills, UK: Palgrave, 2013.

———. "Practice as Research and the Problem of Knowledge." *Performance Research* 11.4 (2006): 105–16.

"Overview." *Practice as Research in Performance: 2001–2006*. Web. www.bris.ac.uk/parip/introduction.htm.

Pape, Sidsel. "Introduction." In *At the Intersection Between Art and Research: Practice-Based Research in the Performing Arts*. Carsten Friberg and Rose Parekh-Gaihede with Bruce Barton, eds. Malmö, Sweden: NSUP, 2010. p. 9–12.

Phelan, Peggy. *Unmarked: The Politics of Performance*. London: Routledge, 1993.

Piccini, Angela. "An Historiographic Perspective on Practice as Research." *Practice as Research in Performance: 2001–2006* (2002). Web. www.bris.ac.uk/parip/t_ap.htm.

"Research Excellence Framework (REF) 2014." *UCL Communications and Marketing*. Web. www.ucl.ac.uk/ref2014/.

Riley, Shannon Rose and Lynette Hunter, eds. *Mapping Landscapes for Performance as Research: Scholarly Acts and Creative Cartographies*. Houndmills: Palgrave, 2009.

Rye, Caroline. "Incorporating Practice: A Multi-Viewpoint Approach to Performance Documentation." *Journal of Media Practice* 3.2 (2003): 115–123. *Practice as Research in Performance: 2001–2006*. Web. www.bris.ac.uk/parip/s_cr.htm.

Scott, Joanee. *Intermedial Praxis and Performance as Research*. Houndmills: Palgrave, 2016.

Werner, James L. "Measuring the Impact of Practice-based Research Networks (PBRNs)." *Journal of the American Board of Family Medicine* (July 2012). Web. http://jabfm.org/content/25/5/557.full.

"Workshops on the Impacts of Research in the Practice-based Creative and Performing Arts, the Humanities and Social Sciences." *Summary Paper*. Research Excellence Framework. December 2010.

Chapter 1

On PAR

A dialogue about performance-as-research

Jonathan Heron and Baz Kershaw

Preamble: This dialogue is an experiment in deploying *performing* as a conduit for discovering some critical qualities of process in transdisciplinarity (TD). It forgoes detailed reference to influential writings and projects that established TD, as well as its growing attraction as a conjunction to well-established fields of scholarly and creative investigation in performance (e.g. Nicolescu, 2008; Daniel, 2009). Aiming to privilege the *doing* of performance, it reports on an experimental launch into an actual field as one way of making a substantive case for the practices of TD. The dialogue then expands its focus to include a consideration of *failing* and PAR.[1]

On 'meadow meanders' and transdisciplinarity

JH: On 17 June 2015 we had a symposium event at the University of Warwick[2] that focussed on your 'Meadow Meander' project. I wonder in what ways this project represents how PAR transcends or transgresses forms of knowledge.

BK: First of all, readers need to understand that a Meadow Meander is a path in a field of meadowland (or other grasses and flowers) that is marked out with a grid of posts, and the grid represents the world. Also, that Meadow Meanders are a key part of my broader long-term project called Earthrise Repair Shop, which explores the notions and practices of performance ecology and – to a lesser extent – performance conservation (Kershaw, 2011). The path is modelled on a global ecological system, deliberately kept secret, but it only approximately follows the model. Visitors are told about the modelling, but not what it is based on, unless they are desperate to know. Also, they can't see the path because the grass is quite long, so from ground level it looks like an untouched field. So 'meanderers' start with a lack of knowledge in approaching this particular outdoor artefact, but also with the knowledge that perhaps it is a rough analogue of some global ecological feature. Therefore, the path is not meaningless, it's not random, although it does weave around and appears not to be going anywhere specific and ends up back where it started. So it's a meaningless path in one sense but in another sense it's saturated with meaning. Anyone entering the path has a problem to solve, but hopefully one that's been framed in a friendly way so that they can try to work out what it might stand for if they'd like to. However, the *meandering* of the path is at least as important as its ecological analogue, because its apparent aimlessness constitutes a lacuna or gap in experience for the meanderer that is potentially profound.

Immediately the path is about becoming. Deliberately abandoning knowledge, purposefully leaving knowledge behind, is a major way of becoming that isn't just about thinking, about what we think we know or don't know, but also about an embodied experience through which something significant that the traveller engages with is undefinable, inaccessible, mysterious, and so on. That's a first step towards a transdisciplinary experience.

JH: And from my own experience of meandering in the meadow, there is a sense that it privileges movement as much as cognition.

BK: That's the aim: an immersive experience which puts the walker/traveller/meanderer into a space that is comfortable because you're not going to get lost if you stay on the path, even though you might be lost as to where you are metaphorically and otherwise, and what *that* means. But you're not completely lost because the path takes you only in the direction that *it* needs to go. At the same time, you are surrounded by the Earth's environment – it is an outdoor situation after all – that can range from a field of commonplace agricultural grass, through a wildflower meadow in the countryside, to an urban city square or a former graveyard or an ex-airport or any kind of place where an invisible or indistinct pathway can be made. So you're always surrounded again by other kinds of saturation experiences. Those environments are always more or less rich and the meanders I've made tend to be placed deliberately in contextually dense places (Bottoms, 2015), such as a former urban graveyard of the nineteenth century in Leeds (2012) or a major ex-airport of a twentieth-century city in Berlin (2013). You're surrounded by matters that you might know something about, but you don't know why you're on this path and/or why it's shaped as it is. The knowledge that you've got becomes a kind of free-for-all playground because you can shift your attention from one thing to another to anything that's around you while you're walking. But you can also simply forget about all that and just immerse yourself and enjoy the walking and the richness of the environment that you are a part of *for its own sake*. I am suggesting that is a transdisciplinary 'space' (or at least a quasi-transdisciplinary space) (see Kershaw and Nicholson, 2011: 6–12).

JH: I would like to stay with that idea of transdisciplinary methods, which we'll be addressing further in the next section of our dialogue. You've described this space as a playground, and in certain forms of play there is a 'not-yet-knowing' (Borgdorff, 2012: 194), which I see as an interplay between knowing and a kind of wilful ignorance. So I wonder how this might relate to transdisciplinary research as an alternative form of knowing and how we might encourage play within a research process.

BK: I think you have to start by turning that question on its head in a sense, because the kind of unknowing that you enter into in a transdisciplinary space is radically different than the kind of unknowing or ignorance that any significant research question or hunch might provide for you. From that point of departure the implication, just before you start your research process proper, is that you've got a problem that you can't extract a question *from*. So therefore you're stepping into the unknown, unless you decide you know where you're stepping from as a continuation of historical knowledge. That is clearly not a first step into a potential transdisciplinary space, where you don't even have those reference points, or even those questions and hunches that you don't yet know the answers to. The radical difference, I think, is similar to that between your becoming aware of an environmental lacuna – say as produced by a heavy mist or a black hole – and you actually entering into it, being part of or integral to that lacuna. Because in engaging a transdisciplinary space, at least initially, *nothing* is known for sure. Therefore it's a very open, flexible, and complex – but also a very common and simple (because apparently empty) – kind of space to explore. Possibly that refracts what Borgdorff calls 'not-yet-knowing', which you link to play: a type of non-*thing*, which practice as researchers might encounter in some kinds of play and improvisation, as you suggest. An embodied, immersive experience, through which your attention has to be totally focussed outwards towards the environment, at least initially, for a large portion of the time.

One paradigm for those processes could be Gregory Bateson's view that 'In the nature of the case, an explorer can never know what he is exploring until it has been explored' (Bateson, 2000/1972: xxiv). That's a very hard place to define because you're trying to avoid defining 'things'; you need to do this in order to discover other 'things' that you might never have encountered if you hadn't entered that kind of 'non-space'. 'Wilful ignorance' might be one way among many to account for transdisciplinary affects/effects, but 'radical failure' might account for it even better: 'Fail again. Fail better' (Beckett, *Worstward Ho*, 1983: 1).

JH: There seems to be a very important distinction here between multidisciplinarity (where various disciplines contribute to a process without blurring epistemic boundaries), interdisciplinarity (where disciplines still claim to know through an exchange between different disciplines or ways of knowing), and TD, which you're describing in terms of practical or ludic knowledge, which seems to be a completely different thing.

BK: TD is some sort of awareness of un-knowledge, which is a completely different kind of experience than learning about knowing through multi- or interdisciplinarity, because by definition you can't define what (or why) it is. Your experience evokes a kind of un-learning, achieved through some sort of deliberate immersion in a state of complete ignorance or, perhaps more accurately, you become involved in an unavoidable lacuna. One's experience is different if you're 'outside' such un-learning, as with various types of multi/interdisciplinary space, and the knowledge they create can become a prelude to TD. When you first 'enter' a transdisciplinary space its inherent lack of definition is an inevitable vector for experiencing its uncanny qualities (Kershaw et al., 2011: 63–85).

JH: This raises some fascinating questions about the terms of engagement between the disciplinary academics and the non-disciplinary artists, and the possibility of being 'undisciplined' when we approach our practice (see Halberstam, 2011).

BK: Let's go back to traditions of theatre to consider that. It's often relatively easy to say historically what different disciplines are engaged in a particular theatre production and/or building, because in that sort of making you have contrasting knowledge domains which are coordinated in relation to each other and that, perhaps inevitably, creates knowledge. So in the usual situation of theatre you're not escaping knowledge directly through interdisciplinarity, at least in the ways that you can in what I'm describing as a radically transdisciplinary space. I say 'radically' because in such a space you have no option but to experience it, at least initially, *as* un-knowledge.

JH: And does this model of TD represent a more 'sustainable' approach to knowledge, as has been recently suggested by Robert Frodeman (2014: 7)?

BK: Although you're in what I've been calling a 'space' (other metaphors could serve just as well), although you're in a transdisciplinary domain and you don't know where (or even *what*) you are, that transdisciplinary zone is not a vacuum. It's not entirely empty of, let's say, 'things'; it's potentially full of 'things' because you're still presumably aware of becoming a part of what's around you (Kershaw, 2009a: 4–5). But you don't know the reality or the unreality of what you're in, in the same way as generally one does in—let's call it 'everyday life'—because you leave behind normative assumptions. A transdisciplinary space encourages you or causes you to abandon assumptions that you usually make about the nature of what's around you. Its 'nature' is there, still, but you can't know what its 'nature' is without engaging with it interactively or, as I prefer to say, *econnectively* (Kershaw, 2012: 11).[3]

This is where you leave knowing behind and enter an environment in which you are freer to shift between thinking (cognition) and not thinking (ignorance, abandoning knowledge). You're free to move in and out of those modes of becoming, and many others. That then gives you more latitude for how you engage with whatever is around you, which you can do from many different kinds of angles than those that exist in normative, everyday situations where we're conventionally imbued by 'knowledge', even constructed *from* knowledge. The difference is that in a transdisciplinary space you are entering into a relationship with your surroundings that potentially leaves you more open to what is happening in those surroundings and the forces, energies, and so forth that are circulating there. In this relationship the environment is likely to be influencing you as much as you are influencing it. TD becomes a meta-interactive space and experience where the nature of what's around you announces itself to you in ways that you haven't otherwise conceived of, or experienced, before. In other words, the environment becomes *in* you, as it were, *flowing through* you. And also you become part of that environment in unpredictable ways because it is performing you even as you perform it (Kershaw, 2015).[4]

On 'formless hunches' and failure-as-resistance

JH: My own PAR project[5] began with a 'formless hunch' (Peter Brook, 1987: 3) rather than the framing of a question. I responded to your definition of PAR as 'a method and methodology in search of results across disciplines: a collection of *transdisciplinary* research "tools"' (Kershaw, 2009a: 5). From this perspective, I conducted practical experiments that crossed disciplinary boundaries (including the arts, humanities, sciences, and philosophy). My PAR therefore engages with theatre practice in order to address experimental performance studies, specifically in relation to TD. While theatre has been one of the greatest resources for multidisciplinary and interdisciplinary encounters between the arts and the sciences, as scholars including Kirsten Shepherd-Barr (2006) and Helen Nicholson (2011) have shown, it has also failed to be consistently transdisciplinary. While a significant part of my work has focused on the experimental theatre of Samuel Beckett, Peter Brook, and Joan Littlewood, my broader analysis considered performance practice in relation to the 'not-yet-knowing' of artistic research (see Borgdorff, 2012). How does this relate to your own interest in TD?

BK: Your description underlines in various ways the crucial function of indeterminacy in attempts to encounter TD through theatre and performance studies, and even in drama as well. While Peter Brook's *'formless* hunch' seems like something akin to intuition or 'intuitive feeling', its oxymoronic status works to compromise the more common meanings of 'hunch' as a push or nudge toward, say, an entirely undefined encounter. Thus the strengths of theatre as a multi- or interdisciplinary phenomenon – especially as it connects with scientific investigation – become a problem of unsustainable access to transdisciplinarity. The genealogical strengths of theatre historically become a weakness in attempts to completely abandon

knowledge and knowing, *beyond* Borgdorff's 'not yet knowing'. For theatre, in almost all its guises, makes the past a burden that it has commonly
looked for over its shoulder, so to speak, even as it may aim to totally dispel
it. I interpret your primary PAR focus on Beckett as an acknowledge-
ment that he is one of the few theatre makers to strip back the art form
to a point of *un-disciplinarity*, which could well be considered as crucially
articulated to TD as a paradoxical shadowing of its profound potentials
for ambivalence and indeterminacy.

JH: I found that both performance-as-research and transdisciplinary research
      enable cultural and epistemological transgressions through their focus
      upon practitioner knowledge, problem solving, and 'failure-as-resistance'.
      As Sara Jane Bailes notes, 'Failure challenges the cultural dominance of
      instrumental rationality and the fictions of continuity that bind the way
      we imagine and manufacture the world' (2011: 2). Following Bailes, I
      treated Beckett's 'failure' as an example of radical failure from a perfor-
      mance studies perspective, but I then became more interested in failure as
      a productive force within the reflexivity of laboratory experimentation. I
      wonder how you deal with failure within PAR processes.

BK: It is not easy – even perhaps impossible – to claim clear-cut distinctions
      between 'performance' and TD because, in my view, they articulate each
      other in complementary ways. Hence, if we consider 'performance' as a
      factor of quantum mechanics – for instance, as indicating a critical opera-
      tional vector of universal energy exchange – then performing-as-such may
      be considered as the 'trans-' aspect of the term 'transdisciplinary'. In other
      words, 'performance' and TD can be mutually involved fundamentally in
      whatever processes the domains of 'un-knowing' may be 'failing' at.

From the perspective of transdisciplinary practices, knowledge and problem-
solving would likely *constitute* 'failure-as-resistance'. Given that, 'failure' may
challenge much more than Bailes suggests – at least at that early point in her
analysis. Your shift from a performance studies perspective to exploring the
processes of reflexivity in laboratory experimentation indicates a potentially
profound commitment to *performing* transdisciplinarity; hence, I suggest, the
widening inclusion of multiple disciplines/disciplinary perspectives in your
research.

As for how I personally 'deal with' failure in PAR, it seems to be a paradoxical
matter of knowingly tricking oneself *out* of pursuing the knowledge, understandings, and so forth that research conventionally aims to create. In meadow
meandering practices, this boils down to forgetting – through unpredictable
meandering as such – everything you thought you knew by aiming to create the conditions for immersion in processes of econnectivity, via which the
abandon of phenomenologically reflexive pleasures ironically becomes a norm,
if only temporarily. Through the doubling back of failure-as-resistance, one
might become a transdisciplinary *re*-searcher.

JH: I would therefore suggest that any revaluation of failure within PAR should take account of transdisciplinary approaches to knowledge. Unlike inter-disciplinary research, transdisciplinary practice makes use of epistemic failure – the 'unknowing' suggested earlier – as an opportunity for future knowledge. Julie Thompson Klein (in Frodeman, 2010) has identified 'four major trendlines' that characterise TD. First: 'the contemporary version of the historical quest for systematic integration of knowledge' (24), from ancient Greek philosophy to 'unification theories' in physics. Second: 'TD is not just "transcendent" but "transgressive", . . . more often as a label for knowledge formations imbued with a critical imperative, fostering new theoretical paradigms (e.g. cultural studies)' (25). Third: 'overarching synthetic paradigms . . . that transcend the narrow scope of disciplinary worldviews (e.g. sociobiology or phenomenology).' Fourth: 'trans-sector TD problem solving [within] contexts of environmental research' (ibid.). I wonder whether you find these 'trendlines' helpful in relation to PAR?

BK: Yes, and no – of course – as there are deep ironies in such *necessary* efforts to 'account for' the 'nature' of transdisciplinary research. For example, the injunction regarding 'overarching synthetic paradigms' appears to imply some limit on TD that belies its full anti-foundational potential. This is particularly the case given the risks inherent in planning to fix on a specific methodological 'entrance' to TD, say, in ways that won't predetermine what's encountered on the 'other side'. So any adequately intelligent attempt to clarify the various ways that 'trendlines' might operate to shape each specific project will likely need to specify what methods are *not* planned as part of its attempts to foster unknowing. The same holds for exits from TD as well, because to decide on what 'happened' within the transdisciplinary domain in retrospect will likely beg many questions regarding what might be agreed upon as adequate descriptions of – or perhaps better – *for* events now past. Not surprisingly, attempts to generalise what might constitute typical 'outcomes' for transdisciplinary projects would be especially fraught – although contradictions, conundrums, and paradoxes would likely feature prominently. So, for example, Bateson's approach to effective exploration I mentioned earlier ironically becomes a foundational mantra for trans-disciplinary research.

JH: I understand Thompson Klein's 'trendlines' as four entangled pathways towards TD, and I recall Frodeman (2014: 7) here in suggesting that this may present a more sustainable approach to knowledge production within the modern university system. However, I echo Katri Huutoni-emi's concern that 'a complementary trend is the "transdisciplinarization" of knowledge, the erosion of the distinction between academic and non-academic contexts of research' (in Frodeman, 2010: 315). This is where PAR can make a specific intervention, in response to Huutoniemi's TD, as 'a form of integrated societal values that emphasizes comprehensive knowledge responsive to political and social needs' (ibid.) by foregrounding *practice*.

My own PAR project explored new futures for performance as transdisciplinary research through a series of performance processes, including *Discords* (2010), *Endlessness* (2011), and *Fail Better Fragments* (2012). Ultimately, I became interested in how experimental theatre practice facilitated disciplinary failure as a form of resistance to the logo-centric epistemologies of contemporary research (see Heron et al., 2014; Heron, 2015). The institutional context for this practice was informed by a transdisciplinary pedagogy (see Monk et al., 2011) that resisted consumerist models of higher education, and instead revalued failure.

BK: 'Disciplinary failure' as a resistant practice strikes me as especially appropriate in a response to current trends within higher education internationally. What other than a 'transdisciplinary pedagogy' could turn the trick of circumventing instrumental learning in all kinds of laboratories – a failure that works in favour of fundamentally reimagining with new generations the nature of the academy as such?

On 'participatory laboratories' and the problem of results

JH: I would now like to focus on the PAR Working Group of the International Federation for Theatre Research and, in particular, the 'participatory laboratory' that takes place within each conference. You developed this particular approach with Mark Fleishman and Anna Birch for the 2009 conference in Lisbon, and since then it has been convened annually (Munich 2010, Osaka 2011, Santiago de Chile 2012, Barcelona 2013, Warwick 2014, and Hyderabad 2015 etc.) and several colleagues have contributed in this design through participation, documentation, and practice.

With regards to this, I wonder whether, for this closing section, we could discuss ways in which PAR enables specific or generic modes of *knowing* and how that might inform an understanding of inter/trans-cultural (as opposed to inter/transdisciplinary) practice in a particularly reflexive manner?

BK: The notion of 'inter/trans-cultural' as a particular form of interdisciplinarity is now pretty standard – even 'historical' – given its emergence through theatre studies in the 1970–80s, for instance in the work of Patrice Pavis (1992). Each person coming into the PAR workshop is from a specific area of the globe; but they're also part, at least potentially, of an international community of particular kinds of knowledge. There is difference associated with where one comes from in terms of everyday lived experience (which, in gatherings like the PAR working group, can constitute a remarkable diversity); let's call it the 'affective world'. But people are also sharing knowledge of an interdisciplinary sort, and that knowledge can be more or less generalised according to its source and original authors. This is where the interdisciplinary problem begins, as people are talking different languages *and* using the same words to create different meanings. That's a useful domain because it generates difference and debate; but it doesn't necessarily take you towards TD in PAR. However, if group members are working through the processes of a culture of *knowing* that they inhabit in their original location, then each member will likely be coming from a very different kind of 'world'. So the differences between the 'knowledge world' and the 'affective world' can be profound in their multiplicity, and that may perform a potential for TD. It is the dynamics between those (and other) various 'worlds' – and particularly through the co-existent *knowings* and *affects* of those 'worlds' that people are bringing with them – that produces the borderlines, the potentially absolute boundaries between an interdisciplinary space and a transdisciplinary space (Kershaw, 2009b: 1–16).

My critical point is that explicit cognitive processes, such as thought, reason, and intellect (which primarily feature through language), in contrast to, say, perception, awareness, and intuition (which arise through somatic experience, embodiment, etc.), can evoke or emphasise those boundaries in unhelpful ways. Whereas, if you work primarily through creative practices in which cognition might figure minimally or even not at all, then the differences in behaviour, in attitude, in emotion – all the implicit differences in those aspects of experience – can come into play more productively. It's those qualities of acute implicit diversity and an environment of inevitable uncertainty and ambiguity within the PAR working groups that make it possible to experiment through TD.

JH: In that sense performance as transdisciplinary research creates not only a temporary play-space but also a durational laboratory as a reflexive space. I think its reflexivity is one of its most important features.

BK: Yes, absolutely.

JH: I have written elsewhere about theatre laboratories and their radical potential within interdisciplinary contexts (for instance Heron, 2015) and experimental reflexivity has been a feature of our collaboration in relation to PAR specifically. What are the values of reiterating one's practice in such a reflexive space, and how do you conceive of that space as a laboratory, specifically a place for new experiments with one's practice?

BK: The reflexivity can appear only through repetition of some kind or another. You must have markers of what's happened in order to know where you are, in order to experiment in where you're going. So as long as the process of repetition and reiteration is done in a way that 'balances' between knowledge and not-knowledge, knowing and unknowing – or shuttlecocks between them – then you're likely going to open up ways of newly experiencing what's going on in the laboratory. This makes for a laboratory that is experimental in the sense that we don't know what's going to happen next, and we're not sure if this is going to 'mean' anything, but nonetheless let's have a go and see what happens and comes out of it. As you immerse yourself in the process of creating work in that way you are moving towards TD. Also, reiteration and repetition always imply the possibility of returning to a point in the past through which to discover other perspectives that can afford you further refractions and reflections on where the group, individually and collectively, has been. This can include moving through areas of cognition, such as thinking. However, the dynamics *between* that cognition and, in particular, the affective aspects of unknowing creativity can be very research-rich, because you're not sure what kind of behaviour or what kind of result will come out of a process that is so radically open-ended.

JH: And with that comes the idea of *result*, which I know is a particular concern of the working group at present. Previously the group has addressed areas such as documentation, repetition, and stratification, and the current conference call (Sao Paulo, 2017) has focused on democracy. I know that an emerging interest – perhaps anxiety – of the group is the need to produce 'results'.

BK: I think the conventional research outcome terms, including 'outcomes' and 'results', sit uncomfortably in relation to TD. This is primarily because, given the intrinsic importance of indeterminacy and unpredictability to its workings, TD tends to create states which are not easily accounted for in terms of cause-and-effect. This will be especially be the case in respect to playful laboratory workshops and similar process-orientated venues. It is very important that such working groups devise methods that take into account the kinds of reflexivity that might be most useful to eventually characterising what went on in their sessions.

The list of broad topics – 'documentation, repetition, and stratification' – may provide clues for clarifying the conundrums that are endemic to TD. They could help provide the reference points for deciding on the types of reflexive orientations that might be best suited for assessing particular aspects in the inevitable mix of complexity and simplicity that circulates in the playful laboratory process. Let's say that 'documentation, repetition, and stratification' are three main aspects of the group's research interests that are part of the workshop's environment. One simple way of dealing with that complexity is for the group to create three subgroups, with each focussing on just one of those topics/aspects. That then could provide a structural 'tool' for tracking the various forms of reflexivity that emerge through the workshop processes – which in turn might enable the workshop members to evolve a simplifying matrix of the different (and/or similar) reflexive methods at play in the overall complexity of the group's overlapping research interests. My hunch is that such a matrix might be an appropriate 'result' to report to interested parties, as it could structurally give access to key co-ordinates of that particular laboratory process. This, in turn, should suggest the kinds of criteria appropriate to assessing the PAR values achieved by the working group.

JH: I think of that 'result' as something to re-iterate *through practice* in future experiments.

Notes

1 With special thanks to Kea Richards (Warwick) for assisting with transcription.
2 The symposium was part of a collaborative project, with Dr Rachel King (Warwick), investigating innovative pedagogies in preparation for a postgraduate module on 'Experimental Ecologies in Practice' at the Institute for Advanced Teaching and Learning (IATL), University of Warwick.
3 This is not to be confused with computing's 'e-connectivity'. Econnectivity is to e-connectivity what total environmental immersion is to observing the same environment on a smartphone (Kershaw, 2011a).
4 This then indicates an *exchange* of performance energies that is highly relevant to the question about sustainability because the optimum state in such systems of exchange is a homeostasis – or equilibrium – that works to at least conserve and enhance diversity in the 'life' of its 'inhabitants' while always working to the crucial ecological rule of 'less is more'.
5 Heron, Jonathan (2015) *A Different Kind of Failure: Towards a Model of Experimental Theatre as Transdisciplinary Performance.* PhD Thesis, University of Warwick.

References

Bailes, Sara Jane (2011) *Performance Theatre and the Poetics of Failure: Forced Entertainment, Goat Island and Elevator Repair Service*, London: Routledge.

Bateson, Gregory (2000/1972) *Steps to an Ecology of Mind*, Chicago: University of Chicago Press.

Beckett, Samuel (1983) *Worstward Ho*, London: John Calder.

Borgdorff, Henk (2012) *The Conflict of the Faculties: Perspectives on Artistic Research and Academia*, Amsterdam: Leiden University Press.

Bottoms, Stephen (2015) Performance Footprint: 'Psi Meadow Meander (Leeds)', http://performancefootprint.co.uk/projects/earthrise-repair-shop/psi-meadow-meander-leeds/ Accessed 21 November 2016.

Brook, Peter (1987) *The Shifting Point: Forty Years of Theatrical Exploration 1946–1987*, London: Methuen.

Daniel, Henry (2009) 'Transnet: A Canadian-based Case Study on Practice-as-Research, or Rethinking Dance in a Knowledge-based Economy', in *Practice as Research in Performance and Screen*, eds. Ludivine Allegue, Simon Jones, Baz Kershaw and Angela Piccini, Basingstoke: Palgrave Macmillan.

Frodeman, Robert (ed.) (2010) *The Oxford Handbook of Interdisciplinarity*, Oxford: Oxford University Press.

—— (2014) *Sustainable Knowledge: A Theory of Interdisciplinarity*, Basingstoke: Palgrave Macmillan.

Halberstam, Judith (2011) *The Queer Art of Failure*, Durham, NC: Duke University Press.

Heron, Jonathan (2015) 'Shakespearean Laboratories and Performance-as-Research', in *Shakespeare on the University and Campus Stage*, ed. Andrew Hartley, Cambridge: Cambridge University Press.

Heron, Jonathan and Nicholas Johnson with Burç Idem Dincel, Gavin Quinn, Sarah Jane Scaife and Áine Josephine Tyrrell (2014) 'The Samuel Beckett Laboratory 2013', *Journal of Beckett Studies* 23:1, Edinburgh: Edinburgh University Press, 73–94.

Kershaw, Baz (2009a) 'Performance Practice as Research: Perspectives From a Small Island', in *Mapping Landscapes for Performance as Research: Scholarly Acts and Creative Cartographies*, eds. Shannon Rose Riley and Lynette Hunter, Basingstoke: Palgrave Macmillan.

—— (2009b) 'Practice-as-Research: An Introduction', in *Practice-as-Research: In Performance and Screen*, eds. Ludivine Allegue and Simon Jones, Baz Kershaw, Angela Piccini, Basingstoke: Palgrave Macmillan.

—— (2011) 'Earthrise Repair Shop', http://performancefootprint.co.uk/projects/earthrise-repair-shop/ Accessed 21 November 2016.

—— (2012) '"This Is the Way the World Ends, Not . . .?": On Performance Compulsion and Climate Change', *Performance Research: A Journal of the Performing Arts*, 17.4, p. 5–17.

—— (2015) 'Performed By Ecology: How *Homo Sapiens* Could Subvert Present Day Futures', *Performing Ethos: An International Journal of Ethics in Theatre and Performance*, 4.2, p. 113–134.

Kershaw, Baz with Lee Miller/Joanne 'Bob' Whalley and Rosemary Lee/Niki Pollard (2011) 'Practice as Research: Transdisciplinary Innovation in Action', in *Research Methods in Theatre and Performance*, eds. Baz Kershaw and Helen Nicholson, Edinburgh: Edinburgh University Press.

Kershaw, Baz and Helen Nicholson, eds. (2011) *Research Methods in Theatre and Performance*, Edinburgh: Edinburgh University Press.

Monk, Nicholas with Carol Chillington-Rutter, Jonothan Neelands and Jonathan Heron (2011) *Open-Space Learning: A Study in Transdisciplinary Pedagogy*, London: Bloomsbury Academic.

Nicholson, Helen (2011) *Theatre, Education and Performance*, Basingstoke: Palgrave Macmillan.

Nicolescu, Basarab (ed.) (2008) *Transdisciplinarity: Theory and Practice*, Cresskill, NJ: Hampton Press.

Pavis, Patrice (1992) *Theatre at the Crossroads of Culture*, London: Routledge.

Shepherd-Barr, Kirsten (2006) *Science on Stage: From Doctor Faustus to Copenhagen*, Princeton, NJ: Princeton University Press.

Chapter 2

Research-based practice

Facilitating transfer across artistic, scholarly, and scientific inquiries

Pil Hansen

Introduction

Motivation and advances

In a 2009 volume of *TDR: The Drama Review* Bruce Barton and I presented a model for research that crosses multiple disciplines of scholarly and creative inquiry called research-based practice (RBP). Instead of researching the implicit knowledge and impact of artistic practice primarily using either artistic methods or scholarly and scientific approaches, we were interested in establishing reciprocal feedback channels that might advance all of these research practices. We proposed to set up discipline-specific spaces of inquiry, which are defined by the respective methodological norms and kinds of utility of each discipline involved, but investigating a shared set of questions. To foster reciprocal exchange, a third space was positioned at the centre of the model with channels to the discipline-specific spaces – channels through which new questions and findings can be transferred into the third space for collaborative exploration. We implied that each discipline-specific space can be established by individual researchers or several spaces can be led by a researcher with multi-methodological literacy. The third space was conceived as a safe lab for rule breaking and novel inter-disciplinary exploration, which is defined by neither methodology nor output objectives. The idea was to facilitate points of connection and contamination while also enabling each discipline-specific space of inquiry to produce 'knowledge' that is fully qualified by compatibility between its method of production and the field it applies to. Indeed, concerns about utility were formative for the design of this model. In the early article, the model was demonstrated through a hypothetical project, which crossed cognitive, behavioural experiments with artistic inquiry and aimed to produce both knowledge about human cognition and dramaturgical strategies for performance creation.

This model has since been realized in *Acts of Memory* (funded by the Social Sciences and Humanities Research Council in Canada). As the lead investigator of a scientific space and facilitator of the third space, my aim with this project was to better understand and make artistic use of the ways in which autobiographical memory is manipulated within systems of dance and performance generation. In pursuit of that objective, challenges, limitations, and strengths of the research-based practice model were revealed. These discoveries are my focus when I return to elaborate on *Acts of Memory* farther into this essay. In particular, I discuss how challenges were overcome and the interdisciplinary utility of the model was increased by strengthening the model's channels of exchange. In order to fully contextualize these results, two preliminary steps are first taken: I briefly position this work in relation to a concern at the heart of the practice as research discourse and account for the trajectory that informs my take on it. Then I take a closer look at the boundaries between the knowledge paradigms that we crossed within this project: the accumulative paradigm of the cognitive sciences, the diversifying paradigm of dance and theatre studies, and the emergent paradigm of PAR and artistic inquiry.

Positions

A comparison of the seminal collections on practice as research (PaR) by Robin Nelson (2013) and Ludivine Allegue et al. (2009) reveals that discussions of politics of knowledge are central to the evolving PAR-discourse. Proposals are made for how the knowledge production of PAR approaches can be recognized independently of established knowledge criteria, in part by advancing what I read as an epistemology of enaction or interaction and a (n)ontology of emergence. With these terms I refer to the notion that phenomena are believed neither to exist ontologically in and of themselves nor to be accessible through objective methods of observation; they emerge relationally, through active and embodied engagement, which also is how they are accessed. In other words, the ontology is epistemological. Artist-researchers are, understandably, raising guards against more established knowledge paradigms in order to evolve research practices on these terms.

The research-based practice model is designed to respond to this priority by rendering artistic inquiry an equal research partner on self-defined terms while facilitating exchange with other forms of research and knowledge within the third space. In this levelled field PAR and artistic inquiry are empowered, and it becomes possible to exchange and collaborate across research practices in artistic inquiry, scholarship, and science with respect for differences.

In addition to addressing unproductive stratification of disciplines, there is a larger social issue that a cross-disciplinary approach is particularly well positioned to solve. The arts and sciences are increasingly facing evaluation measures that emphasize external values, such as entrepreneurial application, impact on policies, or health and education benefits. In the performing arts, the less instrumental values of creative inquiries, processes, and experiences are rarely discussed at the level of policy, in part because they are difficult to measure. I believe that diversified research methods and forms of dissemination are needed to raise the social value assigned to performance. Research-based practice enables a single project to meet the very different criteria of knowledge and utility of artistic, scientific, and social fields; in turn, research results can impact a broad range of discourses at once. In other words, RBP is presented and advanced here as an expansion of the knowledge paradigms and forms of utility that PAR productively can enter into exchange with, affect, and draw upon – that is, while continuing to evolve forms of artistic inquiry that push and pull at the boundaries of the performing arts through the very means that are unique to artistic inquiry.

My choice of working across knowledge paradigms has evolved over time, though the motivation described earlier has remained consistent. Since 2000 I have pursued a series of inquiries into dramaturgy, perception, and memory with an interest in how dramaturgical creation strategies can expand the perceptual capacity of performing artists and spectators. This work has been carried out through a series of professional dance and theatre dramaturgical engagements, in scholarly research projects using PAR and qualitative coding methods,[1] in scientific experiments, and – more on topic – through my pursuit of research and creation models that bring these activities together. I co-developed the research-based practice model to pursue this line of inquiry within a fully cross-disciplinary research design and without losing sight of the artistic values and research validity that I had earned through dramaturgical practice and practice as research projects.

Interdisciplinary challenges

Disciplinary self-segregation in undefined research spaces

My choice of subject matter and disciplines positions my research firmly within the field of cognitive performance studies. In general, this field involves a high degree of cross-disciplinary curiosity and generosity. However, it is a recurrent challenge that the engaged performing artists, cognitive scientists, and dance and theatre scholars speak different languages that render integration of inquiries, exchange, or even just communication highly difficult. This challenge is increased by the fact that inequality in terms of resources and social validation produces stratified roles. In a stereotypical scenario, the scientist is cast as a 'hard' researcher, the humanities scholar is considered the 'soft' communicator, and the artist is reduced to a research subject. New bridges are being built by research networks and projects that explicitly aim to move past this scenario (Cognitive Futures in the Humanities, European Society for the Cognitive Sciences of Music, and Dance Engaging Science) as well as the interdisciplinary, empirical research in cognition and the performing arts of pioneers like Kate Stevens, Jane Ginsborg, and Nicola Shaughnessy (e.g., Ginsborg 2009; Stevens et al. 2011; Stevens et al. 2014; Shaughnessy 2012). In her report from the first symposiums of the Dance Engaging Science research network,[2] the dance dramaturg and performance scholar Freya Vass-Rhee offers a useful example of how difficult it is to break with disciplinary stratification, even in contexts that are set aside from institutional pressures with the intention of achieving equality for artists.

Responding to a series of questions about dance as a form of thinking that were raised by a Forsythe Company dancer in advance of the first symposium, participating scientists were, for example, requesting explicit observations on practice from dancers, and when they received movement demonstrations instead, they began to 'make sense' of what they saw in and on terms that were foreign to the dancers' experience (Vass-Rhee 2014; see also Motion Bank). At the fourth symposium in 2015, which I attended by invitation, the members had been prompted and funded to create smaller research projects in clusters. Neuroscientists and experimental psychologists had separated into clusters, using dancers as research subjects or to design movement manipulations for experiments.[3] Performance scholar clusters established organizational and online platforms for the communication of cognitive science/dance research methods and results to broader humanities readerships.[4] Within these platforms they had begun to map a complex field and develop an expanding network of lenses and approaches. This image of the Dance Engaging Science activities only reflects a selection of movements within the network. The philosopher Alva Noe offered critical responses and collaborated across paradigms, and there also were exceptions in participants who, like me, have acquired research skills in two or three of the represented paradigms and thus were able to move between the groupings. Over time, the full group moreover evolved a set of shared terms and a practice of generosity that resulted in trust, friendship, and respect for different kinds of knowledge production, though most projects continued to prioritize the methodological criteria of a singular paradigm.

Dance Engaging Science offers an example of how a group of scientists, scholars, and artists self-organize when brought into an openly interdisciplinary research space. As such, it invites us to examine the priorities that establish boundaries for interdisciplinary collaboration and make us default to discipline-specific anchors – even when invited to push beyond them. My interest in this examination is to discover productive potential in the differences and soften some of the divides in search of channels of exchange.

Methodological awareness

Performance or dance studies scholars share a meta-subject of study with their respective community, but use theories and methods from a broad range of disciplines to investigate, reinterpret, and categorize subsections of this subject. Philosophy is often used as a foundational measure of validity within its paradigmatic timeframe. Philosophical concepts are used to reinterpret dance and theatre and not often vice versa; critique is about competing interpretations, and it rarely questions the foundation, the philosophy. It is not uncommon that empirical research results from the cognitive sciences are used in a similarly foundational way by theatre scholars (examples can be found in Lutterbie 2011;

Blair 2008; Cook 2010). Such a choice is not made to assign authority of truth to philosophers and scientists; it is made because the lenses they offer are applied in analyses that do not produce philosophical counter-arguments or falsifying empirical results, but rather contribute to a growing network of perspectives on dance and theatre.

Consequently many dance and theatre scholars contribute to proving theories right by applying them to a growing number of subject matters. This practice is not unique to theatre and dance studies or the humanities. Indeed the philosopher of science Thomas Kuhn argued in the 1960s that science is a puzzle and not an accumulation of knowledge surviving falsification attempts, which was the more widely adopted notion of his peer Karl Popper. According to Kuhn, a paradigmatic idea arises and researchers get to work on proving it through application to different fields until accelerating points of resistance destabilize the idea and give rise to the formation of a new paradigm (see Hacking 1999, 219–224).

What is unique about theatre and dance studies (with the exception of dance science) is how eclectically scholars have lifted and combined theoretical concepts and methods from multiple disciplines while liberating them from the often incompatible methodological criteria that qualify them. Differences of interpretation and *thick descriptions* that involve a priori speculations about contexts beyond the researchers' reach become qualitative values, and liberated concepts are not always applied within a new methodological design. In other words, the general strength of theatre and dance studies is not methodological awareness and consistency. The strength, as I see it, is an ability to shift between different lenses and adapt them to serve diverse analyses of theatre and dance phenomena.

Collaborations between performing arts scholars and cognitive scientists thus depend not on negotiation between two methodologies but rather on a discussion as to whether methodology or subject specificity takes the lead.

In PAR projects opportunities for creativity are prioritized throughout the research process. This can, as Nelson argues, mean that creativity is employed as a form of enactive inquiry in a process that also involves more distanced reflection and writing (Nelson 2013, 38–47). However, the priority of creativity can also, as in Kershaw's writing, be associated with a call for methodological mutability and, at times, even a radical dismissal of documentation, analysis, synthesis, or other forms of knowledge extraction (Kershaw 2009, 5). Either way, PAR processes tend to start with a loosely defined field of inquiry as opposed to the specific subject area and questions of scholarly research or the deductive hypotheses and inductive observations of scientific research. The research process is often cyclical (researchers return several times to interactions and materials with new ideas and approaches), it changes course in response to emerging possibilities, and it can involve a stance against systematic methodology that is meant to keep the process responsive to emergence and novel discovery.

When PAR enters our interdisciplinary collaboration, creative emergence thus has to be added to the discussion of priorities.

Methodological incompatibility and differently constituted knowledge

Engaging in this discussion of priorities, the performing arts scholar is likely to have a problem with the ways in which scientific methodology reduces complex artistic practices. What I am approaching here is the price of reductionism and generalization. When undertaking scientific, experimental research about the causal relationship between a phenomenon and an intervention that acts upon it, variables that potentially could affect this process have to be reduced in order to eliminate alternative explanations. In practical terms, variables are eliminated from the space of experimentation in order to ensure that a difference between tests taken before and after an intervention reflects the causal effect of the intervention and not these other variables (compare Cherulnik 2001, 3 and 13). This measure of *internal validity* is met by equally important criteria of *external validity*: in order to contribute to the accumulation of knowledge that Popper first proposed in 1957 and adhere to his criterion of scientific falsifiability, research results must be generalizable (Popper 1999, 65–71). They must apply to a larger population than the research subjects. This is achieved by randomly selecting a group of subjects that is kept uninformed about the objectives of the study, represents a demographic segment, and is large enough to produce statistically valid data and thus conclusions.

Scientific demands for *conceptual and construct validity* (Cherulnik 2001, 3) are more familiar to performing arts scholars. They may phrase it differently, but when conducting hypothetico-deductive research, for example, scholars generally agree that a hypothesis should help answer larger questions (conceptual validity) and that the associated study should test the hypothesis (construct validity). From the perspective of performing arts scholarship the problem is the internal and external validity criteria alone. Dance and theatre practices are inherently complex and deeply embedded in other cultural practices, and it is the relationship between the parts of these performance ecologies that is of interest. As the cognitive theatre scholar Evelyn Tribble concedes when presenting her concept of cognitive ecologies, it is not considered possible to study each part of an ecology in isolation from the others (Tribble and Sutton 2011, 95). Qualitative difference, case specificity, and situatedness are also considered forms of validity that are undermined by generalization.

Artistic inquiry tends to be less concerned with the task of mapping and analysing interconnections that already exist and more invested in bringing something new into the world, at times by severing, isolating, reconnecting, or testing the breaking point of such connections. If hypotheses are used they are *abductive* jumps or kick-starters of a process, not theories to be proven right or wrong. As Charles Sanders Peirce observed when coining the concept, *abductions* are based on neither logical deduction nor inductive observation; they are novel ideas inspired by singular occurrences and associations that offer possible, but unqualified explanations (Minnameier 2004, 78). The most stable and predictable element of artistic inquiry and practice as research often derives from the performance and creation approaches that researcher-artists are trained in – approaches which, as both Nelson and I have pointed out, involve implicit knowledge, skill, and habit (Nelson 2013, 41–44; Hansen 2011, 109–112). The radical arguments against documentation and analysis that Kershaw brings up are met by calls for self-reflection and articulation of such implicit attractors of habitual responses. A focus on self-reflection as a precondition for emergence that pushes beyond the predictable is common within dramaturgy and thus, not surprisingly, furthered in PAR projects with a dramaturgical subject of inquiry. The UK-based Vida Midgelow's research into dramaturgical awareness and memory in dance improvisation provides a useful example (Midgelow 2015, 106–123). Like dance scholars, Midgelow uses theory, in this case cognitive philosophy on enaction and memory systems drawn from Alva Nöe and Thomas Fuchs, as lenses to help her challenge the key notions of a practice. However, the repositioned notions she arrives at are not used to 'make new sense' of the practice through analysis and interpretation. Instead Midgelow brought the notions into a dance studio and used the particular kind of attention they afford to develop a series of improvisation tasks that, one by one, facilitate the improviser's perceptual, enactive, and embodied repositioning in ways that reflect and move beyond her theoretical insights. Midgelow helps dancers achieve agency in improvisation through dramaturgical consciousness about the layers of memory and training that emerge in their choices; how they position themselves in relation to other dancers, space, and audience; how they focus or disperse their attention; and – most importantly – the effect of registering what is generated from such choices while improvising. The full process enables the performer to cause and work with emerging possibilities that otherwise might not be accessible, while making strategic use of trained skills and actively developing new ones. Midgelow is not only articulating her research insights in a way that allows these insights to re-emerge again and again in performance but also training her 'reader's' research readiness by directing them to a practice of self-reflection and attention to emergence.

Though this effect is comparable to what Susan Foster has identified as the PAR embedded in influential dance teaching methods (Foster 2009, 91–97), Midgelow's research has a wider reach and involves more kinds of reflection and insight. Dissemination of her work takes the form of artistic courses and workshops, workshop lectures at scholarly conferences, and publication of workshop tasks inter-spliced with theory, all of which effectively act upon receivers who must dance or imagine themselves dancing to engage with the delivery. She is realizing an enactive epistemology and a (n)ontology of emergence through both her research process and her dissemination of results. Nelson promotes a practice of written reflection and dissemination of PAR results while naming that these texts are purchased at the expense of the exclusively enactive approach, which Foster's examples embody. Midgelow's work leads me to think that this conflict is less between enaction and writing than between becoming and knowing. The moment the PAR practitioner articulates insight as conclusive knowledge the process of becoming is discontinued. The interactions that emerging insight depends upon are lost in ways that mirror the ephemeral and relational nature of live performance[5] – that is unless the articulation, like in Midgelow's case, invites the emergence of insight instead of presenting conclusive knowledge.

In spite of the significant incompatibilities between the three paradigms of accumulative (scientific), diversifying (scholarly), and emergent (PAR) knowledge, there are areas of overlap. Scientists also make abductive jumps to develop novel ideas. If they hold up in subsequent deductive tests and against review of related research, then they may yield a major breakthrough, which can be applied, further developed, and challenged by the scientific community. Performance studies has adapted and produced scholarly approaches that emphasize self-reflective observation and emergence (e.g., performative writing, phenomenological analysis, and auto-ethnography) and concepts advanced by dance and theatre scholars (e.g., theatricality, performativity, and enaction) have since been adopted and used strategically for artistic creation. Perhaps it is not coincidental that it is common for scientists working with dance subjects to have a practical dance background (e.g., Corrine Jola, Elizabeth Waterhouse, Guido Orgs, and Emily Cross). There is a curiosity about whether insights intuited on a personal level as an artist or embedded in a training program can impact more general understandings of embodied, interpersonal cognition and vice versa. These are some of the factors that make us seek collaboration and friendship in spite of our differences and that motivated me to achieve multi-methodological literacy. This search furthermore inspires some degree of methodological adaptation. One of the science clusters in the Dance Engaging Science network did, for example, argue that experiments should take place in the less controlled context of the dance theatre and not a scientific lab to counter negative impact on movement responses caused by reduction (Waterhouse et al. 2014, 12).

However, even when working in these exciting spaces of overlap competing criteria of utility remain intact. There is a significant difference between trying to produce falsifiable knowledge about parts that can add up to a global theory of the natural world; aiming for a vast amount of different insights into the many complex relationships that concern a shared meta-subject; and developing strategies and approaches for how to respond, affect, and create in new ways. These drives behind the research paradigms are not negotiable, and they significantly limit methodological flexibility. It was this realization that led me to work on a cross-disciplinary model.

Acts of memory

One full cycle of exchange between the spaces of the RBP model (figure 2.1) was realized with *Acts of Memory* (completed at the University of Toronto in 2012). As previously mentioned, my main research question was whether personal

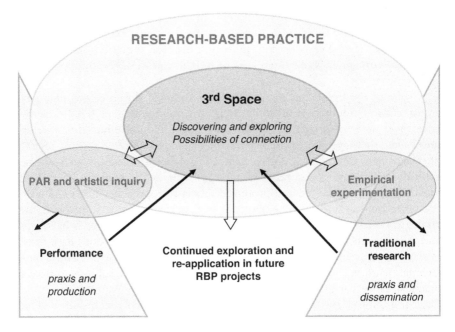

Figure 2.1 Revised version of chart by Pil Hansen; the original is published in Hansen and Barton (2009, 132).

memories that dancers and devisors invest in systematic forms of task-based performance generation undergo change. I had discovered that artistic inquiries into the mechanics of memory often result in the creation of performance generating systems that are designed to repurpose autobiographical memories and recalibrate the perceptual habits they entail. It was the affect of this specific practice that intrigued me. My question was formed while observing the creative inquiries of the Vancouver-based Theatre Replacement and the Toronto-based dance company Public Recordings and offering dramaturgical and scholarly feedback through the lens of reconstructive memory theory (i.e., Edelman and Tononi 2000). Hypotheses induced in that process were then tested deductively in controlled and reductive but not generalizable behavioural experiments with Ame Henderson (choreographer, dancer) and James Long (director, devisor) from the companies. And finally the creative potential of preliminary findings from the experiments was explored in a collaboratively defined *third space*. The outputs from the project are a new performance-generating system, a university course, and a series of conference papers, articles, and book chapters on interdisciplinary methodology, adaptation of memory, and the dramaturgy of performance generating systems (e.g., Hansen 2015; Hansen 2014; Hansen with Kaeja and Henderson 2014).

The model enabled us to move across disciplinary boundaries without sacrificing individual methods and priorities. But it proved more difficult than anticipated to identify and extract aspects from the controlled experiments that carry creative potential. This problem is best unfolded through a more detailed presentation of the *Acts of Memory* experiments.

Artistic inquiry and empirical experiments

In order to enable me to measure the adaptation of autobiographical memory caused by performance-generating systems, we established slightly simplified versions of two systems. This presentation is limited to a dance system called futuring memory (figure 2.2), originally created for Public Recordings' 2010 World Stage commission: *Relay.*[6]

Henderson and Public Recordings' initial creative inquiry was concerned with hierarchies, ownership, and embodied memory in dance. The inquiry started as a playful take on a tendency to avoid unison in contemporary dance. Henderson also wanted to work with the collaborative transfer of ideas from artist to artist, which rarely is reflected when ownership is claimed. In response to these interests she decided to work towards unison without leading or following. The solution to this 'impossible task' that Henderson's group of eight dancers arrived at was a strategic task named *futuring*. When futuring each

Figure 2.2 Public Recordings' dancers futuring in *Relay*. Enwave Theatre, Toronto, Canada, 2010.
Source: Ömer Yükseker.

dancer forms a hypothesis about where his or her co-dancers will be in the moment after 'right now', and then goes there. Copying co-dancers' movement is not an option, but it is allowed to draw upon visual and auditory information about their present movement in order to adjust hypotheses. The group's exploration of embodied, personal memory recall was, in a similar gesture, projected into this future moment in a task called *futuring memories*. In practice, a futuring dancer begins to recall choreographed movements he or she danced in the past when prompted by a physical association. The rest of the group futures the remembering dancer, thereby adapting and rendering collective his or her personal memory.

Prior to designing empirical experiments, Henderson and I published my scholarly discussion of the layers of memory that from a cognitive perspective may be involved in her inquiry alongside her responses to my lens and analysis, including the following conclusion:

> I notice that through a very different lens, this analysis poses questions and reveals the same well of potential that is at the heart of my artistic experiments. The dilemmas that Hansen points to frame my search for task-based performance strategies; but they also point to the increasingly complex revelations about the nature of embodied patterns, group dynamics, and the relationship of these systems to the event of performance.
>
> (Hansen with Henderson 2011, 15)

Henderson's question about embodied, personal memory of choreography and the choice of futuring such memories collectively gave rise to my question about the autobiographical consequences of this work, which in turn facilitated new reflection upon the central dilemmas that fuel Henderson's work. A friendship was born of the kind that makes cross-disciplinary work possible.

In our experiment, I reduced the amount of performers and through them the variables of training and praxis. I also reduced the memory sources used (i.e., the amount of choreographic memories available for recall) and introduced memories incrementally. And finally I reduced the variations over central tasks allowed within the system. The research subjects, Henderson and Long, selected a series of comparable and repeatable memories following a specific set of criteria. These memories served as our dependant variables (or the phenomena studied) and source materials for the systems (see figure 2.3). In order to account for any changes that our intervention might cause, the selected memories were recalled and video-recorded before and after futuring them. Additional tests were done with simple and alternated repetition of comparable memories in order to eliminate simple recall as the cause of adaptation.

When asked, the performers were confident that their pre- and post-recalls of memories were identical, but the data rendered it evident that their memories had been altered significantly: they had become shorter and were performed faster with a loss of range of movement. Each performer had also added qualities

Figure 2.3 Ame Henderson and James Long futuring memory in an *Acts of Memory* experiment. The Theatre Centre, Toronto, Canada, 2011.

Source: Pil Hansen.

that mirrored his or her co-performers' disciplinary strength. Henderson's choreography did, for example, gain emotional expression and intentionality drawn from Long's theatrical sensitivity.

Thus far the experiment has strong internal validity: the causal relationship between the dependant variable and the intervention – the memory changes and the systems – was unchallenged by contaminating variables. However, the produced knowledge was of limited use for artistic development and that limitation hindered third space exploration. We needed to know more about what the biologist Ian Boyd calls the mediating process (Boyd 2006, 25–40). We needed to understand how changes were produced. And like Boyd, I chose to address my case as a complex, dynamical system to meet this challenge.

Dynamical systems theory analysis

As described in the article cited ahead, Ester Thelen and Linda Smith's version of dynamical systems theory (DST) (1994) is a method to analyze the self-organizing dynamic of complex, open systems.[7] The aim of DST is neither to determine whether a system produces change (as in the scientific experiment) nor to interpret the performance it produces (as in hermeneutical or semiotic analysis). DST targets *how* a system generates behaviour through interaction between variables.

> The first step in applying DST involves the identification of the *parameters and variables* that most significantly affect the system's interactions. In *relay* the parameters were the futuring memory tasks and rules, while the variables were the performers' habits and training. The next step is to identify the external source of *energy* that sets interactions in motion and feeds their continued course. This source of energy in relay was memories of choreography from the past. Once these elements are identified, the system is analysed with attention to *order parameters, attractor states*, variables that disrupt stability and generate *phase transitions* and *phase shifts*. In short,

the order parameter attracts a certain form of behaviour within the system. This behaviour continues until another variable becomes a competing order parameter that disrupts stability. The system then transitions into a new phase, attracting a different form of behaviour around the competing parameter until it too is challenged.

(Hansen with House 2015, 67)

Video recordings of our experiment were carefully processed and categorized according to these DST concepts. Each recall of a memory was marked, measured for length and position, and played simultaneously to notate changes. The same was done with pure futuring sections and with the transitions into and out of memory recall within the system.

The findings were complex and rich in detail and can be used to develop dramaturgical strategies within the third space of the research model. I found that the main *order parameters* that attracted patterns of response in our two first futuring memory sessions turned out to be the milestones of a learning curve. The factor that most significantly affected the stability of behaviour, produced by the learning curve, was the addition of new memories: what started out as controlled recall of two memories in the first session became shortened and adaptable recall of four memories in the second session. When the performers arrived at six memories in the third session their recall became fragmented, they initiated the recall of each other's memories, and singular movements from the memories found their way into the pure futuring periods without the performers' awareness. In other words, as the amount of sources was increased and the performers began to learn each other's memories and movement vocabularies, their ability to distinguish their own memories from their partner's deteriorated. Eventually the same happened to the boundary between recall and futuring. The complexity level, which the increased openness towards sources caused, forced the performers to rely more upon their learned implicit memory and relax their conscious control of recall. This process funnelled the system into *phase transition*.

Each stage of the learning curve gave rise to new self-organization. When two memories were futured with control, a pattern of repeated movements for transitioning in and out of recall emerged. When two more memories were added and recall became fragmented, this pattern fell away. Instead a shared movement vocabulary began to emerge while futuring.

The performers' perceptual orientation was also affected. Initially both performers relied on visual information to adjust their hypotheses, but as more memories were added, this reliance ceased to be detectable. Two factors seemed to be involved: the performers learned to adjust to auditory and peripheral visual information and their repetition of vocabularies further increased their ability to base hypotheses on recent memory.

Eventually the performers' growing movement vocabulary, collective memory, and perceptual capacity made them more closely aligned and they did, indeed, produce several instances of self-organized unison (Hansen 2015, 132–137).

Third space

Henderson, Long, and I used these experimental discoveries strategically to explore a new system within the third space. We played with and countered the stages of the performers' learning curve in order to advance their ability to navigate complexity while keeping their effort and attention alive. Scaled increases in energy and new parameters were added to render the system tasks more and more complex to navigate, let alone perform, while ensuring that they continued to generate performance. Incorporating findings from James Long's creative inquiry, rules of response which allowed performers to actively hinder each other's reliance on memorization were devised. This exploration did in turn give rise to questions about the effect of competition (with its end objectives and emphasis on individual performance) within a continuously generating system that depends on collective forms of self-organization. The technical and cognitive insights into the system, which were provided by my analysis of mediating processes, were used to negotiate between the performance principles and different drivers of generation that Henderson's and Long's artistic inquiries had arrived at. Most importantly, we discovered new questions and system possibilities, which neither of our individual research spaces could have produced. Through cross-disciplinary exchange and transference, we achieved non-stratified, interdisciplinary research capacity.

Conclusion

In the case of *Acts of Memory* research-based practice (RBP) solved the problems of methodological incompatibility and stratified roles. In addition to the project outputs previously mentioned, results from the various spaces have also contributed to the creation of new dance and theatre works, workshops, and research projects. Henderson has been working on the possibility of futuring language (in *What We Are Saying*) and Long has been testing the performance-generating limits of competitive structures (in *Winners and Losers* 2012). I have been working on artistic inquiries into intimacy and audience participation through performance-generating systems (in *Crave* 2013 and *Trace* 2014), developing a DST-based dance notation tool (Hansen with House 2015) through RBP, and designing scientific tests of the generating system's effect on working-memory capacity. These projects involve new collaborators from different disciplines, effectively expanding the research spaces and networks that our results, questions, and practices are transferred to and impact. RBP does thus mobilize a process, which can continue to give rise to new emergences across disciplines over longer time, while producing results in a shorter timespan that are valued as knowledge by different fields.

The solutions arrived at were not all reflected in the original model Bruce Barton and I designed. The *Acts of Memory* experiments involved several methodological compromises: the complexity of the intervention (the system) was reduced in order to increase the internal validity of the study. The specificity of the practice and practitioners was, in turn, valued over and above the demand for external validity and generalization. In the spaces of artistic inquiry my dramaturgical feedback was informed by reconstructive memory theory. Looking back, I begin to consider these interferences as one of the preconditions for the productive transfer of subjects, materials, and insights between the different spaces of the research model. The friendship and willingness to not only control our own research spaces but also adapt our methods in anticipation of interdisciplinary exchange are, furthermore, important factors.

That said, the most significant facilitator of interdisciplinary transfer across artistic, scholarly, and scientific inquiries that *Acts of Memory* has produced is the systematic and empirical analysis of mediating processes. With that focus we advance from creating a performance, interpreting its manifestation, or measuring its effect on cognition. We become able to understand performance in terms of the complex mediating processes that generate a cognitive change, and we approach cognition in terms of how it evolves through and affects embodied performance.

Notes

1 Concepts of time in dramaturgical and compositional tools led me to the temporality of perception in philosophy, which in turn directed me towards the cognitive sciences. I set out to develop dramaturgical tools from neurocognitive, reconstructive memory theory and through practice as research experiments with Danish and Canadian dramaturgs. Research methods used were drawn from professional fields of dramaturgy as well as sociology (grounded theory) and linguistics (discourse and speech act analysis). The resulting tool, *Perceptual Dramaturgy*, has empirical anchors in dramaturgical practice, but only hypothetical and theoretical connections to cognitive science (Hansen 2011).
2 Initiated by Scott deLahunta under the Motion Bank Project.
3 Examples of such controlled, neurobiological projects with dancing subjects are Emily Cross's study of how movement expertise affects perception and recall of choreography at Bangor University and Guido Orgs's study of the impact of entrainment (i.e., the tendency fall into rhythm with others) on execution and reception of task-based dance at Brunel University.
4 The theatre and dance lecturer Freya Vass-Rhee headed up a series of Dance Engaging Science guest lectures and helped establish the Beacon Institute for performance and cognition studies at the University of Kent, and the performance studies professor Maaike Bleeker created the Performance and Science Encounters website at the University of Utrecht.
5 Within the field of dramaturgy this problem is known as "closing down" a creative process in interpretation or predetermined staging concepts. See Lepecki (2015) for a dramaturgical strategy of errancy (drifting) that addresses this problem in a creation process.
6 See Hansen "The Dramaturgy . . ." (2015) for a more detailed discussion of this case.
7 This theory and method have evolved from Kelso and Haken's classical model for the dynamics of limb coordination from 1985 (see Kelso 1995; Haken 1987; Fuchs et al. 2008) into two different approaches: (1) a mathematical approach for the calculation and visual representation of complex systems' self-organizing patterns; and (2) a both qualitative and quantitative method for the analysis of human behavior. The second approach was initially proposed by Esther Thelen and Linda Smith in 1994 as a method to analyze the development of cognition and action in early childhood and later used by Van Gelder to argue against a computational model of the mind (Van Gelder 1995; Port 1995).

References

Allegue, Ludivine, Simon Jones, Baz Kershaw, and Angela Piccini. *Practice-as-Research: In Performance and Screen*. Basingstoke: Palgrave, 2009.

Blair, Rhonda. *The Actor, Image, and Action: Acting and Cognitive Neuroscience*. Oxon: Routledge, 2008.

Boyd, Ian. "Studying Complexity: Are We Approaching the Limits of Science?" *Interdisciplinary Research: Diverse Approaches in Science, Technology, Health, and Society*. Ed. John Atkinson and Malcolm Crove. Hoboken, NJ: John Wiley & Sons, 2006. 25–40.

Cherulnik, Paul D. "An Overview of the Research Process." *Methods for Behavioral Research: A Systematic Approach*. Thousand Oaks, CA: SAGE, 2001. Chapter 1: 1–21.

Cook, Amy. *Shakespearean Neuroplay: Reinvigorating the Study of Dramatic Texts and Performance Through Cognitive Science*. Basingstoke: Palgrave, 2010.

Crave. Choreographed by Karen Kaeja, dramaturged by Pil Hansen, danced by Stephanie Tremblay Abubo and Michael Caldwell to music by Sarah Shugarman. Produced by Kaeja d'Dance, Habourfront Theatre Next Steps, Enwave, Toronto, Canada, 2013. Performance.

Edelman, Gerald M. and Giulio Tononi. *A Universe of Consciousness*. New York: Basic Books, 2000.

Foster, Susan Leigh. "Making a Dance/Researching Through Movement." *Mapping Landscapes for Performance as Research: Scholarly Acts and Creative Cartographies*. Ed. Shannon Rose Riley and Lynnette Hunter. Basingstoke: Palgrave, 2009. 91–97.

Fuchs, A. and V.K. Jirsa, eds. *Coordination: Neural, Behavioral and Social Dynamics*. Heidelberg: Springer, 2008.

Ginsborg, J. "Beating Time: The Role of Kinaesthetic Learning in the Development of Mental Representations for Music." *Art in Motion*. Ed. A. Mornell. Vienna: Peter Lang, 2009. 121–142.

Hacking, Ian. "The Rationality of Science After Kuhn." *Scientific Inquiry – Readings in the Philosophy of Science*. Ed. Robert Klee. New York: Oxford University Press, 1999. 216–227.

Haken, H. "Synergistics: An Approach to Self-Organization." *Self-Organizing Systems: The Emergence of Order*. Ed. F.E. Yates. New York: Plenum Press, 1987. 417–435.

Hansen, Pil. "Dancing Performance Generating Systems." *Theatre Topics on Dramaturgy* 24.3 (Sept 2014): 255–261.

———. "The Dramaturgy of Performance Generating Systems." *Dance Dramaturgy: Modes of Agency, Awareness and Engagement*. Ed. Pil Hansen and Darcey Callison. Basingstoke: Palgrave, 2015. 124–143.

———. "Perceptual Dramaturgy: Swimmer (68)." *Journal of Dramatic Theory and Criticism* XXV.2 (Spring 2011): 107–124.

Hansen, Pil and Bruce Barton. "Research-Based Practice: Situating *Vertical City* Between Artistic Development and Applied Cognitive Science." *TDR: The Drama Review* 53.4 (2009): 120–136.

Hansen, Pil with Ame Henderson. "Processing Memory in *300 TAPES* and *Relay*." *Canadian Performance Review on Memory* 14.5 (Winter 2011): 11–20.

Hansen, Pil with Christopher House. "Scoring the Generating Principles of Performance Systems." *Performance Research: On An/Notation* 20.6 (Oct 2015): 65–73.

Hansen, Pil with Karen Kaeja and Ame Henderson. "Self-Organization and Transition in Systems of Dance Generation." With Contributions by Karen Kaeja and Ame Henderson. *Performance Research on Turbulence* 19.5 (Oct 2014): 23–33.

Kelso, J.A.S. *Dynamic Patterns: The Self-Organization of Brain and Behavior*. Cambridge, MA: MIT Press, 1995.

Kershaw, Baz. "Practice-as-Research: An Introduction." *Practice-as-Research: In Performance and Screen.* Ed. Ludivine Allegue, Simon Jones, Baz Kershaw and Angela Piccini. Basingstoke: Palgrave, 2009. 1–17.

Lepecki, Andre. "Errancy as Work: Seven Strewn Notes for Dance Dramaturgy." *Dance Dramaturgy: Modes of Agency, Awareness and Engagement.* Basingstoke: Palgrave, 2015. 51–66.

Lutterbie, John. *Towards a General Theory of Acting: Cognitive Science and Performance.* Basingstoke: Palgrave, 2011.

Midgelow, Vida. "Improvisation Practices and Dramaturgical Consciousness: A Workshop." *Dance Dramaturgy: Modes of Agency, Awareness, and Engagement.* Basingstoke: Palgrave, 2015. 106–123.

Minnameier, Gerhard. "Peirce-suit of Truth: Why Inference to the Best Explanation and Abduction Ought Not Be Confused." *Erkenntnis* 60.1 (2004): 75–105.

Motion Bank. Dance Notation and Research Website Produced by Scott deLahunta at the Prior Forsythe Company. http://motionbank.org/en/content/dance-engaging-science. Visited July 15, 2015.

Nelson, Robin. *Practice as Research in the Arts: Principles, Protocols, Pedagogies, Resistances.* Basingstoke: Palgrave, 2013.

Popper, Karl. "Falsificationism." *Scientific Inquiry – Readings in the Philosophy of Science.* Ed. Robert Klee. New York: Oxford University Press, 1999. 65–71.

Port, Robert F. and Timothy Van Gelder, eds. *Mind as Motion: Explorations in the Dynamics of Cognition.* Cambridge, MA: MIT Press, 1995.

Relay. Choreographed by Ame Henderson (with the ensemble). Perf. Katie Ewald, Matija Ferlin, Claudia Fancello, Marie Claire Forté, Mairéad Filgate, Barbara Pallomina, Brendan Jensen, and Chad Dembski. Harbourfront World Stage at the Enwave Theatre, Toronto. April 2010. Performance.

Shaughnessy, Nicola. "Knowing Me Knowing You: Cognition, Kinesthetic Empathy and Applied Performance." *Kinesthetic Empathy in Creative and Cultural Practices.* Ed. Dee Reynolds and Matthew Reason. Bristol: Intellect, 2012. 33–50.

Stevens, C., R. Dean, K. Vincs, and E. Schubert. "In the Heat of the Moment: Audience Real-Time Response to Music and Dance Performance." *Coughing and Clapping: Investigating Audience Experience.* Ed. Karen Burland and Stephanie Pitts. Farnham: Ashgate, 2014. 69–88.

Stevens, C., J. Ginsborg, and G. Lester. "Backwards and Forwards in Space and Time: Recalling Dance Movement From Long-term Memory." *Memory Studies* 4 (2011): 234–250.

Thelen, Esther and Linda B. Smith. *A Dynamic Systems Approach to the Development of Cognition and Action.* Cambridge, MA: MIT Press, 1994.

Trace. Directed by Bruce Barton with the devisors Michelle Polak and Martin Julien. Dramaturgy by Pil Hansen. Co-produced by Vertical City Performance and Theatre Gargantua. Sommerworks Festival, Toronto, Canada 2014. Performance.

Tribble, Evelyn and John Sutton. "Cognitive Ecologies as a Framework for Shakespearean Studies." *Shakespeare Studies* 39 (2011): 94–103.

Van Gelder, T. "What Might Cognition Be, If Not Computation?" *Journal of Philosophy* 92.7 (July 1995): 345–381.

Vass-Rhee, Freya. "In the Meta-, Somewhat Eluviated: Critiquing Interdisciplinary Metaphors Through Arts-Sciences Research" On the Panel "Why Stratify?: Inter/intra-disciplinary Methodologies for Studying Cognitive Processes through Performance." International Federation of Theatre Research's Annual Conference, Warwick, 2014.

Waterhouse, Elizabeth, Riley Watts, and Bettina E. Blasing. "Doing *Duo* – A Case Study of Entrainment in William Forsythe's Choreography '*Duo*.'" *Frontiers in Human Neuroscience* 8 (Oct 2014): article 812. www.frontiersin.org. Visited July 15, 2015.

What We Are Saying. Created and performed by Ame Henderson, Frank Cox-O'Connell, Katie Ewald, Mairéad Filgate, Sherri Hay, Ame Henderson, Sandra Henderson, Brendan Jensen, Alexander MacSween, Liz Peterson, Bojana Stancic, Stephen Thompson and Evan Webber. Co-produced by public Recordings, Dance4 (Nottingham), Festival TransAmériques (Montreal) and Harbourfront Centre World Stage. The Power Plant Contemporary Art Gallery, Toronto, Canada, 2013. Performance.

Winners and Losers. Created and performed by James Long and Marcus Youssef. Co-produced by Theatre Replacement and New World Theatre. The Gateway Theatre, Richmond BC, Canada, 2012. Performance.

Chapter 3

The daisy chain model

An approach to epistemic mapping and dissemination in performance-based research

Joanna Bucknall

Introduction

There is an inevitable duality in discussing performance as an approach to knowledge acquisition. There are epistemic concerns and issues of ontology in this methodological orientation, and then there is the 'thing itself': the specific, particular and localised research agenda which drives that particular approach. The decision to take up performance as a research methodology comes with various assumptions and relations that impact upon the nature of the insights that can be generated. However, since the 1990s it is this concern with methodology that seems to have dominated the discourse within the various iterations of scholarship that has performance as a central research strategy. I will return to this shortly to give some consideration to the various terms employed to describe those strategies in order to establish my own usage of the terms 'practice as research' (PaR) and 'practice-based research' (PBR). There has, however, been far less concern over the insights and outputs that such an approach contributes to various knowledge communities than the validity of the methodologies that produce those insights.

This imbalance is, of course, something that this very volume seeks to address. Although the battle for the recognition of performance as a rigorous and valuable research strategy is still quietly being fought in very practical ways (with funding bodies, university committees and evaluative processes, such as the Research Excellence Framework [REF]), it is now widely accepted that PaR and PBR have earned their scholarly credentials – at least in theory. In this chapter I will address some of those now familiar concerns over methodology, epistemology and ontology, but with a view to offering a tool that has the potential to marshal, map and disseminate PaR and PBR activity.

The tool that I have developed is called the daisy chain model. Over the course of the chapter I will explain the emergence of the model from my own PaR and PBR activities over the last decade, explicating the nature and function of the model within that localised context, but also highlighting its potentially wider implications and applications. Through a consideration of its function within several of my own performance research projects – *Siren Song*,[1]

You, Hope, Her & Me[2] and *Wish Box*[3] – I will offer insight into the ways in which I have developed my model as a response to the localised peculiarities of my creative practice and context. Further accounting for the ways in which I have employed that model as a tool for marshalling, mapping and disseminating my own rigorous performance-based knowledge acquisition process, I will also offer some of the insights that the process of employing that model has produced. Admittedly, the challenges engaged in my own approach across these three research projects – out of which the model was developed – are of course deeply localised, subjective and contextually contingent. However, I will demonstrate the ways in which the model has potential value and application beyond its originating context. Before I can begin the process of explicating the emergence, development and application of the model, I must first discuss some of the terminology associated with performance-based research and my particular usage of it here.

Navigating the terminological terrain: teleological distinctions

Since the emergence, and more recently the acceptance, of performance as a research strategy, a variety of terminology has been employed to explicate and make distinct the nature of the various roles and practices that such a strategy generates. I will navigate some of those distinctions in order to clarify my own position as a practitioner-scholar and the practice-based approach to research that I employ. The term 'practitioner', at least in its application within the UK, is indicative of the democratic, collaborative, interdisciplinary approach to performance-making that has its genealogy in the paradigm shift into performance of the 1960s. Its usage characterises the slippage between art and the everyday, as well as the dissolution of traditional disciplinary boundaries that have dominated experimental arts practices since the emergence of performance within the arts and cultural studies. According to Henry Bial, 'The field of Performance Studies takes performance as an organizing concept for the study of a wide range of behaviour. A postdiscipline of inclusions, Performance Studies sets no limit on what can be studied in terms of medium and culture' (Bial, 2004: 43). This focus on performance results in an approach that is dominated by a fascination with process: 'the process of doing the work was almost more significant than that which was actually done, the live nature of the work, its actuality, valued more highly than any particularity of content or style' (MacRitchie in Childs and Walkin, 1998: 25).

The distinction of practitioner within the performing arts disciplines simply refers to the role of someone engaged in performance-making of one kind or another. It has become the dominant way to designate the interdisciplinary approach of one engaged in making performance that has been central to experimental, non-text-based modes of performing arts in post-war Britain. Therefore, when I refer to myself as a practitioner or practitioner-scholar I am suggesting first that I am a performance-maker; but more specifically, I am locating myself within that post-war, interdisciplinary, democratic, collaborative, non-text-based tradition. I will elaborate further on the particulars of my own practice and how they inform my research methodology later in the chapter. Employing performance as a research strategy shifts the role of practice from that of the object or subject of academic enquiry to that of the *method* of inquiry. Therefore, when I suggest that I am a practitioner-scholar I am drawing attention to the centrality of performance to my scholarship. It is indicative of the skills, expertise and attitude that I take up as a performance-maker, while at the same time explicitly locating that practice within the wider arena of scholarly inquiry, rather than professional practice *per se*.

There is the potential for confusion and misunderstanding with the acronym PaR; it is crucial, therefore, that I outline my own position in relation to its various definitions and usages. In the UK, PaR refers to 'practice as research' and is a term that has been borrowed from research in the fields of pedagogy, anthropology and sociology. Practice as research (PaR) is a designation that has persisted in discourse surrounding performance practice as a mode of research inquiry in the UK, with further distinctions being made between practice as research, practice-based research and practice-led research. This is not the case outside of the UK academy, however, and in other contexts, such as Australia, PAR is the acronym for performance as research. Robin Nelson, who is a leading voice in the discourse surrounding the development of practice as research in performance and the arts in the UK, suggests that

> PaR involves a research project in which practice is a key method of inquiry and where, in respect of the arts, a practice (creative writing, dance, musical score/performance, theatre/performance, visual exhibition, film or other cultural practice) is submitted as substantial evidence of a research inquiry.
> (Nelson, 2013: 8–9)

Bradley Haseman's definition of performance as research appears to make a similar case to Nelson's:

> At the most basic level, Performance as Research can be defined as pursuing a specific line of scholarly investigation or research into performance – writing, directing, designing, performing, spectating, etc. – by means of performance – writing, directing, designing, performing, spectating, etc. [. . .] Foremost, of course, is the fact that when a researcher conducts research into an aspect of drama, theatre or performance through performance they do not need to translate questions, methods or findings from the creative to the academic in the way that other approaches to research often demand.
> (Haseman, 2007: 148)

Performance as research has its lineage in the theatre and performance disciplines, with strong roots in the Australian academy, but practice as research has a much more interdisciplinary genealogy within the UK context.

The designation of *performance as research* is quite simply a more narrow articulation of the focus of this research approach within the performing arts, whereas *practice as research* has a wider scope that includes any specialist disciplinary mode that might be perceived as *practice*. From this point on in this essay, when I employ the acronym PaR it is in order to abbreviate the UK-centric designation of *practice as research*. However, the specialised practice that I engage in *is* performance; so when I refer to my research as *practice*, I am indeed alluding to my performance-making practice. PaR in both of these senses provides a broad-based definition that, since the early articulations of the field in the 1990s and early 2000s, has developed more nuanced and subtle typologies. These, however, have been shaped by the various research contexts that produce them, such as PhD regulations, funding bodies' criteria and postdoctoral schemes.

In taking up a PaR approach, discourse needs to be developed by the performance practitioner that lays open the tacit understandings emerging out of his or her practice in such a way that does not compromise or subvert them or reduce them to conceptual discourse. Nelson acknowledges the tensions that this produces:

> An acknowledgement that arts innovation cannot be ignored in the academy accompanied by a reluctance to recognize that arts practices might constitute 'research' has led in some quarters to a semantic wriggling which sustains the sense that the arts do not quite meet established criteria.
>
> (Nelson, 2013: 10)

This 'semantic wriggling' has generated two distinct typologies of PaR: practice-led research and practice-based research. Practice-led research places the practice/performance as the central methodology and as the research output. Barbara Bolt recognises that there is a 'double articulation between theory and practice, whereby theory emerges from a reflexive practice at the same time that practice is informed by theory. This double articulation is central to practice-led research' (Barrett and Bolt, 2014: 29). This particular approach to PaR locates tacit knowing as the knowledge itself – knowledge that cannot be expressed outside of the material practice conditions that produced it. Bolt asserts that 'material productivity' (ibid.: 30) is the epistemic nature of practice-led research (PLR); 'the "thing" in question *is* the practice' (ibid.: 30). Practice-based research (PBR) has practice as a central element of its methodology of knowledge acquisition but does not offer a standalone practice-generated output. Within performance disciplines this methodology of PaR has more capacity to achieve the requirements of the academy's interpretation of what might be considered research. My PaR approach is actually a blending of PBR and

PLR research methods. However, this requires that the practice-based researcher ask herself, following Angela Piccini,

> How, then, is this type of research best identified, evidenced and disseminated, if we accept that the academy will continue to demand such activity? And when these research knowledges are translated into other media, what are the best ways to indicate, in the translation, what knowledges are lost or gained?
>
> (Piccini, 2002: 239)

These are some of the questions and concerns that have been the driving force for the development of the daisy chain model.

Localised, subjective and relational negation in existing PaR models

Since the start of my doctoral studies[4] I have been working to develop an approach to PaR that establishes a middle ground between the practice-based and practice-led typologies, to some extent out of necessity. As I have already suggested, in general the UK academy and funding bodies do not accept practice (which is, in this instance, the specialist practice of performance-making) as a stand-alone research output or outcome. Thus, Bolt's typology of practice-led research was never a viable option open to me within the context of doctoral study; nor, in fact, has it been since that project's completion. It is necessary and important to acknowledge the deep impact that doctoral criteria, research funding mandates and the strategic priorities of the Research Excellence Framework (REF) have had on the development of my approach to PaR and the resulting daisy chain model. The practice that is produced by and through my research activity does in fact operate as the tacit knowledge that Bolt suggests is central to the practice-led approach. However, that practice is unable to perform its knowledges as a research output *per se* in my particular context for various reasons. I am required to supplement and support that knowing in more tangible and material ways than performance is ontologically capable of.

The blending of PBR and PLR methods that my own research strategy employs generates what Barrett and Bolt articulate as *praxis*:

> Praxical knowledge implies that ideas and theory are ultimately the result of practice rather than vice versa. Drawing on Heidegger, Don Ihde extends this idea through his elaboration of "technics", which he refers to as: 'human actions or embodied relations involving the manipulation of artefacts to produce effects within the environment' (Ihde, 1979: 3). These 'effects' broadly understood as 'knowledge' emerge through material processes. Because such processes are (at least in part) predicated on the tacit

and alternative logic of practice *in time*, their precise operations cannot be predetermined.

(Barrett and Bolt, 2007: 6)

Blending these two methods has enabled me to produce knowledges that are generated both *in* and *through* engaging in the activity of making performance. It has provided the conditions to generate knowledges that are tacit but that can also be transmitted and transferred beyond the originating site of the praxis. In employing performance as a mode of research inquiry, whether to further performance practice itself or to find ways to understand and conceptualise it, one is dealing with something that is experiential, personal, ephemeral and intangible. It is, in fact, the position of PBR that I am further pressed to occupy by the demands of the experiential nature of the immersive, interactive and participative forms that my practice is concerned with. At the same time, I feel the persistent pressure of my context to ensure that the transferable and transmittable knowledges that the praxis generates are disseminated. Thus, the praxis is never entirely practice-based nor practice-led; the endeavour rests provisionally between the two.

It is a deeply uncomfortable epistemological position that informs my approach to PaR, its documentation and its dissemination. It is the tensions between managing the various knowledge(s) produced in and through practice along with the direct pressures of the academy's requirements to transmit, transfer and disseminate them that have led directly to the development of the daisy chain model. The refusal by the academy in the UK to accept performance *per se* as a rigorous stand-alone output has made it necessary for me to address the same concerns that Rebecca Schneider has voiced when she wonders if 'in privileging an understanding of performance as a refusal to remain, do we ignore other ways of knowing, other modes of remembering, that might be situated precisely in the ways in which performance remains, but remains differently?' (Schneider, 2001: 100). My development of the daisy chain model is, in part, a response to addressing and accounting for those pressures as fundamental from the outset in the design of my PaR method. However, it has also grown out of certain inadequacies of the existing models to address and account for some of the peculiar epistemological and ontological concerns of my own PaR projects over the last decade. Therefore, the decision to employ performance as a research strategy is not in itself a concrete model. Rather it is a decision to adopt a research strategy that foregrounds experiential, embodied, haptic, syn(a)esthetic and kinaesthetic ways of knowing. Choosing to engage in PaR is making an ontological commitment; and '[w]ithout ontologies or the conceptualisations that underlie knowledge, there cannot be a vocabulary for representing [or, in this case, performing] knowledge' (Chandrasekaran et al., 1999: 22).

The daisy chain model has, then, developed out of the gaps and inabilities of the existing models to fully account for, document, map, marshal and disseminate my own process and insights adequately. PaR is necessarily micro in nature; it is localised and subjective, peculiar and particular. In my experience it is precisely the localised and subjective context of the particular practice that is almost always the site of the insights produced by and through PaR activity. When I first began to engage in PaR over a decade ago as a PhD student, I employed Melissa Trimingham's 'spiral model' (Trimingham, 2002: 54) and Nelson's 'dynamic model for practice as research' as tools to structure the methodological design of my praxis. However, it became evident very swiftly that both methods were failing to fully account for the subjective, localised and – more critically – relational aspects of my praxis. Neither model offered the solution to managing the tensions of the regulatory context that I was working within or the significance of the relational elements that impacted upon my praxis. Despite those failings, it is important to acknowledge the valuable contribution to the field of PaR that these models have made and also their influence on the development of my own. Both models focus on the same concerns and propose similar approaches for addressing them. Each is a reflective process that ensures the necessary rigour required of research within a practical context. Both rely upon the concept of *praxis* and situate the researcher in the role of the reflective practitioner – a role previously developed by Donald Schön. It is only through the employment and application of both of these existing models as tools to marshal my PaR activity that gaps, slippages, holes and failures became evident to me.

Choosing to adopt PaR, first with my PhD research and then in my subsequent research projects, was an ontological decision; I was concerned with investigating certain experiential performance practices (to which I will turn shortly), exploring them in both production and reception. I hoped to access insights that could be arrived at only through a direct engagement in praxis. However, that ontological decision required, as with all forms of research, a careful methodology to marshal the material knowledge acquisition and generate a rigorous epistemic logic. The tools that made up my initial PaR methodology for my doctoral PaR project, *Siren Song*, needed to be articulated in order to meet the specific and particular demands of my project. Trimingham's and Nelson's models formed the foundation of my initial approach to devising a robust methodology. Both are designed in such a way that the insights they elicit are contingent to and emergent within the particular research project. As John Freeman succinctly articulates, PaR is 'always a form of re-search':

> [PaR is] a drawing on one's previous experience and developing this into knowledge. Viewed in this way, practice as research is about developing practical work into knowledge by transposing the experience of what it is that one does into data and then subjecting this to the type of reflection, analysis and discipline that is involved in serious compositional study.
>
> (Freeman, 2010: 264)

Through the application of both models I came to realise their inability to account for various, substantive aspects of my own praxis.

Central to praxis is tacit-knowing or knowing-in-action, but these require a certain practical competence. Nelson's and Trimingham's models are both reliant upon the researcher acknowledging her practical competencies and laying these open to self-scrutiny through the dialogic process of reflecting-in-action. This practical competence is one of the ontological concerns that underpin the ensuing praxis; it is that tacit knowledge of performance-making competencies that must be exposed and investigated in order to utilise practice as a mode of research. Reflecting-in-action is a process of investigating, examining and evaluating practice at the moment of its happening, rather than as post-activity analysis (although post-activity reflection is, of course, an aspect of both models as well because it activates the spiral [Trimingham] or the dynamics of the knowledge triangle [Nelson] once insights have been recognised). Reflection-in-action is a way of interrogating practice and its tacit knowing *through* practice: 'In such processes, reflection tends to focus interactively on the outcomes of action, the action itself, and the intuitive knowing implicit in the action' (Schön, 1995: 56).

When reflection-in-action is manifest, it is as experimentation and as a method of practice-based inquiry:

> Through reflection, [the practitioner] can surface and criticize the tacit understandings that have grown up around the repetitive experiences of a specialized practice [in this case performance], and can make new sense of the situations of uncertainty or uniqueness which [s]he may allow [her]self to experience.
>
> (Schön, 1995: 61)

This is one of the central premises of Trimingham's and Nelson's models (Nelson's model appears to be a development of the dynamic spiral of Trimingham's). Trimingham has taken up the principles of action research to devise a model of PaR that in application can structure and lend rigour to the often ephemeral and anarchic nature of the creative process of performance practice. Like Nelson's, Trimingham's model prioritises research questions/ concerns, and to some extent this also suggests reliance upon practical competence. The research questions/concerns and practical competence are the entry point; their dynamic relationship with the creative process creates a reciprocal cycle, with theory affecting the creative process and the creative process affecting the research questions. Trimingham asserts that

> [t]he paradigm model of progress that allows for this [the disorderly reality of creative processes] is the hermeneutic-interpretive spiral model where progress is not linear but circular; a spiral which constantly returns to our original point of entry but with renewed understanding.
>
> (Trimingham, 2002: 54)

Nelson's model is also a dynamic reciprocal process with praxis at its centre. He suggests that it is designed to present the possibility of new understanding through the interplay of the individual elements and is driven by the following modes of knowledge: 'know that', 'know what' and 'know how'. He further suggests that all three perspectives converge during PaR in order to generate an approach to performance practice that is *praxical* rather than *practical*:

> A key observation to reiterate in respect of my epistemological model, then, is that the whole is dynamic and interactive (the arrows along the axes [. . .] consciously point both ways). Theory, that is to say, is not prior to practice, functioning to inform it, but theory and practice are rather 'imbricated within each other' in praxis.
>
> (Nelson, 2013: 62)

It is Nelson's use of *praxis* that 'is intended to denote the possibility of thought within both "theory" and "practice" in an iterative process of "doing–reflecting–reading–articulating–doing" (ibid.: 32). It is, thus, a dialogic process.

Despite the focus on dialogic critical self-reflection in both the models, one that I agree is central to the PaR activity of praxis, there are limitations to these models that have presented my own PaR process with challenges. Trimingham's model is entirely hermetic and does not take into account the contextual relational discourse that also informs and impacts upon praxis. Nelson's model does attempt to account in a limited manner for the relational context of 'know-how' and 'know-what', but the way that this is brought to bear upon praxis is static. It acknowledges the PaR researcher's practical expertise as a specialist practitioner and her theoretical knowledge as components of praxis, but does not account for these explicitly in its design or visual representation. Nelson explicitly discusses the role that these relational practices and discourses play within the construction of the researcher's praxis, which he designates as a 'location in a lineage':

> If we wish to claim that our praxis manifests new knowledge or substantial new insights, the implication is that we know what the established knowledge or insights are. [. . .] In actuality, this means that we know the backstory of our work and experience other people's practice as professional artists typically do.
>
> (Nelson, 2013: 32)

However, his model does not fully account for these factors in its visual representation, nor incorporate their significance beyond their *implicit* contribution to the development of the researcher's praxis. Not explicitly accounting for these relational and contextual aspects that inform and impact upon the praxis marginalises their significance in the dialogic process and ultimately in the generation of discourse. Personally, certain relational and contextual elements have been highly significant in informing my praxis and the insights that emerged out of that dialogic process. Neither of these two models has the ability to account for those relational influencing factors *explicitly*.

Nelson's and Trimingham's models offer an approach which provides the PaR researcher with an intrinsic rigour to her process, one that is driven by research questions/concerns as well as practical competence, in a manner similar to more traditional modes of research methodology. They are models for marshalling the structure of PaR activity, and the praxis that they both generate provides a scholarly approach to performance practice that is essential to validating PaR within the academy. Both models draw into focus the micro aspects of a specific PaR project and make visible the role of the reflective practitioner within that process *through* the activity of praxis. However, this localised and subjective perspective on the praxis is isolated in relation to the PaR activity itself and the questions that drive it. During my own research, I have found this to be deeply problematic; in my experience PaR is impacted and influenced by relational factors outside of the hermetically sealed PaR project and its questions. It has been almost impossible for me to separate my wider context as a scholar from the practical process of the PaR project. It has been even more challenging to account for the influence of these relational contexts on my praxis.

It was this concern that pushed me to shift my thinking about the nature of the process and its epistemic implications. The development of praxis was informed by factors other than my 'tacit knowledge' as a performance-maker, my 'cognitive academic knowledge', and the reflection-in-action that Nelson and Trimingham propose. I suggest that there is a 'flowering' of the relational discursive fields of practice and knowledge sets that is central to not only the development of a PaR researcher's praxis but also the insights that it generates. Neither model accounts explicitly for the process of mapping, documenting or disseminating PaR, nor do they profess to. In order to addresses some of these limitations, I have developed the daisy chain as a more relational model that has the potential to marshal, map and disseminate praxis, accounting for its contextual and relational discursive fields.

The daisy chain model

I developed the daisy chain model during my doctoral PaR activity as a visual representation of the holistic epistemology of my PBR. It is a representation of the methodological concerns that underpinned the practical activity of my PaR and a tool for mapping and disseminating the epistemic logic and discoveries of that practical activity. It is an overriding structure that ensured the research-driven cyclical rigour discovered in the 'spiral model' and the 'dynamic model for practice as research', but in such a way as to account for, marshal and map the relational discursive fields that I had found to impact upon my particular praxis. As such, it grew directly out of my own emergent PaR needs in response to the received methodologies' failure to fully address or account for them.

In order to investigate the central concerns of my PhD research topic[5] – the production and reception of participative performance practices – I designed two distinct research methodologies: (1) the reflective practitioner and (2) the reflective participant.[6] My intention was to engage in praxis as a reflective practitioner in order to gain access to the nature of participative dramaturgies in and through practice, as well as insights about the nature of those dramaturgies' reception. I also developed the concept of the reflective participant as a phenomenological approach to the analysis of immersive, interactive, pervasive and participative performance work that addresses the centrality of experience in those forms. My hope was that the activity I undertook as a reflective participant would supplement the PBR activity that I undertook as a reflective practitioner, providing case studies to demonstrate the location of my own praxis within the wider performance landscape of emergent immersive practices. At the outset I had thought these would be separate strategies that would contextualise and support one another; however, it became evident fairly swiftly that these distinct approaches were actually heavily influencing and impacting upon one another in fundamental and holistic ways. I came to the realization that my 'participation [...] as an audience participant has in fact become a specialist practice; one that is informed by my role as a researcher and the embodied tacit knowledge(s) produced by my significant experience of immersive performance. I am, therefore, locating my participation in (syn)aesthetically constituted performance work as an "audience participant" as a specialist practice' (Bucknall, 2017: 11).

I had not anticipated such a direct relational impact between the two approaches, nor that this would pose such a challenge to the methodological design – a design substantially founded upon a blending of Nelson's and Trimingham's models. The existing models simply did not have the capacity to account for the relationship that had emerged between the praxis produced by my taking up the role of reflective practitioner and the experiential insights gained by the act of engaging in reflective-participation. Therefore, in devising the daisy chain I needed to develop a model that could acknowledge and account for the relational impact that my two research strategies had posed in practice, but one that also had to be dynamic enough to marshal and map the possibility of other emergent relational factors. My model was designed as a way of tracking and representing the development of discourse generated by the interplay between praxis and other non-PBR activities.

As one can see in figure 3.1, not unlike the spiral model, research questions/concerns are the entry point of the process. Each petal represents a research activity or the impact of a relational discursive field, which feeds back into the entry point of the research concerns/questions, influencing and impacting upon the development of the praxis and, ultimately, the insights that it generates. So instead of a single spiral or triangle, there are multiple simultaneous spirals feeding back into the research concerns/questions. Each activity that has a bearing upon the development of the praxis in response to the research questions/concerns is represented as a 'flowering' that both intentionally (actively) or more incidentally (passively) informs and generates the emergent praxis. Each petal acknowledges and represents the direct relational influences of the active simultaneous research activities, such as those undertaken as a reflective participant, alongside the more passive, external factors, such as reading, conferencing and various other feedback instances and

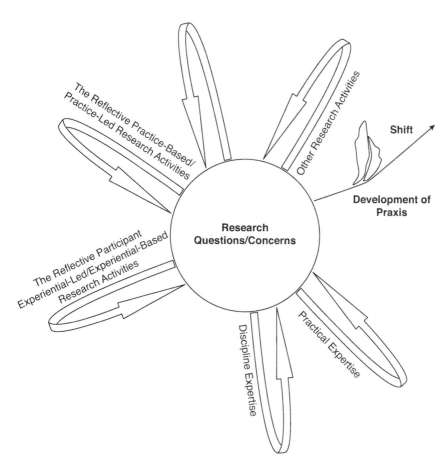

Figure 3.1 General daisy chain single head model.

opportunities. The model serves as a reflective tool that can be employed to recognise the passive and active influences that play a role within the development of the praxis and ultimately the discourse that it produces.

The reflective process of mapping the development of praxis and its relational discursive fields produces a documentation of praxis that can provide the basis for further analysis and interpretation that has potential value beyond the praxis. This can be used to disseminate that process beyond the practice-based context. The act of reflecting in this holistic relational manner produces a very particular approach to managing research activity, but also produces a document that can account for and allow access to the nature and development of the approach itself. I found that managing and recording my research activity in such a holistic manner enabled me to identify the moments when significant insights were generated, and to trace the genealogy of those insights, ultimately producing an epistemic map.

Each single head of the daisy chain model is representative of the relational flowerings that inform the ensuing praxis. A new head is created to acknowledge a shift or renewed focus of the central research questions and concerns, and the whole cyclic process continues: figure 3.2 illustrates the way in which the flowering of new heads produces a continuous chain. The petals feed the head and the head feeds the petals in a symbiotic relationship.

This process is dynamic in two ways: first, it recognises praxis as an emergent activity, generated by and through relational discursive fields; secondly, it recognises praxis as an accumulative knowledge acquisition process, but also one contingent on the interaction between the discursive relational fields and the central research questions and praxis. It is the symbiotic relationship between those factors that creates the dialogic process that produces knowledge and insights. This process is continuous and does not have an end *per*

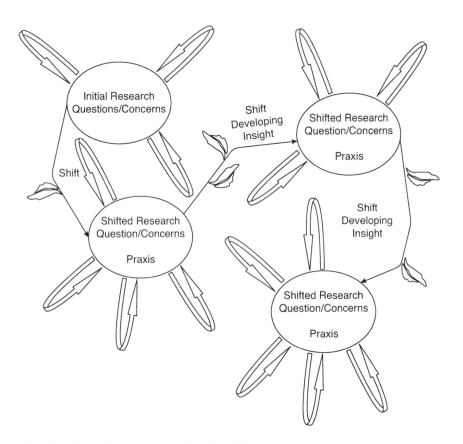

Figure 3.2 General daisy chain multi-head model.

se; it incorporates the continuous nature of praxis as both a method and methodology.

The model provides a tool that visualises the complex relational nature of praxis and the epistemology that informs it. It can be used to marshal the development of the generation of knowledge – the praxis – but it also provides a tool for mapping that praxis. In this way it represents that dialogic process as an enunciated modality. The daisy chain model marshals and disseminates these discursive fields and produces a map of the constellations that come together to form discourse. As such, it has the potential to offer a tool to the practice/performance-based researcher that can visually represent the full range of knowledge(s) produced, along with their epistemic lineage. It thus has the possibility in application not only to marshal and represent the formation of PBR discourse but also to enable its dissemination and the possibility of further and future analysis beyond the PaR that produced it.

I would now like to offer an illustration of the ways in which the daisy chain was employed by an explication of its function within my current PaR project, *Wish Box*, and the role that it played in launching that project.

The peculiarities of my praxis

As well as wrestling with the challenges of PaR as a method, I have had to meet the challenges of the 'thing itself', the particular character of my performance practice, which is the entire reason for adopting PaR in the first place. The practices that inform my expertise lie in forms of performance that are participative,[7] such as immersive theatre,[8] one-on-one performance,[9] pervasive performance[10] and micro-performance.[11]

I am currently in the final year of a PaR project entitled *Wish Box*.[12] I do not have the scope here to describe the entire project; instead I am going to articulate its emergence out of a previous PaR project in order to illustrate the reliance of *Wish Box* on its relational discursive fields epistemologically and ontologically. Before I can start to explicate the nature of that project, I must first set out some contextual background for the epistemic and ontological concerns of *Wish Box* as a PaR project. The research objectives that underpin *Wish Box* are to understand the nature of certain immersive and micro-performance dramaturgies, as well as the implication of those dramaturgies for the nature of the audience's role and, ultimately, experience. My main research objective is to conceptualise the nature of such events and to devise a localised theory of production and reception. In short, I am concerned with the implications of the audience's participative experiences at certain performance events and in finding a critical discourse with which to explicate those experiences.

I am interested in work that implicates the audience in a fundamental way; my research is concerned with understanding existing dramaturgies that engage the audience in this way, as well as developing new ones. My expertise as a live artist and contemporary theatre-maker informs my approach to performance practice. I am very much interested in forms that push beyond simply providing access to the interior of fictive worlds; rather, I am interested in practices that extend a liminoid invitation to the audience and generate an opportunity for them to engage in liminoid acts. Dramaturgies of intimacy, inclusion, participation and pervasion are what constitute and inform my own practical competence and make up my experiential knowledge as a reflective participant. My critical stance is phenomenological and informed by more recent developments in cognitive materialism.[13] Competencies as a participative performance-maker, ten years of experiencing various immersive, pervasive and participative performance works as a reflective participant, and a decade of engaging in praxis through several PBR projects are all factors in the initiation of *Wish Box*.

When the project began in April 2014 I was interested in gaining insight into both the dramaturgy of liminoid invitations and the reception of the resulting liminoid acts. The liminoid invitations of immersive theatre and micro-performance are an invitation to enter into play of one kind or another. Victor Turner suggests that play is a

> Liminoid mode, essentially interstitial, betwixt-and-between all standard taxonomic nodes [. . .]. Play is neither ritual action nor meditation, nor is it merely vegetative, nor is it just "having fun"; it also has a good deal of ergotropic and agonistic aggressivity in its odd-jobbing, bricolage style.
>
> (Turner, 1982: 31)

Turner further suggests 'shallow play' is inherently liminoid rather than liminal. The 'ludic' structure of immersive dramaturgies invites the audience to engage in 'shallow play' with the performers as equals in games, tasks and rules. The invitation is to play, but once accepted, it has the potential to become a liminoid act.

At this stage, in 2014 the project was not called *Wish Box* but instead was simply a set of research concerns that I entered into the performance laboratory with. These questions and concerns were the direct result of the insights gained during my doctoral project, *Siren Song*, and the subsequent PaR project commissioned by the New Theatre Royal, *You, Hope, Her & Me*.

Figure 3.3 maps out some of the relational discursive fields that informed and impacted upon the inception of *Wish Box* as a PBR project: the research questions, the nature of my practical competencies and the embodied knowledge of my reflective participant experiences. This figure employs the model in a broad manner precisely for the purpose of illustrating the function of the model; in reality the heritage of my knowledge(s), experiences and competencies is far more detailed, nuanced and complex than is suggested here. However, for the purpose of explication I want to draw out a couple of the relational discursive fields I have identified here to unpack their direct impact upon the development and design of *Wish Box*.

Siren Song was hugely influential on what constitutes the heritage of the starting conditions of *Wish Box*. *Siren Song* was instrumental in developing and

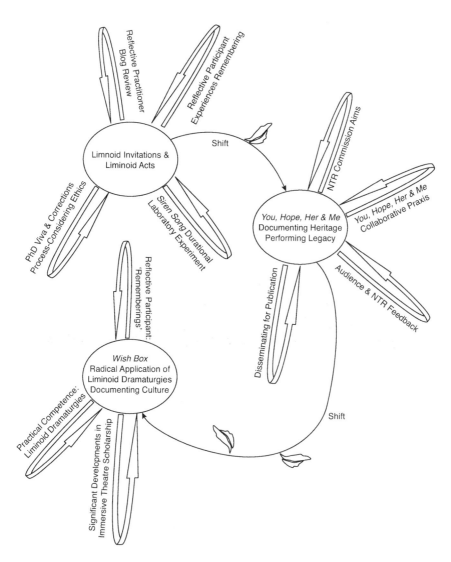

Figure 3.3 Wish Box's discursive relational heritage.

consolidating the reflective practitioner and the reflective participant methods. The insights gained by and through *Siren Song* also consolidated my conceptual, critical and theoretical understanding of immersive, pervasive and participative dramaturgies and their reception. Effectively, this PBR project left me with a new set of questions and concerns that were reached through the discourse generated in praxis.

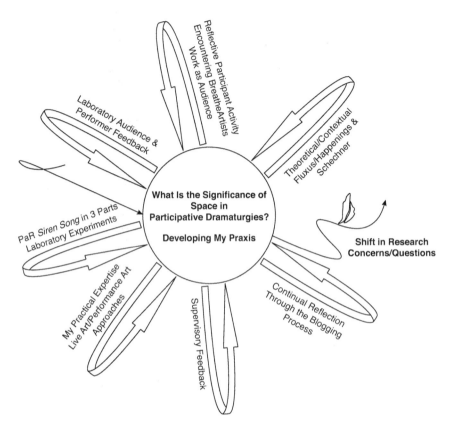

Figure 3.4 Head one: the significance of space.

Figure 3.4 broadly maps out the ways in which the activities that I undertook during *Siren Song* impacted upon the development of my praxis in the early stages of the project in 2006/2007. It represents a crucial moment of insight when the activities of attending a performance at the Edinburgh Fringe Festival in 2007 directly influenced the nature and direction of my work in the performance lab as a reflective practitioner and ultimately led to insights about the significance of liminal space within the participative dramaturgy of immersive and micro-performance.

In the performance laboratory I was developing the first round of *Siren Song* and had been struggling to find a way of inviting the audience inside the world of the performance – to make the shift from spectator to participant. I left for a research trip to the Edinburgh Fringe Festival with these frustrations and unresolved dramaturgical concerns at the forefront of my mind. At the festival I participated in a piece of work by BreatheArtists called *Just To(o) Long?* that

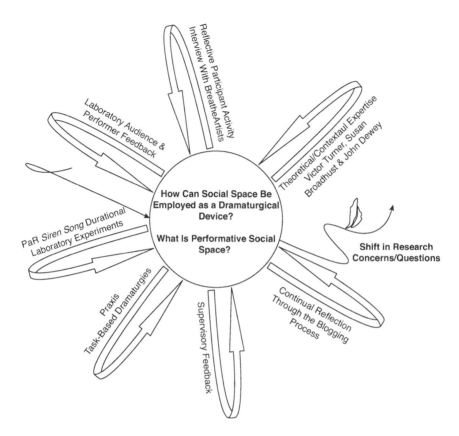

Figure 3.5 Head two: social space.

had found a way to address some of my concerns, and this had a profound effect on my understanding of the nature of liminality and social space. It was the first piece of work where I had encountered a successful invitation to cross into a space of *play* that was not directly fictive. My own laboratory work and its frustrations were reframed by the new insight that I gained through my experience of participating in this work as a reflective participant. It was the confluence of recognising and reflecting upon my own failed laboratory experiments and my experience of BreatheArtists' work that led to a shift in my understanding. The daisy chain enabled me to consider the impact of the new insights reached through my reflective participation by representing that holistic reflection beyond the direct practical activity of the praxis in the laboratory. The daisy chain marshalled the relational and holistic factors and gave me a tool with which to map those emergent developments.

As my research continued in its shifted direction (as represented in figure 3.5), I undertook further activities to address the shifted research concerns. I continued to read but now with a particular focus on space as a concept and as material architecture, which led me to the writing of Gay McAuley (1999), Iain MacKintosh (1992), Victor Turner (1982) and Susan Broadhurst (1999). I have highlighted this particular shift as it was so fundamental to the insights that I gained through the ensuing praxis; but it is also the location of the insight that has underpinned my research in a significant way ever since. Over the next two years of my PhD research project, I came to understand that 'liminal' and 'liminoid' social spaces were central to the nature of 'participative' performance. Over the course of the rest of my doctoral research activity it became clear to me that liminal space[14] was one of the fundamental conditions required in order to be able to make the offer of a liminoid invitation. A liminoid invitation was entirely produced by and through the manifestation of liminal space. This was a significant discovery for me and one that I came to only through the confluence of the activities that are represented in figure 3.4. It was through this four-year process of discovering, mapping and reflecting on the various activities as relational discursive fields that I was able to reach the conclusion that liminoid invitations and liminoid acts were the central tropes of the production and reception of certain participative performance practices, and my completed PhD thesis offered a conceptualisation of those insights. Critical discourse surrounding this mode of performance practice since my work on *Siren Song* in 2006 has shifted, as well, with the term 'immersive' entering popular usage as an index for inclusion and participation. My doctoral research is a significant part of the heritage of the insight, knowledge and competencies that informed my starting point for initiating the PBR project *Wish Box*. However, there is one more significant relational factor that occurred since the completion of my PhD that I would like to identify and discuss.

You, Hope, Her & Me was a year-long PaR project that was commissioned by the New Theatre Royal in Portsmouth in 2013. As part of the *Make Your Mark* rebuild project (see Bucknall, 2013: 140), KeepHouse Performance was offered the opportunity to explore the ways in which performance could be employed as a strategy for capturing localised heritage and to find ways that such a strategy might be capable of generating legacy. The PaR project sought to 'document and map the community's "hopes" for the future of the theatre in light of its redevelopment with the University of Portsmouth' (ibid.: 140). The project was exploring the central question, 'how can we document, map, record, reflect and perform the community's hope for the future of the NTR?' (ibid.: 140). Unpacking the relational fields that were brought to bear on this particular PaR project was a deeply complex task due to the collaborative nature and the scope of the work, so I will focus only on its contribution to the heritage of *Wish Box*.

The insights gained through engaging in collaborative praxis for this project contributed significantly to the development of its entry point because of the shift in focus from my previous PBR activity. *You, Hope, Her & Me* gave me the chance to consolidate my understanding of liminoid dramaturgies, but it also pushed me into considering the possibilities of the radical potential of that form of performance as a tool for lively documentation. As I suggested in my project dissemination,

> The liminoid nature of micro-performance dramaturgy enabled us to achieve those research aims. The various liminoid invitations create the performative opportunities[,] for it is the liminoid acts that perform the heritage and legacy of the theatre[']s community by engaging individuals in play. Through committing such acts, the participants perform, record, document and reflect upon their existing relationship with the theatre and their hopes for its future. Through engaging in 'shallow play' that explores their own past and current relationship with the theatre, they perform the localized and personal heritage of the theatre. By committing liminoid acts that explore their hopes and ideas for its possible futures, they are performing and documenting the possible legacy of the theatre.
>
> (Bucknall, 2013: 152)

What this meant for me personally was that I was left with a shifted perspective about the potential of liminoid dramaturgies as a tool for documentation and social change. Our recognition of our competencies of liminoid dramaturgies enabled Karen and me to explore their possibilities as a mode of capturing heritage and producing legacy. It was the exploration of those possibilities through praxis that led to a further shift in my perspective that then initiated *Wish Box* as a PaR project. That shift and its relational impact upon the development of *Wish Box* is captured and illustrated in figure 3.6.

The insights from my own previous PaR activities (*Siren Song* and *You, Hope, Her & Me*), along with the developments in critical discourse for participative performance practices, became some of the relational conditions for the inception of *Wish Box*. The initial process of devising the PBR project *Wish Box* required me to reflect upon the nature of the competences and research concerns that would underpin it. The daisy chain model became the tool that enabled me to reflect upon, map and assess, in a holistic fashion, the specific aspects that made up the entry conditions of the project. The daisy chain model provided the opportunity to identify the discourse, along with its genealogy, that informed the project. It also provided a tool for me to assess the competencies, knowledge(s) and assumptions of that practical and conceptual 'know how'. It was through making this assessment, mapping it and interpreting it that I was able to formulate the epistemological and ontological concerns of *Wish Box* as a rigorous PaR endeavour. It not only informed my critical process but also provided the opportunity to document that rigour. It meant that I would ultimately be able to disseminate it as a contextual framework for the projects, ensuring its potential to contribute to knowledge beyond the localised PBR activity that would ensue.

Using the daisy chain model gave me the chance to assess and track my epistemological position, and this then meant I could draw out a series of questions

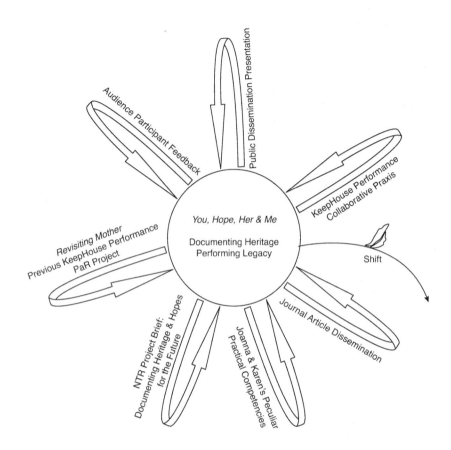

Figure 3.6 You, Hope, Her & Me relational impact.

that were explicitly informed by the assumptions and competencies in relation to my new objectives. Those objectives were to explore and understand the ways in which liminoid dramaturgies operate as a tool for agency, and the potential of that agency for challenging social rituals and traditions. Another objective was to explore the documentational potential of those dramaturgies for capturing and performing identities. It is the analysis of the relational heritage that enabled me to develop a durational performance situation in which I could explore and address my research concerns. *Wish Box* has been designed to provide a site through which the nature of liminoid invitations and liminoid acts can be exercised and explored. The dramaturgy of the performative structures of the event is constructed out of liminoid space and liminoid invitations. Since the inception of the project in 2014 there have been four different laboratory stages, culminating in a final public showing of the piece on 26 October 2016 at the New Theatre Royal in Portsmouth.

I do not have the scope to go into more details about the project here. However, in briefly exploring the inception and initial design of the research project *Wish Box*, I have attempted to demonstrate the significance of employing the daisy chain model as a tool that can be applied to marshal, map, analyse and document the discourse that is produced in and by PBR, as well as the role of relational fields of discourse in the development of praxis. Through interpretation and analysis of the mapping of my own PaR activities over the last decade (albeit very briefly), I hope to have offered insight into my localised practice that might have some methodological value beyond the context of my own praxis.

Conclusion

Documentation and dissemination of PaR are vital if the practice is to function in its capacity as research. Documentation should not simply be an afterthought or a post-process activity; instead it is an integral component that must be engaged with from the very inception of the project. The daisy chain model not only is a visual model for documenting and disseminating the insights generated by and through praxis but also captures the epistemic modelling of those insights. The daisy chain model performs the material praxis of the project and starts to generate a lens through which to approach the localised knowledges being produced through the praxis. It is the epistemic strategy that I employed in my own PaR activity to both map and marshal the knowledge acquisition of my praxis. I am hopeful that in sharing my own ontological and epistemic PaR concerns and the emergent localised solutions I have developed, I can also contribute to the evolving discourse on the tensions of PaR within the academy in the UK and beyond.

Notes

1 *Siren Song* was a series of performance research projects that made up the practice element of my PhD work between 2007 and 2009 at the University of Winchester.
2 *You, Hope, Her & Me* was a year-long PaR project that I undertook with my PBR performance company KeepHouse performance. KeepHouse Performance is a collaboration between myself and Dr Karen Savage (University of Lincoln, UK) that was founded in 2011. You can find more details about KeepHouse Performance and our project *You, Hope, Her & Me* at www.keephouseperformance.org.
3 *Wish Box* is my current (2016) performance research project that has been in development with the University of Portsmouth and the New Theatre Royal, Portsmouth, since 2014. More details about the project can be found at https://www.vexperformance.co.uk/wish-box.
4 I began my PhD at the University of Winchester in 2006 and was awarded the doctorate in 2010. My research activity was further developed during my post as a senior lecturer in drama and performance at the University of Portsmouth in the Centre for Performing Arts and continues in my current post as a Lecturer in Modern and Contemporary Drama and Theatre in the Drama & Theatre Arts Department at the University of Birmingham.
5 My PhD thesis is titled 'Participative Dramaturgy and the Material "Creatorly Participant": A Theory of Production and Reception'.

6 The 'reflective participant' is a term that I have coined to describe the critically reflective activity that I participate in when I attend performances, rehearsals and any other event linked to the making processes of other theatre practitioners. I want to suggest that because of the nature of participative dramaturgies and the burden of creative responsibility placed upon the audience, participation as an audience becomes a *practice* (See Bucknall, 2017).

7 The participation that is offered by 'participative' performance is a material one. It is material because it has the potential to impact upon the performance itself, as well as all the participants' (including the performers') experience of that event.

8 As I have suggested previously, 'immersive theatre' is a term that has been popularised in recent years to identify a mode of practice that invites ambulating audiences into a fictive world of performance in such a way that their participation becomes a material part of the dramaturgy itself. Gareth White acknowledges this as central to a form 'that transform[s] the individual audience member's experience of theatre, without reference to the re-ordering of relationships and experiences outside of it' (White, 2012: 222).

   'Typically in the work of leading immersive companies such as Third Rail Projects and Punchdrunk, the dramaturgy is constructed out of expansive, multi-sensory environments that the audience are invited to explore on their own. Punchdrunk's work has in many ways become synonymous in the UK with the term "immersive theatre"' (Bucknall, 2016: 54).

9 One-on-one performance is a live art trend that has grown in popularity through festivals pioneered at the Battersea Arts Centre in London and Proximity Festival in Perth, Australia. It is work where a single performer directly engages an audience of one in various *acts*. As Deborah Pearson acknowledges, 'because of the intimacy implied by its very structure, [it] encourages audience members to become participants, engaging in intimate and revealing conversations with the performer' (Pearson, 2015: 64).

10 In pervasive performance, immersion is employed in order for both instigator and participant to work together to generate a new liminal space in which an alternative reality is activated through play. Essentially, pervasive performance provides a liminal space in which to create, imagine and try out; it is a safe environment in which to indulge in the act of 'shallow play', free from the usual constraints that culture presents in life praxis and thereby free from weighty consequences. The play of pervasive performance is generated through the collaboration of the facilitators and participants and, for this reason, requires everyone in the game to uphold the fiction and maintain the ruse of the game. The form of pervasive performance is a pregnant scenario, but in order to become born it requires the audience to accept the invitation to play.

11 Micro-performance is a term that I have previously employed, 'in order to make distinct work that has grown out of the live art one-on-one performance trend of the last ten years' (Bucknall, 2016: 55). I want to suggest that micro-performance can be seen as a slippage that sits between the site-sympathetic, experience-centric dramaturgy of immersive theatre and the reframing of the everyday of live art one-on-one encounters. Companies such as Uninvited Guests work in a space between theatre and live art where small audiences are engaged in various social activities/rituals that reframe the everyday through a distinctly theatrical lens. 'Unlike the pregnant scenarios of immersive performance, micro-performance reframes the everyday or social rituals in order to make the offer of a liminoid invitation rather than using the every-day and games to generate a new fictive scenario' (Bucknall, 2016: 56).

12 *Wish Box* is an interactive, immersive experience. For over eight hours the audience and performers work together to testify to the neurosis and aspirations of our times. The audience participants are invited to join the bride and groom as they collect and perform the audience's wishes; without the audience there is no show. In fact, *Wish Box* relies upon a 'ludic' structure to generate the conditions for 'shallow play'. It does this by employing games, tasks and rules; it is a blending of social and performative ritual to create a hybrid

form that I have already suggested might be identified as micro-performance. 'Wish Box's central dramaturgical trope is the re-framing of recognisable cultural practices through game structures' and through this strategy it is able 'to extend its particular liminoid invitation' (Bucknall, 2016: 57).

13 I employ an empirically responsible approach to analysis and criticism, one that is based upon my actual experience of making and experiencing instances of performance. I employ cognitive materialism, an approach that places the experiential at its centre. McConachie and Hart's comprehensive study *Performance and Cognition* (2010) establishes the field of cognitive materialism in a conceptual and theoretical way; my research is picking up that project and applying it in practice. In short, I employ a phenomenological attitude that places emphasis on the centrality of the experiential and perceptival to the various performance events I explore, but also draw on a cognitive epistemology in the collection and conceptualisation of research data.

14 The liminal is a 'marginalized space which holds the possibility of potential forms, structures, conjectures and desires' (Broadhurst, 1999: 12). Turner suggests that '[l]iminality is a temporal interface whose properties partially invert those of the already consolidated order which constitutes any specific cultural "cosmos"' (Turner, 1986: 31).

References

Barrett, E. and B. D. Bolt. (2007). *Practice as research: approaches to creative arts enquiry*. London: I.B. Tauris.

Barrett, E. and B. D. Bolt. (2014). *Material inventions: applying creative arts research*. London: I.B. Tauris.

Bial, H. (2004). *The performance studies reader*. London: Routledge.

Broadhurst, S. (1999). *Liminal acts: a critical overview of contemporary performance and theory*. London: Cassell.

Bucknall, J. (2007). Siren Song Experiments. http://sirensongin3parts.blogspot.com, last accessed on 15th March 2016.

Bucknall, J. (2013). 'You, hope, her & me: liminoid invitations and liminoid acts'. *Performing Ethos*, 3(2), 139–154.

Bucknall, J. (2016). 'Liminoid invitations and liminoid acts: the role of ludic strategies and tropes in immersive and micro-performance dramaturgies'. *Performance Research*, 21(4), 53.

Bucknall, J. (2017). 'The "reflective participant," "(remember)ing" and "(remember)ance": A (syn)aesthetic approach to the documentation of audience experience'. *PARtake: The Journal of Performance as Research*, 1 (2), Article 6.

Chandrasekaran, B., J. R. Josephson and V. Richard Benjamins. (1999). 'What are ontologies, and why do we need them?' *IEEE Intelligent Systems* 14(1): 20–26.

Childs, N. and J. Walkin (Eds.). (1998). *A split second of paradise: live art, installation and performance*. London: Rivers Oram Press.

Freeman, J. (2010). *Blood, sweat and theory: research through practice in performance*. London: Libri.

Haseman, B. (2007). 'Rupture and recognition: identifying the performative research paradigm', eds. Estelle Barrett and Barbara Bolt, *Practice as research: approaches to creative arts enquiry*. London: I.B. Tauris, pp. 147–157.

Ihde, D. (1979). *Technics and Praxis*. Boston, MA: D. Reidel.

Mackintosh, I. (1992). *Architecture, actor, and audience*. London: Routledge.

McAuley, G. (1999). *Space in performance: making meaning in the theatre*. Ann Arbor, MI: University of Michigan Press.

McConachie, B. A. and F. E. Hart (2010). *Performance and cognition: theatre studies and the cognitive turn*. London: Routledge.

Nelson, R. (2013). *Practice as research in the arts: principles, protocols, pedagogies, resistances*. New York: Palgrave Macmillan.

Pearson, D. (2015). 'Unsustainable acts of love and resistance: the politics of value and cost in one-on-one performances'. *Canadian Theatre Review*, 162, 63–67.

Piccini, A. (2002). 'Viewpoint on Mackey's "drama, landscape and memory: to be is to be in place". *Research in Drama Education*, 7(2), 239–242.

Schneider, R. (Summer 2001). 'Archives. Performance remains'. *Performance Research*, 6(2), 100–108.

Schön, D. A. (1995). *Reflective practitioner: how professionals think in action*. Bury St. Edmunds: Arena.

Trimingham, M. (2002). 'A methodology for practice as research'. *Studies in Theatre and Performance*, 22(1), 54.

Turner, V. W. (1982). *From ritual to theatre: the human seriousness of play*. New York: Performing Arts Journal.

Turner, V. W. (1986). *The anthropology of experience*. Champaign, IL: University of Illinois Press.

White, G. (2012). 'On immersive theatre'. *Theatre Research International*, 37(3), 221.

Threads

Linking PAR practice across spectrums

Melanie Dreyer-Lude

The contributions to this volume cover a range of expressive practice: visual art, dance, applied theatre, immersive theater, environmental art, sonic art, intermedial art, urban interventions, and activism. This is not a homogenized collection of carefully shaped essays following traditional academic protocol. The form and language of each essay offer an opportunity to engage with the author's intellect and aesthetic. In most you will find some small act of rebellion, whether against the academic establishment, science-based research standards, or the British government. The authors embrace the challenge of defending what they do and why they do it, recognizing that carefully articulated positions on performance as research are a part of the job. Individually, and as a collected whole, the essays represent a way of working. These are artists who are exploring artistic expression independent of (and sometimes in defiance of) industry norms. Performance as research is practiced in many countries, and the PAR practices in these diverse locales relate to and inform one another, perhaps unconsciously, despite geographic distance. Each of these unique and uniquely expressed essays provides a window into how one engages with performance as research. Many of the contributions to this volume explore related ideas, building upon the work of the others (consciously or unconsciously), or presenting a similar form of practice within a different frame. Conceptual, cultural, methodological, epistemological threads connect many of the essays providing interesting Venn diagrams of artistic practice from multiple perspectives.

In Warwick, England, in 2014, Valentina Signore ("A New Rhetoric"), an architect by trade, attended the working group session for performance as research at the International Federation for Theatre Research conference. What was an architect doing at a PAR conference? Signore had recently witnessed architecture students construct performative doctoral defenses, and had become intrigued by the possibility inherent in demonstrating or 'performing' academic research. While observing the working group, she found that PAR practitioners "reach the limits of spoken language and must go beyond it . . . they develop additional ways of communication that play a crucial role in the sharing of research." What Signore encountered during the conference supported her interest in a new rhetoric for the expression of research knowledge, and because she was seeking to transfer these ideas across disciplines, she sought to identify a way to categorize what she was seeing into a new methodology for communicating that information to her peers. Her outside perspective provides insight into some commonalities in PAR practice. She was surprised to discover that this form of working obligated her to physically engage – her head could not be considered separately from her body. When using all resources available (physical, intellectual, emotional), the experience for her became multivalent in a way that was unfamiliar and stimulating. Signore maps some primary categories to consider when engaging with PAR practice. These identifiers are useful to those who might wish to enter this space as newcomers, as well as to outsiders who wish to transfer this way of working to another disciplinary sphere. Signore concludes her analysis of the PAR working group using her invented methodological frame by offering some challenges and next steps for PAR practitioners, a number of which you will find already in practice within this volume – although probably not as a result of her charge.

Joanna Bucknall ("The Daisy Chain Model") encounters similar struggles in her efforts to define a new methodology for her PAR practice. Responding to leading scholars in the field, as well as the REF (Research Excellence Framework) imposed by the British government, Bucknall articulates her own approach as the "daisy chain model." Bucknall practices various forms of immersive or micro theater, and structures her projects to include audience engagement in her research. She identifies these interactive moments as "liminoid acts" and argues that identifying and documenting quantifiable outcomes that will satisfy the REF can be challenging in her kind of practice. Seeking to find a way to articulate the multidimensional impact of her discoveries and the evolution of her research, Bucknall constructed a model that more accurately identifies her particular process. Her daisy chain model links together previous and current research efforts (along with the entirety of pre-existing knowledge at the moment of investigation), and identifies how experience, knowledge, and analysis intermesh when exploring an idea, the outcomes of which will then lead to another idea – also informed by the just determined knowledge, previous knowledge, current social/political circumstances – that then leads to another idea. . . . Although not labeled the daisy chain model, a number of essays in this volume also appear to practice in a 'daisy chain' fashion. Bucknall's in-depth analysis of her process demonstrates the challenges of articulating the value and measurable outcomes of new knowledge in performance as research.

Signore and Bucknall seek to define their own methodologies for PAR practice. Pil Hansen ("Research-Based Practice") and Göze Saner ("Containers of Practice") structure their PAR practices by articulating the specific ways in which their work extends or amplifies a more standard approach to research endeavors. Hansen does not work against a traditional research paradigm when investigating ideas; she chooses instead to create alongside scientific inquiry, generating what she calls a "third space." Hansen sees value in a 'yes/and' rather than an 'either/or' approach to her artistic collaborations. Because she identifies as a cognitive performance studies scholar, it is helpful for her to find common ground between scientific endeavor and the practice of art. Her third space encourages scientists and artists to continue to rely on comfortable methodologies while also finding a new area of concentricity within which to acquire knowledge. While Hansen uses existing knowledge as a foundation to create a new mode of inquiry, Saner examines the process of 'not knowing.' Both artist/scholars embrace the idea of entering into a project without a clear understanding of where the inquiry may lead. 'Not knowing' is critically important here, as an encounter with a brand-new idea may require the shrugging off of historical paradigms in order to see what is front and center. Like Bucknall, Saner began with one idea based on the history of her experience – solo performance – which then evolved into a process that works against the predictability of performing alone within a recognized performance structure. Her work now includes the public as performers, specifically immigrant women who have little or no performance experience. Saner's previous carefully controlled laboratory (the rehearsal hall and the stage) has evolved into a shared space (echoing Hansen's work) in which her storytelling emerges from a collection of expressive exercises with unpredictable outcomes. This process – helping non-artists discover personal power through storytelling – is held in what she describes as "containers of knowledge." These containers may have finite boundaries determined by the rules of her current project or the exercise of the moment, but they more significantly serve as an open space, a place of invitation, where Saner makes room for knowledge to manifest itself. Like Hansen, Saner has chosen to allow knowledge to emerge rather than to use her work to test hypotheses. Hansen's collaborators are cognitive scientists, Saner's immigrant women. Both depend on the influence outsider knowledge might bring to their investigation. Hansen explores the quality of memory, taking internal information and moving it into shared creative space; Saner begins with universal archetype, which then transforms into personal self-expression. Working within different artistic frames, Hansen and Saner present related arguments for rethinking the ways in which we engage in PAR practice.

Ben Spatz ("Mad Lab") encourages us to reconsider the representation of the acronym PaR/PAR. Is it performance as research? Practice as research? Does it matter? Quite so. Why this distinction? Because, according to Spatz, 'performance' implies 'theater' and the obligatory public event contained therein, while 'practice' opens the field to include not only other forms of performance (music, dance, martial arts) but also other daily events or 'lived lineages' that might also be examined as ritualized practice. Spatz believes that embodied practice holds primary relevance with public performance functioning as an optional rather than required form of expression in PAR. Yelena Gluzman, by contrast, heads in the other direction ("Research as Theatre"). For Gluzman, the performance of research within a standard academic paradigm is fraught with possibility. Spatz wants to diminish the primacy of 'public' performance; Gluzman wants us to acknowledge the ways in which events that may not seem theatrical (like presenting a conference paper) are in fact coded and may be directed just like other performed activities. Gluzman argues that in PAR, one need not separate the creation and the research into separate phenomenological events. The presentation of research *is* performance, and therefore, performance cannot live outside of traditional circles of academic inquiry, but is already embedded within it. Rather than quibbling over performance as research or practice as research, Gluzman creates a new acronym: RaT (research as theater). She does not construct a performance research project and then present her findings at an academic conference; she constructs and engages simultaneously. She turns her paper presentation into a performance in a mildly subversive feat of meta-theatricality, demonstrating how the artistic investigation and the presentation of research discoveries are both performance events.

The challenging tone of Gluzman's essay provides a nice warm-up for Yvon Bonenfant's friendly protest against the demands of the REF (Research Excellence Framework) ("PAR Produces Plethora"). The REF is an outcomes standard imposed by the British government on all who would seek (the unquestionably necessary) funding for arts projects. Using the idea of "plethora" as his platform, Bonenfant rails against the REF requirements by inundating us with his data. They want documented outcomes? He provides an overabundance, thus turning the form of his essay into a written protest. "In harmony with the title of this book, the project I talk about in this chapter wallows in a kind of piggish indulgence in, and even regales you with long lists that illustrate, what we might call data excess." Throughout his carefully articulated and annotated essay, Bonenfant demonstrates his expertise, his legitimacy as a scholar of some standing, and the gravitas of his work, all the while gently poking fun at having to do so. Much of his essay identifies the data he has collected, and it is not until the end that we can finally 'see' and 'hear' what it was that he did to gather his research outcomes. The construction of the essay teases us and rebukes the REF by pounding home his discoveries, and then finally revealing the extraordinary nature of his project. The outcomes are numerous, the accomplishment of his PAR practice significant, but the form of the essay asks – is the data more important than the art? Like Gluzman, the expression of the research becomes part of the project, and perhaps in an echo of Hansen, Bonenfant's plethoric rant about the import of PAR as plethora creates its own third space. Both Gluzman and Bonenfant use their essays as a form of rebellion, defying traditional modes for the dissemination of research while simultaneously providing insights into how and what we might learn from their work.

Two of the chapters in this volume might be considered cultural anthropology. Laurelann Porter's essay ("*Antromovimento*") has no conclusions to offer; she has not yet finished her research. In this instance, Porter allows the reader to witness how a PAR practitioner considers and constructs a PAR project. Porter brings us into the middle of her long-term process examining the embodied practice of ancient religious ritual in Brazil, its contemporary and personal relevance, and its significant cultural/historical value. Porter is careful to state that her work "avoids the study of performance technique for the purposes of developing virtuosity and places cultural anthropology at the center of our process." She is not interested in "professional actor training," but rather "how cultural anthropology can be applied in the form of theatrical exercises that incorporate several modes of learning." This supports Spatz's assertion of the value of "lived lineages." We can also see Saner here, in that the exercises of Porter's *Antromovimento* function much like Saner's containers of knowledge. Because we are brought into the middle of a process, Porter shares how a PAR practice might unfold, particularly when engaging across cultures. Long-term projects have benefits and liabilities, and Porter maps the ways in which unexpected events (like the death of an important participant) shape and determine the continuation of a PAR process (a la Bucknall). Significantly, Porter teases out some of the challenges of the outsider when trying to fully engage with another culture, something Juan Manuel Aldape Muñoz ("Violence and Performance Research Methods") considers in detail in his essay on the Black Lives Matter protests.

Muñoz identifies as a person of color but acknowledges his outsider status as a participant in the die-ins that occurred shortly after the murder of Michael Brown in Ferguson, Missouri, in 2014. Here activism becomes the performance laboratory, and Muñoz examines whether allies of the BLM movement who are actors in this protest drama actually help or hurt the cause. The primary question for Muñoz: can allies effectively support the BLM through active participation or does their participation "erase" or "render invisible" the black bodies they represent? Do the "enduring effects of colonization" cancel out the value of the intent of non-black allies through small acts of "violent empathy"? Like Porter, Muñoz negotiates within the framework of specific cultural parameters, but he is not interested in celebrating, embracing, or promoting cultural practice. On the contrary, Muñoz worries the issue with admirable lucidity. In this case, culturally situated embodied practice is important, but participation without awareness offers a dangerous road. Without considering the impact of cultural dominance, an act of support could turn into just another act of hegemony. One might guess that, given his research subject, Muñoz agrees with Spatz regarding the importance of practice over performance. In fact, Muñoz declares his allegiance with performance rather than practice, stating that the "animacy" of performance is critical to his epistemological efforts. As do others in this volume, Muñoz objects to traditional modes of research and knowledge production, using his position as a challenge to the social construct of academia and the institutional histories it represents. For Muñoz, performance as research provides the appropriate platform (as opposed to performance studies) to examine and consider new forms of knowledge independent of frameworks constructed by institutions of privilege.

Like Muñoz, Manola Gayatri ("PAR and Decolonisation") struggles with the academic system. Recognizing and naming the colonization of artistic practice and arts education, she asks, "Why do I want to be in universities and engage with academia? What does it offer us? Is it really possible to 'change' the system and stamp out traces of colonization from it?" Her essay articulates her concerns by taking us first to India, where we learn about the work of Heisnam Kanhailal and Veenapani Chawla. Both artists work in parallel, exploring, celebrating, and teaching performance practice as archive. In seeking to understand the place of her own work, Gayatri found the live archives of these two artists an active and potent form of decolonizing artistic practice. Negotiating traditional cultural paradigms within a context of contemporary embodied practice, Kanhailal and Chawla construct their own rules by inventing an "aesthetics of hybridity." Now based in South Africa, Gayatri has relocated from one (formerly) colonialized context to another, and is asking hard questions about the value and form of artistic dialogue. Her current interest is 'note-taking,' a process recognized by any student as an imposed construction for the consumption and assimilation of knowledge. Like Bonenfant, Gayatri chooses to appropriate and reframe this 'knowledge structure' in her essay, sharing with us pockets of ideas that jump and shift, dancing forward and backward in time. She consistently amplifies the ways in which global socio-economic concerns inform and influence the lives (won and lost) of artists struggling to free themselves from the capitalization of arts training and artistic practice.

While Porter, Muñoz, and Gayatri focus on projects that examine culturally situated concerns, Monica Sand and Shana MacDonald consider the value of the artistic archive. In her essay ("Resonance in the Steps of Rubicon"), Sand discusses "dance as critical heritage." By re-enacting historic choreography, she hopes to build a bridge from the past to the present, one that is "reactivated in the body." Her project, *Rubicon*, functions as urban activism and as an articulation of another PAR methodology. Sand is particularly interested in the word 'resonance,' specifically as it applies to her research method. For Sand, resonance is "an active response to and a corporeal and sensorial dialogue with public space." Sand intends for the performers and those who witness the performance to time travel – to live in the past and the present at once, and by doing so, to fully experience the city around them. Recognizing the impossibility of recreating history, Sand hopes that her embodied visit to the past will activate contemporary awareness and responsibility to public (particularly urban) space. As with Saner's containers, Sand embraces the concept of dérive, or drifting through a landscape to discover and relish what the encounter might reveal. The psycho-geography of Sand's project is an external link of past and present, while Saner's work describes an encounter with an internal landscape. Both artists value the experience of unfolding rather than pre-determining knowledge through embodied practice.

Shana MacDonald ("The City (as) Place") is a visual art and media studies expert. Like Sand, MacDonald includes urban activism in her practice, using the mediums of art installation and audience engagement. MacDonald's "thick urbanism" intends to move beyond the connection of past to present and into a personal self-awareness. Like Sand, MacDonald structures her projects to activate a political/social consciousness of the effect upon/participation in/culpability for the surrounding urban landscape. In her essay, we witness the evolution of an artist's process (as in Bucknall and Porter). MacDonald begins with specific questions about the public's awareness of their intimate relationship to the local urban landscape by using their trash to make art (*Collect My Junk*). Her second project, *Dear Ruth*, creates the bridge from past to present that Sand describes, by using archival materials to expose the biography of someone otherwise invisible, just prior to the demolition and destruction of all objects that might bear witness to her existence. Her current project, *Mobile Art Studio*, emerged from an interest in more active audience engagement, which, like Saner, pushed her 'knowledge laboratory' out of the art studio and into the public arena. As with Porter, MacDonald ends her essay within the process of creating and implementing her next project, placing us in the middle of her transition from one platform of investigation to another.

In Stephan Jürgens and Carla Fernandes's chapter ("Choreographic Practice-as-Research"), we find links to many of the practices in this volume, as well as a new form of knowledge creation and expression. Their research begins in the past with the conceptualization and performance of a dance by João Fiadeiro (*I Am Here* – 2003). In 2014, Jürgens, Fernandes, and Fiadeiro determine to revive this piece of history, but unlike Sand's reenactment of *Rubicon*, *I Was Here* becomes an entirely new kind of performance event. In the spirit of Gluzman, the artistic team asks Fiadeiro to participate in a lecture-demonstration, what they identify as a research/performance hybrid. Fiadeiro shares with his audience what he discovered when presenting *I Am Here* in 2003, and demonstrates excerpts from the piece. The resulting public performance becomes a combination of lecture, recollection, and re-creation, and contains within it an improvisational structure. The shape and duration of each subsequent performance of *I Was Here* depend upon the mood and inclination of Fiadeiro, and his relationship with the public before him. The archive of his former dance piece (like Sand) becomes the material for a conversation with the public (MacDonald and Saner), which then shapes and creates a research object that is then performed for the public (Gluzman). Jürgens and Fernandes's particular contribution to PAR practice with *I Was Here* is the way digital technology informs the creation of the art and the analysis of the research. Qualitative data becomes quantitative data presented in images that are themselves forms of artistic expression. Here one might reflect back to Hansen's interest in interdisciplinary collaboration as Jürgens and Fernandes "see a high potential in the research design and approach . . . for further case studies in the field of contemporary dance and beyond." In *I Was Here*, media does not represent just one layer of expression of the idea (as with MacDonald), but becomes a conversation partner in the generation of information and aesthetic.

Annette Arlander also uses media in her PAR practice. Arlander works with a camera and the natural world to investigate the boundaries between human and non-human subjects. In her essay ("Agential Cuts and Performance as

Research"), Arlander interrogates the writing of Karen Barad, a physicist/ philosopher/feminist known for her theory of agential realism. Barad asserts that in research (as in artistic practice), the observer and the observed are entangled and therefore influence one another. The objects of research are considered phenomena that contain within them boundaries or "agential cuts" that frame and shape what emerges from the investigation. Knowing and being are not separate experiences. We are in the world – we shape what we create and are shaped by it. In Arlander's practice she sits on a swing, or stands on a frozen lake (or some other natural context), and records the event with a camera. The consistent human object appears in relief against a changing landscape – forefronting the temporality of the relationship between man and nature. The agential cuts in her research include geographic location, costume, camera frame, duration, repetition – all of which inform as she enacts and interacts with the surrounding environment. Arlander controls the perception of time and space through the many choices that determine the intervals of each recorded moment – many times a day, several times a year, several years in a row. Like Gluzman, and Jürgens/Fernandes, the documentation of the research project and the knowledge produced become part of the performative event. All objects – human, environmental, or inscribed – are entangled in the exploration of an idea and the expression of its discovery. The embodied practice informs the documentation, which informs the embodied practice (as in Bucknall). Arlander asks, "Should we consider only the impact of the finished artwork or include the effects of the process of creating that work?" In an echo of Muñoz, Arlander challenges the PAR practitioner to consider impact and entanglement as influential components of the pursuit of new forms of knowledge.

In Jonathan Heron and Baz Kershaw's essay ("On PAR") we encounter multiple threads of connection. Kershaw's work, like Arlander's, concerns itself with the artist/spectator's relationship to nature. Arlander's digital recordings of her humanness within a natural environment simultaneously reduce the world to the size of the viewing screen and expand its scope to present one small being against a backdrop of vast wilderness. With Kershaw we find the reverse equation. In *Meadow Meander*, a small field of wild space represents "the whole world." Arlander's work is mediated through the camera frame, her editing, the platform used to view it. Kershaw's work must be experienced first-hand; it does not exist outside of each participant's individual (and lived) experience. The spectator of his work (named a 'meanderer') walks the field and attempts to 'see' with little or no context for guidance. This lack of context is important to Kershaw's definition of a transdisciplinary experience. One must enter as a tabula rasa – willing to encounter the work on its own terms. "Your experience evokes a kind of un-learning, achieved through some sort of deliberate immersion in a state of complete ignorance." One must engage in dérive (as with Sand) and allow the environment to work upon the psyche. Like Saner's approach of not-knowing, of leaving room for unexpected knowledge, Kershaw's transdisciplinary space involves "[d]eliberately abandoning knowledge, purposefully leaving knowledge behind." Harking back to Arlander's investigation of Barad, Kershaw insists "the environment is likely to be influencing you as much as you are influencing it." Structure also plays a role in this essay. It is not a theoretically positioned concept paper – it is an interview, a conversation, just two guys talking about PAR. Yet within this casual format, one finds important ideas about the ways in which PAR encourages alternative practice and alternative thinking. Heron, the emerging scholar, debates with Kershaw, the veteran in the field, and this substantive conversation provides insight into some key concepts in PAR practice.

A woman stands on a frozen lake, a chorus of voices chant a research paper, a brown body lies beside black bodies, children scream and sing and shout. These are distinct examples of PAR practice. It is difficult to categorize or systematize a practice that deliberately opens the field for any embodied work seeking new forms and new knowledge. This volume testifies to the fact that, though the range of expression may be vast, and the artists may be practicing within wholly independent spheres of engagement and intent, PAR practitioners are generating common ground. What is emerging is a series of connecting threads that demonstrate that PAR practitioners are moving independently but in synchronicity with the evolution and growth of this new field of artistic practice.

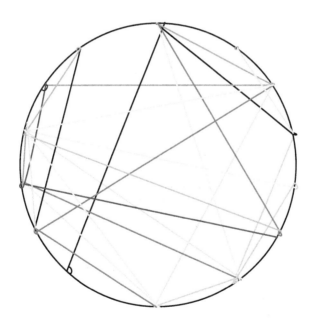

Chapter 4

A new rhetoric

Notes on performance as research in academia

Valentina Signore

Introduction

If you want to know more about the frontier of live presentation in artistic research you should join the Performance as Research Working Group. This is what I told myself when I signed up to attend the International Federation for Theatre Research (IFTR) Conference in Warwick in July 2014. Aware that my architectural background made me an outsider in this context, I was moved to attend the PAR Working Group by a curiosity that arose while attending several recent PhD defences in architecture and built environment at Royal Melbourne Institute of Technology (RMIT).[1] During these doctoral defences, PhD candidates were using the space and their bodies in such a free and inventive way that I started to look at their presentations as "performances". I began to wonder how far one could go in this direction.

In this essay I report on what I learned that week in Warwick at the meeting of the IFTR Performance as Research Working Group. In this way I tackle the question: What can performance as research teach to other academic fields? My answer is that PAR opens new paths in the field of live presentation and may play a crucial role in the development of a *rhetoric* for artistic research – namely in that specific component of classical rhetoric called *"actio"*.

The place of live presentation in artistic research

One could argue that across academia live presentation is the disreputable outcast of scientific communication in comparison to the authoritative firmness of the written text. However, I claim that for artistic research and *research by design* (another term used in architecture), the live presentation plays a crucial role, even though it has been neglected as a subject of reflection.

The story of Phryne serves to introduce my preliminary argument. Phryne was a legendary ancient Greek courtesan, condemned to death for the transgression of impiety. Standing before the Greek tribunal, she was rescued by the public speaker Hyperides (figure 4.1).[2] At the climax of his defence, instead of attempting to justify her life through words, Hyperides made it evident by

Figure 4.1 A white silhouette replaces the naked body of Phryne in the painting by Jean Léon Gérôme. The image suggests that in artistic research unspeakable insights may be made present to the audience by means other than words. The original painting is part of the collection of the Kunsthalle Hamburg.

revealing her naked body. The judges decided to spare her life. In this pointedly gendered story, the beauty of Phryne represents the unspeakable in artistic knowledge, while Hyperides is the researcher who presents that knowledge to the public.[3] As in this story, the kind of knowledge and insight pursued in creative fields (not only performance and theatre but also design, architecture, music and arts at large) often needs to be expressed in ways other than words.

My observation of live presentations in Warwick and at RMIT shows how researchers more and more resemble Hyperides while presenting their work to a public: they reach the limits of spoken language and must go beyond it. This doesn't mean that they discard the use of words as such, but that they develop additional ways of communication that play a crucial role in the sharing of research.

The "hegemony of the alphabetical" has been much debated in artistic research. However, in the literature relatively little attention has been paid to the format of the live presentation and to the non-verbal level of the communication that it entails. On the other hand, it is apparent that new experimental approaches are taking place in the academic scene, showing a natural tendency towards performance that arises not from a theoretical, top-down standpoint but rather from the pragmatic needs of researchers. With this essay, I hope to return the discussion of artistic research to what is happening in academic practice. By doing so, I wish to counter what I consider a significant lack of theoretical discussion and also to foster further development of experiments in live presentation.

Epiphany

> "*I will serve you today a presentation in five parts (. . .) this is my little allotment . . .*
>
> [CJ Lim points at a wooden structure containing his drawings]
>
> *. . . and from this, I will then translate it into the field, of which I will feed you the information later.*"[4]

(RMIT University 2014a)

CJ Lim started his PhD viva by making an explicit analogy between food and knowledge and referring to himself as the one who serves it to the jury. The whole scenography literally expressed this concept: the examiners sitting behind a table were given some dishes and cutlery (in paperboard, designed by CJ). Gradually, all along his speech, CJ served them a series of drawings – food. The last four drawings – one for each member of the jury – were served with a special emphasis: a folded paperboard showed the white surface when laid down on the jury's plates:

> *Would you like to start dinner? Or rather, dinner itself? . . . Would you like to open it? . . . One . . . two . . . three . . .*
>
> [The examiners open the paperboards and look at the drawings. Long silence.]
>
> *That's it. Thank you very much.*

[Applause] (ibidem)

The conclusion of CJ Lim's viva was a simple act of showing.[5] Like Hyperides, he was confident that he had reached a point where the jury didn't need words any more, but just to 'see'.

Frankly, I couldn't say to what extent his performance was crucial to convince the jury. As part of the general audience, in fact, I had a completely different experience than the examiners. From my point of view, this defence turned out to be not just unusually structured but also an "extreme" experience, comparable to some powerful live performances I attended. It was a kind of epiphany for me that ultimately brought me to write this essay. Imagine now that you are sitting on a plastic chair for one hour, observing CJ's elegant, sumptuous and repetitive movements to "serve" his drawings to the jury. Imagine now that there is no way to see these drawings, nor to properly follow his speech: you can't really see his eyes as he shows his side to the public in order to face his examiners; nor you can see his drawings arranged on the jury's table: they are too small, too far and too low. And then, as with optimism you notice a projector, you must realise that the wall of the projection is perpendicular to you, so that the images are completely flattened and illegible.

Everything seemed to be meticulously designed to let the public feel violently excluded from the scene. It was like being invited to a delicious, never ending dinner, but being forced to just observe other people eating. Fighting my own discomfort and annoyance, looking for the sense of so many coherent choices against any possible enjoyment of the viva, I persuaded myself that there should have been a strong reason behind all that. Certainly, I told myself, CJ Lim wanted to communicate something to the public that he was unable to say otherwise. He, whose work is about envisioning utopian cities and triggering new imaginaries in people, was certainly trying to provoke some specific effect in his public. No matter the answer that CJ gave me when I asked him for confirmation of my hypothesis right after his defence: I became aware of the power of the mutual disposition of public, presenter and artefacts of a live presentation, and, most important, of the need to know and use this power to consciously deepen the understanding of the public. Thanks to CJ Lim's viva I also realised that something experimental was happening in the nature of the PhD defence. To what extent was this an isolated phenomenon? To what extent could one push the boundaries of academic presentation to communicate artistic research? And who better than researchers in performance and theatre studies to show me the way? These questions led me to what I now consider a pioneering area in this aspect of artistic research: the arena of performance as research.

In this essay I analyse four sessions of the Performance as Research Working Group held in Warwick[6] and will refer more loosely to some PhD defences at RMIT.[7] The Working Group sessions and the PhD defences by the RMIT candidates are undoubtedly different in nature and I do not intend to set up a direct comparison between them. My intention is rather to make these two worlds resonate, revealing the potential for a reciprocal process of inspiration. On the one hand, I envision PAR's "extreme" experiments in research presentation triggering new possibilities in fields such as architecture. On the other hand, the RMIT examples show that experimental approaches to research presentation are not limited to closed scholarly working groups, but are also beginning to challenge one of the most institutionalised of academic presentations, the PhD defence.

Towards a new rhetoric for artistic research

The art of persuasion has always been part of the formation of scholars, and only in the last decades has it been nearly abandoned – in science because it is too emotional and not objective enough, and in the humanities because of its overly formal set of rules. In the past few years, some voices have begun to ask how rhetoric might again play a role in academia, not only in artistic research (Mullin 2011) but also in philosophy of science and of the humanities (Kjørup 2002).

Historically, however, rhetorical thinking has been very much in service of the analysis and composition of the written text, mainly discarding the analysis of its culminating moment: the delivery of the speech itself, what was called in antiquity "*actio*".

I now consider the basic elements of classical rhetoric as they apply to the examples studied here, underlying the elements of innovation.

Preparation

A major change that all our case studies introduce concerns the basic program for preparing a speech. As it was inaugurated by Aristotle (1984), five steps are required: collecting the material for the speech (*inventio*); composing the speech (*dispositio*); choosing accurately words and phrases (*elocutio*); learning the speech by heart (*memoria*); and delivering the speech (*actio*).

Looking at the live presentations by PAR Working Groups and RMIT candidates, this agenda needs to be revised: main steps, such as *dispositio, elocutio* and *memoria*, must make room for improvisation (i.e. in the case of PAR), and some new additional operations should be introduced:

1   Choosing a specific setting for the speech, itself able to convey a certain message;
2   Arranging the space of the speech, including the displacement of the audience(s);
3   Revising the rules of engagement of the audience.

With these kinds of additional operations, our orators become authors not only of a "speech" but also of a new reality, a distinct presentation-specific context.

Genera

In classical rhetoric, analysis of the context of the speech was essential. Students were trained to recognise the appropriate type of oratory according to three branches or *genera causarum: juridical, deliberative* or *epideictic* oratory (Aristotle 1984). Typical academic lectures are similar to the juridical genre, for they try to prove the truth of some claim (and to show that other claims are false). So one would expect a similar format in the cases in our study. However, at a deeper examination, not only can one find very few "truth claims", and moreover each of the presentations creates its own context that is superimposed on the strictly academic one. The result is that the presenters approach the speech in completely different ways. In the RMIT scene this ranges from CJ Lim serving his drawings to "feed" his jury's members to Pedra Pferdmenges[8] using her "farm truck" as an interactive showcase of her socio-artistic projects. In the PAR arena we can pass from Juan involving the audience in a political act to John and Melanie disappearing from the scene to let the participants experience the framework they had prepared in advance.

Audience

Rhetoric has always been preoccupied with its audience. In antiquity, the kind of audience depended on the settings or occasions in which genres of oratory were practiced. In our case studies, an important aspect of innovation is the relationship that the presenters develop with their audiences. As aforementioned in reference to preparation, presenters take the freedom to set up presentation-specific relations and rules of interaction; they construct perspectives and fields of view to achieve their aims; and they establish their own rules of engagement for the audience. All of this influences the communication game.

Memoria and kairos

Learning the speech by heart was an essential step in classical rhetorical training. However, "memory" meant much more than memorising a complete speech and was always tied to the improvisational abilities of a speaker. In this sense, *memoria* is strictly related to the concept of *kairos*: the opportune occasion for speech. Only through a sensitive receptiveness to the context, to the contingencies of a given place and time, can the orator deliver an effective speech. In the RMIT defences the candidates, with or without the support of a written text, know their speech by heart and show an improvisational mastery in the moment. In this sense they are close to the rhetoric tradition. On the contrary, the PAR presenters observed in Warwick did not rely on already defined texts, although their interventions were based on previous writings. In fact, the register of their speech can be completely different than that of the written text: it can indulge in many more doubts, uncertainties, questions, wandering, and contaminations, as in the case of Myer, Johanna and Emma, who brought together the diversities of their research topics to trigger a common conversation.

To highlight how each PAR presenter or group of presenters concretely interpreted these main rhetorical elements, the case studies will be analysed according to the following parameters:

1   Spaces/setting/scenography: What kinds of spaces were explored by the presenters?
2   Presenters and audience: What kind of relationship was established between the presenters and the audience?
3   Rules of engagement: What kinds of rules of engagement were established? How were they made explicit?
4   Memoria/improvisation: Relation between written text and speech.
5   Documentation: Who was documenting who/what and how were they doing it?

In addition to these elements, I will also refer to my own *body-mind involvement*, which may offer additional clues about the experience of the audience in each presentation.

The matrix

To facilitate a meta-perspective across several examples, I developed a matrix (figure 4.2) that presents a general overview. To highlight the innovative strategies used by the presenters, a generic session by (what may be, generally speaking, understood) an "orthodox" scholar is included as a reference.

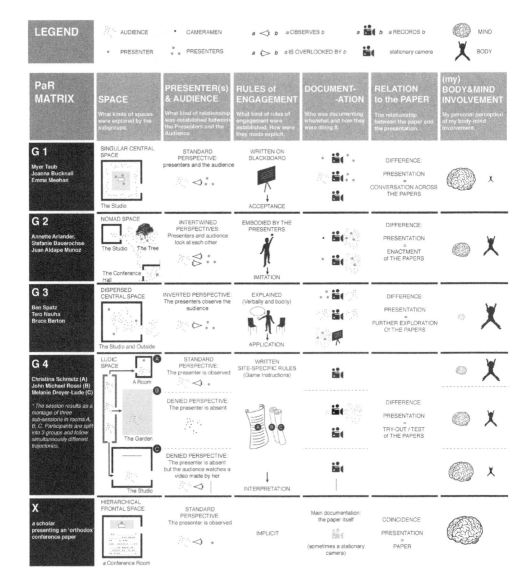

Figure 4.2 The matrix offers an overview of the four PAR sessions analysed in this essay, in contrast with a "generic" academic presentation. The matrix is an elaboration of the author.

Purpose

Rhetoric is known as the art of persuading the audience. However, these case studies show a possible new interpretation. While the RMIT candidates act in continuity with rhetoric's original purposes, ultimately attempting to persuade the examiners of the validity of their PhD research, the PAR presenters show a different vocation that seems to hint at a new direction for academic practice: the presentation before a public audience is no longer meant to *persuade* it of its own correctness, but would be intended to *produce* new insights with the active participation of the audience.[9]

Power

The case studies, with their experimental approaches, seem to resist certain consolidated forms of power. Acting in a field where the rules are based on practice more than written regulations, they arguably reconfigure power dynamics in relation to the audience. At the same time, one should not forget that these new formats and strategies also establish new power relations. This may no longer be a hierarchical, normative and repressive form of power, but rather takes a "performative" shape (McKenzie 2001) in which power shows its a-hierarchical, permissive and excessive side.

PAR in Warwick: challenging the conference presentation

The four sessions analysed here were led by twelve researchers in theatre and performance studies who gathered as part of the Performance and Research Working Group at the IFTR Conference in Warwick (July 2014), in which I took part as a participant. The conference theme was "Theatre and Stratification." These PAR sessions challenge the notion of "research output" as a stable and definitive form in which knowledge acquired in advance is communicated. The PAR sessions do not just communicate already produced and "definitive" knowledge (in a highly alternative way), but rather engage the audience in the process of producing knowledge by creating conditions to keep such processes open and productive.

Before I analyse these PAR sessions according to the six categories enumerated earlier, I will briefly consider the same categories for what, generally speaking, one would consider an "orthodox" academic presentation (see in the matrix the "X" row). Of course, this is an abstraction and generalisation, as there is no properly standardised format for academic presentations. But virtually any conference, no matter in which country or institution, one expects certain aspects, starting with the conference's *space*: you would expect to enter a building and to find a room in which rows of seats define the audience's place, where you can take a seat. You shouldn't be disappointed if you look for a focus point (a podium, a desk or another small area) that will indicate where the presenter will speak from, and you are pretty sure that the rows of seats will be facing that point. Along with this disposition, you would probably take for granted a certain *audience-presenter* relationship – what I would call the "standard perspective" of an academic presentation: the presenter is the one who is observed by the audience, and it doesn't matter if an audience member takes notes or writes an email on his tablet PC or yawns, his behaviour will not be deemed inappropriate.

Even though there is no formal etiquette of academic presentation for the audience, one implicitly knows the basic *rules of engagement*, because the presenter and audience have clearly distinguished roles: the first is a speaking and active subject, while the second is a listening and passive one. You know you can take notes, and unless the speaker gives different indications, only at the end of his speech may you intervene with questions or comments.

Normally, it is well known, there will be very little room for *improvisation*, and very probably the presenter will be reading a text, as suggested by the revealing term "conference paper",[10] which indicates how the written text itself stands as the primary *documentation* of the session. This is sometimes supplemented by a fixed camera, but in many cases that is limited to major conference papers and keynote lectures. Finally, if you are aware that you need a lucid *mind* to properly follow the presenters' speech, you give little thought to your *body*, sitting there at the service of your brain, eventually able to comment on the comfort offered by your seat, the room temperature and the illumination.

There is nothing new in all of this. But now, just try to forget it, as I will guide you into some sessions of performance as research working groups.

Spaces/setting/scenography: What kinds of spaces were explored by the presenters?

"The studio" was the space assigned to the PAR Working Group by the IFTR conference organisers. It was a squared space with a semi-sprung harlequin floor and black curtains all around, provided with stacking plastic chairs, and surmounted by an overhead wired grid for the lighting bars.

Within this quite neutral space, each PAR group arranged a completely different setting (figure 4.3). The first group (G1: Myer, Joanna, Emma) created a *singular central space* by means of a main focus point in the middle of the room: a black carpet, at its corners four heaps of white powder (for the presenters to dip their feet into) and in the middle a desk with various objects and chairs for the presenters. The audience was sitting all around; however, as suggested by the rules of engagement on the blackboard. What, participants were encouraged to enter the central space (a couple of people did so at the end of the presentation). The table was more than a scenographic element: it was the physical catalyst of the whole collective operation. What do the concept of "catastrophe" explored by Myer, the Dublin Contemporary Theatre investigated by Emma, and the "daisy chain model" proposed by Joanna have in common, after all?[11] Perhaps nothing at all, until Myer, Emma and Joanna sat around that table and put their research

Figure 4.3 Different spaces explored by the PAR working groups (clockwise from top left): a singular central space (G1), nomadic space (G2), ludic space (G4), dispersed central space (G3).

topics one next to the other, like any other possible object displayed there, and initiated a free conversation.

The centre of the studio is used also by the third group (G3: Ben, Bruce, Tero), but in the form of a *dispersed central space*. This is achieved by having several focus points in the centre of the room, and by displacing the chairs in pairs. Here the participants take the stage in the middle of the room, sitting and moving around the chairs, following the instructions given by the presenters: touch hands, touch voices, touch organs, for variable durations (five or twenty seconds, one or five minutes). Ben, Bruce and Tero stand at the borders of the room, observing and documenting what is going on. In the very last part of the session the whole group of participants explores together the instructions, and as if moved by a centrifugal force, goes outdoors. The result is literally an empirical experimentation, as Ben's previously submitted working paper was hinting at (Spatz 2014).

A *nomadic space* is generated altogether by participants and the presenters of the second group (G2: Annette, Stefanie, Juan), moving throughout the different "ambiances". The transition from one atmosphere to the other is fluid and progressive: a brief introduction inside the studio is followed by moving outdoors, where different actions take place, each of them led by one presenter. First Annette invites the participants to rock on a swing hung on a tree, and right after to answer a list of questions about performance and research. Then Stefanie climbs on the branches of the same tree and, followed by the participants, initiates a collective reading of a passage of Shakespeare's *Venus and Adonis*. Finally, under the guidance of Juan, following a sudden launch of apples, presenters and participants jumped down from the tree and marched towards the main university conference hall, thus enacting what he sees as a general attempt of PAR actions to "occupy institutionalised academic processes".

A *ludic space* is the playful result of the free montage of different sections and locations led by the last group (G4: Christina, John, Melanie). The articulation of different spaces (A, B, C in the matrix) does not follow a predefined sequence; there is no hierarchy among them. Instead, participants are split into three groups and follow different trajectories. The transition from one space to another occurs by means of written "game rules" given to the participants on rolls of paper. The choice mirrors a common preoccupation of the presenters with the audience's changing role in contemporary theatre and performance practices.

Similarly, one can observe how RMIT candidates occupy the same creative space for a viva, even though the formality of the event leads to less extreme solutions in comparison to the PAR working groups.[12] In some exceptional cases, a candidate can choose a peculiar location for his defence. For instance, architect Tom Holbrook[13] set up his viva in the market hall of the city of Ghent in Belgium, designed by Paul Robbrecht and Marie José van Hee. Such a location, its architectural features along with its public setting, embodied main distinctive features of his practice: a constant search for a complex dimension between the intimacy of the "furniture" and the public sphere of the "infrastructure". The arrangement of the space generally results as a support to the main argument of the PhD research and as a concrete reference to the actual work of the practitioner for the audience. Often quite literally, the RMIT researchers open their talks by explaining the main themes of their speech in relation to several elements of the space (see the defence by Thierry Kandjee[14]). In this way, the *method of loci* introduced by the rhetoric tradition as a mnemonic device for the orator becomes for the audience a sort of spatial reference for the whole discourse.

Presenters and audience: What kind of relationship was established between the presenters and the audience?

The PAR sessions constituted four different examples of active audiences, with significant differences between the natures of audience participation across the groups. The visual relationship between audience and presenter is treated here as a practice of "surveillance" (Foucault 2014), in that the observation of subjects is analysed as a means of controlling the audience in addition to self-control on the part of the presenters.

In what I would call the *standard perspective* (X), the presenter is the one who is observed by the audience. This direction of sight is used also in some PAR sessions, like the first working group (G1: Emma, Myer and Joanna), that chose a main focus point from which to speak. However, they create a centre rather than a front, as the participants are sitting on three sides of the room, and they invite participants to enter the central space, so that some spectators temporarily become part of the "observed" group. The configuration used by Christina (G4, Room A) is also very interesting in this regard, because it plays with the conventional configuration: a row of chairs for the public and the presenter behind a desk. Christina subverts the power relations of the configuration by eliminating the main characteristic feature one expects from a presenter: speaking. Through her strong and silent presence, she compels the audience to feel observed by her (as well as by a fixed camera).

The third group (G3: Ben, Bruce, Tero) experiments with an *inverted perspective* in which the audience is observed by the presenters. Ben, Bruce and Tero give instructions to the participants for an activity and then observe them from outside. The second group (G2: Annette, Stefanie, Juan) combines its nomadic space with *intertwined perspectives*: presenters and participants look simultaneously at each other while engaged in the same activities. This two-directional perspective reinforces the presenters' attempt to overcome the subject/object dichotomy and its implied power relations.

An extreme solution is achieved by the choice of a *denied perspective* (G4, room B and C). In this case the presenter is absent from the space and can neither look at the audience nor be observed. The presenter's presence is evident only in the written instructions given to the participants (G4/B) and in a video projected in the studio (G4/C). At the same time the audience is asked to document the sessions using cameras and becomes responsible for a kind of self-observation.

While in the RMIT examples the formality of the occasion greatly constrains the audience's engagement,[15] this becomes central in the PAR sessions. The audience's position can vary significantly: at the margin or at the centre of the space, they can be asked to swing and then to climb a tree (G2: Annette, Stefanie and Juan), or to lay down on the floor (G1: Myer, Joanna and Emma). All these variable relationships between presenters and audience are the symptom of a changing power relations and mirror quite clearly current trends in theatre and performance practices.

Rules of engagement: What kinds of rules of engagement were established? How were they made explicit?

The degree of engagement of the public is probably the most obvious difference that distinguishes a PAR session from an "orthodox" one, as made clear by the fact that the audience in the PAR context is referred to as "participants".[16] The rules of engagement concern the way the audience engages in a presentation. A first distinction can be made between implicit and explicit rules. In a generic

Figure 4.4 Rules of engagement (clockwise from top left): rules written on the blackboard (G1), embodied rules (G2), site-specific written rules (G4), explained rules (G3).

academic presentation (X), the rules of engagement are implicit and there is no need to explain how the audience should behave. (Indeed, a presenter who specified that the audience is expected to sit down, to listen in silence, to take notes and to raise a hand at the end to pose questions or comments would sound ridiculous.) In contrast, in a PAR session the desired participative nature of the audience requires that rules be made explicit, precisely because none of the usual tacit norms can be expected to hold. In these PAR sessions, rules were conveyed through diverse mediums, had different natures, and demanded that the audience take different approaches (figure 4.4).

Two groups (G1: Myer, Emma, Joanna, and G4: Christina, John, Melanie) use *written rules* that are not explained or negotiated with the audience. In one case (G1) they serve to expand the perceived possibilities: on a blackboard it is written that the audience is allowed to enter the space, to interrupt, to freely document the session and so forth. Before the session started, participants were invited to read them, and since they were quite simple, there was neither special explanation nor negotiation with the audience. In another case (G4) the rules were written on site-specific rolls of paper given to the subgroups of participants. Here they served to introduce the audience to the sessions A, B and C and were subjected to a higher level of interpretation. *Explained rules* are conveyed by the presenters of the third group (G3: Ben, Bruce, Tero) by means of words and examples until their content has been properly understood by the audience. Ben and Bruce explain the rules not only in words but also by providing a practical demonstration of the proposed exercise. Here the audience relates to the rules in terms of the application and execution of an assigned task. *Embodied rules* (G2: Annette, Stefanie, Juan) are not written or explained, but are embodied by the presenters so that the participants naturally follow them in an attitude of imitation.

The new function of presenters to "legislate" on what is allowed or not in a conference room can be seen as a criticism of "orthodox" presentations. The paradox is that while such a fact shows its liberating power, the audience members turn out to be less "free": they have many more tasks and constraints, they mustn't be distracted, and to a certain extent they are "forced" to be interactive in a certain way. What I want to suggest here is that the spectrum of "interpassivity" (Pfaller 2017; Žižek 1996) accompanies PAR practices and should be considered as a point for critical reflection.[17]

Memoria/improvisation: relation between written text and speech

The PAR presentations are developed in response to an earlier phase of work that was based primarily on written texts. Prior to the conference, the researchers had each written a paper and shared it with the group. They were then divided into sub-groups and asked to create a PAR session based on their shared concerns as found in the papers. Thus the presentations are the result of a collective process originating in written text. However, there is always a relation of difference between the written text and the presentation. Each PAR session, as well as a standard academic presentation (X), is preceded by work on a written text. However, while this paper is standardly *read aloud* to the audience, in PAR presentations there can be many other relationships between the text and the presentation.

The first group (G1: Emma, Myer, Joanna) brings their working papers into an *ongoing conversation*. Very diverse questions, concerns and ideas discussed in their texts become part of an open conversation in which they mix, contaminate and enrich each other in an organic way.

The second group (G2: Annette, Stefanie, Juan) proposes an *enactment of the working papers*: Questions, concerns and ideas discussed in the working papers are put into practice in the here and now of the session through situations created by the presenters for that purpose: hanging her swing on a tree, Annette involves the public in her embodied reflection on "performing with plants"; Stefanie lets her copy of *Venus and Adonis* – frayed from use – go from hand to hand and from voice to voice of the participants; Juan involves the public in a march, demonstrating his claim that PAR's practices are attempting to occupy academic processes in a similar way as the Occupy Movement seeks to inhabit political discussion. Unlike the first group, here the presenters keep the distinction between the different working papers: each author leads a distinctive part of the session. A sense of unity is given to the whole session only by the smooth transition between its parts.

The third group (G3: Ben, Bruce, Tero) develops a *further exploration of the working papers* with the help of the audience: questions, concerns and ideas discussed in the working papers are pushed forward through a sort of experimental setup, led by the presenters, in which the participants take part. The fourth group (G4: Christina, John, Melanie) carries out a *try-out or test of the working papers*: questions, concerns and ideas discussed in the papers are revisited in order to test their potential in the context of the conference. The session, articulated in three rooms, mirrored the three different contributions. The chosen frame of the game gave a sense of unity: a theme which was explicit in John's contribution allowed emphasis on the participation of the audience, which was the common thread in the three different working papers.

Concerning the relation between what is written beforehand and what is spoken in the session, the four PAR working groups in Warwick present some extreme situations. Christina abolishes any use of words to deeply estrange her audience. In the same working group, Melanie and John suppress not just their voices but also their presence, being absent on the scene. Sometimes just a little part of the written text can be used in the presentation, as in the case of Annette, who reads from her article some questions about PAR to interrogate the participants while they swing. Also notable is Stefanie's use of one of the materials used for the *inventio*: a passage from Shakespeare's *Venus and Adonis* that participants are asked to read from the branches of a tree.

The empahsis on improvisation in PAR's presentations is certainly related also to the collective nature of the sessions. It is not just about re-enacting one's own research but also about finding ways to establish a relationship with the research of others. In those cases in which the session was articulated in separate parts, each under the lead of an author, the relationship between writing and performance was more evident, with performance thus clarifying the written elaboration and making it more concrete and accessible.

Documentation: who was documenting who/what and how they were doing it

Documentation plays a key role in all the PAR sessions. Every session has multiple layers of documentation, mainly achieved by the use of cameras. The different patterns of documentation largely mirror the presenter/audience relationships, but also expand it, adding additional directions of sight intended for future viewers and researchers.

A *fixed camera* records the whole session of the first working group (G1: Emma, Myer, Joanna), providing a "neutral" point of view. The use of *personal photo cameras* is also encouraged. Even during the presentation the presenters themselves took pictures of what was going on, while being "on the stage".

These moments of interruption of the flow give a live clue to the purpose of documentation: it provides an external eye that brings a higher self-awareness of tacit yet apparent aspects.

In the second case (G2: Annette, Stefanie, Juan) an *external cameraman* follows the group, thus capturing presenters and participants at the same time. Only Annette Arlander held a camera to record in a close-up the answers of the participants after having swung.

In G3 (Ben, Bruce, Tero) documentation was made by means of a *fixed camera*, *personal photo cameras* and a *blackboard*, which was used during the session to annotate emerging aspects, to be later discussed collectively. In the last working group (G4: Christina, John, Melanie), each sub-session was recorded by a *fixed camera*, providing a "neutral" point of view. In room B, the instructions suggested one of the participants also record what was going on, thus adding a "personal" point of view.

Overall, one can notice how an external camera is often used to record the whole session, providing a "neutral" point of view that does not represent the perspective of any presenter or participant (G1, G2, G3, G4). In addition, personal cameras were used in combination with the former and may be passed from one person to another in order to involve multiple perspectives on the event (G2). Only in one case (G1) the documentation is assumed as an integral part of the reflection of the moment, while in all the other cases it refers to a "post-production" moment. The use of the blackboard to make annotations during the session collects emerging aspects that can be discussed collectively just after the session (G3).

Documentation requires technology and additional work to process the material after the "actio". Why is documentation so important? What are the effects of the employment of such a tool?

I believe that documentation can today play a similar role to that played by the development of writing at the origin of classical rhetoric. As Kjørup puts it, "the systematics of rhetoric would be impossible to invent and to preserve without writing" (Kjørup 2002: 3) as writing originally allowed rhetoric to develop because it made it possible to meticulously analyse, reflect and fully structure the text for a speech, now the documentation permits us to analyse, reflect and thus better structure the actual performance of the speech, including the "kairos", the body language, the physical setting and the use of the space. Documentation plays a crucial role also in RMIT PhD defences. While traditional academic PhD defences are rarely filmed or electronically registered in any way, RMIT provides a highly qualitative record of the session, which is made available online. The viva is in fact considered the third component of the PhD completion (along with the exhibit and the dissertation). Altogether they provide a wonderful database for further exploration. Also, intermediate presentations of RMIT PhD candidates are often recorded and they constitute a tool for the researchers – and their supervisors – to meticulously analyse and reflect on the presentation.

(My) body-mind involvement: clues to the experience of the audience

The emotional involvement of the audience is an essential task for rhetoric, and a presenter can often sense when he or she is achieving this ephemeral yet powerful target. With no claim to objectivity, I refer here to my personal experience of the PAR sessions in order to compare it to my usual feeling after attending an academic presentation (X). A main difference I can highlight is that not only are my intellectual qualities stimulated but also my body is deeply involved. Emotions then become much more complex than the usual battlefield between agreement and disagreement with the presenter, or between surprise, interest and boredom. Each PAR session triggered multiple aspects of engagement – intellectual, physical and emotional – in different ways and proportions. Of course, it has to be said that body and mind, as well as emotions and other levels of being, are all intertwined, so that a purely bodily experience (as well as a purely mental one) does not exist as such. However, it is indubitable that listening to a paper presentation while sitting on a chair demands less bodily engagement than climbing a tree. In this regard, I experienced an interesting juxtaposition in the session involving a tree (G2: Annette, Stefanie, Juan): just after I had been in the air on a swing attached to a tree branch, I was asked to verbalise, on camera, my answer to a question about performance as research. Emotions also played a central role in my perception of my body, as I experienced in the session led by Christina Schmutz (G4, room A): despite the fact that I was seated and silent, I can remember minimal yet intense body sensations – such as my heartbeat, breath, the smallest sensations on my skin – an intensified awareness of my senses, affected by her enigmatic presence.

It has been widely demonstrated how the body affects the learning process (Bresler 2004; Hannaford 2005; Kjørup 2006). But I am not saying that any body sensation is in itself relevant: it must be pertinent to the message to be conveyed in order to coherently facilitate the communication.

In some working groups (for instance, Ben's or Annette's), the attention on the embodiment was a central topic in the working papers themselves, so the emphasis on the body experiences proposed during their presentations is coherent with their research focus. In other cases, this attention is less evident in the text as well as in the presentation (which doesn't mean that the presentation is less effective).

Conclusions

One may be surprised that when writing about rhetoric, I don't comment on the "persuasiveness" of all these innovative devices. The reason for this is twofold. First of all, being an outsider to the performance and theatre studies domain, I do not have appropriate field knowledge to estimate in depth the relevance of the working groups' research topics, and how they effectively impact on their research field. However, some cases struck me with their clarity, especially in contrast with the previous understanding I had from reading their working papers. To mention some among others, this passage written by Christina sounded absolutely abstract to my ears:

> (. . .) the critical potential of theatre today consists in new distances between actor/stage and audience (. . .) For Eiermann this distance is a necessary consequence of an "interruption of the rule" (Lehmann 2011: 36) and a prerequisite for the creation of a triangle that consists of actor, spectator, and a third instance.
>
> (Schmutz 2014: 2)

But it suddenly made sense once I was sitting still in her silent presence. Similarly, the philosophical concept of "It thinks" explored in the paper of Annette suddenly became concrete while I was swinging under the tree. Next to this, I can also assert that while I tried with little success to follow more traditional sessions within the same conference in Warwick, I could with almost no problem enter into the proposed work and themes of the PAR working groups. This seems to prove the fact that these new rhetorical devices are at least useful to open research to a non-expert public.

The second and most important reason for abstention regarding persuasiveness of the presentations is that the main shift achieved by the PAR session seems to require changing the central criteria to judge the success or failure of a rhetorical operation. If there is not a real need to "persuade" the audience, but rather to involve it in the process of research, then this "involvement" and its capacity to affect the research development should be judged. Then one shall envision how to estimate if and what kinds of new insights are produced through the active participation of the audience. In this light, everything that happens after a presentation gains importance: the feedback of the participants, the processing of the documentation and the rewriting of the working paper.

As the matrix simply shows (figure 4.2), this chapter reassembles a few examples and tries to look across them according to some general criteria. Its purpose is not to provide a set of devices that can be emulated successfully. There is not a perfect mix of choices that can work for any research. As the set of examples clearly shows, each researcher should find his or her own peculiar way to best communicate or co-develop research work. This means, I believe, reaching a real state of necessity. Rather than choosing an extravagant solution for its own sake, one should arrive at new solutions as a result of a real, concrete need, like Hyperides, who unveiled Phyrne only once he was facing the concrete possibility of losing her.

The term "matrix", from the Latin *mater-*, refers to something with or from which something else originates, develops or takes form. This is the sense of the matrix and of this chapter as a whole. I made reference to four specific situations of the PAR sessions in Warwick, but I hint at the generation of many new other possibilities and configurations, and more generally to the rise of a deeper awareness of the possibilities and responsibility of such intense moments called live presentations.

Such a rise of awareness should naturally go along with some operations that, to conclude, I would like to suggest:

- Make explicit the choices made and articulate them coherently in relation to the research.
- Give all the necessary support to the audience to understand the proposed situation/experience, providing, for instance, a frame of reference before the presentation (i.e. in a written text) or after it (i.e. in a moment of discussion).
- Map and reflect on the impacts of the session on the development of the research.
- Map and reflect on the impacts of the session on the audience.
- Document and monitor the shifts between expectations and the actual delivery. Sometimes things are planned but don't go as intended. Sometimes the moment offers unforeseen opportunities.[18]

Notes

This project has received funding from the European Union's Seventh Programme for Research, Technological Development and Demonstration. Funding provided under Grant Agreement No. 317325.

1 The defences took place within the framework of the ADAPT-r program (Architecture, Design and Art Practice Training-research), which is a groundbreaking, practice-based research model in an emergent field of research across a range of design and arts disciplines. ADAPT-r involves seven institutions in Europe and was developed on the basis of the Royal Melbourne Institute of Technology model developed over the past twenty years (http://adapt-r.eu).
2 The scene is depicted in Jean Léon Gérôme's *Phryne Revealed Before the Areopagus* (1861).
3 The story of Phryne suggests a highly gendered narrative according to which the vulnerable feminine body of the artwork is unveiled by the masterful masculine rhetor. However, for the purposes of this essay I leave that aside in order to emphasise the affection that the rhetor had towards Phryne and his deep fear of losing her. In this light the act of unveiling can be seen as an extreme action required by a life-or-death situation. Hyperides's extreme action was not just a clever idea, but also the desperate action of a man who wanted to save his beloved – he was in fact one of Phryne's lovers.
4 A recorded video is available online at https://vimeo.com/84726131 (RMIT University 2014a).
5 Referring to the "viva" or "defence", I will mainly consider only the presentation part of the PhD examples, not the questions-and-answers part. The latter, one might say, is the real "disputation", both with the examiners and with "opponents from the auditorium", "ex auditorio", which traditionally has been the most important part. My choice is related to the focus and purposes of this essay: to present innovative strategies developed by the presenters, and not necessarily analyse all the elements of the presentations (that is, I will discard also the analysis of the text, central in rhetorical analysis). Since in the examples under study the question-answer part with the jury is quite formal and

doesn't present particular elements of interest, I consciously discard it from my analysis, even though it certainly plays a crucial role in the communication and evaluation of the research work.

6 I will refer to these working groups using the first names of their presenters: Working Group 1: Myer Taub, Joanna Bucknall and Emma Meehan; Working Group 2: Annette Arlander, Stefanie Bauerochse and Juan Aldape Muñoz; Working Group 3: Ben Spatz, Tero Nauha and Bruce Barton; Working Group 4: Christina Schmutz, John Michael Rossi and Melanie Dreyer-Lude.

7 These doctoral students took part in a PhD program of creative practice research through which creative practitioners – architects, landscape architects, designers, musicians, visual artists and others – inquire about their own practice to disclose the tacit knowledge embedded in their work. In these cases, the urge to manifest research insights beyond words seems to reach its climax at the culminating moment of the PhD journey. However, also before the completion, RMIT candidates are encouraged to experiment with the presentation space and various mediums in order to engage other levels of communication while discussing their works.

8 https://vimeo.com/155621980 (RMIT University 2015).

9 To some extent this is a function of the working group environment and not specific to PAR. However, the extent to which the audience may be integrated into the act of research in the moment of presentation also relates specifically to PAR as a discipline occupied not with "truth claims" but with the "production of a new reality" (Bolt 2008).

10 With the interesting result that if originally rhetoric needed the written text to deliver a well-structured speech, now the written text is spoken in a conference room only as a mid-step, before the achievement of its ultimate purpose: to be published in the proceedings.

11 In his writing Myer explores the concept and problem of "catastrophe" as a historical, literary and personal frame of reference. Joanna develops the daisy chain model as an epistemic approach to mapping and marshalling PAR activity. Emma reports on the exploration of Irish Dublin Contemporary Dance Theatre (DCDT) through a performance as research investigation into the "embodied archives" of original company members.

12 Artefacts, scale models, drawings, books, sketchbooks, projections, screens, posters, lighting, but also the chairs of the audience and the position of the examiners – they all become integral parts of the preparation of the speech. As with any other project, candidates make sketches, drawings and scale models, and they explore different solutions and discuss them with their peers and supervisors.

13 https://vimeo.com/98989809 (RMIT University 2014c)

14 https://vimeo.com/85316486 (RMIT University 2014b)

15 The audience's active engagement is generally limited to receiving some artefacts, drawings or books from the presenter and letting them circulate among the public.

16 However, the matrix also makes clear that not every PAR session challenges all the typical aspects of an "orthodox" academic presentation. For instance, session G1, ahead, gets quite close to it concerning both the use of space and the relation of the audience to presenters.

17 Interpassivity is a concept that merges the concepts of "interactivity" with its supposed opposite of "passivity". It refers to a state of passivity, when a medium (namely works of art and media) sometimes provides for its own reception. The term was coined by Slavoj Žižek and Robert Pfaller.

18 Holbrook, for instance, provided some blankets for the audience in order to communicate the "regime of care" present in his work, but the weather was too inclement for the public to feel comfortable. At the same time he couldn't have foreseen that the city

of Ghent was going to provide a benign series of dramatic interventions (bystanders walking through, a cyclist shaving a scale model, the aroma of a sewage pumping truck) that helped him to make his point about the complexity and richness of cities, and how designers could operate responsively within them.

References

Aristotle, 1984. *The Complete Works of Aristotle: revised Oxford translation*. Edited by Johnathan Barnes. Oxford: Oxford University Press.

Bolt, Barbara. 2008. A Performative Paradigm for the Creative Arts? *Working Papers in Art and Design* 5.

Bresler, Liora (ed.). 2004. *Knowing Bodies, Moving Minds Towards Embodied Teaching and Learning*. Dordrecht, Boston, MA, and London: Kluwer Academic.

Foucault, Michel. 2014 [1975]. *Surveiller et punir: naissance de la prison*. Paris: Gallimard

Hannaford, Carla. 2005 [1995]. 7 and 13. In *Smart Moves: Why Learning Is Not All In Your Head*. Salt Lake City, UT: Great River Books.

Kjørup, Søren. 2002. 'Notes on the Humanities: Material for the Basic Course in Philosophy and Theory of Science and of the Humanities'. International Cultural Studies, Roskilde University, Spring Term.

Kjørup, Søren. 2006. *Another Way of Knowing: Baumgarten, Aesthetics, and the Concept of Sensuous Cognition*. Sensuous Knowledge 1. Bergen: Bergen National Academy of the Arts.

McKenzie, Jon. 2001. *Perform or Else From Discipline to Performance*. New York: Routledge.

Mullin, Johan. 2011. Rhetoric: Writing, Reading and Producing the Visual. In Michael Biggs and Henrik Karlsson (eds.), *The Routledge Companion to Research in the Arts*. London: Routledge.

Pfaller, Robert. 2017. *Interpassivity: The Aesthetics of Delegated Enjoyment*. Edinburgh: Edinburgh University Press.

RMIT University. 2014a. *prs- CJ Lim* [video file] https://vimeo.com/84726131

RMIT University. 2014b. *prs- Thierry Kandjee* [video file] https://vimeo.com/85316486

RMIT University. 2014c. *Tom Holbrook* [video file] https://vimeo.com/98989809

RMIT University. 2015. *prs- Pedra Pferdmenges* [video file] https://vimeo.com/155621980

Spatz, Ben. 2014. *Stratum Sediment Self: Embodiment as the Primary Site of Critical Realism*. (Performance as Research Working Group IFTR Warwick 2014).

Schmutz, Christina. 2014. *Face-to-face//artistic and scientific strategies of new theatre formats*. (Performance as Research Working Group IFTR Warwick 2014).

Žižek, Slavoj. 1996. *The Plague of Fantasies*. London: Verso

Chapter 5

Research as theatre (RaT)

Positioning theatre at the centre of PAR, and PAR at the centre of the academy

Yelena Gluzman

0   Intentions

The very existence of this volume testifies that it is no longer outrageous to claim that performance can be a method of investigation, knowledge production and scholarship, but also testifies to the fact that there is work to be done in exploring how particular performance practices can be commensurable with the accumulation, verification and dissemination of what counts as academic knowledge. Yet, even in thus articulating the problem, there is a presupposition that performance is just one (unruly) member of a broader category of (otherwise adequate) scholarly methods. In this formulation, performance is the outsider looking in, and thus assumes the burden of justification and assimilation as it attempts to enter the academy. The presumed adequacy of more conventional research methods – always in relation to the purported *objectivity* of the scientific method – still dominates tacit understandings of normative academic knowledge production, and inflects the ways in which *performance as research* (PAR) is theorized as both challenge to and member of the academy. In this chapter, instead of conceptualizing performance as a type of research, I begin with the inverse premise, that scholarship is a type of performance.

There are two senses in which scholarship – the process of reading, collecting data, teaching, communicating with disciplinary peers and disseminating research outcomes[1] – can be understood as a kind of performance. One would be the claim that research is *performative*; this is the notion that scholarship, even when it is concerned with simply describing an aspect of the world, not only is acting upon and shaping that world but also is itself constituted as scholarship through a "citational" reiteration of ritualized norms and accepted modes of speech (e.g., Nelson 1999; Dewsbury 2000; Cabantous et al. 2016). This sense of the performativity of scholarship is heavily indebted to Austin (1962), who suggested that, though some utterances seem to be performative (like the assertion, "I promise"), even non-performative speech acts (like the statement "I am writing") impact the situation in which they are uttered, shaping the constraints on meaning for present and future utterances. Also crucial for this sense of scholarship as performative is Judith Butler's (1988, 1990, 1993) specification of *performativity* as a process in which seemingly stable, naturally occurring phenomena (like gender identity or subjecthood) are produced through citations or reiterations of preceding practices. These citational acts, occurring on a massive social scale, shape a nexus of authority that undergirds the logics and form of subsequent acts. Building on these two notions of performativity, then, we might begin to suspect that to acknowledge the *performativity of scholarship* is to call for reflexive attention to the compulsory citations that shape the research process, and to the identities, relations and objects that emerge as facts through these acts of research.

While the argument in this chapter relies on this first sense of *scholarship as performative*, it is the second sense of scholarship as performance that I want to develop, a less popular view that considers *scholarship to be a kind of theatre performance*.[2] In making a distinction between performativity and theatre, I continue to cite both Austin and Butler, who each famously distinguished performative acts from theatrical performances. Austin excluded theatrical speech from his argument about performative speech acts because theatrical speech is *artificial*[3] and thus an "etiolation" (or weakening) of language (Austin 1962, 22). Butler specified performativity as distinct from theatricality because theatre and its role-playing presumes an *intentional subject*, one who can realize or "de-realize" (1988, 53) an identity, masking the crucial "compulsory" nature of the citationality through which that subject is formed (1993, 22).[4] Though neither Austin nor Butler is concerned with developing a theory of theatre, by specifying performativity against the artifice and intentionality of theatre, both Austin and Butler add fuel to the complex logics of a long-standing anti-theatricality that permeates Western philosophy (Barish 1981; Puchner 2002) and inflects the position of theatre studies in the US academy (Jackson 2004).[5]

Needless to say, the exclusion of theatre from the notion of performativity is a familiar story for many readers of this volume. Lest my dredging up the anti-theatrical prejudice seems gratuitous, I may as well admit my intentions: here, I hope to suggest that theatre performance is central to the performativity of scholarship, allowing scholars to engage not with *fact* of ongoing performativity but rather with the concrete, situated *processes by which scholarship is materialized*. So, instead of directly considering this volume's titular issue of "performance as research" (PAR), I hope to suggest that *scholarly research of all stripes* might take seriously commitments to performativity by engaging *experimentally* with their *theatrical underpinnings*. In other words, rather than directly addressing the complexities of PAR (in relation to a normative notion of scholarly methods), I'd like to consider RaT, or *research as theatre*: the notion that theatre is central to all scholarship, and thus available for experimental inquiry into the relations and knowledges produced through scholarly work. Here, I use "theatre" to mean the intentional, contingent, semiotic arrangement of materials, entities and temporalities for an audience; similarly, "theatricality" is used to refer to the particular arrangement of manipulable resources. While this may seem general to a fault, my definition of theatre is guided precisely by characterizations of theatre in contradistinction to performativity: namely, that it is intentional (addressed to an audience) and artificial (crafted).

To consider the artifice and intentionality inscribed in theatre, allow me to get personal (and by doing this, let me also assert the importance of *situated, subjective experience as a basis for knowing* what happens in theatre). In my experience of theatre, from my earliest memories of sitting among the audience as a child, I was never in doubt that what unfolded in those spaces was (forgive me) real. Yet this is not to say that I doubted the artifice of the event. Even then I understood intuitively that an actor being kissed on stage was receiving a *different* kiss than one received in private, but it was nonetheless a powerful (not *etiolated*) kiss, with consequences not only for that actor's mind and body but also for myself, for everyone in that room, and indeed for what I could only dimly conceive of as a totality of experience that transgressed the closed doors of the theatre. As I grew up watching theatre, I became more sceptical of the fuzzy totalities that I'd intuited, yet what never flagged was my conviction that what happened in the theatre constituted an exemplar of the inseparability of representation and action. In other words, while recognizing the particular arrangements of space, time, architecture and entities that constrained the operation of a piece of theatre, I could also see that such "artificial" constraints could never resist or reduce the complexity of interactions that they made possible. Is this theatre artificial? Yes. But importantly, as asserted by a number of theatre scholars (Diamond 1997; Jackson 2004; Worthen 1998; Ridout 2006), the representationality and artifice of theatre were performative through and through, challenging the idea that theatrical acts were specially "hollow" (Austin 1962, 21) or could be "de-realized" (Butler 1988, 527). As Donna Haraway puts it, "I learned early that the imaginary and the real figure each other in concrete fact, and so I take the actual and figural seriously as constitutive of lived material-semiotic worlds" (Haraway 1997, 2).

Later, when I became interested in theatre as a field of engagement, I "made" performances, an activity that was relentlessly laborious, terrifying and rewarding. I qualify the word "made" because a vivid aspect to the experience of "making" theatre was in fact the ambiguity of authorship and agency; one both is racked with the weight of responsibility of composition, of introducing a gesture or speech-act into a public space that did not necessarily ask for it, and at the same time, must come to terms, over and over, with the fact that any such occurrence is neither an "introduction"[6] nor in one's control.[7] When taking into account the great hubris of theatre-making at the same time as honouring its extreme contingency at every moment, theatre begins to look more like the sort of material-semiotic interaction that Haraway described, in which "the imaginary and real figure each other in concrete fact" (1997, 2). Is theatre intentional? Yes, it is not only intentional but also impossible, requiring enormous coordination of energy and matter to realize. Yet this intentionality is not in opposition to theatre's necessary citationality and, as suggested earlier, potent consequentiality in iteration. And, above all, the consequentiality of the theatre doesn't presuppose its illocutionary success, since its intentions are never simply realized, but always contingent, thwarted and undone.

This last point is worth unpacking a bit further, since it proposes that the intentional arrangements implicit in theatre shape the events, relations and meanings that emerge from it, while simultaneously acknowledging that these effects are indeterminate and contingent not only upon intentions and arrangements but also on a much more complex field of situated encounters. For example, as Nicholas Ridout points out, it is especially in moments when the planned theatre event slips, "corpses" and stutters that the smooth flow of representation that is its promise is interrupted, embarrassed and exposed as contingent upon the material and interactive conditions of the event. As Ridout says, "Something fails to take place amid what does take place" (Ridout 2006, 32), and this, like Lucy Suchman's notion of plans as situated actions,[8] is an opportunity to theorize intentionality *alongside* not only its compulsory citationality but also as deeply contingent on its situated material forms. Thus, when looking at theatre performance as a performative – that is, re-iterative – event, there is an interesting conundrum between what is intended and what is produced.

This conundrum can perhaps be explored by taking up the argument of feminist scholar Rebecca Herzig, who critically examined science and technology studies (STS) notions of performativity alongside the performativity articulated by performance studies, and asks why both disciplines assume the compulsory and unproblematic productivity of performance.[9] In her words,

> Here, I wish to draw attention to a second, and largely unacknowledged feature of the vocabulary of motive evident in these studies: namely, that the activity described in such studies is invariably *productive*. Diseases, ships, natural philosophers, and termites appear equally governed by an imperative to produce some rhetorical or material effect.
>
> (Herzig 2004, 135)

Herzig suggests that the implicit functionalism of such an "inexorable logic of production" (ibid.) can be avoided by acknowledging the *excess* of performance. Relying on a familiar distinction between theatre and performativity (and reminding us of the subtle anti-theatricality of such a move), she pits the "excess" articulated by *performativity* against the functionalism of *theatre*:

> Unlike the theatrical sense of the word, the critical feature of the deconstructive performative, Eve Kosofsky Sedgwick points out, is its 'necessarily "aberrant" relation to its own reference' (. . .) In the hands of writers such as Paul de Man, J. Hillis Miller, Jacques Derrida, Gayatri Chakravorty Spivak, and Judith Butler, the performative tends to maintain this sense of unavoidable excess: slippage, perversion, or occlusion necessarily conditions every inscription.
>
> (Herzig 2004, 136)

Herzig makes an important point about performativity that is, I argue, even more characteristic of theatre – namely, that its artifice and intentionality is marked by, and undone through, excess. This is precisely Ridout's point in gesturing to the slippages of the highly contingent event of theatre, as it inadvertently (or, in some cases, experimentally) exposes the methods and conditions of its own production.

I "What are we doing" in science and technology studies (STS)

> *To study technoscience requires an immersion in worldly material-semiotic practices, where the analysts, as well as the humans and non-humans studied, are all at risk – morally, politically, technically, and epistemologically.*
>
> (Haraway 1997, 190)

I began with the suggestion that a consideration of PAR can be founded on the premise of RaT: that scholarly research not only is performative but also operates theatrically. I have argued that the theatrical underpinnings of scholarship can be unearthed by appealing to previous anti-theatrical characterizations of theatre's *intentionality* and *artifice*, as it is enlivened or undone through the *contingency* and *excess* of their material enactment.

Here, I turn to the literatures of science and performance studies to consider the claim that RaT may have radicalizing potential for academic work writ large. STS literatures are relevant for a number of reasons: they have taken up performativity as a way to describe the production of scientific knowledge, have called for greater reflexivity and methodological experimentation, and, most importantly, STS has long been concerned with the question of *knowledge production*. Even before its disciplinary formation as STS,[10] sociological, historical and philosophical studies of science were already, in one way or another, interested in scientific knowledge: how it is produced, disseminated and applied, how it changes and how it differs from other sorts of knowledges. Whereas such scholarship in the first half of the twentieth century tended to understand science as an exceptional type of knowledge production (Merton 1938, 1942), after the 1960s – as science joined the growing list of institutions of power to be dismantled by an increasingly anti-institutional public – the tenor of social studies of science shifted towards the critical. One of the targets of such critiques was science's purported objectivity. Much of this post-1960s STS work argued that scientific facts do not pre-exist their discovery, but are rather socially constructed.[11] STS literature on objectivity in science (like Daston and Galison 2007) unsettles – if not displaces – the grounds for an assumed primacy of the scientific method among scholarly research methodologies.

By the late 1970s, a small group of STS scholars became interested in shifting from sociocultural accounts that undermined scientific claims of objectivity to looking at the material, daily practices by which scientific knowledge was made. Assuming roles of laboratory participant–observers, these scholars imported the ethnographic methods of anthropology into what had previously been designated a historical, philosophic and/or sociological study of science. This new orientation, taken up by Knorr-Cetina (1981), Latour and Woolgar (1986 [1979]), Lynch (1985), Traweek (1988) and others, was to examine science in daily practice, scientists in their natural habitats, and scientific facts in the making. If, as Knorr-Cetina proposed, an STS concern with the "problem of facticity" could be more profitably seen as a "problem [. . .] of fabrication" (Knorr-Cetina 1981, 3), the attention to practices was a way to characterize *how* this fabrication occurred.[12]

The growing focus on laboratory practices initiated what became known as the *practice turn* in STS. Despite the ephemerality implied by the word "turn," the impact of the practice turn for the emerging STS discipline was formidable. Rather than a short-lived conceptual trend, a focus on daily practice continues in STS (e.g., Schatzki, Knorr-Cetina and von Savigny 2001; Gad and Jensen 2014). Further, the understanding of scientific facts as being contingent on the daily practices of scientists was foundational for subsequent STS approaches; the practice turn undergirds both actor-network theory (ANT, an approach that stresses the co-construction of facts through interactions of networks of human lab members, non-human entities, material artefacts and inscriptions) and feminist STS and new materialism (a view that argues for the inseparability of the material and discursive).[13]

Thus, there is a continuity in stressing the descriptive aims of such work between Knorr-Cetina's 1981 attention to "how" scientific facts are fabricated and, two decades later, a 2002 statement by Annemarie Mol (a scholar indebted to both ANT and feminist STS) that "Methods are not a way of opening a window on the world, but a way of interfering with it. . . . The question to now ask is *how* they mediate and interfere" (Mol 2002, 155). Both Knorr-Cetina and Mol share a commitment to the "how," based on the conviction that scientific facts do not pre-exist their discovery by scientists, but are constituted through situated networks of scientific practices, disciplinary methods and daily interactions. Yet, there is also a subtle *discontinuity* between the argument posed by Knorr-Cetina and that of Mol, most crudely summarized as the difference between the *constructed nature of scientific facts* (Knorr-Cetina's "facticity") and the *construction of the natural world that those facts describe* (Mol's "world"). It is precisely this shift that is amplified, theorized and justified by the uptake of *performativity* into the STS discourse on practices that occurred in the decades between those two publications.[14] Thus performativity in STS is oriented to the practical effects of action, and to specifying the ways that scientific descriptions or models of the world themselves act upon and shape that world.

Annemarie Mol's 1998 article ("Missing Links, Making Links: The Performance of Some Artheroscleroses") was an influential text taking up the language of performativity to describe the ways that a disease is not a single, pre-existing entity, but is enacted variously by different members of a hospital. Four years after the publication of this chapter, Mol published *The Body Multiple*, a book-length analysis based on the same study of artherosclerosis (Mol 2002). Though Mol's central argument is quite consistent across these publications, two concerns appear in the book that do not figure in the earlier article. One of these, discussed widely not only in regards to Mol's articulation of it but also across STS since the rise of the practice turn, was a grappling with the reflexive implications of a turn to practice, especially within the framework of performativity. The problem, in a nutshell, was the realization that, just as scientists continually performed the world they sought to describe, so too do STS scholars perform the world *they* sought to describe.

Though the concern with reflexivity preceded the uptake of performativity (e.g., Latour and Woolgar 1986 [1979]), it gained a more urgent tenor when articulated together with performativity, since the world-making stakes of performativity were so high (Law and Singleton 2000; Law 2004; Law and Urry 2004). Thus, through the lens of performativity, a concern with practice spilled over into an anxiety about methods, particularly the methods of STS researchers themselves. In the book, Mol expresses this concern explicitly:

> Self-reflexive desperation about the foundation of our (whose?) knowledge is no longer required. We would be wiser to spend our energy on trying to come to grips with what we are doing when crafting academic knowledge. What are we doing – when we go into fields, observe, make notes, count, recount, cut, paste, color, measure, slice, categorize, and so on. What are we doing when we tame materials, when we publish, give talks, stage stories for various audiences.
>
> (Mol 2002, 158)

This sort of imperative appeared in other STS texts of the early 2000s,[15] and continues to inflect STS's interest in how the methods of scholarship may be rethought. Yet, as I will describe later, the calls for re-thinking scholarly methods have vastly outnumbered methodological responses. Before pursuing the question of scholarship, however, there is another seemingly unrelated difference between Mol's chapter and the book published four years later, one that echoes the discussion on performativity and theatre in the previous section.

The second, important point in Mol's 2002 monograph that differed from her 1998 chapter is in her use of the word "performance" to refer to performative events. The earlier text used the terms "perform" and "performance" throughout (including in the chapter title), but in the later work Mol writes, "Even if I have been using the term performance elsewhere in the past, I have carefully banned it from the present text" (2002, 41). Mol objects to various resonances of the term performance; she doesn't like that it connotes a stable achievement or effect, since her argument is premised on the ongoing, practical labour that allows objects (as multiplicitous entities) to be held together as singular ontological identities. But also (and perhaps primarily) objectionable is the resonance of "the stage," the theatrical implication of a backstage reality occluded by onstage social performances – a view Mol attributes to Goffman (Mol, 34–6).

The disavowal of theatre in STS discourses on performativity is not limited to Mol's work; it continues to echo in more recent STS projects that develop feminist new materialism, like that of Karen Barad, a scholar whose uptake of performativity has reinvigorated the use of the concept in STS. Recalling the subtle shift between Knorr-Cetina's concern with the ways in which practices fabricate *facticity* and Mol's attention to methods that interfere with the *world*, Barad (2007) goes further in explicitly arguing that practices do not constitute ways of knowing the world, but *the physical world itself*. So while performativity is a way for Barad to describe how entities are enacted through practices, she insists upon the material contingency of these entities' ontology. Indeed, Barad's argument makes use of quantum physics experiments as an exemplar of a performative interaction that produces difference. Like Haraway's notion of the material-semiotic, Barad suggests that models, measuring devices and theories are themselves *material-discursive*, both manifesting a material world and being in turn manifested within that world. Interestingly, Barad's claim about the material-discursive differentiation of objects of knowledge and ways of knowing is made by a reiteration of performativity specified against theatre:

> A performative understanding of scientific practices, for example, takes account of the fact that knowing . . . come[s] from . . . a direct material engagement with the world. Importantly, what is at issue is precisely the nature of these enactments. Not any arbitrary conception of doings or performances qualifies as performative. And humans are not the only ones engaged in performative enactments (*which are not the same as theatrical performances*).
>
> (Barad 2007, 49; italics added)

Like in the case of Butler's claim about the performative emergence of subjecthood, Barad's use of theatre is understandable as a way to stress that the process of performative enactment does not presuppose the human.[16] Still, that Barad's project – to theorize the emergence of difference through material interaction – cites the old distinction between performative enactments and theatrical performances is, I argue, a clue to the broad problem of how to track such enactments while taking into account one's own participation as researcher.

Let's imagine that, *pace* Herzig, Butler, Mol, Barad and others, theatre can be considered central to the performativity of scholarship. What might it offer that performativity theory doesn't already deal with? Recall the performativity invoked in ANT and feminist STS. Here, in its simplest form, performativity is understood by the axiom that to *act* (to speak, to observe, to behave, to relate) is to contribute to the creation of a world that shapes the ability to act. As we've already seen, some STS scholars have foregrounded *practices* over psychological factors, conceptual frameworks or historical institutions; they have sought to displace ontological categories naturalizing, for example, objecthood, causality and agency; they have attempted to describe ways in which a confluence of practices is not limited to a shift in concepts and inscriptions, but is entangled with shifts of being, calling into question the division between the ontic and epistemic (e.g., Haraway 1997; Barad 2007). It is precisely this understanding of performativity as enacted through practical action that allows a case for theatre as a material-discursive practice par excellence.

At the same time, the uptake of performativity in STS foregrounded the imperative for researchers *to take account of their own practices*, resulting in calls for various degrees of reflexivity, and even for measures *beyond reflexivity*. Recall Annemarie Mol's plea for scholars "to come to grips with what we are doing when crafting academic knowledge" (Mol 2002, 158), and, keeping in mind crises of reflexivity in other fields (most notably in anthropology – e.g., Clifford and Marcus 1986), consider the plethora of like-minded frustration from STS:

> The argument, then, is that social science is performative. It *produces* realities. But what to do with this claim? (. . .) We have suggested that the issue is one of 'ontological politics'. If methods are not innocent then they are also political. They help to *make* realities. But the question is: which realities? Which do we want to help to make more real, and which less real? How do we want to interfere (because interfere we will, one way or another)?
>
> (Law and Urry 2004: 69)

Or this:

> It's no use speaking of "epistemological breaks" any more. Fleeing from the past while continuing to look at it will not do. Nor will critique be of any help. It is time to compose – in all the meanings of the word . . .
>
> (Latour 2010: 487)

The second quote indexes the movement from Latour's critique of critique (Latour 2004) to his proposal that deconstruction should be abandoned in favour of construction (Latour 2010). Consider this alongside the dedicated attempt by John Law's *After Method: Mess in Social Science Research* (2004) to propose that methods might be reformulated by STS scholars by championing mess and indeterminacy as methodological strategies; we might even include Pickering's account of early cybernetics as a precursor to what such methods might look like (Pickering 2010).

Still, despite so much interest in rethinking methods, attempts at methodological reflexivity or measures beyond have been primarily limited to literary strategies in monographs, as early as Latour and Woolgar's 1979 book *Laboratory*

Life and as explicitly as Mol's 2002 *The Body Multiple*. However, these print "performances" have had a difficult time doing more than reflexively acknowledging their performativity while continuing to adopt the problematic distance of participant-observer, shifting scripts as they move between field sites and disciplinary peers. And, despite more than 20 years of growing concern for how to move beyond bare-bones reflexivity in STS, substantive, widespread methodological reconfigurations of research methods outside the monograph did not follow. In fact, foreshadowed perhaps by Mol's rejection of the term "performance," the popularity of the performance idiom seems to have declined[17] in the STS literature, especially in the US.[18] This might suggest that, in STS at least, the difficulties in methodologically responding to the reflexivity of a performative framework point to the *limits of performativity*. For me, as I will discuss in the following section, this limit of performativity (which, on its other face, delineates the limits of what may count as scholarly method) begs the question of what lies "beyond" performativity. I argue that the resources for *methodologically* addressing the performativity of scholarly methods are to be found in precisely the *artifice* and *intentionality* that have historically marked the theatre as outside the borders of performativity, as well as the *contingency* and *excess* that complicate a simple causality of theatre's productive effects.

Because, as STS scholars have indicated, our scholarly practices are constructive, not only of our knowing but also of what we seek to know, indeed of the "we" that can know, must we not reflect on the *material staging of scholarship itself*? Might it be possible to consider the methods of scholarship as consistent with the intentional *and* contingent manipulation of boundaries, temporalities and entities that characterize the theatre? In this fourth section of the chapter, I talk about how a material-discursive understanding of theatre might reframe the possibilities for doing scholarship that takes the co-construction of the world that it reflects upon, and through which it is constituted, as a *matter of concern* (Latour 2004) or a *matter of care* (de la Bellacasa 2011) by attending to the fragile bodies formed through practices of scholarship.

II   RaT at the podium

> So your lecturer is meant to be a performer, but not merely a performer.
>
> (Goffman 1981, 166)

If my use of the term *theatre* is broad, so too is my definition of *research*. I consider research to include a range of scholarly activities, including surveying the literature, collecting data, writing, teaching and communicating with disciplinary communities. While all of these can be understood and approached as theatre in the sense of intentional yet highly contingent arrangements or stagings, in the following analysis, I will look at two cases of scholarly lectures, both presented at academic conferences. While the first presentation is situated in a more conventional arrangement, and the second presents itself as an intervention, it is important to note that both are acts of theatre in non-trivial ways. In other words, I do not wish to suggest that one is more or less theatrical than the other, but that for both, theatrical arrangements are available to and inseparable from the perlocutionary effects of each talk. Thus, in the following examples, I invite you to consider historically theatrical arrangements, including scenarios, divisions of observer/performer, temporary animacies[19] and particular configurations of architecture, light, sound and bodies, as crucially relevant to both the methods of scholarship and the multiple ways this scholarship is taken up.

To begin, I bring your attention to an elegant lecture given by theatre scholar Martin Puchner at the 2013 conference of Performance Philosophy,[20] a newly launched scholarly organization bringing together academics with interests spanning performance and philosophy to consider the question, what is performance philosophy? Puchner proposed one interpretation, a genealogical tale in which performance philosophy emerges through the intersection of early "literature" and "scenes of instruction." Literature, for Puchner, begins when the first writing technologies move beyond functions of record keeping and begin to transcribe oral stories. As stories are inscribed, they are sorted and assembled by anonymous scribes into larger texts. These author-less assemblages of text become what Puchner calls "foundational texts," which come to exert great influence on their culture. The existence of these foundational texts makes possible, then, the first scenes of instruction, in which teachers (those who read and interpret foundational texts) surround themselves with a community of students. These master teachers – Puchner means Socrates, Confucius, Buddha, Jesus and Mohammed – do not themselves write, but their teaching circulates through the reports and writings of their students. These students, in turn, constitute prototypically scholarly communities in the sense that they are "held together by devotion to their teacher." These communities of students are "held together by the knowledge that something important is happening in this teaching scene, something world-shattering. A new way of thinking and viewing the world has emerged."[21]

Puchner's account invites us to imagine the origins of scholarly communities in these scenes, where, as students produce texts to communicate and interpret their masters' teachings, the academy, as an institutional assemblage of such students, writers and lecturers, emerges through these students' inscriptions and interactions. So, although other modes of performance – song, storytelling, gesture and so forth – may perhaps have preceded the development of writing, Puchner claims that performance philosophy doesn't emerge until these first scenes of instruction, where what is taught is grounded by, *but always exceeds*, the spoken content of the teaching. What is taught cannot be separated from the scene of teaching itself.

> And soon the students will go out and proselytize for that, they will transmit their teacher's words. But not just the words! Equally important are

> the teacher's gestures, the teacher's way of living, dietary habits, everything. Everything matters. Everything in this supercharged teaching scene is connected to this new way of thinking.[22]

His most salient claim, as I understood it, was that philosophical knowledge is developed and interpreted through the excess of interpretive performances, where situated, multimodal and seemingly extraneous meanings pervade and shape what might be otherwise mistakenly understood as abstract or conceptual knowledge.

Yet, the import of his account unfolds in its delivery, since Puchner is making a genealogical argument that explicitly extends past Socrates and Confucius to Wittgenstein and de Saussure, and, implicitly, on to the scene in which he himself appears when he gives this talk. Although Puchner never comments upon this implicit extension, it raises the question, is Puchner taking the role of a teacher when he delivers this lecture on 26 June 2013? The scene of instruction that Puchner describes is very particular: it features a master teacher, one who reads and interprets, but rejects writing, and draws students' fervent loyalty and interest in their quest for new ways of thinking and living. Yet, as these students (who do write, and debate, and proselytize) become teachers, and mastery multiplies, new networks of peers are formed. The academic lecture, particularly one given at a conference or gathering of peers, is perhaps not a scene of instruction in the foundational way Puchner described it. A scholar embedded in such peer networks (unlike Jesus or Mohammed) must not only succeed at attracting and producing devoted students but also be *constituted as a member of the community* through the now-institutionalized community of his academic peers. In a one-to-many academic lecture, these peers provisionally and theatrically take the role of students in order to give him the floor, as it were, and receive his argument in an extended and thoughtful manner. This obviously theatrical site – the conference lecture – is framing these performances of community. Not surprisingly, then, the conference lecture is a form giving rise to the single author, *solo voce* recitations making possible audibility, attribution and thus, perhaps, accountability; at the same time, it is a form that gives rise to the audience, the community that constitutes the author as member, in which the coherence of membership is declared *a una voce* by the cooperation of those assembled.

In this particular instance, Puchner's talk is one of six plenary lectures, and as a keynote speaker, he is acknowledged by the conference organizers as having achieved mastery among the peers and students assembled there. Held at the historic Sorbonne University, the lecture itself occurred in a large, domed neo-classical auditorium called the Amphitheatre du Richelieu. Puchner, a white, male Harvard professor with Clark Kent glasses, a white button-down shirt and a casual grey suit, waited on the side of the stage while he was introduced. After being introduced, praised and linked to various institutions and publications, he was invited to move to the centre of the wooden stage and began his talk, facing the many rows and balconies of wooden benches reminiscent of church pews, which the audience filled out nicely. Puchner, a gifted and experienced lecturer, spoke into a hand-held microphone; lacking a podium, he used a music stand for the notes he referred to in the course of his talk. The lights in the auditorium were on, though the stage was even more illuminated, thanks to four theatrical lights positioned, two by two, on the right and left upper walls flanking the stage. These lights created a subtle spotlight and marked the position of the speaker.

I had been among the audience during this presentation, but relied on a video recording available online for the description I offer here. It was by looking at the recording, for example, that I could report the presence of theatre lights; in my live experience of the event, these lighting arrangements receded from my attention even while they directed my attention to the speaker. When I consider the theatrical arrangements of ordinary scholarship, it is these sorts of arrangements that seem most salient, ones that are often so conventional and seemingly superfluous as to appear beside the point.

This superfluity recalls sociologist Erving Goffman's account of theatricality, in which theatrical presentations of the self draw upon particular social identities and props in order to articulate a "footing" upon which interlocutors can access intended content or meaning (Goffman 1981, 2012 [1959]). For Goffman, these theatrical machinations are meant to recede, the process of production becoming transparent to allow the product – social meaning – to surface. In the case of Puchner's lecture, this meant that I could focus on the stories and emerging argument of the talk, quite apart from its lighting, the wooden pew in which I sat, and the gestures Puchner used while speaking. But could I? Goffman's claim – one that I agree with – is that all these extraneous events require particular sorts of work to ignore, and that they are nevertheless communicative of a particular frame of interpretation which marks their irrelevance. Goffman discusses this point in his essay "The Lecture," a transcript of a live lecture he delivered in 1976, published as a chapter in his book *Forms of Talk*. He said,

> During lectures, some equipment and encoding faults are inevitable; they imply that a living body is behind the communication and, correspondingly, a self in terms of which the speaker is present and active, *although not relevantly so*. A place is made for this self. It is okay to self-correct a word one has begun to mispronounce. It is okay to clear one's throat or even take a drink of water, providing that these side-involvements are performed in speech-segment junctures – except, uniquely, this one [lecture that I am now giving], this being the only juncture when so minor a deflection would not be that, but some overcute theatricality, of merit only as a frame-analytical illustration of *how to go wrong in performances*. In sum, such attention as these various manoeuvres get either from speaker or hearer is meant to be dissociated from the main concern. *The proper place of this self is a very limited one.*

> (Goffman 1981: 184; italics added)

Here, Goffman considers a central and recurring event in the life of academics: *the lecture*, an activity in which he is himself engaged while making this argument. Goffman identifies the living body of the presenter, along with other distractions, as meant to be dissociated from the content, or "main concern" of the lecture. Yet, despite this dissociation, Goffman thinks of these excesses as a form of what he elsewhere called *ritualization*, in which "the movements, looks, and vocal sounds we make as an unintended by-product of speaking and listening never seem to remain innocent . . . [but] acquire a specialized communicative role in the stream of our behavior" (Goffman 1981, 2). While Goffman finds these non-innocent excesses arising primarily from the behaviour of human participants, it is not much of a stretch to claim that such communicating excesses are also to be found in stages, seating arrangements, temporal divisions and lighting instruments, and that these never function in isolation but always together.

Connecting this point back to Puchner's lecture means taking the scene of his instruction seriously; perhaps his lived body, presented to us on the stage of the Sorbonne, does not teach us how to live (as in the case of the original masters he talks about), but it does teach us how to live as scholars. In this sense, Puchner's clothes, way of speaking, his physical elevation and vocal amplification, and the many names and titles associated with his own name are all far more impactful than his literal lecture about what it means to be a member in this particular community.

Goffman was not the only scholar who used theatre as frame by which to analyse social behaviour (see, e.g., Peckham 1965), but his was the account most taken up subsequently. For later theorists of performativity (both in performance studies and in STS) Goffman's theatricality had to be disavowed, and the basis for this was usually the fact that his accounts of "on-stage" behaviour, role-taking, and other theatrical devices were critiqued for their implicit assumption of a "back-stage" reality behind the artifice of social identity (Butler 1988, 528; Mol 2002, 35–6). While this is an arguably valid critique, at least of Goffman's earlier work, my own dissatisfaction with Goffman's analysis is not with his assumptions about an essential self behind a theatrical one, but with his neglect of what STS scholars might call the performativity of his own account. For Goffman, attending to the theatrical machinations of social presentations of the self is the job of the sociologist; he does not see his description as an intervention, and is careful to separate the two acts. As is clear in the excerpt quoted earlier, Goffman performs a forcefully normative version of the "proper" lecture, in which he is careful not to "go wrong" in his own performance, and thus stresses and propagates the "very limited" place for a lecturing self.[23] Unexamined and unproblematic, all sorts of norms are swept in with the argument; thus, in Goffman's description, a male lecturer will "clean his glasses" while a female one will "finger her pearls" (Goffman 1981, 183). Crucially, for Goffman, culture informs and shapes the speech acts he studies, but it is a silent presence in terms of the *resources for* and *consequences of* his own scholarly work.

A very different attitude towards the theatricality of scholarship is to be found in the writings of anthropologist Margaret Mead. Mead did not explicitly use the idiom of theatre, but in a modest monograph published eight years before Goffman delivered his lecture, Mead talks about the material arrangements of scholarly communication. She characterizes the one-to-many form of lecture (that is the subject and vehicle of both Goffman's text and Puchner's talk) as one that maintains hierarchy. She wrote,

> The presence of hierarchy has been manifested in the construction of build-ings, in the elevated pulpit, the raised lecture platform, the special seat for a cabinet minister, all giving elevated and visible status to those who spoke versus the permanently or temporarily humble positions of the auditors who were to be informed by those who spoke.
>
> (Mead and Byers 1968, 4)

Mead's attitude to these observations is profoundly experimental, being at once interested in the way a particular lecture shapes outcomes and at the same time interested in what other outcomes are made possible *had it been arranged differently*. And in fact, her book *The Small Conference: An Innovation in Communication* advocates for another arrangement for scholarly communities, what she calls the "small substantive conference," a face-to-face gathering of a group

> small enough to sit around one large table, called together for a specific purpose, at a specific place, for a limited time. . . . All members of such a conference are accorded participant status; the method of communication is mutual multisensory interchange with speech as the principal medium; attitude, shifts in attentions, gestures and the type of expressiveness that can-not be adequately represented in print, play an important part.
>
> (Mead and Byers 1968, 5)

In contrast to Goffman's lecture, then, Mead acknowledges that the "noise" of extra-linguistic gestures, shifts of attention, boredom and fidgeting *can* be in the centre of explicit proceedings, and acknowledged as pertinent information in the flow of scholarly communication. For this to occur, however, Mead redraws the procedural and material arrangements of the communication event.

What is relevant about Mead's analysis is that it focuses on how the arrange-ments of bodies, gazes, voices and time constrain and enable particular sorts of status relations, articulations and interactions. In the vocabulary of the cyber-neticists with whom Mead developed such small conferences,[24] these differences of arrangement *made a difference*; in the parlance of feminist new materialism, where emergent status relations, articulations and interactions are both material and discursive, one might say these differences *matter*. For my own argument here, I am claiming that such arrangements partially constitute what Goffman called the *theatricality* of scholarship, but that, *contra* Goffman, this theatricality is not determined; *it can be staged differently*. Further, to also push gently against Mead's optimism, manipulating the theatrical arrangements of scholarship is not necessarily for the greater good; on the contrary, as making theatre has taught me, the meanings and effects of such arrangements always exceed their intent. In this way, intervening in the theatre of scholarship is not an answer of how best to do scholarship, but a question about how the doing of scholarship *does* what it does.

If intervening in the theatrics of scholarships is not for the greater good, then what is it good for? Allow me to address this by introducing a second example, a conference paper I myself presented at the same Performance Philosophy conference mentioned earlier.[25] The form of the conference panel is not the same as a plenary lecture format, but it is even less similar to the "small conference" model described by Mead. A conference panel does not have the indeterminate structure of a small conference, where all are authorized to speak; instead, conventionally, three to five speakers are given 10 to 20 minutes each to speak in an uninterrupted fashion. Like the plenary lecture, speakers are temporarily given the floor, and responses are admissible during a scheduled "question-and-answer" period following each talk, or sometimes following the completion of all talks. At the Performance Philosophy conference, the panel to which I was assigned had three speakers, and was held in a medium-sized neoclassical room, called the Amphitheatre du Descartes. Though much smaller than the Amphitheatre du Richelieu, where Puchner gave his lecture, the Amphitheatre du Descartes was filled with similar wooden benches in the auditorium, descending to a recessed stage with a large table, tabletop microphones and a chalk board.

Here, instead of "giving a talk" or "reading a paper" (an act typical of scholarly communication), I asked the panel's audience to read my paper aloud. My presentation, which sought to intervene in (but not dismantle) the conditions that constituted an authorial, scholarly utterance, began with this uncontroversial phrase: "Hello. My name is Yelena Gluzman." It was spoken by all the people in the room. Three voices spoke the next sentence: "Rather than describe my research, I would like to attend to the material conditions that make possible this panel presentation." In this way, the paper went on to consider the limits of performativity, the historical exclusion of theatre from the theory of performativity, and the theatrical arrangements that made possible scholarship as it was being done. Throughout, the talk used the experience of dispersed vocalizing as an experiential lens to ground these claims.

The paper was distributed in the form of prepared booklets, where text to be read was highlighted, and these highlighted portions differed from booklet to booklet.[26] So, certain parts of my paper were spoken by many voices, some parts by a few, some by just one voice. When preparing the talk, I had scored the text according to how many voices spoke each part, and printed unique booklets for each different voice. At the panel, after being introduced by a moderator (by name, but lacking any further affiliations), I asked the audience assembled who was comfortable reading aloud in English; to the people who raised their hands in response, I distributed booklets scored with the most text to be spoken. To the others, I distributed the remainder of the booklets. My instructions, spoken while I moved around the room handing out booklets, asked the participants to read the highlighted parts out loud. The reading began.

Sonically, there was no ideal spot from which to hear the talk, since the dispersal of voices, both when booming *en masse*, as in the first sentence, and stumbling in a trio, as in the second sentence, were hard to hear. The acoustics of the room were constructed for a sonic source to originate at the stage. The Performance Philosophy organizers, who did a wonderful job documenting all the talks either on video or audio, recorded the talk, but because the recording was localized to the tabletop microphone at the front of the room, most of the sound was registered by the digital recorder as noise and fades in and out on the existing recording. In this way, the dispersal of voices caused trouble for a stable point from which either a spectator or a recording device could have an overview of the proceedings; if such a position did exist, it was located at the physical object of the booklet. However, since each booklet (unlike a playscript) contained only one scoring (making it impossible, e.g., to predict how many voices would speak the next line), even this position could not access an overview. And, since the experience of speaking and listening was itself the object of the talk's consideration, a post hoc reading (or worse yet, a description, like I am giving here) of the printed text does provide an overview, but is arguably a view from very far away.

What was the point of such a performance? I respond by posing two questions that emerged from writing, performing and observing it: (1) What are the relationships between the *form* of scholarly communication and the *object* of scholarship? and (2) What are the conditions that constitute a scholarly utterance as such?

To consider how these questions have been articulated in the literature, I turn to Dwight Conquergood's meditations on ethnographic participant-observation as it relates to the ethnographic texts produced by participant-observers. He writes, "Recognition of the bodily nature of fieldwork privileges the processes of communication that constitute the 'doing' of ethnography: speaking, listening, and acting together" (Conquergood 1991, 181). While he champions the embodied, intersubjective complexity necessary for ethnographic fieldwork, Conquergood mourns the undoing of this complexity in ethnographic monographs:

> Although ethnographic fieldwork privileges the body, published ethnographies typically have repressed bodily experience in favour of abstracted theory and analysis. . . . The *interpersonal contingencies* and *experiential give-and-take* of fieldwork process congeal on the page into authoritative statement, table, and graph.
>
> (ibid; italics added)

Though Conquergood is referring specifically to ethnography and the ethnographic monograph, it may be fair to generalize this loss of complexity and intersubjectivity even when talking about other methods of scholarship as they congeal into scholarly communication. This, I argue, is true also for the presentation of papers at scholarly gatherings. It goes almost without saying that paper presentations have a fairly typical structure: the presenter is placed in front of a group and proceeds to either read a previously prepared text verbatim or speak from notes or in tandem with PowerPoint slides. The audience watches and listens and, when appropriate, engages with the speaker by asking questions. Regardless of the topic of the presentation, or the argument advanced by the speaker, certain relations are already activated. So, not only is a great deal of the complexity of the research process necessarily smoothed over in the conference talk, but also other effects follow. For example, through the conventions of presentation (i.e. one body facing many, one speaking while others listen), the speaker is constituted as an author. The subject of the talk is positioned as a phenomenon that is outside of, and unaffected by, the unfolding presentation and interactions therein. The rules of engagement between participants are constrained, and these constraints are actualized through their enactment. Even time (so precious and enforced in the 20-minute conference talk) is both a condition and product of such proceedings.

Beginning the talk with multiple voices saying, "My name is Yelena Gluzman" was my way to reorient the proceedings, an aporia that was meant to focus on the complexity of authorship. To be clear, I do not consider this choral introduction to undermine authorship; all the voices declaring their name to be Yelena Gluzman were reading from a script, after all. However, the foregrounding of a named author by its dispersal through a room-full of audience-speakers was intended to acknowledge that it was the presence of this audience, an audience that is iterative through its very presence, that constituted my authorship and identity as scholar.

The issue of authorship isn't simple, and the subject/object relations, which are built in (and built from) authorship, are multiple. At the Performance Philosophy conference, immediately before the session in which my paper was presented, there was a staged reading of Anne Carson's *Antigonick*, directed by Ben Hjorth. A number of extremely respected performance studies scholars read the parts, including Judith Butler as Creon, and Avital Ronell as Antigone. After the staged reading, there was a large Q&A in which Ronell expressed her discomfort in reading Carson's text, since she disagreed with some of the text's philosophical allegiances. Was her responsibility as an actor to uncritically speak the words given to her by the text, she asked the assembled audience, or was her responsibility to the criticality of her scholarship?[27] This question echoed in the choral presentation of my talk that followed the staged reading. One of the members of the audience was performance scholar Kélina Gotman, who expressed a similar discomfort: did speaking my text suggest her complicity? This discomfort suggested that the voices in the conference room were harnessed rather than liberated by the performance paradigm of this "distributed" talk; therefore, though authorship itself is foregrounded in its vocal distribution, it is also reinforced by the script that so tightly orchestrated the audience's participation.

To take this a step further, we might say that Avital Ronell's description of the tension between affirmation-through-participation and responsibility-through-criticality speaks to the sort of complexities experienced in ethnographic fieldwork, as described by Conquergood. For Conquergood, the intersubjectivity of the ethnographic encounter is positive; it is embodied, processual and embedded in interactions, and has no recourse to an Archimedean view-from-above. On the other hand, the scholarly monograph, according to Conquergood, smooths out this complexity of experience into a rhetorical singularity in which the author *responds* to the process of research, and *directs* her response to a specialized community that is situated elsewhere. Whereas the messy process of fieldwork (or archival research, or thinking, for that matter) is experienced through multiple encounters in which agency and objecthood are continually re-emerging, the elegant scholarly argument is possible only through situations that pre-empt the instability of subjects and objects.

What then are the repercussions on subject/object relations that emerge during the conference talk? As I see it, the issue of authorship implies the co-constructive relations between a singular author/performer and a community of spectator/participants. My (for it is "mine") particular conference performance *reinforces* such a division while at the same time putting its dividing apparatus (constituted primarily by the script as *rubric*) into the literal hands of all those present. However, flowing from (and constituting) authorship there is another aspect of subject/object relations as they exist in typical scholarly communications, and that is the reification of the object of research *as* object. This is the something that Conquergood argues against. I would like to suggest that the distributed conference talk was fundamentally reflexive, asserting its own enactment *as a research encounter*. So, while it reinforced the authorial act, it also made both authorship and voice the moving target of collective consideration. In other words, the distributed conference talk both highlighted authorship through the discomfort of uttering scripted words and at the same time asked speakers to consider this experience of vocalizing as the object of the research being presented.

The experience of vocalizing en masse is a funny one, and all three times I have attempted this presentation, people have remarked on their self-awareness of shifts in rhythmicity in response to an emergent rhythm of the group's vocalizing. Here, in attempting to speak out loud, participants found themselves engaged in what Conquergood called an *"experiential give-and-take"* (Conquergood 1991, 181). Though I have no video recording of the talk at the Performance Philosophy conference, there is a video record of this presentation at an STS conference in 2015, held in a large hotel in Denver. The camera was pointed towards the audience, and for the most part, the video shows that people's gazes were oriented downwards, towards the booklet in their hands. One man, smiling, took out his smartphone and filmed the unfolding scene. When voices "entered," some looked up, away from the booklet, to locate the person who was speaking. Most interesting, though, is that when multiple voices spoke the same text, they almost always ended in unison. Thus, although they were not speaking in strict synchrony, people tended to coordinate their speed with others, and were thus attuned to the emerging rhythmicity of collective speaking. In one part of the written text (pictured in figure 5.1), this rhythmicity is both commented upon and tested, as disintegrating words make coordination more difficult for speakers.

Here, the text in bold was spoken by everyone in the room, while the italicized text was spoken by one voice. Though true for all parts of the text, but particularly

---

What are the relationships between the form of scholarly communication and the object of scholarship?

and

What are the conditions that constitute a scholarly utterance as such?

and

What is my part in this paper presentation?

What have I done to constitute a legitimate author, to make possible the legibility of the talk?

How do the multiple voices that carry, trip, alter, and drop this text negotiate with each other, even when (shout out to Garfinkel) the linguistic social conventions of this negotiation disintegratekbjegbvb
jsbdughbxz
kmdnkjbd
dmnkdsbnkf
dd
khiue
kjhgyyewoihzblioooo
piqnninxx ejijiee
eeeknnk
iiiii

Figure 5.1 Page 10 of the lecture booklet given to the conference audience.[28]

in the nonsensical jumble of letters, participants had to attune to an emergent voice, involving themselves in a moment-to-moment give-and-take of rhythm, speed and enunciation. In the video recording of this moment, some people laughed, others did not, but there seemed to be a heightened, effortful attention to each other's sound as voices found their way to the end of the phrase. It was this attunement that was foregrounded as a phenomenon of interest in the attempt to consider the material-discursive conditions that make possible the conference presentation.

III   Situating PAR through RaT

My essay is not suggesting that theatre *should be* levied as a method of scholarship, but that it already is. At its base, my argument assumes that the process of scholarship is partially constituted by its material-discursive arrangements, and that those arrangements tend to reify multiple divisions between subjects and objects that then serve to differentiate scholarship as such. Yet, instead of simply acknowledging this to be the case, as has been done in, for example, STS confessions of methodological performativity, I am interested in how scholarship can actively incorporate these theatrical arrangements as part and parcel of its objects of research; this is the move from theatre to *experimental theatre*. Thus far, I have given two examples of lectures organized theatrically. In one, although the theatricality of instruction is the topic of the lecture, the theatricality of the lecture itself is not commented upon, and, as is typical in such contexts, allowed to recede in order for the topic of the lecture to enter the spotlight. In the other example, the typical arrangements are redesigned so that attention to *the argument* must necessarily traverse attention to *the form of the occasion*.

Focusing on the site of the academic lecture has allowed me to consider a particular recurring event in scholarship, one where membership and the community are dynamically creating each other, and has allowed me to consider this in light of historical work on such events, by both Goffman and Mead. However, I do not wish to imply that the conference is the only site of academic theatre; on the contrary, I suggest that all stages of scholarship, from reading and discussing the literature to collecting data in the field or the archive, to writing, publishing, teaching and attending conferences, are all theatrical practices whose forms are both conventional and particular. By exploring particular theatrical arrangements in each of these, I propose that meaningful interventions are possible in the spirit of Mol's "grasping our own methods" (2002, 158). By theatrically grasping them, we not only acknowledge our complicity in their constraints and affordances but also, in the spirit of Mead's experimentality, can explore *how* boundaries, relations and meanings shift when methods are done differently.

To return to the question posed at the outset of this chapter, does this proposal for research as theatre meaningfully address recent debates around the institutionalization of performance as research, or does it further marginalize art- and performance-based methodologies from legitimate academic work? The issues around performance as research touch on two main areas, one usually framed as the promise of PAR, and the other framed as an obstacle to its institutionalization. As its promise, it has been suggested that PAR, by insisting upon experiential and embodied methods, may contribute to a lineage of expanding what counts as knowledge. In alignment with my own genealogical links between PAR and the practice turn as it occurred in STS, Robin Nelson and others see practice-centred, phenomenological and poststructuralist projects as important precursors to making practice as research (Nelson 2013, 49–57) or performance as research (Riley and Hunter 2009) justifiable and legible. Further, by addressing what constitutes legitimate knowledge-production, PAR also has the potential to influence new policies and visibilities in the university; as Piccini and Kershaw ask, "What kind of academy do we wish to create?" (Piccini and Kershaw 2004, 86). Yet Piccini and Kershaw have more to say about the institutional obstacles to practice as research in the academy, focusing on a long list of questions: how are PAR dissertation projects evaluated? What is required for them to count as "research"? Must they be accompanied by a written work, and if so, what is the status of this work vis-à-vis the performed component? What sorts of resources and infrastructures are needed for PAR? How are the "results" of such projects published, disseminated and critiqued? To consider each of these questions in turn, these authors, and many other members of the conversation, presuppose a normative academy – founded on positivistic ideals – that must be negotiated, coddled and appeased in order for institutional space to be made for PAR.

My proposal, to shift from an idiom of PAR to one of RaT, is not meant to deflect from the particular problems raised by PAR work, nor to ignore the obstacles to its institutionalization. Instead, I hope to shift the conversation from prematurely getting stuck in the impossibility of generalizations (and therefore policies) about what PAR should do, and instead endorse scholars to consider theatre methods as a way to *address these obstacles* in their work. Thus the question of audience is crucial for RaT that is well aware that meaning is situated at local sites of encounter (even when these sites and encounters are shaped culturally, historically, grammatically).[29] By foregrounding the always-already theatrical arrangements of scholarship situated in (and situating) particular discursive communities, I question the efficacy of invoking the abstraction of the normative academy in PAR discussions. This attention to situated particularities addresses the problem of how PAR projects can be evaluated and disseminated, how they can enter broader academic discourse, and how they might be cited – textually or performatively. The suggestion of the inversion I propose here (PAR > RaT) is that assessment, legibility and dissemination do not need strict guidelines but rather already emerge as actionable problems through an extended engagement with particular discourse communities. This is not to say that these engagements are necessarily happy or without friction. It is the tension or contradiction sometimes found in such encounters that is the potential for criticality (always in part a self-criticality, if engagement is to continue) and insight. For example, Piccini and Kershaw point out that the multiple locations and forms of practice as research might introduce problems around "authorship, ownership and ethics." They offer this hypothetical problem:

> If a mix of academic and professional practitioners together with students, technicians and designers collaboratively devise a performance that is staged on two nights, one in the university theatre, the other in the city's public art space and it is funded by a mix of AHRB and local arts council money and is eventually submitted as an RAE output, how do we deal with those potentially conflicting agendas and systems of value?
>
> (Piccini and Kershaw 2004, 90)

Here, I argue that an orientation to RaT, research as theatre, allows these complexities described by Piccini and Kershaw to open up as actionable the very practices underlying issues like authorship, ownership and ethics, not to mention issues of collaboration, expertise and publics.

It must be noted, also, that in the literature on PAR, we can see resistance to taking up the complexities of the term *performativity*. For example, Robin Nelson, one of the most vocal participants in PAR discussions, argues for practice as research while explicitly avoiding the idiom of performativity, which for him is too "contested and multi-accented," an objection similar to that expressed by Annemarie Mol in her rejection of the term *performance*. Retaining the idiom of theatre as relevant to discussions about PAR (as is the case with the re-orientation of RaT) is, I argue, a way to recuperate theatre and theatre studies as integral to PAR work across disciplines. For theatre departments in the US, which lag significantly in embracing PAR frameworks compared with departments of visual arts (Riley 2013, 175–77),[30] putting theatre at the centre of PAR might impact concrete institutional policies that support an experimental approach to research methods and, more importantly, facilitate local legibility for such work.

Further, inverting the usual understanding of theatre as one instance of performance (alongside music, dance, sports, rituals, etc.) and considering performance as research (PAR) as *one instance* of research as theatre (RaT) allows for generative and necessary discourse between theatre, other forms of performance, practice-oriented social science methods, materialist STS and feminist theory, to name only a few possible intersections. How such conversations might proceed, how they might share risk and what institutional spaces might enable them are open questions that, in my sense of current imperatives towards interdisciplinary, are gaining traction.

Acknowledgement

While all faults are my own, this text has been enriched through the comments, feedback and engagement of Morana Alač, Nadine George Graves, Patrick Anderson, Cathy Gere, Fernando Dominguez Rubio, Sarah Klein, Michael

Berman, Tina Hyland, Don Everhart, Jacob Hellman, Rebecca Hardestly and Christina Aushana. A first draft of this paper was developed in the Performance Philosophy working group convened by Will Daddario and Ioana Jucan at the 2015 conference of the American Society of Theatre Research (ASTR). Thank you to Nadine George Graves and her graduate students for allowing me to learn with, and from them in their *Performance as Research* seminar. The first version of the distributed talk discussed in the chapter was presented at a workshop with Karen Barad, when she visited UCSD as Student Choice Speaker in March 2014. I am grateful to her, Emily York, and the other participants of that workshop for their generous engagement. The first instances of my theatre-thinking occurred when my mother and father took me to see theatre as a child; I thank them for sharing with me these indelible experiences.

Notes

1 Throughout this chapter, I use "scholarship" and "research" interchangeably to refer to this range of activities.

2 See, for example, Crease's examination of scientific experimentation as theatrical arrangements (Crease 1993).

3 The status of theatrical speech as *artificial* is related to the *mimetic* or *representational* project that, for Austin, marks the theatre as separate from authentic and impactful *action in the world*.

4 In Butler's "Critically Queer," she does attempt to re-specify theatre performance through drag as resistance to compulsory gender norms through a hyperbolic display of those norms (Butler 1993). However, I will argue for a more central role of theatre that is not based in its hyperbolic representation of social norms, but rather in its double-ness: as an intentional crafting of possible experience and simultaneously as an event supremely contingent on situated conditions that always exceed those intended.

5 Shannon Jackson's influential discussion of the disavowal of theatre by Austin and Butler in *Professing Performance* (2004) argues that the evacuation of theatre from performativity (and theatre studies from performance studies) was more than just another instance of an even longer-standing antitheatrical bias (Barish 1981; Puchner 2002; Ackerman and Puchner 2006). Jackson suggests multiple ways in which the exclusion of theater forms a *constitutive absence* around which the attributes of theater and performativity are defined in opposition to each other: theater studies becomes associated with traditional cultural formations, craft and manual action, while performance studies is associated with inter-disciplinarity (speaking to concerns in anthropology, sociology, cultural criticism and critical studies) concerned with, and articulated through, theory (performativity theory in particular) (2004, 189).

6 "But where and when does a *performed gesture* draw its force . . .?" This is my theatre-focused variation on Butler's question from "Critically Queer": "But where and when does such a performative draw its force?" Butler argues that performative acts are a form of "authoritative speech," but whose originating authority is not an individual subject but rather "a reiterated acting that *is* power in its persistence and instability" (Butler 1993, 17). I am suggesting that theatrical compositions are performative in their reiteration of available semiotic precursors, even while they are introduced by an authorial subject.

7 Texts on theatre-making are therefore very concerned with the techniques and technics needed to reproduce a performance night after night. This is an obsession because such repetition is constantly thwarted by any number of contingencies, from emergent moods in performers and/or audiences to unruly costumes to slips of the tongue. Likewise,

authorship in theatre performance, an event often made by multiple collaborators, is vexed (Worthen 1998).

8 Suchman, a feminist STS scholar who has written about human-machine interaction, stresses that although plans (like intentions) certainly exist, they are better understood as representations of a problem or opportunity than as an explanation of subsequent action. Action, for Suchman, is contingent upon, and emergent from, situated *interaction* (Suchman 2007).

9 This productivity has also been referred to as "efficacy" (Bottoms 2003).

10 The first US professional organization for STS, the Society for the Social Studies of Science, was convened in 1975 (http://www.4sonline.org/society).

11 This is a large body of work across sociology, history and philosophy. For an overview of some of the key players of the 1970s from the perspective of the early 1980s, see Collins (1983). For a critical account of the development of STS, see Zammito (2004).

12 See Knorr-Cetina's elaboration of this point in the section titled "From the Question Why to the Question How" in *The Manufacture of Knowledge* (1981, 20).

13 See, for example, Haraway (1997), Coole and Frost (2010) and Barad (2007).

14 Texts that introduced and developed the notion of performativity in STS include Pickering (1995), Callon (1998), Mol (1998), Law (2004) and Barad (2007).

15 For example, John Law and Vicky Singleton (2000) described how a turn to a performative idiom was not only a rejection of previous STS modes but also necessarily a commitment to reflexively considering how scholarly acts figured into these performances. They argue, "[Previous STS approaches] choose, often knowingly, to ignore the performative consequences of their own descriptions. By contrast, actor-network theory and, to a greater extent, feminist technoscience studies choose to wrestle with the fact that they (and therefore their own accounts) are socially located, *noninnocent*, and therefore political performances. This suggests that they don't offer simple descriptions, but make a difference" (767, italics added).

16 Understandable, but fraught, since in the case of the split-screen experiments that Barad cites, as well as in her own articulation of this argument, human researchers are ever present, both as conditions for and products of such action. This isn't to say that performativity (or theatre) presupposes the human, but that human observation or description of a phenomenon will shape and couple both the category of human and the attributes of the phenomenon.

17 With the important exception of Karen Barad's work, as discussed earlier.

18 Particularly in STS work coming out of Northern Europe, performativity continues to be invoked, sometimes alongside formal innovations in how scholarship is done (Fitzgerald and Callard 2015; Zuierent-Jerak 2015; Jensen 2014). It is an open question whether the academic climate for such formal experimentation might be more hospitable *because of* the relatively more integrated place that practice as research has in UK institutions (Nelson 2013).

19 "Animacy – or we might rather say, the set of notions characterized by family resemblances – has been described variously as a quality of agency, awareness, mobility, and liveness" (Chen 2012, 2).

20 Delivered by Martin Puchner on 26 June 2013 at the Sorbonne University. Video recording available at http://labo-laps.com/videos-theatre-performance-philosophie-tpp-2014. Accessed 16 December 2015.

21 These and subsequent quotes were transcribed from the publicly available video of the lecture.

22 From an STS perspective, Puchner's lecture can be troubling. It troubles because it is only at the site of the primordial academy that Puchner recognizes a scene of instruction and knowledge-making that counts as performance philosophy. The characters of his stories, both masters and students, are men, "sitting cross-legged, or reclining on chairs." If analogous scenes of instruction occurred among women, slaves and others

not authorized to participate in such gatherings, these might well be indispensable for subsequent cultural formations, but are certainly not included in the performance of legitimate and institutionalized knowledge that is understood by Puchner's evocation of philosophy. From an STS perspective – rooted in decades of deconstructing narratives glorifying the lone great men of science – Puchner's story problematically restricts instruction to one sort of scene.

23 Indeed, Goffman is very concerned with being taken seriously by his audience, and spends much of the first part of the lecture assuring his audience that he is not "yet another self-appointed cut-up, optimistically attempting a podium shuck" (Goffman 1981, 162). To me, Goffman's anxiety reveals how deeply he relies on the norms of the lecture form, even as he points to their social mechanisms.

24 Most famous among these were the Macy Conferences, held yearly between 1946 and 1953. As Mead herself points out, these highly interdisciplinary gatherings of scholars interested in systems, broadly speaking, were also themselves opportunities to experiment with systems. She writes, "In the late 1940s, use of a cybernetic model for cross-disciplinary communication was developed within a series of conferences which themselves exemplified the newly realized principles of feedback and error correction" (1968, 10).

25 This paper, with textual variations, was first presented at a workshop with Karen Barad at the University of California, San Diego, in 2013, and presented again at the annual conference for the Society for Social Studies of Science (4S), in 2015.

26 In a later version of this paper, given at the 4S conference in 2015, text to be spoken was printed in bold typeface, and all other text was printed in italics.

27 A decidedly Brechtian concern, as one reviewer pointed out.

28 Figure 5.1 is from the presentation at the 4S conference in 2015, since that is the one that has video recording available. The 2014 booklet used at the Performance Philosophy conference has a similar gesture of disintegrating text.

29 Thus, when considering my distributed conference presentation discussed earlier, it should be noted that the institutional and conventional space of each conference where it was presented was already positioned to read such a text; in all cases, the talk took seriously and addressed particular concerns of that community. And for each presentation, I re-wrote parts of the text to orient it to a site-specific conversation. Thus, I would not endorse a generalization of this particular scholarly act as method; rather, I would propose a keener attention to repercussions of particular theatrical arrangements of particular acts of scholarship in particular disciplinary and discursive communities, including those outside the academy. That said, the method of this distributed conference talk was subsequently taken up and adapted by disability studies scholar Louise Hickman for her conference paper "Distributing Crip Socialities" (Hickman 2016).

30 As Shannon Rose Riley argues, this fact may be attributed to entrenched characterizations of academic theater as a manual, non-theoretical field, a trend that Shannon Jackson related to the anti-theatrical bias of performance studies (Riley 2013; Jackson 2004).

References

Ackerman, Alan, and Martin Puchner, Eds. 2006. *Against Theatre: Creative Destructions on the Modernist Stage*. Basingstoke: Palgrave Macmillan.

Austin, John L. 1962. *How to Do Things With Words*. Oxford: Oxford University Press. Web. Accessed March 10, 2014 from www.metaphilo.fr/Livres/ Austin%20How%20to%20 do%20things%20with%20words.pdf.

Barad, Karen. 2007. *Meeting the Universe Halfway*. Durham, NC: Duke University Press.

Barish, Jonas A. 1981. *The Antitheatrical Prejudice*. Berkeley, CA: University of California Press.

Bottoms, Stephen J. 2003. "The efficacy/effeminacy braid: Unpacking the performance studies/theatre studies dichotomy." *Theatre Topics* 13(2): 173–87.

Butler, Judith. 1988. "Performative acts and gender constitution: An essay in phenomenology and feminist theory." *Theatre Journal* 40(4): 519–31.

———— 1990. *Gender Trouble and the Subversion of Identity*. London: Routledge.

———— 1993. "Critically queer." *Gay & Lesbian Quarterly* 1: 17–32.

Cabantous, Laure, Jean-Pascal Gond, Nancy Harding, and Mark Learmonth. 2016. "Critical essay: Reconsidering critical performativity." *Human Relations* 69(2): 197–213.

Callon, Michel. 1998. "Laws of the markets." *Sociological Review Monograph* 46(S1): 1–272.

Chen, Mel Y. 2012. *Animacies: Biopolitics, Racial Mattering, and Queer Affect*. Durham, NC: Duke University Press.

Clifford, James and George E. Marcus. 1986. *Writing Culture: The Poetics and Politics of Ethnography*. Berkeley, CA: University of California Press.

Collins, Harry M. 1983. "The sociology of scientific knowledge: Studies of contemporary science." *Annual Review of Sociology* 9: 265–85.

Conquergood, Dwight. 1991. "Rethinking ethnography: Towards a critical cultural politics." *Communication Monographs* 58(2): 179–96.

Coole, Diana and Samantha Frost, Eds. 2010. *New Materialisms: Ontology, Agency, Politics*. Durham, NC and London: Duke University Press.

Crease, Robert P. 1993. *The Play of Nature: Experimentation as Performance*. Bloomington, IN: Indiana University Press.

Daston, Lorraine and Peter Galison. 2007. *Objectivity*. Brooklyn: Zone Books.

de la Bellacasa, Maria Puig. 2011. "Matters of care in technoscience: Assembling neglected things." *Social Studies of Science* 41(1): 85–106.

Dewsbury, John-David. 2000. "Performativity and the event: Enacting a philosophy of difference." *Environment and Planning D Society and Space* 18(4): 473–96.

Diamond, Elin. 1997. *Unmaking Mimesis: Essays on Feminism and Theater*. London: Routledge.

Fitzgerald, Des and Felicity Callard. 2015. "Social science and neuroscience beyond interdisciplinarity: Experimental entanglements." *Theory, Culture & Society* 32(1): 3–32.

Gad, Christopher and Jensen, Casper Bruun. 2014. "The Promises of Practice." *The Sociological Review* 62(4): 698–718.

Goffman, Erwin. 2012 (1959). "The presentation of self in everyday life." In *Contemporary Sociological Theory*, 3rd Edition. Edited by Craig Calhoun, Joseph Gerteis, James Moody, Steven Pfaff and Indermohan Virk. 46–61. Hoboken, NJ: Wiley-Blackwell.

———— 1981. *Forms of Talk*. Philadelphia: University of Pennsylvania Press.

Haraway, Donna. 1997. *Modest_Witness@Second_Millenium.FemaleMan©_Meets_ Onco-Mouse™*. London: Routledge.

Herzig, Rebecca. 2004. "On performance, productivity, and vocabularies of motive in recent studies of science." *Feminist Theory* 5(2): 127–47.

Hickman, Louise. 2016. "Distributing Crip Socialities." Paper presented at the Composing Disability: Crip Ecologies Conference. George Washington University, April 8.

Jackson, Shannon. 2004. *Professing Performance*. Cambridge: Cambridge University Press.

Jensen, Caspar Bruun. 2014. "Experiments in good faith and hopefulness: Toward a post-critical social science." *Common Knowledge* 20(2): 337–62.

Knorr-Cetina, Karin. 1981. *The Manufacture of Knowledge: An Essay on the Constructivist and Contextual Nature of Science*. Oxford: Pergamon Press.

Latour, Bruno. 2004. "Why has critique run out of steam? From matters of fact to matters of concern." *Critical Inquiry* 30(2): 225–48.

———— 2010. "An attempt at a 'compositionist manifesto'". *New Literary History* 41(3): 471–90.

Latour, Bruno and Steven Woolgar. 1986 (1979). *Laboratory Life: The Construction of Scientific Facts*, 3rd Edition. Princeton, NJ: Princeton University Press.

Law, John. 2004. *After Method: Mess in Social Science Research*. London: Routledge.

———— 2009. "Actor network theory and material semiotics." In *The New Blackwell Companion to Social Theory*. Edited by Bryan S. Turner. 141–58. Hoboken, NJ: Wiley-Blackwell.

Law, John and Vicky Singleton. 2000. "Performing technology's stories: On social constructivism, performance and performativity." *Technology and Culture* 41(4): 765–75.

Law, John and John Urry. 2004. "Enacting the social." *Economy and Society* 33(3): 390–410.

Lynch, Michael. 1985. *Art and Artifact in Laboratory Science*. London: Routledge & Kegan.

Mead, Margaret and Paul Byers. 1968. *The Small Conference: An Innovation in Communication*. The Hague: Mouton.

Merton, Robert K. 1938. "Science and the social order." *Philosophy of Science* 5(3): 321–37.

———— 1942. "Science and technology in a democratic order." *Journal of Legal and Political Sociology* 1: 115–26.

Mol, Annemarie. 1998. "Missing links, making links: The performance of some artheroscleroses." In *Differences in Medicine: Unraveling Practices, Techniques and Bodies*. Edited by Marc Berg and Annemarie Mol. 144–C65. Durham, NC: Duke University Press.

———— 2002. *The Body Multiple*. Durham, NC: Duke University Press.

Nelson, Lise. 1999. "Bodies (and spaces) do matter: The limits of performativity." *Gender, Place & Culture* 6(4): 331–53.

Nelson, Robin. (Ed.). 2013. *Practice as Research in the Arts: Principles, Protocols, Pedagogies, Resistances*. Basingstoke: Palgrave Macmillan.

Peckham, Morse. 1965. *Man's Rage for Chaos*. Philadelphia: Chilton Books.

Piccini, Angela and Baz Kershaw. 2004. "Practice as research in performance: From epistemology to evaluation." *Research in Mathematics Education* 15(2): 86–92.

Pickering, Andrew. 1995. *The Mangle of Practice: Time, Agency and Science*. Chicago: University of Chicago Press.

———— 2010. *The Cybernetic Brain: Sketches of Another Future*. Chicago: University of Chicago Press.

Puchner, Martin. 2002. *Stage Fright: Modernism, Anti-theatricality, and Drama*. Baltimore, MD: Johns Hopkins University Press.

Ridout, Nicolas. 2006. *Stage Fright, Animals, and Other Theatrical Problems*. Cambridge: Cambridge University Press.

Riley, Shannon Rose. 2013. "Why Performance as Research?—A U.S. Perspective." In *Practice as Research in the Arts: Principles, Protocols, Pedagogies, Resistances*, Edited by Robin Nelson. 175–87. New York and Houndmills: Palgrave Macmillan.

Riley, Shannon Rose and Lynette Hunter (Eds.). 2009. *Mapping Landscapes for Performance as Research: Scholarly Acts and Creative Cartographies*. Basingstoke: Palgrave Macmillan.

Schatzki, Theodore R., Karin Knorr-Cetina and Eike von Savigny. 2001. *The Practice Turn in Contemporary Theory*. London: Routledge. Society for the Social Studies of Science Website. Past Officers Page. Accessed December 2, 2015 from www.4sonline.org/past_officers.

Suchman, Lucy. 2007. *Human-Machine Reconfigurations: Plans and Situated Actions*. 2nd Edition. Cambridge: Cambridge University Press.

Traweek, Sharon. 1988. *Beamtimes and Lifetimes: The World of High Energy Physicists*. Cambridge, MA: Harvard University Press.

Worthen, William B. 1998. "Drama, performativity, and performance." *PMLA* 113(5): 1093–107.

Zammito, John H. 2004. *A Nice Derangement of Epistemes: Post-Positivism in the Study of Science From Quine to Latour*. Chicago: University of Chicago Press.

Zuierent-Jerak, Teun. 2015. *Situated Intervention: Sociological Experiments in Health Care*. Cambridge, MA: MIT Press.

Chapter 6

Agential cuts and performance as research

Annette Arlander

In this text, I develop some ideas of physicist and queer theorist Karen Barad in relation to performance as research and to my practice of performing landscape. I suggest that Barad is especially interesting in the context of performance and performance studies, as well as artistic research,[1] as she proposes a new understanding of how discursive practices are related to the material world. She criticizes Judith Butler's theory of performativity for a re-inscription of the nature-culture dualism and for privileging discursive over material concerns (Barad 2003; Barad 2007, 34–35). While performative accounts by social and political theorists focus on the productive nature of social practices, Barad's 'agential realism' acknowledges that the forces at work in the materialization of bodies are not only social, and that the bodies produced are not all human (Barad 2007, 33–34).

In relation to the themes of this book – knowledge, method, and impact – Barad is relevant because of her insistence that knowing and being are inseparable and entwined with ethics. Her ideas are important for problematizing our relationship to the environment, which is also one of my key concerns. In the following I will present two of her core concepts, 'agential separability' and 'agential cut', approaching them through my work of performing for camera in some works created by Lake Kilpis in the north of Finland in Spring 2014.

Barad emphasizes that practices of *knowing* and *being* are mutually implicated, and she introduces the term *onto-epistemology* to describe the study of practices of knowing in being (Barad 2007, 334). Those with experience of performance as research will probably find it easy to agree with Barad when she states, "We don't obtain knowledge by standing outside the world; we know because we are *of* the world. We are part of the world in its differential becoming" (Barad 2007, 185). For Barad, separating epistemology from ontology is part of "a metaphysics that assumes an inherent difference between human and nonhuman, subject and object, mind and body, matter and discourse" (ibid.). Barad suggests we need "something like an *ethico-onto-epistem-ology* – an appreciation of the intertwining of ethics, knowing and being" (ibid.).

For Barad,

> experimenting and theorizing are dynamic practices that play a constitutive
> role in the production of objects and subjects and matter and meaning . . .
> [they] are not about intervening (from outside) but about intra-acting from
> within, and as part of the phenomena produced.
>
> (Barad 2007, 56)

Following physicist Niels Bohr, she maintains that apparatuses are productive
of the phenomena they measure. This does not mean, however, that reality is
a product of human concepts; rather, concepts are specific material arrangements (Barad 2007, 334). Knowing for Barad is a physical practice of engagement: "Scientific practices are specific forms of engagement that make specific
phenomena manifest" (Barad 2007, 336). In a similar manner, artistic practices
are specific forms of engagement that make specific phenomena manifest. The
artist-researcher is literally producing phenomena – artworks or performances –
and not only observing them.

Among proponents of artistic research, the subjectivity of the artist-researcher
is usually considered an asset rather than a disadvantage. For instance, scholars
coming from the qualitative research tradition have pointed out that "[t]he
starting point for artistic research is the open subjectivity of the researcher and
her admission that she is the central research tool of the research" (Hannula,
Suoranta, and Vadén 2005, 160). An entanglement of researcher and what is
researched can rarely be avoided. Moreover, from the point of view of systemic
thinking, there is no point in separating organism and environment, as they are
aspects of the same system. In the famous words of Gregory Bateson, "[w]hat thinks
is the total system which engages in trial and error. . . . The unit of survival is
organism plus *environment*" (Bateson, quoted in Kershaw 2007, 248).

As humans, Baz Kershaw observes, we are totally imbued with earth's bio-
sphere, and cannot survive without it, so how could we possibly access a critical perspective that would be beyond it? How can we solve a problem whose
solution is another version of itself (Kershaw 2007, 52)? After presenting this
recursive dilemma, Kershaw brings in Po-chang's ox and paradox. "Asked about
seeking the Buddha-nature Po-chang says: 'It's much like riding an ox in search
of the ox!' The quest is a search for itself" (ibid.). This is the dilemma not only of
the artist-researcher who is mixing the object, method, and outcome of her
research but also of all of us who study landscapes within them. Barad's notion
of agential separability can be useful for tackling this 'conundrum'. Referencing
studies on colonies of slime mould, Barad asks,

> How can we expect the notion of an organism understood as an individual
> that is situated in a container we call the environment to begin to speak to
> the complexity of the intra-active reconfiguring of bodily boundaries that
> defines the slime mold's astonishing material existence?
>
> (Barad 2012, 77)

Particularly relevant in the context of performance is Barad's realization that, rather than being something given, the split into subject and object is enacted in each case, through various *intra-actions* (a neologism she has created as an alternative to interaction). For her no predetermined subjects and objects exist that could interact, form networks or assemblages; both subjects and objects are constituted through specific intra-actions (Barad 2007, 339). For Barad, 'observer' and 'observed' are merely two physical systems intra-acting in the marking of the 'effect' by the 'cause'. Thus, the "reproducibility and unambiguous communication of laboratory results are possible because the agential cut enacts determinate boundaries, properties and meanings, as well as [. . .] the 'measured object' ('cause') within the phenomenon" (Barad 2007, 340). I will return to the agential cut later in the text.

In creative research 'reproducibility' is rarely strived for, although some form of experimental dimension distinguishes artistic research and much practice-led research from traditional forms of social sciences and humaniora. The Finnish philosopher Tuomas Nevanlinna proposes that artistic research can be experimental although it cannot be an exact science; it can produce knowledge, albeit knowledge of the singular. He sees artistic research as an heir of the "aesthetic research" proposed by Alexander Baumgarten in the eighteenth century (Nevanlinna 2004, 83). "It cannot be generalised into laws in itself, and it applies only to the unique, but it is knowledge nevertheless and makes truth 'happen' in a singular way" (ibid.). Not all performance as research, however, is concerned with the unique, as art is traditionally expected to be.

More recently the notion of experimental systems developed by Hans-Georg Rheinberger has been explored related to artistic research, starting with the observation that artworks can be considered as matters of fact or manufactured pieces of knowledge, at least in some sense (Schwab 2013, 5). Rheinberger suggests that matters of fact are complex spatiotemporal entities that emerge not in individual experiments but rather in complex experimental settings or experimental systems, which provide the context against which an experiment has meaning (Schwab 2013, 6). Experimental systems "inextricably cogenerate the phenomena or material entities and the concepts they come to embody" (Rheinberger quoted in Schwab 2013, 7).

This approach, which tries to find common ground between scientific and artistic experimentation without conflating them, seems congenial with Barad's ideas, at least on a superficial level. This is not surprising, as Barad is reinterpreting the thinking of physicist Niels Bohr and developing his ontology beyond his humanist bias. As does Bohr, Barad moves beyond an epistemological conception of objectivity and replaces it with an ontological one. Bohr realized that the boundary between the observer and observed is not given, but articulated by the apparatus in each case. However, for Bohr the experimenter is still a liberal subject who freely chooses among apparatuses and then notes the marks on bodies (Barad 2007, 153). What is required for objectivity, according to Bohr – unlike Einstein, for whom separability between observer and observed is the condition of objectivity – is an unambiguous and reproducible account of marks on bodies (Barad 2007, 173–174).

Barad does not assume the knower to be a self-contained rational human subject; "we are not outside observers of the world," she points out. "Neither are we simply located at particular places in the world; rather we are part of the world in its ongoing intra-activity" (Barad 2007, 184). For Barad, knowing is a distributed practice that includes the larger material arrangement, a practice where "a specific engagement of the world . . . becomes differentially intelligible to another part of the world in its differential accountability to or for that of which it is a part" (Barad 2007, 342). Knowing is "not a play of ideas within the mind of a Cartesian subject that stands outside the physical world"; rather, "knowing is a physical practice of engagement" (ibid.). This will not come as news to artist-researchers engaged in performance; knowing as a physical practice has been emphasized by scholars in the field as diverse as Conquergood (1999), Bolt (2004), Riley and Hunter (2009), Johnson (2011), and Spatz (2015), to name a few.

According to Iris Van der Tuin, one of the few writers to introduce Barad in the context of artistic research – or what she calls 'creative research' – Barad wants us to study practices. "Such practices happen *in being* and they are *of knowing*" (Van der Tuin 2014, 259). She maintains that understanding the onto-epistemological nature of all research practices foregrounds the 'how-question' (i.e., how are research practices enabling or constraining?): "How do they open up or buy into the anthropocentric schema of the authoritative scientist objectifying a muted entity with the help of a mediating instrument in a neutral environment?" (Van der Tuin 2014, 260). A social-constructivist, or what she terms *linguisticist*, approach is equally anthropocentric, Van der Tuin claims, and she asks whether academic research and creative research are so different (ibid.). She criticizes the wish "to posit that artists produce 'other' knowledges from their non-scientific studios, holding up the ideal of knowledge production in clean laboratories and restricted-access libraries and archives" (ibid.). She argues that "the heightened attention to onto-epistemology, even if not labelled as such, in creative research teaches positivists and linguisticists alike something about their practices" and suggests that "all these practices are at once specific in the terms of the knowledge produced and generic in onto-epistemology" (ibid.).

Like a physicist, the artist-researcher is literally producing phenomena and not only observing them. Some kind of agential separability is necessarily at play, however. We can benefit by not only acknowledging our subjectivity and entanglement with the object of research but also examining how we enact some separation with the phenomena at hand, such as splitting temporarily into observer and observed. Following Barad, the important thing is that this split is not given in advance; there is no neat division into subjects and objects to be found in the world. Rather, this cut is and can be enacted each time anew. I will return to the 'agential cut' later in this text.

Barad emphasizes the rejection of 'particularism' – that is, the idea that the world consists of individuals with properties (Barad 2007, 333). This stands in contrast to current ideas of object-oriented ontology,[2] although attempts to find connections to new materialism have been made (Bennett 2015). For Barad, however, the primary units are phenomena rather than objects:

"phenomena do not merely mark the epistemological inseparability of 'observer' and 'observed'; rather, *phenomena are [. . .] ontological entanglements*" (Barad 2007, 333). Thus, phenomena are not only what is observed in laboratories but also "the basic units of existence" (ibid.). The basic units are not 'words' and 'things' but 'material-discursive practices' and 'phenomena'. The primary *ontological* units are phenomena – that is, dynamic topological reconfigurings or entanglements or relationalities or (re)articulations of the world. The primary *semantic* units are material-discursive practices, through which both ontic and semantic boundaries are constituted. According to Barad, this dynamism is *agency*, which "is not an attribute but the ongoing reconfigurings of the world. The universe is agential intra-activity in its becoming" (Barad, 2007, 141).

For Barad, following Foucault, discourse is not a synonym for language and meaning or intelligibility is not restricted to humans: "Discursive practices are the material conditions for making meaning [. . .] [and] meaning is an ongoing performance of the world in its differential intelligibility" (Barad 2007, 335). Bodies are not objects with inherent boundaries and properties but material-discursive phenomena, and human bodies are not inherently different from non-human ones (Barad 2077, 153). Barad turns from linguistic representations to discursive practices and from apparatuses as "laboratory setups to an understanding of apparatuses as material-discursive practices through which the very distinction between the social and the scientific, nature and culture, is constituted" (Barad 2007, 141). By using the term *material-discursive practices*, Barad consequently refuses to separate discourse and materiality. This is, of course, relevant for performance and for artistic research, where knowledge is often both produced and shared by means other than written language. Before considering Barad's ideas any further, I will describe some examples of my practice (see figure 6.1).

How to be here with Malla? How do you speak to a mountain, asked the cloud? How do you

Figure 6.1 A Day with Malla (text), video still.

Ars Bioarctica Residency

A few works created during Spring and Summer 2014 at the Helsinki University's Biological Station by Lake Kilpis in the north of Finland, near the Norwegian border and the Polar Sea can serve as examples. I visited this place for one week in April and another in June as part of the Ars Bioarctica Residency organised by the Finnish Bioart Society.[3] When applying for the residency, I explained how my work is related to landscape rather than bio art in a strict sense and described my aims:

> I would like to explore the landscape in Kilpisjärvi and see how I could document changes taking place in the landscape during the spring or early summer. For twelve years I have performed landscape on Harakka Island, off Helsinki, by documenting the changes in the environment either once a week for the duration of a year or with two or three hour intervals during a day and night. [. . .] Some of the techniques I have used on Harakka could probably be utilized in Kilpisjärvi as well, for instance documenting a day and night with three-hour intervals. [. . .] Ideally I would like to come at a time when the snow is melting or almost gone and there is a lot of light.

During my first week in the north in April, ice covered Lake Kilpis and there was 150 cm snow on the ground. However, there was indeed plenty of light. The proximity to the Polar Sea makes the weather in the area extremely changeable, which was interesting for my purposes, as the landscape changes character constantly.[4] I used the same technique I have used elsewhere, performing for a camera on tripod in the same place repeatedly, creating a rough form of time-lapse videos. Walking out on the ice, wearing a dark blue scarf, turning my back to the camera, I stood for a while looking at Malla Fell in front of me, again and again.

During my second week in June, the ice was almost gone, and spring was approaching quickly.[5] There was no possibility of returning to the same spot on the lake, so I stood on the shore using a composition I had used once before on Harakka Island, with only a part of my shoulder wrapped in the scarf visible to the left in the image. I also performed sitting on a rock at the shore during a full day and night, again with two-hour intervals between the performances, and recorded one image in real time for approximately twenty minutes.

The works later edited of the material created in April on the lake are *A Day with Malla (text)* (4 min. 25 sec.) and *Meeting Malla* (10 min.). The first one was performed on 7 April 2014 (7 am – 9 pm), with two-hour intervals. The second combines material performed on two consecutive days, 3 April (2 pm – 8 pm) and 4 April (8 am – 10 pm), again with two-hour intervals. As the title indicates, the first one included a voice-over text, written and recorded during my stay at the station. I also edited an installation version of the same material, *A Day with Malla 1–2* (8 min. 10 sec.), juxtaposing two images of the same landscape, one of me standing on the ice and the other without a human presence. All these works show a view of Lake Kilpis and Malla Fell with a tiny human figure standing on the lake, while the colours and shades of the land-scape change with the time of day and the shifting weather.

When returning in June I wrote the following on the Ars Bioarctica blog:

> What is changing, what remains the same? I tried to recreate the image I repeated for a day in April, and found almost the same spot for my camera tri-pod; the wooden construction I used as a signpost was still there. Almost, that is, because the shores are open, I cannot walk on the ice, of course, and even the slight shift in the angle of the camera transforms the image. I will probably make a version, one day every second hour, without the human figure, never-theless. Everything changes; perhaps something remains the same.
>
> What should I change and what should I try to maintain as the same? A delicate balance; in some sense nothing is ever, ever the same. That is the beauty of it, the whole point of performing landscape; it changes all the time. And that is why repetition is needed, to somehow artificially produce an impression of something remaining the same, in order for all the small changes to become discernible.[6]

The works edited from the material created during the June visit, where I had to remain on the shore, include *Looking at Malla* (9 min. 20 sec.), recorded on 5 June (10 am – 10 pm) with two-hour intervals, showing only part of the scarf on my shoulder on the left in the image. *Day and Night with Malla 1–2* (30 min. 20 sec.) is an installation version edited from the material recorded during a day and night, between 7 June (noon) and 8 June (noon), which combines an image of me sitting on a rock at the shore, looking at Malla (part 1; see figure 6.2), with the same view without the human figure (part 2). Another version

Figure 6.2 Day and Night with Malla, video still.

of sitting on the rock was performed on 6 June as a real-time session and edited using very long crossfades into an installation, *Moment with Malla 1–2* (26 min. 10 sec.), where I am slowly disappearing from one image while slowly appearing in the other. In these works, the view with Lake Kilpis and Malla Fell include a part of the shore to the right with some rocks and vegetation; the human figure is fairly large in the foreground. Apart from changes in weather and light, the movement of the melting ice and the water on the lake provides the main action.

Agential cut

Based on my practice, described earlier, as well as previous conversations in the Performance as Research (PAR) Working Group of the International Federation for Theatre Research (IFTR), I suggest that Barad's notion 'agential cut' can be useful in the context of research involving practice. Barad explains:

> Intra-actions include the larger material arrangement (i.e., a set of material practices) that effects an *agential cut* between 'subject' and 'object' (in contrast to the more familiar Cartesian cut which takes this distinction for granted). That is, the agential cut enacts a resolution *within* the phenomenon of the inherent ontological (and semantic) indeterminacy.
>
> (Barad 2007, 139–140)

According to Barad, the boundaries and properties of the 'components' of phenomena become determinate through specific agential intra-actions and in that way particular material articulations of the world become meaningful. A specific intra-action, which involves a specific material configuration of the 'apparatus', enacts an agential cut, effecting a separation between 'subject' and 'object'. The agential cut resolves the ontological and semantic indeterminacy (Barad 2007, 333–334).

This means, to put it simply, that differences are made, not found, and dichotomies derive from specific cuts (Barad 2012, 77). The boundaries and properties of the parts of a phenomenon become determinate only in the enactment of an agential cut that delineates the 'measured object' from the 'measuring agent'. The intra-action of one part of the phenomenon with another part marks a correlation between the 'causal agency' (cause) and 'measuring agency' (effect) (Barad 2007, 337). Thus, Barad reworks causality as intra-activity: "What is a 'cause' and what is an 'effect' are intra-actively demarcated through the specific production of marks on bodies" (Barad 2007, 236).

A measurement is the intra-active marking of one part of a phenomenon by another; nothing in the nature of a measurement makes it irreducibly human-centred (Barad 2007, 338). No human observers are required, because 'observer' and 'observed' are merely two physical systems intra-acting in the marking of the 'effect' by the 'cause'. Humans may emerge as part of such practices but they are not necessary. Objectivity is a matter of accountability to marks on bodies. The agential cut delineates object and instrument, but the role played by any part of the experimental arrangement varies depending on the details of the intra-action, due to the mutual exclusivity of the conditions for definability (Barad 2007, 326). For example, a device that can be used to define and measure 'momentum' cannot be used to define and measure 'position'.

What is crucial for Barad is the accountability to marks on bodies – that is, an accounting of the apparatuses that enact determinate causal structures, boundaries, properties, and meanings (Barad 2007, 340). She stresses the importance of *"the proper accounting of agential cuts within the specific phenomenon in question"*, and the key point for her is "that *agential separability is enacted only within a particular phenomenon"* (Barad 2007, 345). Although there are no determinate, pre-existing entities with determinate properties, there are determinate marks on bodies produced through specific intra-actions – and these need to be accounted for.

Here the artist-researcher could take note. How do we account for the apparatuses we use or are used by – and for the marks on bodies they create? The task for an artist-researcher is, then, not only to acknowledge her subjectivity and entanglement with the object of research but also to account for the agential cuts within the phenomena at hand – that is, what is included and what is excluded from mattering. Perhaps we could consider agential separability as an ongoing process or as a continuous choice of focus: to experiment with one aspect of the practice as a method or 'measuring apparatus', while leaving other aspects to react, respond, or become 'measured'?

Barad further specifies the nature of agential cuts as follows: "Intra-actions enact agential cuts, which are a cutting together-apart (that is, entangling-differentiating), as one move (not sequential acts)" (Barad 2012, 80). Although this seems paradoxical, "it goes to the very nature of the agential cut, which cross-cuts itself", she states (Barad 2012, 80). Moreover, "the world can never characterize itself in its entirety; it is only through different enactments of agential cuts, different differences, that it can come to know different aspects of 'itself'" (Barad 2007, 432, chapter 4, footnote 42). We cannot study or look at everything at once: "Only part of the world can be made intelligible to itself at a time, because the other part of the world has to be the part that it makes a difference to" (ibid.). Therefore, it is important for an artist-researcher to focus on articulating the apparatuses used, the specific agential cuts enacted, and especially the marks on bodies generated. What is part of the apparatus and what is part of the body being marked or measured can change from case to case and within a specific case from time to time. An effort to account for the various entanglements of a practice in changing circumstances (see figure 6.3) and the inclusions and exclusions involved could take us far towards articulating agential separability in performance as research.

Figure 6.3 Looking at Malla, video still.

Agential cuts in practice

We can understand the idea of an agential cut, albeit in a simplified manner, with the help of my video practice described earlier, since the framing of an image enacts an agential cut of sorts. The camera produces an image by creating a split between what is within and what is outside the frame, between what is part of the image and what is not. Nothing of this division pre-exists in the landscape; the framing emerges through the action of video recording. This intra-action between equipment and environment involves material-discursive practices, like the properties of the lens of the camera, or my preconceptions of what constitutes a good view, or the condition of the ice on Lake Kilpis, and so on. And these, too, are created through intra-actions. What is apparatus and what is object, what is equipment and what is environment are not given but produced in each case.

The practice of performing for a camera on a tripod could be described as a measuring apparatus that produces difference. The specific choice of who or what performs the subject or observer as part of the 'measuring apparatus' (behind the camera) and who or what performs the observed, the object or 'causal agency' to be 'measured' (in front of the camera), is decided in each case. The tripod enables me as an artist to act in both roles, in turn. When I split into a performer in front of the camera and a witness behind it, we can speak of an agential cut of sorts, since the division of labour is not predetermined or given but contingent to the situation. With the help of a camera on a tripod the same person can act as photographer and model. I can put the camera to record and to function as a witness and enter the image, engage in the action, and then return behind the camera to control the result. This enables a practice less dependent on funding, planning, and so-called production values. Moreover, because of video technology there is the potential to correct mistakes *in situ* and reuse the material, as the result can be checked immediately afterwards. Which moments to use and which moments to discard can also be decided later, while editing.

Another kind of apparatus, or measuring agency, is the choice of time schedule. A temporal framing, a literal cut, takes place when I repeat the action once every two hours, picking 'slices of time' of the landscape. Everything between the recorded moments is excluded from the video, as a consequence of the cut or jump created by the schedule or the measuring apparatus. Another schedule, another 'temporal framing' – such as returning to the same place once a week or once a month for a year, as in my works based on the Chinese calendar – would produce another view of the changes in the landscape. This is demonstrated by comparing, for instance, *Day and Night with Malla*, which consists of 'slices of time' (I sit on the rock by the shore for a moment every two hours for a day and night), and *Moment with Malla*, which is recorded in one sequence.

A further type of apparatus or measuring agency is activated in the editing process. In these cases, the appearance of a (new) reality is produced by removing, rather than adding, slices of material while editing. Usually I use all takes in the order of recording, leaving out only the parts where I enter and exit the image. Thus, an illusion of continuity is created in the final work, a rough form of time-lapse imagery. When the performer stands immobile on the ice on the lake or sits motionless on the rock at the shore, an illusion of her being there while time passes and the weather changes is produced, especially if I manage to return to precisely the same spot, if the camera stays immobile, and if the clips are combined with soft crossfades.

Such processes do not involve only human decision-making, as Barad points out. Because I am using the automatic functions of the video camera, the technology has a great deal to say in this case. The light meter and white-balance calculator, automatic focus, and other technological devices included in the functions of the camera constantly react and readjust to changes in the environment caused by weather and wind, time of day, passers-by of all species, and the actions of the performer. The rain at the end of the video *Meeting Malla* exemplifies this; the automatic focus of the camera chooses to focus on the raindrops hitting the lens, and to blur the landscape behind, which is thus hidden from view by the drops. This takes place behind my back, unbeknownst to me, while I am standing on the lake and the camera intra-acts with the weather. The editing process as well, the choice of what images to use and how to combine them, is interplay between human choice, recorded environmental circumstances, and the affordances of technology.

In these cases, all the following could be understood as agential cuts in a broad sense: (1) the framing of the image; (2) the shift between the roles of performer and observer/witness; (3) the schedule of when to perform and record; and (4) the principles used during editing. Each clearly makes a difference in the resulting videos by defining what is included and what is excluded on each level. This could be understood as a simple demonstration of Barad's statement, "[s]ince different agential cuts materialize different phenomena – different marks on bodies – our intra-actions [. . .] contribute to the differential mattering of the world" (Barad, 2007, 178). It is not only a question of choice, however, since, according Barad, cuts are not agentially enacted by wilful individuals but by the larger material arrangement of which they are a part. She insists that we are responsible for the cuts that we help to enact, not because we choose or are being chosen but because we are an agential part of the material becoming of the universe. This also means that "'others' are never very far from 'us'; 'they' and 'we' are co-constituted and entangled through the very cuts 'we' help to enact" (Barad, 2007, 179). Although I choose the apparatus and the moment, the combined environmental circumstances that the camera reacts to produce the image.

The ice melting on the lake, the rock on the shore, and the water moving between them are co-constituted and entangled in a way that changes over long periods of time. But how could the boundaries between the rock and the human being sitting on the rock change? However much I would feel at one with my surroundings, I am aware of what is part of the rock and what is part of me. How are we co-constituted and entangled? At least we consist of the same minerals, and the cold wears and tears the surface of both of us. For Barad, however, the point is not only to incorporate both humans and non-humans into the apparatus of bodily production. Humans do not merely assemble different apparatuses for their knowledge projects; they are themselves part of the ongoing reconfiguring of the world (Barad, 2007, 171).

Barad dismisses both humanist and anti-humanist accounts; human subjects do not exist prior to their involvement in natural-cultural practices; nor are they the effects of human-based discursive practices. Human subjects are neither outside observers of apparatuses nor independent subjects that intervene in the workings of apparatuses; nor are they the products of the social technologies that produce them (Barad 2007, 171). Rather, human bodies are like all other bodies; they are not entities with inherent boundaries and properties but phenomena that acquire specific boundaries and properties through the dynamics of intra-activity (Barad 2007, 172).

What would this mean in terms of my material-discursive and natural-cultural practice of performing landscape? Does it mean that I, too, like the lake or the ice on it or the rock on the shore, acquire specific boundaries and properties through the intra-actions involved? That I change the environment through my actions, as when I create a path in the snow by repeatedly placing the tripod in the same place? That the environment changes me, as when I get a cold by standing in the wind and rain? That my ideas of what is an enjoyable temperature to be outdoors or what is needed for a beautiful view change over time? That I change and transform together with the environment? Yes, indeed.

And the same holds for the video works thus created, which can be shown in other places at other times and which could potentially change, for instance, the way the viewers imagine that specific place or the north in general. When *Looking at Malla* was shown in Mediaboxi, at Gallery Forum Box in Helsinki in March 2015, I realized how the associations related to images of ice melting on a lake have changed in recent years. What used to be an image of hope – spring finally returning after a long winter, even in the high north – now has ominous overtones of melting glaciers and rising sea levels due to climate change.

For Barad, the fact that humans are emergent phenomena, like all other physical systems, does not diminish our responsibility, as all situations entail an ethical obligation. We have to intra-act responsibly in the world's becoming, to contest and rework what matters and what is excluded from mattering (Barad 2007, 235). To intra-act responsibly means understanding that 'we' are not the only active beings – although this in no way deflects our responsibility (Barad 2007, 391). Intra-acting responsibly in the world as a human being without assuming a humanist subject who can freely choose is not easy to realize in practice. What agency remains for us?

For Barad, agency is an enactment, not something one has, nor an attribute of subjects or objects; agency is distributed over nonhuman as well as human forms (Barad 2007, 214). This distributed agency is evident in my practice of performing landscape as well. The lake, the ice, the rock, the scarf, the clouds, the snow, birds and humans, barking dogs, snowscooters, passing cars, and the litter on the shore are all entangled parts of the same material becoming of the world in the image. The camera, the tripod, the pieces of wood at the shore under the tripod, the biological station I stay at, and all other 'components' only indirectly impacting the image have agency, too. In the video imagery, the boundaries between what or who seems to perform can shift; the scarf can turn into the main actor, as in *Looking at Malla*. Or the raindrops can assume centre stage, as at the end of *Meeting Malla*. In terms of agency, in creating the image we all are part of the intra-action.

As Barad suggests, "[a]ll bodies, including but not limited to human bodies, come to matter through the world's iterative intra-activity, its performativity. Boundaries, properties, and meanings are differentially enacted through the intra-activity of mattering" (Barad 2012, 69). She adds, however, that differentiating is not about radical exteriorities, not about 'othering' or separating, but about making connections and commitments: "the very nature of materiality itself is an entanglement. Hence, what is on the other side of the agential cut is never separate from us. Agential separability is not individuation" (ibid.). We are responsible to others we are entangled with through the various ontological entanglements that materiality entails: "Ethics is about mattering, about taking account of the entangled materializations of which we are part, including new configurations, new subjectivities, new possibilities. Even the smallest cuts matter" (ibid.). Ethics is not about the right response to a radically exteriorized other; it is about responsibility and accountability for the relationalities of which we are a part (ibid.).

The relationalities involved are too numerous to keep count of in most cases of performance as research. This is evident when considering these few examples of my work. The connections involved are not limited to my participation in the Ars Bioarctica residency and recording moments in the life of Lake Kilpis, Malla Fell, and the landscape around them, but include all the relations the resulting artworks might engender. This difficulty of imagining not only the past but also the future of a work relates to discussions of impact, which are problematic in many ways. Barbara Bolt has suggested that artist-researchers should consider the transformations that have occurred through an artistic practice or the effects an artwork engendered, which can be material, affective, or discursive (Bolt 2008, 6). Should we focus our attention on the experience of the viewers, or on the transformation of the performer(s)? Should we consider only the impact of the finished artwork or include the effects of the process of creating that work? What about possible side effects or unwanted consequences, like a heap of waste produced by the process? As I understand Barad, we are responsible for all of them, and more.

Performances for camera that are recorded, edited, and distributed in digital form, like the ones in my examples, can be endlessly copied, but also destroyed with one click of a mouse. They are seemingly 'immaterial' and light, although heavily dependent on technology and electricity; they could easily dissolve into the general flow of disposable media images but could in principle be watched hundreds of years from now as strange souvenirs from a distant past. The entanglements involved in their production are too numerous to even imagine, much less to account for and articulate in detail. Consider, for instance, the automatic focus of the camera intra-acting with the weather (see figures 6.4 and 6.5). To

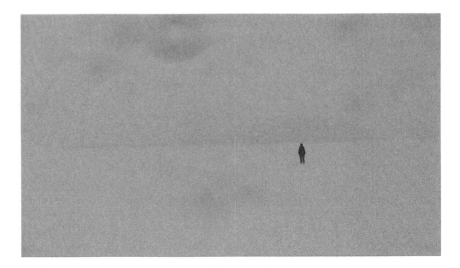

Figure 6.4 Meeting Malla, video still.

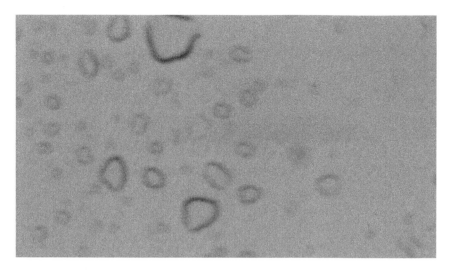

Figure 6.5 Meeting Malla, video still.

imagine their potential future consequences seems almost impossible. Nevertheless, following Barad, I should try to account for the cuts of inclusion and exclusion involved and the marks on bodies generated.

By way of conclusion

Barad's idea of an agential cut is useful for efforts to make artistic research understandable for those who work in other disciplines, who can find the entanglement of the subject and object of research or the mixture of method and outcome in artistic research difficult to accept. It is important to remember, however, that the principle of agential separability concerns all forms of research. By creating a bridge between science and humanities Barad makes space for a wide variety of experimental practices artist-researchers might engage with. Barad's ideas do not necessarily present any 'new tools' to artist-researchers engaged in performance. Her ideas can, however, be interpreted as a challenge to account for the cuts of inclusion and exclusion we make, the apparatuses we use and are used by, as well as the marks on bodies generated by them. This could, in turn, help us see the research aspect in artistic work more clearly. Personally, I find her notion of material-discursive practices particularly helpful. In this text, I have focused on the notions of agential cut and agential separability. Other concepts she uses, like diffraction rather than reflection, could be worth looking closer at in the future. Barad radicalizes the idea of performativity and makes it material in a way that is widely acknowledged as crucial today. Her insistence on taking both human and nonhuman bodies into consideration is a challenge for performance as research, which, like performing arts in general, tends to regard human bodies as the interesting ones.

Thanks to the Finnish Bioart Society for the possibility to spend time at the Ars Bioarctica Residency in Kilpisjärvi.

Appendix 1

Blog posts
Ars Bioarctica Residency blog
archived at https://www.researchcatalogue.net/view/266988/351018
Arlander, Annette "Performing Landscape in Kilpisjärvi 1–15"

1   April 2, 2014 https://bioartsociety.fi/projects/ars-bioarctica/posts/performing-landscape-in-kilpisjarvi-1
2   April 3, 2014 https://bioartsociety.fi/projects/ars-bioarctica/posts/performing-landscape-in-kilpisjarvi-2
3   April 4, 2014 https://bioartsociety.fi/projects/ars-bioarctica/posts/performing-landscape-in-kilpisjarvi-3
4   April 5, 2014 https://bioartsociety.fi/projects/ars-bioarctica/posts/performing-landscape-in-kilpisjarvi-4
5   April 6, 2014 https://bioartsociety.fi/projects/ars-bioarctica/posts/performing-landscape-in-kilpisjarvi-5
6   April 7, 2014 https://bioartsociety.fi/projects/ars-bioarctica/posts/performing-landscape-in-kilpisjarvi-6
7   April 8, 2014 https://bioartsociety.fi/projects/ars-bioarctica/posts/performing-landscape-in-kilpisjarvi-7
8   April 9, 2014 https://bioartsociety.fi/projects/ars-bioarctica/posts/performing-landscape-in-kilpisjarvi-8
9   June 4, 2014 https://bioartsociety.fi/projects/ars-bioarctica/posts/performing-landscape-in-kilpisjarvi-9
10   June 5, 2014 https://bioartsociety.fi/projects/ars-bioarctica/posts/performing-landscape-in-kilpisjarvi-10
11   June 6, 2014 https://bioartsociety.fi/projects/ars-bioarctica/posts/performing-landscape-in-kilpisjarvi-11
12   June 7, 2014 https://bioartsociety.fi/projects/ars-bioarctica/posts/performing-ladscape-in-kilpisjarvi-12
13   June 8, 2014 https://bioartsociety.fi/projects/ars-bioarctica/posts/performing-landscape-in-kilpisjarvi-13
14   June 10, 2014 https://bioartsociety.fi/projects/ars-bioarctica/posts/performing-landscape-in-kilpisjarvi-14
15   June 13, 2014 https://bioartsociety.fi/projects/ars-bioarctica/posts/performing-landscape-in-kilpisjarvi-15

Arlander, Annette. *Performing Landscape* blog
"Malla – Mountain in the North" (blogpost 5.4.2014)
http://annettearlander.com/2014/04/05/malla-mountain-in-the-north/

"Meeting Malla again" (blogpost 5.6.2014)
http://annettearlander.com/2014/06/05/meeting-malla-again/

Appendix 2

Videos produced of the material created during the Ars Bioarctica Residency:

A Day with Malla (text) 2014, HD video, 4 min. 25 sec.
www.av-arkki.fi/en/works/a-day-with-malla-text/
Wrapped in a dark blue scarf I am standing on the ice on Lake Kilpis, looking at Malla Fell for a day, with two-hour intervals between 7 am and 9 pm, on 7 April 2014. In the voice-over I wonder how to be there with Malla.
Looking at Malla 2014, HD, 9 min. 20 sec.
www.av-arkki.fi/en/works/looking-at-malla/
With a dark blue scarf on my shoulders I am standing on the shore of Lake Kilpis, looking at Malla Fell, on 5 June 2014, between 10 am and 10 pm with two-hour intervals.

Meeting Malla 2014, HD, 10 min.
www.av-arkki.fi/en/works/meeting-malla/
Wrapped in a dark blue scarf I am standing on the ice on Lake Kilpis, looking at Malla Fell, on 3 April (2 pm – 8 pm) and 4 April 2014 (8 am – 10 pm) with two-hour intervals.

A Day with Malla 1–2, 2014, HD, 8 min. 10 sec.
www.av-arkki.fi/en/works/a-day-with-malla-1-2/
Two-channel installation
Part 1. Wrapped in a dark blue scarf I am standing on the ice on Lake Kilpis, looking at Malla Fell, on 7 April 2014, between 7 am and 9 pm with two-hour intervals.
Part 2. Malla Fell videoed on the same occasions.

Day and Night with Malla 1–2, 2014, HD, 30 min. 20 sec.
www.av-arkki.fi/en/works/day-and-night-with-malla-1-2/
Two-channel installation
Part 1. Wrapped in a dark blue scarf I am sitting on a rock by Lake Kilpis, looking at Malla Fell, for a day and night between noon on June 7 and noon on 8 June 2014, with two-hour intervals.
Part 2. Malla Fell videoed on the same occasions.

Moment with Malla 1–2, 2014, HD, 26 min. 10 sec.
www.av-arkki.fi/en/works/moment-with-malla-1-2/
Two-channel installation
Part 1. Wrapped in a dark blue scarf I am sitting on a rock by Lake Kilpis, looking at Malla Fell, on 6 June 2014, and then slowly disappearing from the image.
Part 2. I am slowly appearing in the image to sit on a rock by Lake Kilpis, looking at Malla Fell, on 6 June 2014.

Other videos mentioned:

Year of the Horse (Sitting on a Rock), 2003, DV, 12 min. 28 sec.
www.av-arkki.fi/en/works/year-of-the-horse-sitting-on-a-rock/
Single-channel video in two parts.
Part 1. I am standing with a blue scarf on my shoulders close to the camera, obscuring part of the view from the cliff, on Harakka Island, 64 times, approximately once a week from January 2002 to January 2003.
Part 2. I am sitting with a blue scarf on my shoulders on a rock in the landscape below the cliff, 64 times, on the same occasions.

Year of the Horse – Calendar 1–2, 2015, HD, 11 min. 10 sec.
www.av-arkki.fi/en/works/year-of-the-horse-calendar-1-2/
Two-channel installation
During the year of the horse 2014, I revisited once a month the site on Harakka Island, which I visited once a week during the year of the horse 2002, wearing the same dark blue scarf.
Part 1: I stand on the hill in front of the camera, covering most of the view.
Part 2: I sit on a rock on the slope.

Notes

1 In the context of this text I do not distinguish between performance as research and artistic research. Artistic research is usually undertaken by artists and often involves art making, while performance as research can involve the performance or execution of various types of actions for the purposes of research, 'research by doing', and is not necessarily concerned with art.
2 For recent discussion related to object-oriented ontology, see for instance *O-zone/A Journal of Object-Oriented Studies* (o-zone-journal.org).
3 See http://bioartsociety.fi.
4 The blog posts "Malla – Mountain in the North" (5 April 2014) and "Performing Landscape in Kilpisjärvi 1–8" (2–9 April 2014) describe my first visit.
5 The second visit is described in the blog posts "Meeting Malla again" (5 June 2014) and "Performing Landscape in Kilpisjärvi 9–15" (4–13 June).
6 Extract from the blog post on 4 June 2014, "Performing Landscape in Kilpisjärvi 9". https://bioartsociety.fi/projects/ars-bioarctica/posts/performing-landscape-in-kilpisjarvi-9.

References

Arlander, Annette (2014). From interaction to intra-action in performing landscape. In Beatriz Revelles Benavente, Ana M. González Ramos, Krizia Nardini (coord.). New feminist materialism: Engendering an ethic-onto-epistemological methodology. *Artnodes*, 14, pp. 26–34. Available at: http://www.raco.cat/index.php/Artnodes/article/viewFile/303309/392962

Barad, Karen (2003). Posthumanist performativity: Toward an understanding of how matter comes to matter. *Signs: Journal of Women in Culture and Society*, 28(3), pp. 801–831. Available at: www.jstor.org/stable/10.1086/345321

Barad, Karen (2007). *Meeting the Universe Halfway: Quantum Physics and the Entanglement of Matter and Meaning.* Durham, NC: Duke University Press.

Barad, Karen (2012). Intra-actions. *Mousse*, 34, pp. 76–81. (Interview of Karen Barad by Adam Kleinmann). Available at: www.academia.edu/1857617/_Intra-actions_Interview_of_Karen_Barad_by_Adam_Kleinmann_

Bennett, Jane (2015). Systems and things: On vital materialism and object-oriented philosophy. In Richard Grusin (ed.) *The Nonhuman Turn*. Minneapolis, MN: University of Minnesota Press, pp. 223–240.

Bolt, Barbara (2004). *Art Beyond Representation: The Performative Power of the Image*. London: I.B. Tauris.

Bolt, Barbara (2008). A performative paradigm for the creative arts? *Working Papers in Art and Design*, Volume 5. Available at: http://sitem.herts.ac.uk/artdes_research/papers/wpades/vol5/bbabs.html

Conquergood, Dwight (2004 [1999]). Performance studies. Interventions and radical research. In Henry Bial (eds.) *The Performance Studies Reader*. London: Routledge, pp. 311–322.

Hannula, Mika, Suoranta, Juha and Vadén, Tere (2005). *Artistic Research – Theories, Methods and Practices*. Helsinki: Academy of Fine Art and Gothenburg: University of Gothenburg.

Johnson, Mark (2011). Embodied knowing through art. In Michael Biggs and Henrik Karlsson (eds.) *The Routledge Companion to Research in the Arts*. London: Routledge, pp. 141–151.

Kershaw, Baz (2007). *Theatre Ecology – Environments and Performance Events*. Cambridge: Cambridge University Press.

Nevanlinna, Tuomas (2004). Is artistic research a meaningful concept. In Annette W. Balkema and Henk Slager (eds.) *Artistic Research: Lier en Boog Series of Philosophy of Art and Art Theory*, Volume 18. Amsterdam: Editions Rodopi B.V., pp. 80–83.

O-zone/A Journal of Object-oriented Studies. Available at: o-zone-journal.org

Riley, Shannon Rose and Hunter, Lynette (eds.) (2009). *Mapping Landscapes for Performance as Research – Scholarly Acts and Creative Cartographies*. Basingstoke: Palgrave Macmillan.

Schwab, Michael (2013). Introduction. In Michael Schwab (ed.) *Experimental Systems: Future Knowledge in Artistic Research*. Leuven: Leuven University Press, pp. 5–14.

Spatz, Ben (2015) *What a Body Can Do: Technique as Knowledge, Practice as Research*. London: Routledge.

Van der Tuin, Iris (2014). The mode of invention in creative research: Onto-epistemology. In Estelle Barrett and Barbara Bolt (eds.) *Material Inventions: Applying Creative Arts Research*. London: I.B. Tauris, pp. 257–272.

Chapter 7

Antromovimento

Developing a new methodology for theatre anthropology

Laurelann Porter

Introduction

For the last three years I have been working in collaboration with Brazilian cho-reographer Mestre Monza Calabar in the planning and initial stages of research on a long-term project we are calling *Antromovimento*. This project proposes to use performance both as a pedagogy for teaching Afro-Brazilian culture and history through dance and as an epistemic orientation to anthropological research. In *Antromovimento*, the objective is to learn the myths and histories of Afro-Brazilian Candomblé culture through theatrical investigations designed to elicit visceral, corporeal responses. This method reflects a need to devalue the emphasis on text-based analysis and verbal approaches to learning and empha-sizes the value of embodied learning, a concept crucial to understanding Can-domblé and Afro-Brazilian culture. For initiates of Candomblé, the tellings of ancient myths through rhythm, dance, and song are acts that evoke the presence of the Orixás in material form. For Candomblé initiates, the ancient myths of the Orixás are enacted by everyone, but cultivated by people of faith, of *axé*.

In my work with Mestre Monza, we acknowledge that these myths – related, understood, and retold through dance and movement – offer individuals an embodied entry to understanding these Afro-Brazilian cultural histories. By exploring the archetypes of mythic narratives, such as Ogum, the warrior, or Iemanjá, the mother of all, students in our workshops can begin to find a vocabulary for understanding and expressing the consciousness of this mythol-ogy. The movement qualities and characteristics come from a specific history. Mestre Monza explains the details of these histories as he teaches. I remember a moment when he demonstrated the position of his foot to students of dance in our first class together: his knee bent, foot in the air, deliberately flat, not arched (see figure 7.1). He proclaimed loudly that this was not a delicate foot, pointed for ballet, but it was the *"pézão do negão!"* (the big foot of the big black man).

He explained that these dances have survived through 500 years of slavery and oppression. He acknowledged that sometimes, the way he teaches these dances might seem harsh or even violent, but this is the way the dances have survived. This is the way slaves resisted. In this regard, the dance practices allow for a mythic consciousness to inform the historic consciousness.

Figure 7.1 Monza demonstrating foot position.
Source: Porter (2014).

In this essay, I will articulate the theoretical underpinnings of the work and the proposed mode of engaging with theatre, dance, anthropology, religious studies, and performance studies. I will present a description of how the work has been developed thus far, initial responses from participants, and an outline for moving forward with the development of the project to the next phase. I will also describe the genealogy of the knowledge we have gained from our two very different paths: Mestre Monza as an initiate of Candomblé and dancer/choreographer with decades of professional experience in this area, and my own path as a performance maker and scholar of performance and ethnography.

Genealogy: the journey to this point

The paths that have led Monza and me to work together have been as different as we are. Monza's path has followed that of a Candomblé initiate who became a professional dancer, choreographer, and teacher specializing in Afro-Brazilian dance. My path has followed that of a US-based theatre student who became familiar with dances of the Orixás through an interest in physical theatre training, which began at Boston University, and then continued at the Double Edge Theatre in Massachusetts, the Odin Teatret in Denmark, and ultimately with late Brazilian choreographer Augusto Omolú, an Odin resident performer from 2002 to the time of his death in 2013.

As with any ceremony in the Candomblé tradition, I must pay homage to my intellectual ancestors, the mentors who have guided me here, and the theoretical influences that have shaped my thinking and this collaboration. I first met Augusto Omolú in May of 2005 at a one-week workshop in dances of the Orixás he taught in Bristol, England. I had met and worked with several people who had studied with members of the Odin Teatret; I myself attended one of the Magdalena Festivals of Women in Theatre founded by Odin member Julia Varley. At the Odin I became familiar with the way Eugenio Barba works with his actors, the rigor of their training, and the virtuosity of the company members. Several people connected to the Odin recommended I meet Augusto Omolú and learn from him because of my interest in Brazilian culture.

In 2005 I decided to take the opportunity. During that workshop Omolú introduced us to four principal sets of movement vocabularies: the dance movements of Iemanjá, Ogum, Oxossi, and Oxum. Iemanjá, the Orixá associated with the oceans and considered to be the mother of all living beings, possessed a fluid, almost lyrical quality to her dances. The movements of the waves have a softness to their quality, yet the power of the tides carries the body with momentum. Ogum, the Orixá associated with metals and highways and considered to be the warrior archetype, provides the vocabulary of percussive moves, simulating the violence of warriors in battle. His gestures are firm. The arms embody his machetes. Hands must be flat like blades. (See Monza demonstrating correct hand position for Ogum in figure 7.2). Oxossi, the Orixá associated with forests and considered to be the supreme hunter, requires the body to incorporate agility and quick movements. He leaps through the forest or rides his horse,

Figure 7.2 Monza teaching correct gestures for Ogum.
Source: Porter (2014).

always light on his feet and with the eyes of an eagle to secure his prey. Oxum, the Orixá associated with freshwater and rivers, is often considered to be vain, a temptress, a supreme lover. When it came time to learn and practice her movements, I felt the relief from the jumping and violence of Oxossi and Ogum. Her movements were smooth and slow. A constant gentle undulation served as a physical base upon which gestures were placed: gazing into the mirror, applying lipstick, admiring her bracelets, running her fingers through her long hair, and dipping into fresh, cool water to wash her face. It was delightful to see all the participants, including masculine Englishmen, embody these movements.

Omolú codified these movement vocabularies over the course of years in collaboration with Eugenio Barba so that he could teach what he called the dramaturgy of the Orixás. He taught these sets of movement languages in order to tell a variety of stories using movement. His most widely known example of this was the performance *Oró de Otelo*, wherein he utilized drumming and the soundtrack from Verdi's *Otelo* to serve as the soundscape for a movement score that told the story of Othello, each character represented by the particular movements of a unique Orixá. The movements of Ogum, the warrior, represented Othello. Oxossi, the hunter, represented the actions of Iago. The movements of Oxum portrayed Desdemona. The Orixá dances become the vocabulary for telling stories on the level of archetypes, legible across different cultures.

The workshop was physically intense. Augusto demanded that we push ourselves to our limits and beyond. I remember him shouting out to us, "There is no *cansaço*! [tiredness]. There is only *axé!* [sacred life force]." Even more important than my experience pushing my boundaries physically, I came away from that workshop, and from the daily post-workshop chats with Augusto, with a few important takeaways. Any actor or dancer has the capacity to incorporate the qualities of these varied Orixás. In terms of acting training I began to use this in my teaching to help actors broaden their expressive potential. Additionally, through the daily conversations with Augusto about his life in Candomblé and the basic philosophical tenets of the religion, I came to understand the worldview that no one human being is inherently good or inherently evil. We all have the potential for both. Because I had been raised in an intensely religious Christian household, these were fresh ideas for me. Augusto and I agreed that the kinds of polarizing arguments that dominate the US-American political landscape are evidence that my own country's cultural influences could benefit from a philosophy that reduced the urge to demonize others of different viewpoints. Augusto and I agreed that we needed to do work together for communities in the US, particularly in my hometown of Phoenix, with its divisive border politics.

I took a three-week intensive workshop with Augusto in Salvador, Bahia, in 2008, where I also met Monza. Augusto and I continued our discussions of how we could collaborate further through 2010. However, at a fundamental level, our basic research questions were slightly different. Augusto was most interested

in speaking of the ways the movements are used for dramaturgical development, as movement-based vocabularies for telling stories. I, however, was formulating a research question rooted in understanding how the movement practices themselves might be useful for cultivating a deeper understanding of the culture form whence they come, the ways we understand its stories and myths, the world around us, and our relationship to it. We put the collaboration on the back burner and continued with our own individual projects. Then Augusto was taken violently from this world in June of 2013. For Monza, Augusto's death was devastating because they were childhood friends with a bond as close as brothers. To a lesser degree, I felt the loss personally. Monza and I both felt the loss professionally. Because Monza and I had already begun our own conversations about possible collaborations outside of the work of Augusto, we suddenly felt the urgency to re-energize this new collaboration: one that would honor Augusto's memory while developing our independent professional identities.

In initial stages we were adopting the term *Antropoloteatral*. We selected this term with an awareness of the problematic histories of how the disciplines of theatre and anthropology have been intertwined. One of the most strident critiques of theatre anthropology comes from Indian theatre and performance scholar Rustom Bharucha. In his essay "Somebody's Other: Disorientations in the Cultural Politics of Our Times", he describes the discourse surrounding orientalism as "this layered reality by which the history in post-colonial societies continues to be assumed, named, designated, theorized, and represented for 'us'" (Bharucha 1996, p. 198). While he does not cite Eugenio Barba by name, Bharucha denigrates concepts and terms coined by Barba. He specifically cites the "'anthropology' of theatre" and "pre-expressivity", as well as Barba's idea of the *bios* as the actor's "being", and links them to a tendency to flatten the "specificities of particular cultures" (Bharucha 1996, p. 207). Bharucha describes this form of intercultural theatre as representative of a "neo-colonial[ist] obsession with materials and techniques from the 'third world'" (Bharucha 1996, p. 207). While his critique has merit, Bharucha also acknowledges that intercultural performance (and by extension collaborations between the fields of theatre and anthropology) can have value as long as they follow certain guidelines. He calls for cautious interaction between self-sufficient agents. He asks for a negotiation that can create "new narratives with shared responsibilities, if not a shared history". He claims this will also entail a more "critical openness" and "a greater sensitivity to the ethics involved in translating and transporting other cultures" (Bharucha 1996, p. 208).

Because we are including in our methodology concepts and strategies from both theatre and anthropology, I must distinguish what we are doing from what Eugenio Barba has done through his International School of Theatre Anthropology. Ric Knowles describes the generally accepted opinion in academia about Eugenio Barba and his work, categorizing him as "universalist", along with Antonin Artaud, Jerzy Grotowski, and Peter Brook. He cites Barba's downfall as the fact that "he is determinedly ahistorical, removing elements of performance from the social, cultural, and theatrical or ritual contexts that produced them and where they produce their meanings" (Knowles 2010, p. 19). Barba, however, deliberately and distinctly claims that his work is not to be confused with cultural anthropology.

Our work with *Antromovimento*, in contrast, avoids the study of performance technique for the purposes of developing virtuosity and places cultural anthropology at the center of our process. We are not interested in the study of professional actor training across different cultures, but rather the study of how cultural anthropology can be applied in the form of theatrical exercises that incorporate several modes of learning: engaging in daily practices with the *quilombo* communities wherein the workshops take place; learning the myths and histories via oral storytelling from Mestre Monza and other community members; learning the dance movements of the Orixás and their archetypal associations; and engaging in critical reflections in group dialogue about how these combined activities contribute to our sense-making of Afro-Brazilian culture. We intend for these activities to be of use to a variety of diverse audiences. To contrast this with Barba's theatre anthropology: rather than an interest in the "extra-daily" use of the body in performance, we are interested in the ways the use of the body in performance exercises can illuminate daily, quotidian realities, influenced by mythic narratives of cultural archetypes.

We recognize that the dances and movements of the Orixás are not universal, but rather come from a long history of African peoples in the Diaspora. Understanding these dances and movements is always already a study in translation. As such, there will necessarily be places where the translation falls short or where concepts or movements become untranslatable. We do not seek to gloss over these spaces or moments. We seek to work through those moments to find places of encounter where the original meaning might very well remain a mystery, but a connection to another's own lived experiences can offer what we might call a metaphorical handshake. This metaphorical handshake serves as a gesture of agreement that "I recognize my experience cannot be equated with yours, and that my parallel understanding of it can only capture a fragmented understanding of your experience." I propose that this fragmented understanding, with its acknowledgment that it is fragmented, is a more honest approach to translation than the assumption or belief that through translation one can wholly know a foreign concept or phenomenon. Gayatri Spivak elaborates on this kind of fragmented understanding in her essay "The Politics of Translation", where she describes an important "three-tiered notion of language" that includes rhetoric, logic, and silence (Spivak 1992). She points to the need to allow for rhetorical silences so that untranslatable moments and concepts might not be glossed over by hegemonic language practices that privilege accessibility to the majority over a diligent attention to specificities and differences. It is a humbling experience to remember that we can never know everything about the other. We can only hope to find some points of intersection to help people from diverse backgrounds coexist in the same physical and ideological space.

Julie Stone Peters, in her 1995 article "Intercultural Performance, The-atre Anthropology, and the Imperialist Critique: Identities, Inheritances, and Neo-Orthodoxies", provides an overview of some of these key challenges in intercultural theatre and theatre anthropology. She acknowledges that late twen-tieth-century intercultural theatre has a genealogy rooted in imperial conquest and the exoticism of putting the "other" on display, but she also asserts that each individual performance event must be analyzed on its own terms. She cat-egorizes the bulk of arguments against modernist theatre anthropology and its derivatives as arguments that assert that these practices reinforce and reinscribe the kinds of dualisms (Western/non-Western, us/them, anthropologist/primi-tive) that anthropology has constructed. However, she also acknowledges that, as contested as these histories have been, the potential for valuable and ethical work can still be envisioned (Peters 1995, p. 205). After one year of entertaining the possibility of adopting the term *Antropoloteatral*, Monza and I opted to adjust the term we coined to reflect a stronger emphasis on the movement practices of Afro-Brazilian dance and the implicit links to social justice movements of the African diaspora. While we acknowledge that our work is highly influenced by our deceased friend and mentor, Mestre Augusto Omolú, and his work with Eugenio Barba, we have theoretical orientations that diverge at a basic level from those of Barba and the International School of Theatre Anthropology.

Our proposal seeks to enrich the fields of performance, anthropology, and religious studies. The histories, mythic narratives, and daily practices are learned corporeally through this work. Students will be invited to gather fruit, fish, and cook with members of the local *quilombo* community. *Quilombos* are communi-ties descended from escaped slaves. They have a long and rich history in Brazil and pride themselves on their ability to resist oppression by existing off the land, outside of official state infrastructures. For detailed histories of these com-munities across Brazil, see the forthcoming anthology edited and published by Diasporic Africa Press (see Reis and Gomes 1996). Transforming trash or other refuse into usable goods honors the aesthetic of these communities, which seek to exist in harmony with nature. The sacred movements of Candomblé dances become the vocabulary utilized to learn religious myths in a visceral sense. Performance practices become a way to understand histories, mythologies, and religious practices. Our work reflects the importance of the telling of ancient myths, not necessarily for ritual purposes but for the purposes of deepening intercultural understanding. While the stories in ritual context certainly have their value, we do not propose to lead religious rituals while conducting this investigation. Our reasons for this stem from the well-established historical need for Candomblé houses to keep their ritual practices secret. While more and more Candomblé houses are increasingly making their ritual practices acces-sible to the general public, I honor Mestre Monza's religious orientation, which demands certain aspects of the sacred life of these communities remain hidden.

Initial responses from the open class held in Ilhéus, Bahia, in 2014 indicate that this practice may also be useful for *intracultural* understanding. The most enthusiastic participants were those initiated in African-derived religions eager to find ways to articulate the manner in which embodied knowledge can be revalued in their own communities. One participant indicated that in his community there has been a wave of religious intolerance towards members of African-derived religions, such as Candomblé and Umbanda.[1] He suggested that this kind of articulation of *Antromovimento*, with its emphasis on cultivating embodied practices and linking our understandings of history and resistance with our embodied experience and memory, offers him an avenue for explaining some of the benefits of preserving this cultural heritage in a way that does not require non-practitioners to understand the theological orientations in order to see the value in the work. We seek to contribute our work with *Antromovimento* to the ongoing efforts in Brazil to reduce religious intolerance and revalue the kinds of embodied practices that have been central to the epistemologies descending from Western Africa that have found themselves spread throughout the Americas as a result of colonization and the transatlantic slave trade.

Situating the methodology between and within theatre/performance studies, anthropology, and religious studies

In the introduction to *The Archive and the Repertoire*, Diana Taylor describes performance as a means for transmitting cultural knowledge: "If performance did not transmit knowledge, only the literate and powerful could claim social memory and identity" (Taylor 2003, p. xvii). Here Taylor identifies an important concept for articulating *Antromovimento* as a research methodology: performance as an act of transference of knowledge. For our work, the emphasis is on performance as a process for understanding cultural histories of Afro-Brazilian peoples. Current trends in the ethics and methods of performance ethnography indicate that the most ethical way of creating a work of performance or art based in anthropology or ethnography is through a collaborative dialogue between the researcher and the person(s) being studied. In Dwight Conquergood's essay "Performing as a Moral Act" he explains the pitfalls that have befallen certain "performative stances", in ethnography (2013). Conquergood describes what he calls a "dialogic performance", wherein the performance that results from ethnographic work implies a genuine conversation between the group being studied and the group assuming the role of the spectator. In this dialogic performance, an awareness of cultural difference is maintained and the performance text can "interrogate, rather than dissolve into the performer" (Conquergood 2013, p. 71–75).

Amira de la Garza (writing as María Cristina González) has proposed a set of ethical guidelines for postcolonial ethnography. The first guideline is accountability (being transparent about how the ethnographer came to know the story being told). We honor this ethic by placing Mestre Monza in control of what information about Candomblé life gets disseminated and how. De la Garza's additional ethics are: context (being clear and detailed about the descriptions of the environment from whence the story came); truthfulness (being transparent about how our own motivations have played into the research); and community (ethnographers must acknowledge that the study is the beginning of a committed relationship) (González 2003). The fourth of these is most salient to my work with Mestre Monza because we both understand the need to examine what the research can do for the community. We intend to maintain an ongoing and dedicated commitment to a permanent relationship with the various communities in which we work. In addition to de la Garza's ethical orientation, she also writes of an important shift in ontology in her essay "The Four Seasons of Ethnography" (González 2000), in which the researcher makes effort not to separate herself from the process of conducting research. She claims, "It is never the same to merely watch a ceremony as it is to participate in it" (González 2000, p. 642). With this assertion she underscores the importance of acknowledging that any ethnographer enters the field in order to learn "through his or her own experience" (González 2000, p. 635). This relates specifically to our work together in that it allows for a genuine recognition of the importance of experiential and embodied knowledge, which is central to Afro-Brazilian histories and religious cosmologies.

An example of such ethical negotiations occurred during my conversation with Mestre Monza about a particular symbol that was being used in the *carnaval* design for the carnival group where Monza is one of the principal choreographers. He explained that, for people within the Candomblé community, the symbol of the trident is instantly recognizable as a symbol of Exú, the Orixá whose domain is the roads and crossroads and who is responsible for communication, the theme of that year's *carnaval*. Common perception outside of the community considers Exú to be an evil entity because of his syncretic association with the Catholic devil. But Monza insisted, "*Isso não tem nada que ver!*" [This has nothing to do with it!]. These facile assumptions about Exú's significance have led to continued marginalization and intolerance towards Candomblé religious practices. Monza described the way the symbol must be treated with care, because of its association with Exú. Exú might not be evil but he is "*bravo*".[2] His symbol cannot be taken into the streets "*de qualquer maneira*" [in any old way]. Monza pointed out how the artist who designed the image for the *trio elétrico*[3] made the symbol with some modifications to its form, adding some bends and crookedness in a way that implied movement and aliveness, rather than the overt symbol of a trident, which, per Monza, would be too harsh a symbol to take to the streets (Exú's domain) in the open. He also indicated that the object itself, once designed, would be taken to a house of Candomblé for preparations "*que não se pode falar*" [that we cannot speak about] in order to ensure that the symbol would not be used for purposes contrary to the needs and desires of the religious community.

Another way that our approach differs significantly from traditional approaches to anthropology lies in the way we view participant observation. One of the foundational methods for engaging in anthropological fieldwork is Clifford Geertz's "thick description" (1973). Having trained in the skill of thick description, it is a method I use regularly in my ethnographic research. One of Geertz's contributions to the field of anthropology lay in his assertion that the act of taking field notes and writing the anthropological report of findings is an interpretive act. Geertz recognized that a wink might be interpreted (or misinterpreted) in a number of ways. With careful attention to details and diligent observation, an anthropologist can interpret those details and the social discourse they represent into an interpretive tale or account of the life and culture of those being studied. To date, my participation in Candomblé ceremonies has been as a participant-observer in a limited capacity. My introduction to Candomblé religious life has been through the invitations I have received from my friends and colleagues Mestre Omolú and Mestre Monza. In both cases, I was instructed to be present and open to whatever might occur but that, out of respect for the process and hierarchies within the community, I was not to impose my presence in ways that might be construed as invasive. For these reasons I have largely erred on the side of more "passive" observation and less active participation. In one community I was permitted to take photographs, in another it was forbidden. In one community the ritual meal was delivered to me in my seat right in the space where the ritual occurred. In another community I waited until I was invited to partake at the table outside the ceremonial space, after everyone else in the community had been served. Mestre Monza has dubbed me a *"Frequentadora de casa de Candomblé"* [person who frequents Candomblé houses]. He uses this as an affectionate term for people he knows who are sympathetic to the needs of the religious community but, for whatever reason, have not been initiated.

I have often wondered if or when I might become an initiate myself, either for a deeper theoretical understanding or were I to feel a spiritual call to do so. Having read the work of dance anthropologist Yvonne Daniel and dancer and ethnographic filmmaker Maya Deren, two researchers entering similar fields at two very different times in recent history, I have a deep respect for those who answer a call to enter the sacred space as both researchers and initiates. The works both of these women produced have affected me profoundly. Daniel's detailed and well-crafted study on dance practices in Brazilian Candomblé, Haitian Vodou, and Cuban Yoruba offers the reader the kind of intimacy that only someone with years of exposure as both observer and participant can provide (2005). Her work and Deren's also reflect a deep respect for these ritual practices and the need to be skeptical about the academic gaze. The challenges Maya Deren and Yvonne Daniel both faced continue to be valid concerns today. One of my colleagues from the Kàwé research group told me of her experience as an anthropologist in one of the local *terreiros*. Her *Mãe de Santo* made it explicitly clear to her that just because she was undergoing a rite of passage to be named a daughter of the house did not mean she was an initiate of Candomblé. She seemed to scoff at anthropologists she has encountered who are permitted this small level of entry to the culture, only to write about the experiences as if they had some degree of authority that was simply not present. Daniel speaks of the phase wherein she was "half-seated" (somewhere between "*frequentadora*" and "initiate") and establishes that this phase is not generally considered advisable for a long period of time. In both Deren's case and Daniel's case, their work and research occurred over years of time in the field cultivating healthy relationships with the communities being studied.

Participant observation often assumes a particular situation of privilege and access. The privilege to be an outsider from a wealthier nation (usually North American or European), coming to the setting with institutional support from one of these wealthier nation's universities, arriving with a desire to know the foreign other, already implies a particular power dynamic. Someone I met during my time conducting fieldwork asked me, "Why are you foreigners always so interested in our religions?" (field notes 2014). I stumbled over my response because I knew, from my training and orientation in postcolonial ethics, that merely because I desire to know something doesn't mean I have the right to know it. De la Garza describes entitlement as a taken-for-granted assumption that "simply having a question is seen as grounds for being able to attain one's 'answer' upon demand" (González 2003, p. 631). A more ethical approach is to cultivate an awareness of what is and is not appropriate to ask in a given setting.

While participant observation continues to be an essential component to any anthropological fieldwork, Mestre Monza and I will encourage the student participants in our workshops to engage in participant observation with a deep critical reflexivity. Group discussions about the observations made by the individuals will be conducted with members of the community in order to better understand how the practices are being perceived, documented, and translated. The process of observing, then describing, and then translating and interpreting poses several challenges. Firstly, any individual's account will be shaped by his or her personal history, experience, and worldview. Secondly, the process of translation will always present situations where a word, a concept, a feeling, or a phenomenon will be either untranslatable or mistranslated. The act of writing down the ethnographic tale or the anthropological analysis implies a process of translation that often elides these moments of mistranslated or untranslatable experiences. Our intention is to honor the approach of postcolonial scholars, such as Rustom Bharucha, Gayatri Spivak, Amira de la Garza, and Ruy Póvoas, with a diligent and rigorous process of critical self-reflection to try to account for these natural and inherent biases. By making these documentation processes a collaboration and dialogue between the students and the community members we hope to serve as a model for these kinds of important debates in intercultural theatre, ethnography, and anthropology.

In order to support these efforts our approach holds two main tenets. We do not (and cannot) teach the mysteries of the Candomblé religion. There are processes that have been kept secret for generations and must continue to be kept secret. The second main tenet follows the suggestions made by one of the university's key administrative coordinators who has supported the Kàwé group for the last several years: the work to support academic education of Candomblé religion and culture is not theological, but should rather approach an understanding of the religion through analyses and examinations of the social dynamics within the context. Scholars within the Kàwé group have approached their work from perspectives of linguistics, sociology, communications, and educational pedagogy, among others. My work with Monza supports these objectives by understanding the mythic archetypes and their symbolic interactions in quotidian life and in interpersonal relationships. In the work of *Antromovimento*, we place the ordained Ogan[4] in the position of controlling the way information is shared and interpreted. Mestre Monza, as both an ordained Ogan in the Candomblé religion and a child of the *Movimento Negro* in Bahia of the 1960s and 1970s, offers a mode of instruction that includes the pointed and violent histories of both ancient myths and recent movements for racial and social justice in Brazil.

Kinesis and corporeal understanding

We seek to revitalize and renew the memory of ancestral lives present in the myths, legends, histories, and real-life events of Afro-Brazilians living lives dedicated to Candomblé. We seek to understand and to articulate how these presences are already incorporated in daily life. Within the rituals of Candomblé, ancestral spirits are incorporated in a literal, bodily sense. But in dialogue with the anthropology of the quotidian, we seek to understand how they are incorporated in other ways as well and how daily realities of the past may be compared to daily realities of the present. For Mestre Monza, a life in Candomblé offers a "Living Bible" for such understandings. This bible is not a written bible but a lived or embodied text. Placing the focus on bodily movement, we are proposing a vision of dance and cultural expression that incorporates aspects of daily realities of Candomblé life. Through these investigations, we seek to offer participants who work with us a level of understanding unavailable to those who merely read a written account of these cultural histories. While our primary target audience for these workshops will be dancers, actors, anthropologists, and students from outside of Candomblé, we recognize that the possibility also exists for members of the local Candomblé communities to deepen their awareness of how these histories are narrated and strengthen their consciousness of how they can articulate the value of these practices.

One illustrative example of these methods for cultivating an embodied understanding of the myths lies in the plans currently underway for our next workshop. Our intention is to explore the dynamics, actions, energy, and metaphors of Ogum, the Orixá associated with ores, metals, metalsmithing, technology, and wars. He is often called upon for the purposes of overcoming obstacles and paving pathways. In his essay "Kinesis: The New Mimesis", Joseph Roach claims that dance and movement as performance allow for a different kind of "corporeal empathy" (Roach 2010, p. 2). He claims that "Mimesis, rooted in drama, imitates action; kinesis embodies it" (Roach 2010, p. 2). This idea is central to our work. First, in our next workshop Monza will teach the participants the movements and rhythms of Ogum, the warrior archetype. Second, we will take physical objects into the dance laboratory and create obstacles in the space. Directions will be given to the participants to achieve certain simple goals – that is, getting to the other side of the room following a particular pathway, using the movements of Ogum. Different roles will be assigned: traveler, obstructer, and so forth. At the break, the group will collectively discuss and reflect on how it felt to perform each of these roles and any connections it might have evoked about their own particular stories. Connections will be drawn to the documented stories of historical figures who embody the characteristics of Ogum as well as narratives about Ogum from Candomblé mythology. In the second segment of the workshop, the physical obstacles will be removed and the participants will be asked to repeat the journey from the previous exercise, maintaining an awareness of the affective sensations of the exercise when there were physical obstacles present. Final stages of the workshop will involve the participants drawing parallels from the narratives of Ogum's mythology to the narratives of their own lives while dancing the dances of Ogum to the rhythms associated with him. Our intention is to offer participants an opportunity to see how an awareness of Ogum's presence in the world can fortify a person with the strength of a warrior when needed.

I have a personal memory of how this works from a workshop I took with Augusto Omolú back in 2008. Partway through the intensive workshop I discovered that my debit card had been cloned after I had used it at an unprotected ATM on the street in Salvador. I lost about $1,000 from my bank account before I found out the card had been compromised and was able to contact my bank. I felt shocked, angry, and scared. I had no money to last the remaining ten days in Brazil. Shaking and sick to my stomach, I went to Augusto and said, "I can't do this. I can't dance today." He looked at me and smirked. "No, you have to do this today. This is exactly when you need to do this." Then he sent me to the dance floor and directed the drummers to begin playing Ogum's rhythms. He led us across the floor like the invincible warrior I believed him to be. That day I slashed my hands through the air like machetes with a vigor I hadn't felt before. Then I heard Augusto shouting at me, "*Isso ai, Laurinha! Pega aquele ladrão!!*" [That's right, Laurinha! Go get that thief!]. That was my first experience of understanding how the embodied awareness of these stories and their archetypes can relate to our own lives. One possible avenue for future research with regard to this aspect is the parallels here to the field of drama therapy and working with cultural archetypes. It is certainly possible that the danced gestures of the Orixás might provide kinesthetic deepening to understandings developed during mimetic drama therapy.

Performance-making practices

While performance ethnography often remains in the academy, where it reaches a mostly academic audience, Monza and I aim to bring this form of *Antromovimento* to a broader public. The first way of doing this is teaching workshops to those in Bahia who are hungry for both movement practices and the language to articulate their importance. The second way of reaching a broader public is for the process to culminate in a performance event where students take what they have learned and present it to their communities. This requires a dedication to the collaborative process between Monza, musicians who also have knowledge and experience with the sacred rhythms, and the workshop participants. While we certainly plan to produce performance events for a general audience, our main purpose with this ongoing project is the process of understanding myths through dance and theatre exercises. A final product will be offered as a way of sharing stories and sharing experiences, always privileging the process as epistemic act, rather than emphasizing spectatorship.

Monza's aesthetic for this work utilizes found objects, refuse, and items otherwise considered waste by the dominant social order. In our planning meetings for a collaboration in a US academic institution, he told me,

> I don't need a lot of money for materials. Yes, I'll bring some key items from Brazil. But mostly I want these students to go with me out into the trash to find our materials. There are so many things we can make from the items other people throw away. We will make our scenery, our costumes, the objects we hold, out of garbage.
>
> (Personal communication 2014)

By engaging the students in the process of finding items of waste with the potential for renewal and reuse, Monza leads them in a process of self-transformation that revalues materials previously considered valueless. This serves as an active metaphor for the ways Black people have been considered expendable and embodies a process of revaluing their cultural histories in a tangible way. When I pointed out this metaphor, Monza's response was "Isso aí, Laurinha!!!" (That's right Laurinha!!) This approach honors a *quilombo* aesthetic.

Our greatest challenge is in developing strategies for documenting this work in a way that honors the intent while also being legible to academic audiences and readers. While anthropology and ethnography have tended to privilege text-based records of cultural stories, Monza and I emphasize a process-based transfer of knowledge wherein the act of writing culture becomes a shared movement experience. Participants read the movements as narrated by the body of Mestre Monza. They retell those movement-based stories within our seminar setting as a process-based performance practice. And the participants share their experiences of the intersecting stories as a way of reflecting on the bodily understanding that was transferred through movement-as-writing.

Because this work reduces the emphasis on the written word, the documentation of the work will be a multifaceted challenge. We will be collecting responses through video and through shared experiences. Both the workshops themselves and the discussions surrounding the work will be videotaped. Additionally, private post-workshop "postmortem" discussions between Monza and myself will be videotaped. We will also utilize questionnaires and surveys designed to stimulate fruitful discussions relating to the process of learning through movement. These questionnaires will include both open-ended questions to elicit personalized responses and a small sampling of questions designed to understand if or when affective responses to the exercises created links to the participant's own memories and lived experiences.

Roach's essay on kinesis offers a theoretical entry to the basis for our work, but it could be read as suggesting that dance is some kind of universal language, similar to Barba's concept of pre-cultural expression. Taking up the suggestions of Susan Leigh Foster, I would like to question the assumptions behind this assertion (Foster 2009). Are movements understood the same way across different cultures? We believe they are not. Do they require some kind of mediation or translation of the movements? Perhaps. We respect and admire the long-time collaboration between Eugenio Barba and Augusto Omolú and the valuable fruits of their labor in the form of Omolú's codified dance vocabulary of the dances of the Orixás and the performances they developed together. For personal and professional reasons, we honor them as theoretical ancestors. However, we do not believe that there can be pre-cultural expression or any kind of universal movement language. All gestures come from a specific culture. We aim to help people understand this culture through performative pedagogies. I recognize a risk that our work might result in oversimplifications about cultural identity through an uncritical embracing of an "other" culture. However, I refer to a quote by Antoine Vitez, which I use as a mantra: "[I]t is impossible to translate, but at the same time, it is intolerable not to translate" (quoted in Pavis 1996, p. 122). I have often been asked to address or help produce theatrical works where these questions have arisen. The easy choice would be to walk away. But the most ethical approach is to acknowledge the potential for problems, misinterpretations, and appropriation and proceed with an awareness that sensitivity and humility are required for the project to offer new insights to all participants.

Acknowledging material realities and outlining next steps and objectives

As I iterated earlier in this essay, Monza and I are not proposing that we teach sacred practices of Candomblé. To even attempt to do so would be a violation of his religious commitment. Additionally, I have been reminded on multiple occasions that my position as an outsider has to be acknowledged. In order for our work to proceed, we have to solicit a formal ritualized acknowledgment that our objectives are in harmony and in balance with the entities with which Monza has worked for so long.

Recently, Monza and I made plans to offer a free workshop in the community where I conducted fieldwork last year. On the day he was supposed to leave to come to Itacaré for the workshop, Monza sent me an urgent message that he could not get away because of an incident in his hometown. A small group from a criminal faction entered a public square and opened fire on innocent bystanders, killing two people. Some people very close to Monza were present and were deeply traumatized by the incident. Monza felt he needed to be with his community. Many of my Brazilian friends commented that this kind of activity is becoming more and more common across the country. One friend from Itacaré bemoaned how this is yet another manifestation of the veritable genocide against poor people and people of color in Brazil.

Monza and I realized we had not yet conducted the proper ritual offering to the sacred entities responsible for opening pathways and ensuring our work is in line with the objectives of social justice. This might seem like a step that renounces rational inquiry. Perhaps it is. It might also seem like a gesture that ignores the politics and places hope for social justice in the hands of some divine entity rather than in the hands of people on the streets fighting, literally, for their lives. Looking at the histories of my two friends and colleagues who have been working diligently to teach, dance, and choreograph the African histories in their communities in Bahia, and to see how often their lives are touched by violence, I cannot deny that the work is risky. In fact, it is risky merely to be a Black person in Bahia, in Brazil, and in many other parts of the world. Additionally, if I look at the histories of Candomblé practitioners in Brazil, whose very beliefs and specifically their religious practices were demonized and criminalized for centuries, I should also remind myself and my readers that these practices have always been rooted in social resistance to oppression. I cannot pretend to know that rational inquiry should remain separate from ritual practices and offerings or that either of those aspects of the project can be separated from the sociopolitical realities of the time and place in which we work. The trained academic in me continues to pursue this work as a rational mode of understanding. The performer in me trusts that the intersections of rational knowledge and embodied performance need not be mutually exclusive. The activist in me knows that nothing exists outside of politics or ideology. The spiritual wanderer in me recognizes that we are to tread lightly in this arena. For the safety of my dear friend Monza, and for the ability of our professional journey together to continue, we have taken the necessary steps to be certain our motives are in balance with the energetic presences of these divine Orixás. For now, we are preparing our offerings, being attuned to the messages we might be receiving, and remaining open to the pathways this journey presents to us.

Our next phase will open what we are calling an *Aldeia Afro*. *Aldeia* is a term that implies a community, such as a village, oftentimes existing outside of official municipal structures and implying a communal ethic of reciprocity.

This will begin within the next two years in a rural region of Bahia to be determined by Monza. The site will be a place of study where we can invite students of dance, theatre, religion, and anthropology to participate in these seminars in a setting where students can partake of a *quilombo* lifestyle, living off the land and in harmony with it, while studying the dances, music, percussion, histories, myths, and culture of the African peoples in Bahia, Brazil. Once this has been established, first through crowd sourcing and volunteer work in Monza's community, and later through the continued marketing of our work, we will seek opportunities for this work to travel to North America and Europe, recognizing that the mode of participant observation we will be modeling in Bahia will be very different from this model once it has been transported to other settings.

Our specific objectives for this project and its desired outcomes are multiple. On a micro level, we seek to provide students interested in Afro-Brazilian cultures and histories the opportunity to investigate these myths through dance and theatre in such a way that the corporeal knowledge gained becomes a deepening of knowledge they may have garnered through intellectual studies. On a macro level, we hope to achieve three main goals. We hope that our model and methodology can be adopted by other artists and scholars working at the intersections of Afrocentric performance practices and the preservation of Afrocentric culture and history. Additionally, we seek to invite students from within Brazil to engage in this work as a strategy for revaluing Afro-Brazilian cultural histories in their own communities and on the national scene as well. Lastly, for other scholars and artists working in the field of intercultural theatre, we hope that our ethical and theoretical orientations might guide their own performance practices in such a way that the current shift in the fields of anthropology and performance studies towards a revaluing of embodied knowledge can be deepened.

Notes

1 Umbanda is a syncretic religion in Brazil that combines Yoruba traditions and sacred entities with indigenous practices and spiritist practices developed by Allan Kardec in the late nineteenth century.
2 "Bravo" can be translated as mad or angry. But in this case, when referring to Exú, because of his trickster nature, this use of the word more likely means something like "wild" or "unpredictable". The word "bravo" also hints at Exú's ambiguous moral stance and his ability to disrupt one's path and purpose if proper respects are not paid.
3 *Trio elétrico* is a kind of parade float that has a live band and a massive speaker system playing the music of the band to which dancers for a half a block in either direction can dance, while drummers play on the street with the dancers.
4 The term "Ogan" refers to different roles in different regional manifestations of Yoruba religious practices (from Brazilian Candomblé to Haitian Voudun). In this context, as explained to me by Mestre Monza, the Ogan is one of the religious leaders responsible for the drumming and music for the Candomblé ceremonies and festivals.

References

Bharucha, Rustom. (1996). "Somebody's Other: Disorientations in the Cultural Politics of Our Times." In Patrice Pavis, Ed. *The Intercultural Performance Reader.* London: Routledge.

Conquergood, Dwight. (2013) "Performing as a Moral Act." In Dwight Conquergood and E. Patrick Johnson, Eds. *Cultural Struggles: Performance, Ethnography, Praxis.* Ann Arbor, MI: University of Michigan Press.

Daniel, Yvonne. (2005). *Dancing Wisdom: Embodied Knowledge in Haitian Vodou, Cuban Yoruba, and Bahian Candomblé.* Urbana, IL: University of Illinois Press.

Foster, Susan Leigh (Ed.). (2009). *Worlding Dance.* New York: Palgrave MacMillan.

Geertz, Clifford. (1973). *The Interpretation of Cultures.* New York: Basic Books.

González, María Cristina. (2000). "The Four Seasons of Ethnography: A Creation-Centered Ontology for Ethnography." *International Journal of Intercultural Relations.* Vol. 24, 623–650.

González, María Cristina. (2003). "An Ethics for Postcolonial Ethnography." In R.P. Claire, Ed. *Expressions of Ethnography: Novel Approaches to Qualitative Methods.* Albany, NY: SUNY Press.

Knowles, Ric. (2010). *Theatre & Interculturalism.* London: Palgrave MacMillan.

Pavis, Patrice. (1996). *The Intercultural Performance Reader.* London; New York: Routledge.

Peters, Julie Stone. (1995). "Intercultural Performance, Theatre Anthropology, and the Imperialist Critique: Identities, Inheritances, and Neo-Orthodoxies." In J. Ellen Gainor, Ed. *Imperialism and Theatre: Essays on World Theatre, Drama, and Performance.* London: Routledge.

Porter, Laurelann. (2014). "Dismantling Illusions in and of Paradise Through the Gift of Refraction in the Terra do Exú: An Ethnography with Women of Rural Bahia." Diss. Arizona State University.

Reis, João José and Gomes and Flávio dos Santos (Eds.). (1996). *Liberdade por um fio: história dos quilombos no Brasil.* São Paulo: Cia. Das Letras.

Roach, Joseph. (2010). "Kinesis: The New Mimesis." In Emily Coates and Joseph Roach, Eds. *Postglobal Dance.* Spec. Issue of *Theater.* Vol. 40, Issue 1.

Spivak, Gayatri Chakravorty. (1992). "The Politics of Translation." In Lawrence Venuti, Ed. (2000). *The Translation Studies Reader,* 2nd edn. New York: Routledge.

Taylor, Diana. (2003). *The Archive and the Repertoire: Performing Cultural Memory in the Americas.* Durham, NC: Duke University Press.

Chapter 8

PAR and decolonisation

Notemakings from an Indian and South African context

Manola K. Gayatri

1.0 Introduction un/settling names: nomenclature of practices and ownership

> *Naming is inevitably genealogical revisionism.*
> Kimberly W. Benston, "I Yam What I Am" (3)

In this chapter I offer notes from the early stages of a project that investigates traditional forms, contemporary political struggle and hybrid artistic collaborative practice through embodied research and which speaks to the decolonisation of our epistemes, pedagogies and art making. I make an interlocution between performance-as-research and the practice and discourse of decolonisation through my research in India and South Africa in the context of the work of two contemporary Indian theatre practitioners – the late Heisnam Kanhailal and the late Veenapani Chawla – the #FeesMustFall student movement in South Africa and an ongoing performance-as-research project that I am co-leading in Pretoria.

It is worthwhile to start these notes on the discourse and practice of PAR and decolonisation with a reflection around the politics of naming and ownership, the 'unsettled' nature of practice – be it that of PAR or decolonisation – and the political potency of this unsettledness. The question of naming assumes an importance for two reasons. First, the naming of things has been one of the first acts of colonising and the un-naming of these an important aspect of decolonisation. Second, what is named as performance-as-research here is a method and practice that has other names associated with it, such as artistic research, practice-as-research and practice-led-research, and the significance of this is that PAR in itself as a named practice has not yet 'settled' into a given name. I would like to argue that this unsettled state of its own nomenclature has political potency, especially in the context of the decolonisation discourse. Through the processes of naming and settling, I'd also like to raise another key concern in decolonisation discourse, which is around settlements leading into land, capital rights and access to resources as non-negotiable factors in decolonisation practice and what this might entail for research practice in PAR.

Finding a name for my practice made a significant difference to the course of my own research. My research on breathing in performance compelled a practice-based research enquiry that led to my synthesising the findings through short performance experiments in phenomenology, *ecriture feminine* and other discourses around the body. My encounter with PAR as a named methodology and 'way of knowing' was not simply a discovery of PAR. Even before the discovery of PAR as an emerging methodology, my research already included practitioners for whom the dichotomy of practice and research was made fluid in their own processes. Their end goals differed. The naming of PAR as a methodology in the Western academic context needs to be carefully negotiated in contexts where research through practice has had its own trajectory. This is not to say that the two are necessarily the same. I am not for example advocating that Indian performance practitioners have been doing PAR for two thousand years or even necessarily for the last forty years. But it may be valuable to consider how the role of practice has a place in epistemological enquiry and what makes this different from the ways that PAR in Western academia places and historicizes itself.

1.1   Practice as archive: Heisman Kanhailal and Veenpani Chawla

In considering decolonised performance utterance and the question of performance archives in this, the work of the Adishakti Laboratory of Theatre Research and the work of Kalakshetra Manipur, envisioned respectively by the late Veenpani Chawla and Heisnam Kanhailal, are two models that I find useful. I came to closely study their work while researching breath practices in theatre between 2010 and 2014. Coming from different political and cultural contexts within India, engaging with their search for a contemporary decolonised utterance in the findings of their own research and practice, will enable us to also establish a continuity in a historical trajectory of practitioners and thinkers in performance who have over the decades dealt with these key issues.

The theatre of Heisnam Kanhailal and Veenapani Chawla offers models of practitioners whose research into traditional forms may be understood as engagement with live archives as they developed their own vocabulary for a contemporary theatre. For theatre, music and dance practitioners and scholars, it is not unfamiliar to think of practice as archive. Practice-as-archive especially resonates in contexts where performances have not been visually or aurally documented and where therefore the live practice passed down is what makes itself available as the archive or the live archive. For Kanhailal and Veenapani, the traditional performance and martial art forms that they studied became these live archives. These traditional performances continue to exist as part of the repertory of classical forms. It seems obvious that the nature of such a live archive in performance must mark an ontological difference from a more documentary and record-based archive through its experiential and phenomenological constitution. In this chapter, my interest is looking at what I'd like to propose as an artefact of the live performance archive through my own practice-based research – that is, breath – and to reflect on how practitioners have engaged with this artefact in an attempt to create a new aesthetic for the theatre.

Both Veenapani and Kanhailal developed a theatre aesthetic that gives central importance to the actor's body and the physicality of performance. Their actors underwent intensive and particular physical training and much of the dramaturgy of each play was developed through physical vocabularies rather than linguistic text. It is possible to speculate on the different impulses that led them to the intense physicality of their theatre aesthetics. Kanhailal's tryst with theatre began in his youth and later he was accepted for study at the National School of Drama. He quit the course early and has often spoken of how his discomfort with Hindi as a medium of instruction was one of the reasons for it. Coming from the military occupied state of Manipur, which continues to suffer a political struggle based on ethnicity, he was primarily familiar at that time with the Meitei language. Returning to Manipur, he began to teach himself as he developed a vision of contemporary theatre that would emerge from his own ethnic and cultural sensibility. He conducted research for over ten years in different art forms of Manipur and from them developed a series of physical and vocal exercises that would train the actor to become sensitive to 'energy flows', as he describes them. He sought a 'universal language' of theatre that would be sensitive to the organic body of the actor, one that he nurtured also through sensitivity to the rhythms of tribal life and nature. In recent times he called his new form "Theatre of the Earth" – a title that befits Kanhailal's long interweaving of political, ecological and moral concerns through an organic acting and a dramaturgy that constantly interconnects political and sexual exploitation with exploitation of the earth and seems to seek and propose solutions that establish ecological and political harmony.

Gokhale (2014) describes how the physicality of Veenapani's theatre began with her disenchantment with realism and with the Stanislavsky method of memory recall for actors. Tired of administrative overbearing in institutional teaching, she resigned from her job at St Xavier's college in Mumbai and moved to Pondicherry to experiment with a new theatre. Veenapani's concerns were philosophical. Realism and method acting were already no longer options. A brief interest in Meyerhold opened up the body's potential to energise actors and a deeper interest in Eugenio Barbra's work. Grotowski, whom she met during his India travels, interested her because of his own search for physical expression for the actor, but she found an alternative to his notion of sacrifice. For Veenapani the body was an instrument of perfecting *sadhana*. From her engagement with Indian traditional forms, such as Chau, Kalaripayattu and Koodiyattam, she began to find the tools to shape her own particular theatre vision.

Kanhailal's research into traditional forms took place over a period of ten years. Then, having evolved a system of physical training for the actor, he moved on to creating a variety of works over his forty-year professional life as the director of Kalakshetra Manipur. Veenapani's research and engagement with traditional forms, however, continued through her life and beyond into the present at the Adishakti Laboratory for Theatre Research in Pondicherry. The Adishakti campus is housed next to a Kalari Gurukul (residential school) and the two share a symbiotic relationship while remaining autonomous institutions. Adishakti's focus on research and experimentation can be seen as a development of Veenapani's compelling vision of a contemporary Indian theatre that could express philosophical dilemmas about the individual's relationship to the collective, archetypes and choice, hybridity and belonging, and most importantly a search for self that unlike Grotowski's vision was not based in sacrifice (Auslander: 2002) but in cultivation and celebration.

The performance archive that Veenapani dipped into remains part of a living tradition of classical art form in Kerala – for example Koodiyattam and Kalaripayattu. She also studied Pranayama, Chhau and Ashtanga yoga, and trained at the Royal Central School of Speech and Drama in London. All of these influences helped carve the specific 'hybrid' sensibility of her contemporary theatre. But Veenapani's investigation of 'theatrical pasts' was not accomplished only through accessing the live archive that the traditional forms in many ways continue to be. It also involved practice-led investigations and experimentations with India's ancient dramaturgy text, the Natyashastra. The Natyashastra's Rasa theory or theory of affect in performance describes in detail several basic emotions as well as the contexts in which they may be expressed and some physical characteristics that they hold. For example a description in the Natyshastra of *Adhbuta* or wonder includes 'gaping of the eyes, staring unblinkingly, shedding tears, choking etc.' (NS: pg83), while *bhibhatsa* or disgust includes 'squeezing of limbs, moving of head to and fro, rolling eyes, spitting etc.' – all of which have corresponding breath patterns to enable this state. From scant clues in the existing text and insights from her exposure to Koodiyattam's work with breath and emotions, Veenpani began to elaborate a system of emotional expression for performance that depended on physiology rather than emotional recall. The findings of this research are still offered to contemporary actors who travel from across India and the world to participate in ten-day Source of Performance Energy workshops that are held at the Adishakti campus through the year. Thus for Veenapani's work, the live archive in conjunction with practice-led investigations in ancient dramaturgical texts offered a relationship with the past that informed and gave shape to present practice and allowed for the creation of a contemporary theatre vocabulary and actor's presence.

1.2 Hybrid utterance, new subjectivities and PAR

> Silence remains two, and perhaps even three, in the construction of history: the future must stay partly silent so that the other can construct it together with me.
>
> Luce Irigaray, *To Be Two* (65)

Describing her theatre as an 'aesthetics of hybridity', Veenapani outlined her own position as a cultural thinker and theatre maker. The alternatives that appeared before intellectuals and cultural agents in post-independence India – either (a) creating a derivative culture that accepted Western universals to the obliteration of difference and otherness or (b) attempting the resurrection of an imagined 'authentic tradition' – seemed to her unrealistic and inadequate. In her work, as with other contemporary Indian performance makers, one is able to see a wrestling with new subjectivities that the idea of hybridity may help give aesthetic form in performance.

The work of both Kanhailal and Veenapani offers distinct models of theatre-makers whose practice was also a search for the articulation of a decolonial aesthetic and episteme and a new political subjecthood. The relevance of breath in this process is perhaps not such a strange phenomenon after all. Breathing – the inhalation and exhalation of air with short periods of retention or completed expulsion – is a process that has undergone various experimentations by voice trainers as well as somatic bodyworkers and meditation practitioners. Luce Irigaray identifies breathing or respiration as the first 'autonomous act' that articulates our presence in the world. It is the first act that the newborn baby does outside the womb. Moving on from this basic respiration, Irigaray writes about the cultivation of breath being linked with the birthing of the self. Conscious breathing and the activation of subtle breathing are related to a conscious becoming.

Breathing technique in theatre is indeed an area of research that requires an involvement through practice. What drew me to the work of Kanhailal and Veenapani was a specific relationship with breath that both of them discovered and in varying degrees made a significant part of their actor training. Breath as an element of embodied performance is inextricably tied to embodied liveness and presence. Theatre produces a presence through the breathing body of the actor that can awaken a sense of the temporal as distinct from the historical. An actor's presence is a breathing presence. Irigaray asks for a return to the cultivation of breath as a way back into being alive in the moment. Yet this aliveness in a moment can be apprehended only though a sense of the historicity of that moment. Derrida's critique of Artaud's *Theatre of Cruelty* and its call for a pure presence is also relevant insofar as an unrepeated act is one that closes off the possibility of meaning-making. Artaud imagined a live theatre in the sense that life does not and cannot repeat itself.

Scholarship focused on the 'agonizingly relevant body of the performer' (Phelan 1993: 150) predicates itself on an ontology of disappearance. For Peggy Phelan the disappearing image re-enacts itself in memory. Breath in performance, however, is linked with immediacy and with the circulation of shifting breath patterns and is therefore the *force* of the corporeal, undivided by the Cartesian duality of mind and body, consciousness and inert physicality. The process of breathing in performance lends itself to a circular temporality. The actor breathes in, exhales through word or sometimes in breath aligned with movement, and then inhales again. Even with shifting rhythmic patterns there is repetition and the meaning of variation is predicated on this repetition. What disappears at the end of the performance is not simply the images and the meanings you make of it through your re-enactment of it in memory, but crucially your participation in the circulation of breath. There is a particular relationship with time present and past that a temporal element such as breath activates in theatre.

At the same time, in practice-led research into breath traditions, breath becomes an artefact that may be studied, replicated and understood as a specific cultural practice that enables specific outcomes, such as the expression of *adhbuta*/wonder or *bhibatsa*/disgust. Wartofsky's praxis theory is useful in allowing transferrable skills and techniques to be understood as artefacts (1979: 200–201). In this context, breath techniques are also artefacts belonging to a live archive. The Adishakti actor's experiment with breath also becomes an artefact subject to change over time.

My own project picks up certain impulses from my exposure to the theatre of Kanhailal and Veenapani and seeks to find expression through specific interests and concerns, such as the body as materiality and sign in embodied research and its place in academia, in new or partial subjectivities produced at the collision of cultures, and inner and outer states of being and becoming that enable a relational sense between the self, other and ecology. Veenapani's focus on breath and emotions, combined with her foregrounding of body centres from a tantric mapping of the body, offered me the tools for an embodied exploration of Self and the Other that I had already begun as part of my own site-specific performances based in authentic movement.

1.3 Universities, research practice and decolonisation

A part of me wonders about the university itself as a space of contestation in the postcolony. Why do I want to be in universities and engage with academia? What does it offer us? Is it really possible to 'change' the system and stamp out traces of colonisation from it? The different education systems and the institutions that hold them are themselves products of colonisation. India and South Africa, the two countries where I have lived and worked, had other systems of learning and sharing knowledge, or valuing what is knowledge and knowing, prior to colonisation. Within many healing and performance traditions, these ways of knowing continue to exist and even flourish. But some of these systems are self-contained and do not interact with the world.

I have valued university education for its apparent and explicit goal of universal accessibility. Traditional knowledge systems have specific modes of exclusion – for example based on gender, ethnicity or caste. There is also nepotism – for example in dance teaching. In independent India any student may have access to dance classes in the city if she pays a fee, but the highly individual and personalised pedagogic process is often unfair and leads to biased training of students. Certain healing traditions stay within the family or community, usually along caste lines. Women were certainly not allowed to learn many art forms as part of this 'exclusion', so to me a university model that has apparently more objective criteria is valuable. Yet in practice exclusion and systemic exclusion also happen in and through the university. This reality is constantly raised by student movements in both India and South Africa in their struggle for quality, accessible, free education for all.

How then do we decolonise this conversation?

Is it really possible to decolonise the university or this discourse?

At the outset I am sceptical of how decolonisation may be achieved. In South Africa and other parts of the African continent, the need to decolonise the syllabus and universities has emerged as one of the main agendas of the student movement. It is also a goal that intellectuals and academics are invested in achieving. Yet the way forward to this end remains unclear.

2.0　PAR project: queer notes

> The crisis lies precisely in the fact that the old is dying and the new cannot be born yet.
>
> Antonio Gramsci, *Prison Notebooks*

When Italian neo-Marxist philosopher Antonio Gramsci was imprisoned, he wrote his thoughts and reflections on a wide range of issues. Many years later, these were compiled and published as the *Prison Notebooks*. What interests me in this moment about Gramsci's *Prison Notebooks* is that they are not in the style of essays or articles. In fact the use of the word 'notes' to describe these writings is very apt. Also of interest are the conditions under which he wrote them. Written in prison, in poor health that was savagely deteriorating through concentrated neglect and prison conditions, Gramsci wrote in what theatre critic Samik Bandhopadhyay called 'a historical and political time when it was not possible to do anything more than take notes' (2012). This was the late 1930s in fascist Italy, a moment when Gramsci's people were caught in the ferment of political, economic and social turmoil. The time and space for reflective analysis and processing of the conditions of the time to write a tract or text had not yet come. All one could do was take notes.

The conceptualising of note-taking as a reflexive strategy of meaning-making in tumultuous historical contexts occurred to me after watching an amateur production in Soweto. After several weeks in South Africa, I went to see the play *Rocks and Roses* by at the Soweto theatre. It was a piece that through the trope of 'alliances and betrayals' touched on gender and sex games, sexism, political corruption, exploitation, 'white capital' and corporate hegemony, all played against a churning social unrest and disillusionment. At the same time, through a heightened farcical, physical aesthetic the play celebrated and constantly interrupted its own tensions. A scene of gruesome torture was followed up by an unbelievable and hilarious seduction of the prison guard by the tortured semi-heroine. At the end of the play, when the despot is being shot at by a defected military officer, who has just joined forces with the henchmen of the white capitalist, his death resembles the decelerated motion of *The Matrix* scene where Neo avoids bullets. Only here the despot is hit and takes a long, long, tiring and finally funny time to die. The audience is screaming with laughter by the end while the white capitalist hoisted on the shoulders of his newly bought army yawns. The dying despot representing the old regime is not simply dying but taking an unbelievably long time to die. The message is clear and grim: the old system is not going to give way easily and the new system is a terrifying unmasked face of naked capital interests.

How does one describe this as a theatrical event? Can this be classified within a genre? Written by a leader of the ANC's youth wing, the play claimed to be a critique of party politics and a hyperbolic account of a series of incidents about which it revealed some insider information. It can also be described as a hybrid between political farce and physical comedy. Yet some moments were chillingly 'unfunny', as when the white capitalist burns a young woman's hand while declaring that he loves the smell of 'Brai'. Despite its criticism of party politics, the ideological safeguarding of the ANC is also apparent in this work. But in the string of incidents woven together into a plot, and the many issues touched upon in seriously playful ways, it seemed to make sense as a set of 'notes' on a particular political moment. It was not yet a text or a thesis, not yet quite a full play, but more like notes in the context of Gramsci's notebooks and my idea of note-taking in fraught moments. In this way the play offers multiple insights and acts as a commentary on its time. At this moment in South Africa, can we do much better than faithfully – and with relentless honesty and perhaps some humour – take notes? This is what I propose the *queer flaneur* does. This is what I intend to do here, offering some notes out of my experience here in the last few months. I interweave this with memories and moments from other cities and spaces as I sense my way through being in South Africa as postdoctoral fellow, researcher and performer today.

So how does the queer flaneur take notes? Impressionistically at first. In words, images, gestures and symbols. In residues of feelings and emotions that stay accessible within a register of remembering events experienced. In recordings of exchanges with citizens through formal interviews, choreographed meetings and spontaneous conversations. In becoming also a teller of stories and working through different means of collaboration.

Notemakings 1: technology and space

In a special edition of *Café Dissensus* called *The Idea of the University*, several scholars interrogated the idea of the university. This was also spurred by a concern in the Indian context that the "twinning of 'saffronization' and 'financialization' in the imminent fortunes of the university are [*sic*] neither new nor unprecedented, and must of course produce in its wake the rage of a resolute defiance" (Bhattacharya 2016). During the Fees Must Fall student protests in South Africa, student leaders announced that their generational agenda or call was to resist the corporatisation of education. The goals of corporate capital and liberal education may to a large extent be at odds with each other. "Educating someone to pursue the open-ended search for deeper understanding has to be a kind of preparation for autonomy" writes Stefan Collini (2012: 8).

I arrived at Pretoria for a postdoctoral fellowship in the Drama Department in June 2017, optimistic about being part of a Global South network that would exchange and learn from each other's histories and political contexts and develop new pedagogies and epistemes, especially taking into account embodied research. Decolonial debates and discourses, such as subaltern theory and postcolonialism, seemed to need an update, taking into account neo-liberal capital and technology through methods involving co-thinking and writing as well as collaborative practice. Attending the World Social Forum for the first time in Mumbai in 2004, I was left with questions around social justice mostly framed through the discourse of capitalism and socialism. Speaking to an ideologue and underground activist from the 1970s, I asked what he felt the left intellectuals' task now was. His response was simply this: to recognise that we had lost the battle against capitalism. In the last few years of experimenting with various communal living and economic arrangements, I am coming to terms with what this means and realising that there must be new strategies for going forward.

At that time of the Mumbai World Social Forum I was in the first semester of my master's in women studies in a partially private college in Bangalore, South India, which was on its way to becoming an autonomous institution. More than ten years later, I taught at the same institution before coming to Pretoria. One of my more disturbing experiences while working there was of the faculty herding around a machine at 9:30 every morning and 5:30 every evening to log in and log out our entrance and exit from the college. Thumb impressions were needed. One of the first and more expensive apartments that I moved into there had a similar system of finger impressions that unlocked two levels of entrance and exit from the building. One regimented my time on campus and the other regimented access. I could not leave keys to the apartment with a friend or lover. I had to be present to fingerprint my entrance and exit. This was purportedly for security.

I'd like to take a moment to think about the advancement of technologies, the increasing regimentation of spaces, and the intensity with which corporate capital pervades our personal and professional lives – robbing us of our agency, of the ways we choose to live and with whom, and ironically doing this with money we are paying. The corporatisation of the university also involves regimentation of access and identification of an 'other'. Adam Habib recently said that one of the key things that disadvantaged labour in the era of neo-liberal capital was technology being used by corporations and management to intensify control and regulate production (2016). We have seen how online teaching and assessment have been a sharp blow to the 'Shut Down UP' (University of Pretoria) students' movement. This is all obvious. But the question of mediation through technology also demands scrutiny of teaching methods and the value of embodied presence and oral transfers of knowledge: a question around embodied presence that has indeed been a central concern within performance studies discourse.

Notemakings 2: Nkosinathi Gaar's Engyn Room

When I was preparing to come to South Africa, I wrote the news to a friend from Pretoria who I had met in India in 2010. His first question back to me was if I needed a place to stay. I'd said that the university was making some arrangement and I should be fine. He was a theatre-maker and enrolled as a master's student here after many years of professional work. When we met he greeted me as an international scholar. "More like wandering book hustler", I replied. We both laughed, understanding the interest in street scholarship and learning in and out of the system. He took me to a space that he had invested the last few years of his life building – I should say, creating. He called it the Engyn Room. It was housed in a set of industrial buildings that he had converted into studios, a performance space, and a screening room, installing a bar and setting up rooms where artists lived and where he had hosted residencies focused on building and activating the Pretoria art scene. When I walked in I was immediately struck with the thought of Warhol's Factory. Needless to say Nkosinathi was thrilled at the comparison. His reasoning behind the space was that artists needed a place to showcase high-quality work that still wasn't finished. He'd felt there was sufficient support and space for showcasing developed work but not enough serious spaces of engagement for work that was still developing but required a critical showcasing. He also wanted as a theatre-maker to be able to dwell in and inhabit his sets. He did not want to make the sets and have to break them down at the end of each rehearsal. He wanted to be able to immerse himself in the sets.

Listening to my friend, I laughed with the thrill of his ambition and its contradictions. At a time when performance discourse was showcasing itself as an ephemeral experience, it appeared to me that he was attempting to build an anti-ephemeral theatre. I caught the excitement of his vision and we made plans about how to take the work forward, which included my moving into the space in a few weeks. In a bizarre set of events that spiralled out of control, the artists residing at Engyn Room were asked to move out of the space and my friend took his own life one Sunday evening. There were stories about administrative mishaps with his scholarship, about his needing financial support from a family not supportive of the arts. And also his unwillingness, I think, to see his anti-ephemeral theatre shut down. His death has been a painful loss to many friends and family but a loss also felt keenly within the young arts community in Pretoria, in which he had taken a role of leadership. Today, in lamenting the loss of ideas of spaces that help us dream and think and imagine new ways of living, I also lament the loss of Nkosinathi Gaar – loss that is not simply personal but has come to take on symbolic value in the contexts and violence of our times.

Notemakings 3: Mthubi the Hub and the Old Fire Station (Tshwane Arts Hub)

I'd like to pose, alongside the idea of the university as space, the idea of space as relationally driven. Mthubi the Hub is an arts collective on Arcadia Street, a stone's throw away from the university gates. It has artists in residence that have 'occupied' the building. The artists living there in strained conditions re-imagine possibilities even as they try to sustain the Hub and chart a new direction through creative fundraising art events. The struggle of the artist, like that of the researcher in neo-liberal times, is in legitimising the value of what he or she does in monetary terms. The hardship is also endured for goals that are not as immediately tangible.

The Mthubi Arts Hub is a residential community, newer in comparison to the Tshwane Arts Hub, popularly referred to as the Old Fire Station because of the buildings they occupy. The Tshwane Arts Hub is best described as a coalition of several independent artists and a cluster of independent art organisations that have their base here. There are craft studios, exhibitions spaces, intimate performance venues, residences, and organisations' offices within the compound. Both hubs reflect the tensions of post-Apartheid land politics, where they represent an assertive Black arts movement that believes in occupying abandoned spaces even if that occupation is deemed illegal by state bodies. Both hubs have faced threats of eviction, which they continue to battle through legal means as well as by continuing to 'occupy'. The internal dynamics and pressures of both the hubs, the gendered negotiations of space, and the managing of internal conflicts and abrasions often reflect the difficulty of accountability in such conditions. Is there a sense in which the conditions of living and ownership in a space like the Hub may be compared to university space? Is there a way to enter strategic relations of support with such spaces?

In *The Slow Professor*, Maggie Berg and Barbara K. Seeber write that "many of us are searching for meaningful exchange about what it feels like to be an academic in the corporate university, and we seem to encounter the fact that the corporate university actively militates against us having these exchanges" (2016: 85). While justice seems to prefer to operate at a systemic level – the authors argue for reactivating professorial agency and taking back power from administrators in terms of setting the direction and culture of the university – I would also like to argue for the political potency of relational exchanges through friendship, work, love and interpersonally negotiated institutional collaboration with different spaces as a means to arrive at spatial justice. In times when the mechanisation of corporate systems threatens both academic and artistic free-dom, we need to regain lost rights and in the performance of last rites recover the political agency of friendship to help us in these quests for spatial justice. I agree that we are in a time of loss but I argue for a point of recovery from here too. As examples of negotiating strategic support and extending interac-tions with artistic spaces, site-specific classes from the Drama Department were conducted at the Tshwane Arts Hub and the artists from the two hubs were invited to speak and participate at the Department's annual arts festival. Other art ventures from the university such as the S.L.O.W. project have also collabo-rated with this space for events and exhibitions.

Notemakings 4: "Darshan" – finding utterance in South Africa

I am not made in god's image
She is not made in mine
Ancient temple builders
Across the Deccan landscapes
pick their tools
Hand against hammer against stone
Tap, chisel, carve, breech
their way
through the hills
turning rocks into gods
These craftsmen
staring at long slabs of stone
drawing from inner mystery
to vision the divine

Which image of their self did they make the Almighty in?

These gods . . .
staring at devotees through half lidded eyes-
slender dancing erect penised gods
gripping round breasted devis,
slanted hip against hip and
languid
carrying enlightenment in their hands –
Dread locked Siva fucks Parvati on the mountains of Kailash for a 1000
    years and goes celibate for another 1000
Parvati who makes childrens from the dirt of her own skin when all the
    available sperm is condom wrapped or falls to the ground
Part-animal winged and fiery creatures
Tearing through the worlds of maya

flap furious feathers
against my third eye still unopened

Whose gods are these that will not be left behind when I wear metal wings and fly oceans and continents to reach your lips?

Bags. Lost. In transit. I come. Burning townships. Angry debates. Ethnicity of a new mayor.
Tribalism says the taxi driver from Thambo Airport to Cum Laude 3.
Tribalism says the law student at the bar with the golf coach.
He wants free lessons and is betting on my accent and my skirt.
Durban, London . . . no India. Yeah actually India. Because India is a city like Africa is a country hey?
3 glorious fucks later. The unasked I don't do relationships conversation later.
Part time law student, full time pimp offers to hook me up with packs of men. You can make good money on the side he promises.
Welcome to South Africa he smiles.
You're not South Africa I say and leave.
South Africa is not Africa my Zambian philosopher friend tells me.
Corpse cold July night.
News of lives taken in hospital beds.
I dream again. With a half-fluttering third eye that now begins to get restless. I dream again. Of other lawyers and other law students.
Of a Mandela prison that changed how we saw political possibility. Made us think Hindus and Muslims, post Godhra, post Babri Masjid, post partitions could still find a way to reconcile,
Of Biko behind a truck. Your mind is your most powerful weapon he said and the fuckers bashed his brains in.
Of blackness that still made nights like this magical.
Of a Famished Okri road that has fed my spirit with oranges and a dead father's wisdom for over 14 years.
Of Tess Onwueme dancing war against three male directors desecrating her play in the halls of a New Delhi performance.

Which image of our many selves did I make my Africa in? My third eye gets restless . . .

Ever since I arrived my love for you has been an uphill battle
Crossing fuck boys and dead lovers
Stolen cards, broken hearts, bruised rainbows
Sistas for whom my skin is never ever dark enough

Sistas whose skin is too light for kinship
New lingo I learn to make up Randy as in rand starved as in

Freedom Children speaking of chains that tie them like unwelcome
    Randy dogs outside university gates

Ever since I've arrived my love for you has been an uphill battle

    Stopped short when 24 rubber bullets were pumped into the back of a
        student leader
    Gasping for breath in a hospital bed
    I finally agree I didn't see you S Africa . . .
    Whose image did I make you in before I arrived?
    But I find the Gods who will not be left behind, Gods who dance
      destruction and recreation watch these new Gods . . .
    Gods whose temples are jail cells broken open
    and the backs of trucks that trundle through restless sleep less awakenings,
    Gods whose prayers are new constitutions
    Warrior gods unleashing wrath against 94 promises broken
    Goddesses whose hair makes Moses' burning bush envious.

The gods of this country and that country drum a chant

    I am not made in god's image
    She is not made in mine

But each day we are making each other as a third eye opens.

References

Auslander, Philip (2002) *From Acting to Performance: Essays in Modernism and Postmodernism*, London and New York: Routledge.

Bandhopadhyay, Samik (2012) *Seminar, Theatre and Performance Studies Forum*, New Delhi: Jawaharlal Nehru University.

Benston, Kimberly W. (1984) 'I yam what I am: The topos of un (naming) in Afro-American literature,' in *Black Literature and Literary Theory*, ed. Henry Louis Gates Jr., New York: Routledge.

Berg, Maggie and Barbara K. Seeber (2016) *The Slow Professor: Challenging the Culture of Speed in the Academy*, Toronto: University of Toronto Press.

Bhattacharya, Debaditya (2016) 'What "use" is the liberal ruse? Debating the "idea" of the university,' *Café Dissensus* 29, Special Issue: *The Idea of the University*. Online: <https://cafedissensus.com/2016/09/15/contents-the-idea-of-the-university-issue-29/>.

Collini, Stefan (2012) *What Are Universities For?* London: Penguin Books.

Derrida, Jacques (1978) 'The theatre of cruelty and the closure of representation,' in *Writing and Difference*, Chicago: The University of Chicago Press.

Gayatri, Manola K. (2014). *Breath, Radical Faith and Intersubjectivity in Poetic Utterance*, PhD Thesis, New Delhi: Jawaharlal Nehru University.

Gokhale, Shantha. (2014) *The Theatre of Veenapani Chawla*, New Delhi: Oxford University Press.

Habib, Adam (2016) 'The unrest of the South African psyche', Keynote address, Annual Consulting Psychology Conference, Department of Industrial and Organisational Psychology, University of South Africa, Pretoria.

Irigaray, Luce (2002) *To Be Two*, London: Bloomsbury.

Nair, Sreenath (2007) *Restoration of Breath Consciousness and Performance*, New York: Rodopi.

Phelan, Peggy (1993) *Unmarked: The Politics of Performance*, New York: Routledge.

Wartofsky, Marx (1979) *Models: Representations and the Scientific Understanding*, Dordrecht: D. Reidel.

Chapter 9

Containers of practice

Would you step into my shell?

Göze Saner

> *The tortoise shivered: 'Now I'm cold*
> *I wish I hadn't been so bold.*
> *I think I've lost the urge to roam.*
> *I think I'd like to go back home.*
> *Without my shell, I don't feel right.'*
> *But her shell was nowhere in sight . . .*
> Buckley and Carle 2009

Preamble

19 January 2013, North London Community House. I hoover, then mop the wooden floor of the banquet room and arrange fifty chairs in two rows facing each other. After warming up, I balance my wooden plank precariously on its base, put my ukulele, shoe box and umbrella down in their corners, and lay out three rocks as if over a brook and step on them a few times to see they are not slippery. I arrange my eggshells and cover them with sand. A brief look around, then I start letting my guests in and showing them to their seats. They are surprised by the lack of curtains or lights, and the particularly maternal comment on my lack of footwear. Once everybody sits down I take my place crouched by the wooden plank and using my hands as puppets I tell the story of the Foolish Tortoise who leaves her shell in search of freedom, lightness and fastness but upon much suffering decides to return to its security. Unfortunately, in the version I tell, when she gets back to where she has left it, there is no shell to be found. And thus begins a journey interweaving fragmented images, actions, songs and stories of many lost, shell-less tortoises wandering in search of a home.

I am playing *ev·de·yol·da/at·home·on·the·road*, in Turkish, for an audience of Turkish/Kurdish migrant women. The performance is free and has been organised in collaboration with the Women's Committee of DayMer, an advice and service organisation for Turkish-speaking migrants based in London. The event, including a Q&A, is intended to serve as an invitation to women to take part in a community theatre project planned to start in the autumn. I am sharing my work on the tortoise and asking, quite literally: would you like to do this? Would you step into my shell? With the same action, I am also leaving the security of my shell behind. I am departing from the safety of laboratory theatre and for the first time stepping into the wholly unknown territory of community performance.

This essay examines the questions, problems and challenges that accompany such a step. It interrogates the kind of knowledge generated by laboratory theatre processes and questions if and how it can be made accessible and relevant within a community theatre context. By drawing an affinity between laboratory theatre practices and practice as research (PaR), particularly where research into the craft of the actor is concerned, the essay also proposes a reconfiguration of knowledge generated through PaR.

Step into the background: from *at·home·on·the·road* to *migrant steps*

I am an actor who devises theatre, alone or collaboratively, through processes informed by the actor's work on herself (Carnicke and Benedetti 1993; Stanislavski 1993, 2008; Richards 1995; Christoffersen 1993). My research during, and since completing, a practice-based PhD has been concerned with articulating the myriad ways in which performance can facilitate an engagement with archetypes (Saner 2009). My emphasis on research and commitment to long-term processes without imminent results resonate with the way of working associated with the laboratory, often presented as 'a place where scenic life can be investigated and develops independently from performance and audience' (Christofferson 2004, 6) – a safe space, free from commercial concerns, where the craft of theatre can be studied as an end in itself, where elements of uncertainty, chance and serendipity and different modes of knowing and sharing knowledge can be embraced (Christofferson 2004; Schino 2009; Spatz 2015).

But what does it mean to study craft in itself, when craft means building or making things, such as performances? I find Heidegger's example of the cabinetmaker's apprentice an apposite analogy here. He argues that in order to become a true cabinetmaker, the apprentice does not just 'gain facility in the use of tools' or 'gather knowledge about the customary forms of the things he is to build' (1993: 379). Rather, 'he makes himself *answer and respond* above all to the different kinds of wood and to the shapes slumbering in the wood' (379). Heidegger shifts the attention from the person and the skills to the raw material to be crafted, a shift that I believe is reflected in the theatre laboratory where the researcher is able to delay the quick turnaround of outputs in order to cultivate the silence to respond to the *matter* of performance, which in my case, as an actor, is the body, imagination, voice, space, time, action, sensation, memory, to name a few. Rather than developing expertise in conventional methods of working, the apprentice learns to learn by returning to the basics. The laboratory not only hosts an experiential mode of investigation as the scientific connotation of the word implies but also permits, even encourages, not knowing.

Discoveries are often not outcomes but rather *forms* of listening and asking.

Such an approach resonates also with my focus on archetypes. My intention in engaging with the basic materials of the actor is to search for theatrical forms that can instigate an archetypal engagement. The term 'archetypal engagement', as opposed to representations of archetype, derives directly from my adopted methodology of archetypal psychology. While the Jungian articulation of archetype has been problematised from a number of fronts, including postmodern, feminist and post-colonialist critique (Cambray and Carter 2004; Casement 1998; Hauke 2000; Stein and Jones 2010; Young-Eisendrath 2004), the post-Jungian school of archetypal psychology offers a processual, phenomenological approach that shifts the attention from making universalist claims on archetype *per se* to conceiving an *archetypal methodology* that aims to return autonomy to the culturally specific, multiple, messy and deeply particular material manifestations of the psyche – images, dreams, artistic or cultural products (Samuels 1985; Davis 2003). David Tacey summarises how archetypal psychology thus revolutionises Jungian thought: 'diversity replaced unity, phenomenology replaced metaphysics, imagination replaced the unconscious, and uncertainty and openness ('not knowing' or *via negativa*) replaced knowing' (1998: 219).

Two methodological principles underpin archetypal psychology and guide me in drawing the borders of my laboratory: specificity and the unknown. The precise, detailed nature of psychic material – for example a dream – is respected by consciously resisting unifying interpretative tendencies. Rather than moving towards exhaustive analyses, the archetypal psychologist surrenders to not knowing and submits to a process in which knowledge or, in better words, a kind of kinship with the material may arrive gradually, in time. James Hillman argues that only by 'sticking to the image and staying in the unknown' (1977: 78) is it possible 'to hold back the hermeneutical desire' and 'to let the image elaborate itself' (2008: 18). Following these principles, in my search for archetypal figures, the tyrant and later the tortoise, I let my practice yield non-representational forms that I am unable to identify until much later, while staying close to the incomprehensible details that appear and reappear. I try to work 'with an eye attuned to the dark' (Hillman 1977: 82), and to use Heidegger's metaphor, I respond to the matter of acting to find the theatrical shapes slumbering therein that can serve to facilitate and contain archetypal encounters.

At·home·on·the·road was concerned with the archetypal image of a wandering tortoise. During the three years of preliminary research, I looked for ways of embodying and meeting the tortoise in the studio, working with actions, objects, songs and stories that provided repeatable shapes which could serve as an invitation to this archetypal animal – to meet, to befriend or perhaps to possess me. In the final year, I experienced a moment of crisis in my personal life. I was feeling out-of-place at the shared house where I lived, and in hindsight, in my life as a whole. One Sunday morning, unable to stay 'at home' any longer, I stepped outside, banged the door behind me and started walking, until I was utterly lost. The next Sunday, I went again. Without realising, I had started a practice of drifting, wandering aimlessly but in response to my environment, with weekly *dérives* in the manner of the Situationist International (Debord 2006, 62–66). Gradually I drew the connection between the work in the studio and on the streets. In the studio, I started looking for the form of observations I scribbled during drifts. Notes such as 'You always aim somewhere (there is no absolutely aimless wandering) but you change your mind or something else is as likely to draw you as where you were headed in the first place'[1] transformed into exercises exploring walking, changing direction, decision-making. Conversely, I was engaging with the streets as an actor by staying in my body and giving myself instructions for improvisations: 'Stalk a building.'[2] Eventually the autobiographical narrative, notes as well as photographs from my walks, became one of the many tortoises whose stories the performance followed.

The touring of the piece embodied a similar process. Thanks to a departmental sabbatical, from October 2011 to January 2012, I sublet my room and travelled abroad to visit collaborators who had been home to me in the past, as far away as Bakersfield, California (see figure 9.1). With them, I reworked and performed *at·home·on·the·road* in two languages and five countries (Saner 2011). One of my stops was Odin Teatret. While in Holstebro, through a set of

Figure 9.1 Göze Saner in *ev·de·yol·da/at·home·on·the·road*, 5 January 2012, The Empty Space Theatre, Bakersfield, California.

Source: Matthew Woodman.

chance encounters, I ended up performing for an audience of Turkish-speaking Kurdish women in Trivselshuset, the leisure centre of a housing estate occupied primarily by migrant families. The majority of my spectators had never been to the theatre before and were not familiar with the physical/vocal language of a non-naturalistic devised solo performance, with only fragments of narrative, a multiplicity of characters, and minimal props and costumes. Yet it worked. The piece truly found its home. After the performance, members of the audience came up to me to tell me they too were tortoises. They voiced such a deep connection with the central archetypal figure that I was compelled to follow through. Eventually I got in touch with Turkish/Kurdish organisations in London, arranged to share the performance in a similar non-professional context as the one in Holstebro. *Migrant Steps* was thus conceived with the intention to open up the work on the tortoise to other migrant women, not just as audiences but also as performers.

Migrant Steps is a community theatre project where I worked with Turkish-speaking migrant women living in London. In collaboration with DayMer and the North London Community Centre (NLCH) in Bruce Grove, I led walks and workshops every Sunday for three months starting in October 2013. While the intention was to eventually produce a piece of theatre, these sessions were non-committal and open to women of all age groups. Our journeys, literal and metaphorical, on the streets and in the studio, were accompanied and documented in a short film by filmmaker Alev Erdoğan. We also used shared journals passed on from person to person every week to collect our experiences and impressions. In January 2014, I set out to formalise our work in a more intensive devising and rehearsal programme, and out of approximately twenty-five women who had participated, eight decided to continue. I received an Arts Council grant and a Goldsmiths University Enterprise Fund in order to direct and produce a theatre performance, working with the group of participants as performer-devisers as well as enlisting the help of professional Turkish-speaking migrant women artists, such as Zeynep Kepekli, a lighting designer and production manager, and Zeynep Bulut, a sound designer, and ensuring the continued collaboration of Alev Erdoğan. The resulting performance was an ensemble-led piece, interweaving stories, moments and text from the aforementioned shared notebooks as well as actions and scores developed in the workshops, bracketed by traditional songs and dances. After an open dress rehearsal on 7 March 2014, the piece, also named *Migrant Steps*, was presented along with the documentary film on 8 and 9 March 2014, in celebration of International Women's Day.

Step out of the laboratory

'Accidentally on purpose' discoveries are at the heart of articulations of the laboratory (Christofferson 2004; Schino 2009). The performance in Trivselshuset is such a serendipitous experience, confirming the efficacy of the work and indicating a new direction, perhaps even a leap. Considering the underlying research on archetype – a concept that is by definition collective – the step from the solo project towards the territory of community theatre appears to be an organic migration. Yet, however wilful, extending my practice into a new context, with its wholly new set of unknowns, is also an act of displacement. It is a *dis-location* in the sense employed by Baz Kershaw as he argues, 'the most crucial effect of performance practice as research is to *dis-locate* knowledge' (2009: 105). In the following section I will outline the challenges in translating my laboratory-based methods in a community project and question how and if knowledge can indeed be dislocated and transmitted in different contexts.

The laboratory, particularly laboratories constructed around the actor's work on herself, relies on long-term, continuous processes. Over years, even decades, the actor trains through psychophysical blocks or tendencies in order to develop a way of working that is at once spontaneous – ready, alive, responsive – and precise – aware, detailed and free from behaviourisms. The limited time-span of the project is thus my first challenge: I am to work with untrained participant-performers, for roughly five months, around work and family commitments, and towards a given performance date: International Women's Day. Can I achieve a level of spontaneity and precision quickly with untrained performers?

My second challenge is aim. Participants do not want to train to be performers. Even if we had unlimited time, the intention is not a deepened understanding

Figure 9.2 Göçmen Adımlar/Migrant Steps collaborators. Clockwise from top left: Carine Koleilat, Alev Erdoğan, Margarida Correia, Ayşe Yılmaz, Göze Saner, Perihan Tan, Zeynep Kepekli, Nia Wood, Eylem Nalan Karaoğlan, Leyla Kepez, Dilek Koca, Naciye Yurdakul, Gülhan Küpeli, Güllü Kuşçu.

Source: Steve Kessel.

of craft or the building of expertise in psychophysical technique, but rather to enable participants to have their own encounters with their own tortoises and to shape their own narratives to share with an audience. Can I transmit forms of archetypal engagement without relying on a framework in which the ultimate aim is to investigate and develop performance technique? Without the elements of long-term-ness, training outside the constraints of a set production date, and technical competence, what is there left to my laboratory?

Knowledge as method

Considering how knowledge can be transferred from one setting into another leads to another question: what kind of knowledge? There are a number of articulations of knowledge understood in PaR, specifically knowledge within the laboratory. One is through practitioners' theories. Shannon Riley observes that 'Rethinking theatre as a laboratory can be seen as an attempt to theorise (perhaps legitimise – perhaps protect) the theatre arts from a modern, scientific perspective' (2009: 140). Theories in the shape of methods, sets of principles, rules and value schemes often emerge out of laboratory processes and help formulate and formalise the practice of the specific practitioner/laboratory for posterity. Yet as Riley points out in her use of the word 'protect', the configuration of the laboratory also underlines the subjective nature of knowledge, which is acknowledged further in another model: embodied knowledge. Ian Watson argues that theatre laboratories are deeply resistant to developing quasi-scientific formulas that can be readily isolated from the space in which they are found: 'This embodied research model denies both the tenet of objectivity and the reproduction of findings by other parties that is so central to scientific discovery' (2009: 87).

The terms 'theory' and 'method' imply the work can be taken and repeated by somebody else, elsewhere. Yet knowledge generated through laboratory processes resists such a dislocation. The wish to legitimise, by presenting knowledge in the form of *technique* which can be adopted/tested by others, stands in opposition to the need to acknowledge the complex circumstantiality of the discoveries made in a laboratory. One solution is to distinguish between tacit and explicit knowledge, which offers a way of protecting methods within the *body* of laboratories – within physical spaces and the bodies, minds and histories of the laboratorians – while proposing certain modes of transmission. Watson calls these *applications*: 'Unlike scientific research, which is grounded in the discovery of universals, performance research is rooted in the personal, in the findings of individual actors and/or researchers in particular circumstances which are, in turn, *applied in future situations*' (2009: 85). In this model, tacit knowledge, which is necessarily subjective, becomes objectively demonstrable always and only through something else. In the list drawn by Jonathan Pitches, this can be through performance, writing, as reflexive practice or otherwise, 'translating embodied processes and discoveries into written registers' (2011: 138), or teaching as a 'vertical transmission' (2011: 139).

Following this model, the leap into *Migrant Steps* appears to be a textbook example: a laboratory practitioner working in *applied theatre*, transposing previously developed embodied methods into a new context and thus 'applying them in a future situation'. Yet I have misgivings with this approach. Intending to apply an already-completed set of techniques on new material would imply numerous ethical problems by presenting my methods as a cookie cutter and reducing the amateur participants to dough. Neither am I comfortable with the position of a teacher as bearer of knowledge; I feel participants should take priority over the techniques and I adamantly want to spare them 'terms such as "lineage" and the related issues of status, legitimacy and authority' (Pitches et al. 2011: 139). I also question if such an approach would involve a proper dislocation. It would be a re-enactment perhaps, but would it be research in the sense of listening in for new knowledge?

The notion of application does not quite do justice to my objectives or my principles. I want to share my laboratory, to repeat the experiment and to do it *anew*. As I observed earlier, the laboratory embraces not knowing and does not necessarily *produce* knowledge, to use the paradigm of academic research, but, like searching for cabinets hidden in the wood, the laboratory *hosts* knowledge, it *calls for* or *allows* knowledge, or knowledge *resides* in the laboratory. The difference between producing and hosting would remain semantic if I attempted to dislocate knowledge without relocating the process of calling and response therein. How is it possible, then, to conceive of a process of dislocating, transmitting and translating forms of not knowing?

Containers of practice

An adjustment to the image of knowledge in the context of the laboratory and PaR helps to underline this kind of knowledge that embraces not knowing. I would like to argue that complementarily to the notion of embodiment, knowledge in the laboratory can be conceived through a model of *containment*, and understood as contained in various shapes, forms, *containers*. The difference here is subtle and containment can be seen as yet another form of embodiment itself. The metaphor operates in the image of a container that has a shape and a hollow interior. It is empty unless it is filled by someone or something, indicating that it holds a process of not knowing, a potentiality, a way of asking, which can be shared and transmitted from context to context independently of the practitioners who have created, adopted, stolen, learned or taught them. Many exercises and tools operate in such a way; to give a few examples, Stanislavski's infamous affective memory, Meyerhold's iconic shooting from the bow, Brecht's street scene and Grotowski's the Cat are each containers of a certain way of working as they make a process of (not) knowing available outside the physical, historical, subjective circumstances in which they were conceived (Barba 1997). The suggestion here is that techniques/methods can and do exist independently of the practitioners and laboratories that have discovered or shaped them, that

Figure 9.3 The tortoise as container. Naciye Yurdakul, Dilek Koca and Gülhan Küpeli in
        Göçmen Adımlar/Migrant Steps, 8 March 2014, North London Community House,
        Tottenham, London.
Source: Steve Kessel.

they are things-in-themselves, epistemic objects in their own right (Spatz 2015).
It follows that the laboratory is a place that hosts, indeed generates, perfects and
gradually transforms repeatable experiments in the shape of containers, such as
exercises, actions, structured improvisations or scores, sometimes literally, in the
shape of umbrellas, as seen in figure 9.3, rather than a place that produces master
practitioner-researchers.

A container: the Cat

Let us take a brief look at the Cat. The Cat is one of the corporeal exercises
developed by Grotowski in the early sixties, with its roots in Hatha yoga, Meyerhold and Delsarte and its branches in numerous contemporary approaches to
actor training (Kapsali 2010; Kumiega 1985; Slowiak and Cuesta 2007; Wangh
2000). Eugenio Barba describes it in detail as he records the Theatre Laboratory's work during the years 1959–1962 in *Towards a Poor Theatre*. 'This exercise
is based on the observation of a cat as it awakes and stretches itself. The subject
lies stretched out face downwards, completely relaxed. The legs are apart and
the arms at right angles to the body, palms towards the floor. The "cat" wakes
up' (Barba 2002: 135).

Barba's description is sandwiched between two qualifying notes, the first of which urges that 'the actor must justify every detail of this training with a precise image, whether real or imaginary' (Barba 2002: 135) and must align the body fully with this image, at times becoming light and supple and at others hard and solid. The second note points out, however, that it is problematic to do the exercises purely mechanically as a show of physical skill. In bold it states, **'The exercise serves the research.** It is not merely automatic repetition or a form of muscular massage' (Barba 2002: 136). Pitting exercises that 'repeat' against those that 'investigate' the note also articulates what the research might involve:

> The body's centre of gravity, the mechanism for the contraction and relaxation of the muscles, the function of the spine in the various violent movements, analysing any complicated developments and relating them to the repertory of every single joint and muscle.
>
> (Barba 2002: 136)

Grotowski's prescript to the section explains that the exercises are later transformed from a 'positive technique or, in other words, a certain method of training capable of objectively giving the actor a creative skill' towards a way of working 'orientated towards a quest for contact' (Barba 2002: 133). According to Margaret Croyden, by 1963 the Cat becomes 'the basic corporeal exercise . . . designed primarily for energy and the suppleness of the vertebrae' (Croyden 1974: 163), resonating with Slowiak and Cuesta's description of the exercise's aim: 'engagement of the sacrum-pelvis complex and flexibility of the spinal column' (2007: 95).

Even within a span of four years, within the same laboratory, differences appear in how one might occupy the Cat, each pitting one set of givens against a set of unknowns. On the one hand, it is possible to use the Cat to chip away at the body's resistances: take inspiration from the image of an animal to find total balance, flexibility, rigour, strength and wakefulness. On the other hand, the mechanical, skilful repetition of the exercise to reach physical virtuosity is later seen not an end in itself but rather a means to an end. What is required of the actor next is to move beyond physical mastery towards 'research', to use the form in order to investigate other operations of the body. Then *via negativa* emerges: use an exercise that takes you to precarious balance to investigate gravity, use something that effectively blocks out the arms and legs to explore the range of movement in the spine, indirectly identify and work through the actor's resistances. Yet Grotowski's note indicates a wholly other direction, to continue from being the 'whole organism' to being a whole organism with someone else.

What do these variations indicate in terms of the knowledge discovered through and contained within this exercise? The container has its own life; it develops and grows as the given boundaries of the exercise, the knowns, and its aims, the research or the unknowns, continue to shift and change places. Kumi-ega identifies what is essential to the shaping of a container, such as the Cat, as she articulates the overall non-method of Grotowski dialectically, as

> techniques and ethics. Techniques we can understand as the minutiae of method, the practical directives which, in certain combinations, produce the verifiable results which are usually classed as method. Ethics are what inform the use of technique – the how, when, why and which of the technique.
>
> (1985: 111)

While technique is the pragmatic, descriptive, factual, quantitative aspects of the exercise, the ethics is the set of principles and values with which it is qualified. In the same way that the description of an exercise is parenthesised by a number of notes, the technical aspects of methods are complemented by questions. What is the aim? Where is the attention? How is it observed? Be it the mechanistic rendering of the Cat, or the one in which the attention is on encountering the other *via* the exercise, certain rules or instructions shape the container and a set of principles informs the way of doing. The dialectical inter-play of these two sides constitutes the container in its entirety.

What happens when containers are removed from their original context and adopted by others? Hunter suggests that the value of the theatre laboratory is grounded in the observation that its experiments cannot be repeated, as she argues:

> But the signal difference between the laboratory of the scientist and that of the artist is that the former aims to construct a method by which anyone in the world can duplicate the experiment. Whereas the potential instabil-ity and unrepeatability is something that scientists worry about, it is the lifeblood of arts practitioners.
>
> (2009: 4)

Does this observation suggest that exercises such as the Cat do not survive?

Kumiega's pairing of techniques and ethics functions as a powerful mecha-nism for understanding how containers can transmit knowledge. Often, when practitioners borrow methods, they do so within these parameters; techniques are adopted in order to embrace precisely the non-tangible elements described as ethics, or a parallel ethical predisposition renders a technique attractive. When exercises such as the Cat are misunderstood, it is not due to issues of lineage, which operates as an elitist way of questioning one's allegiance or proximity to the source practitioner, but due to a lack of ethics, which marks a particular disposition regarding the aesthetic, interpersonal and moral values underpinning the work, or a lack of care in terms of technique, which demands precision. When an exercise is displaced in a way that leaves either the technique or the ethics behind, it ceases to be. Yet returning to Hunter's observation that artistic containers derive their value from their unrepeatability, one can argue that such transformations are inevitable and indeed desirable. The same Cat, and Grotowski's relationship with and intentional disruption of the lineage of yoga out of which the container emerges, suggests that discontinuity is an essential aspect in the life of a container.

Perhaps there is a misleading identification of repetition with sameness in Hunter's claim, as indicated by the word 'duplicate'. I propose to rethink artistic (un)repeatability by making reference to another model of repetition which should be understood, specifically in theatrical terms, as intricately and essentially linked with difference. Deleuze's formulation of 'presence as perpetual variation' (Cull 2009: 12) and his 'ontological prioritisation of difference' (Cull 2009: 1) indicate that the interplay of difference and repetition is much more complex and playful, especially when it comes to performance, than the scientific model of duplicating experiments. As opposed to a vague promise of regurgitating the same results, containers can be seen to operate in a Deleuzian framework where each repetition becomes as such by way of its difference, of its ability to be the unduplicatable *first*.

Repetition and difference

In *Difference & Repetition*, Deleuze argues that repetition is experienced essentially as difference and uses theatre as his model to problematise definitions of repetition as generality, analogy, sameness and similarity. Repeated actions, instances or occurrences cannot be accumulated, put side by side, and understood, judged, evaluated and categorised according to relative factors or according to how truly or skilfully they *represent* an origin. On the contrary, each repetition is its own origin, always a first: 'This is the apparent paradox of festivals: they repeat an "unrepeatable". They do not add a second and a third time to the first, but carry the first time to the "nth" power' (Deleuze 1994: 1). Translating the 'paradox of festivals' into the vocabulary of another work by Deleuze, one could argue that a festival 'proceeds not by addition, but by subtraction, by amputation' (1997: 239). Each time the festival happens, it leads not to 'one more' Edinburgh, but rather to 'one less'. The apparent reversal of common sense here serves as an operation to destabilise the ontology of performance that sees difference as an indifferent by-product of repetition by claiming that it is indeed the primary condition of repetition.

A rhizomatic image of time might help explicate what Deleuze suggests here. If time is conceived as a more or less linear progression of moments, it logically follows that any festival (or repetition) that comes after a previous version would add onto it. The festivals would collect in time like beads on a string and they would be defined as repetitions by the fact that they repeat something identifiable: the colour red, a certain shape, or beadness. Yet for Deleuze, what defines a festival is its unrepeatability, its uniqueness and firstness. The moment we identify what exactly is repeated in each festival, it ceases to be one. The festival maintains its festivalness so long as it is different. Yet its difference becomes, or becomes understood or experienced as, repetition by the way it reorganises the past from a handful of beads thrown in the air to a constellation or a rhizome of beads. One less festival as yet another constellation is ticked off, exhausted.

Deleuze's proposition resonates with my conceptualisation of containers as a way of negotiating their multiplicity. There are many cats within the Cat, each of which necessarily presents a variation. Something remains and might appear to be overtly repeated – the name, the visible form, the physical constraints – yet Deleuze teaches us that it is not this recognisable similarity but the very variation that enables the Cat to be repeated at all. Each version already constitutes one less Cat, even without having travelled out of Grotowski's hands into other contexts. Rethinking containers in terms of repetition and difference suggests that what remains and what changes in each rendering is incalculable, ever-shifting. Within such a dynamic interplay, it is mandatory to allow for a playful dance between the knowns, givens or set of instructions of a container and its unknowns, points of research, sense of direction.

While it is tempting to equate technique with repetition and ethics with variation, the reverse is equally plausible; the relationships between the inner and outer components, and between technique and ethics, in containers are too complex and interwoven to allow clear-cut divisions. Perhaps the festivalness of a container derives from a third component which further qualifies Kumiega's dialectic of technique and ethics: experience. In addition to the physical and mental rules and instructions that constitute the Cat, there is an experience of doing the Cat that is irreducible to any of its parts and is repeated differently every time anyone does it somewhere in the world: one less Cat.

The addition of experience has implications regarding how containers transport knowledge, or the possibility of knowledge. Viewing a form not as a thing in itself that changes or stays the same over time but as a container for a lived visceral, somatic, psychophysical, phenomenological experience aligns knowledge with the experience of that form rather than with its name or shape. While maintaining the two sides of technique and ethics, this approach resists the temptation to prioritise either. It allows the practitioner to be aware of and indeed relish the shifting playfulness between the specific givens and the unknowns in any one form. Viewing exercises, actions or improvisational structures as containers thus renders it easier and more organically possible to let what is known and what is unknown to swap places – thus, to dislocate knowledge.

Another container: Stepping

I would like to now turn to Stepping, one of the central containers used in both *at·home·on·the·road* and *Migrant Steps*, in order to elucidate how seeing an exercise as a container that operates within the dynamic interplay of difference and repetition allowed me to circumvent some of the challenges I laid out earlier. As it appears to be the case with many of my findings, the discovery of this container was also serendipitous. While it coincided with my work on the tortoise, it was born outside the space of my research, while teaching a practical workshop introducing Odin Teatret.[3] Given the vastness of the material and the limitations of time and my own position as a researcher as opposed to a member of the company, I had decided to dedicate the session to one practical concept: *sats*. *Sats* is action in stillness or stillness in action, best described with reference to a pendulum's moment of pause at the top or with the image of 'a frozen waterfall' (Grotowski 1997b: 303). My objective was to offer a number of ways in which students could have a physical, experiential and observational understanding of *sats*.

I started with a basic version of Iben Nagel Rasmussen's wind dance (*Bridge of Winds* 2015). Students were quick to learn the step. The tempo-rhythm of the wind dance was there, yet not the dance itself in that there was no wind, no *sats*. Judging that this had to do with students not using their weight, I instructed them to pay attention to how they engage with the floor: 'Think about the centre of gravity bouncing off the floor,' 'Work with the spine of the foot, feeling the floor move from the ball of the foot to the heel and back,' 'Use the breath to really allow your weight to drop' and 'Imagine the surface as a big bouncy ball.' Nothing worked. In the end, I decided to do something radical and break the dance down. I thought it would take a few minutes to demonstrate what I meant; little did I foresee that I was about to stumble upon the key container for the tortoise that would occupy me for years to come.

I said: let me put them in touch with weight and bounce. Let us take a step and retract.

I stand in a neutral stance, feet parallel, weight distributed equally between both feet and on the soles of the feet. I shift my weight between various places on the feet before I find this place in the middle somewhere. I let my body sink comfortably into the floor via the feet, making full firm contact with the floor, while I simultaneously rise off the floor, my spine is long with breathing space between the vertebra and my head is nicely balanced on top. Each breath that enters and leaves my body moves me ever so slightly but on the whole I am still and balanced, grounded and light. It is from this place that I let one foot lift off the floor, shifting the weight completely to the other, what I will call the anchor foot. The other, lifted foot (which I will call the traveller foot) travels away from the rest of the body, in any direction, until it lands on a spot, some distance from where it had originally been. I redistribute my weight and shift it onto the traveller foot, until I am almost wholly transported to this new place. I could almost lift the anchor foot off the floor (a state where I can stay as long or as little as desired) when I retrieve my weight back onto the anchor foot (which can be done as slowly or quickly as desired) and return the traveller foot back where it had started. I then start again, with the traveller foot once again lifting off the floor and this time flying away from my body in some other direction, at some other pace, at a different height off the floor, and in order to stay where it lands a different amount of time than before. And again . . .

I asked students to use the exercise to turn their attention to their weight and notice what happens as they shift it from one foot to the other, gradually, paying attention to the minute movements, eventually transferring their full weight back and forth but not assuming or glossing over any of the moments in the process. I asked them to continue to do the whole action again and again, in new directions, trying new distances, and gradually I added different elements to do with the mechanics of the action, suggesting that they play with its tempo-rhythm and duration. All along I wanted them to stay with their experience on the action: What happened at that moment the weight tipped over to the other foot? Could they slow the moment down so much that the edge of the balance could be more pronounced for them? Alternately, could they speed up the whole process while maintaining the minutiae, to borrow Kumiega's term?

The group was becoming too good at the exercise. Students were challenging themselves physically, really stretching their limbs, really breathing with their feet and their spines, yet eyes were glazed, in that 'Look I am so focused!' stare. Nothing was happening. I stopped the work and suggested we add another variable to the equation, the eyes. Could they make a choice about where they placed their gaze each time they repeated the action? When they lifted the traveller foot, were they looking at it? Were they looking out, towards where they were going? Or were they looking in another direction entirely, back over the shoulder?

I stand in neutral, feet parallel, weight distributed equally between both feet and on the soles of the feet; each breath that enters and leaves my body moves me ever so slightly but on the whole I am still and balanced, grounded and light. I imagine a circle around me; I see it lightly as boundaries on the floor or an invisible glass wall surrounding my body, like a glass fanus or an aura. It is from this place that I let my eyes wander; with a clear ocular gesture I make a choice and look outside the circle. Following this impulse, I let my foot lift off the floor, break the invisible barrier and travel outside it, until it lands on a spot, some distance from where it has originally been. I follow, until I am almost wholly transported to this new place (where I can stay as long or as little as desired). I look around. I see something and I retrieve myself back into the circle (which can be done as slowly or quickly as desired). I then start again, with my eyes taking the lead, while paying attention to my weight and balance, the sensation of the floor, the tempo-rhythm and spatial dynamics of my movement, while following the impulse of another ocular gesture. And again . . .

So far I had given only one image to students. For those who found it very difficult to work on taking a step, I had suggested imagining standing in the middle of a circle and allowing one foot to exit that circle, step on the other side and then draw back in. They could think of the size of the circle to help them vary the length of each step, if it helped. (Through this formulation, it seems the tortoise must have been present from the beginning.) The eyes added a whole new set of possibilities, a previously unchartered pocket within the container, with multiple dimensions. One could turn the gaze this way or that, look afar or near, with or against the distance of the step; one could work with the plasticity of the eyes, play with correspondences or disharmonies with the rest of the body; one could find stimuli in the world to trigger the action, both the step and the retreat, and these stimuli could be real sights of actual people in the room, or sights from memory that working with the eyes can unlock. But of course I didn't tell them any of this. I asked simple questions: What do you see? Is it something you see that makes you move? Are your eyelids heavy or light?

As soon as the eyes became alive, fuller images with more detailed outlines began to appear. The silhouette of each moment traced by each student seemed to touch the world in more intricate and unpredictable ways; while on the one hand students appeared more aligned, on the other hand, paradoxically, their actions were more complex, multifaceted, sometimes self-contradictory, articulating multiple points of contact. The room also became interconnected as students had opened themselves up to real, uncalculated impulses from each other. Even though they were not asked to and were not pursuing direct relationships, ripples of actions and reactions travelled through the space. I stopped the exercise, praised the shift in energy, quoted Grotowski like you do ('You have to be passive in action, active in the seeing'; Grotowski 1997a: 378) and moved on, returning eventually to the wind dance after a long-winded digression.

Yet the Stepping exercise did not stay behind but became the core of my work in search of the tortoise. The dynamics of stepping away from oneself, outward into unchartered territory, coupled with the ability to retreat, captured something essential about the tortoise. It also resonated with my drifts. I continued working with this form with a collaborator on an initial attempt at encountering the tortoise and later during my solo devising process. When faced with the dislocation into the context of community theatre, the Stepping exercise was one of the containers of practice and research which served and still serves, as can be seen in the photograph from a recent workshop (figure 9.4), as my anchor foot.

Figure 9.4 Göze Saner does Stepping holding an umbrella.
Source: Scott Robinson.

Migrant stepping

I started working with the Stepping container in *Migrant Steps* initially during the workshops preceding the rehearsal/devising phase. Later, I revisited the form while generating and scoring material and it eventually became the main action of an ensemble scene, which I will describe ahead. Working with the exercise as a container, I was able to rely on the numerous entrances and exits that it contained, all of which had emerged as possibilities even in that first workshop at Rose Bruford. Prioritising the experience of the container, I found that different trajectories in and out of the form can coexist non-hierarchically; they are equally important and valuable to the experience of the person occupying it. However, they afford a kind of flexibility and a multiplicity of possibilities, allowing the experience of the container to remain fresh, able to surprise the person doing it, as well as the person leading it.

15 December 2013. In an initial attempt at the container, I note how it contains certain principles of acting and implicitly trains the person occupying it. Due to the precarious balance found in the repeated action of shifting weight from an anchor foot to the other displaced foot, the container serves to build physical awareness and draws attention to weight, balance and subtle mechanisms of the body. It sensitises the doer to the spine, breath, toes and feet, centre of gravity, and opens the chest and back to the world in all directions. This can be seen as the layer of mechanics, as well as that of self-awareness. Working with a small group of participants, I find this particular focus fruitful yet challenging. To the participant-performers, focusing on the body comes naturally; the simple instructions of a container like the Stepping exercise already indicate a number of things to do, repeating the verb 'notice.' They do just that and do not assume awareness in the way a more seasoned performer might. Participants later feed back details encountered – that they are impressed with how much flexibility they discover in their feet or how they hear themselves breathing through their noses. The space and time opened up to observe one's own physicality translate into an experience of dilated self-awareness. However, at this level the exercise is short-lived; without the focus on training, participants find it difficult to sustain the kind of research or investigation into the workings of their bodies that Barba mentions in his account of the Cat, for example. The exercise is repeatedly interrupted: one participant notices a detail, say the specific way in which she holds her shoulders, and immediately wants to stop and report, having completed that task.

In order to counteract this obstacle, I try to give another objective, with the hope that it will help sustain the container a little longer: the sense of music. I suggest hearing a song in their heads, listening to the voices, the instruments, the varying beats. I know from previous work that the playful relationship with tempo-rhythm, duration and pace, coupled with the active, noticed breath, sometimes allows the exploration to become musical, opening up a broad range of steps, from graceful and attentive to clownesque and staccato. Rather than asking for an abstract sense of musicality, I propose starting with a known song. While this layer emphasises artistic play and works only if it comes after establishing a minimum degree of self-awareness, I anticipate that it will shift the attention away from the body and give space for creativity. Yet this musicalised step, and even my rather casual demonstration of it, intimidates participants. They ask me to teach the dance, if they are to dance. Are they supposed to rhythmically repeat the step in certain directions?

I let this go and move to the imaginary world emerging around the container. Drawing an imaginary shell around one's person implies both a journey out of oneself and the thought of entering another person's. The image of a threshold becomes prominent; many doors are opened and many fences climbed. In the same way the Cat finally serves to create relationships between performers, the stepping container also has a layer of relationality through this image; the steps are not self-generated but rather reactions to others in the space. In order to make explicit use of this potentiality, I ask participants to pair up and repeat the exercise with the added element of musicality in pairs. They stand close to one another with their partners, so that each step is inevitably entering into the other's sphere. A sense of music is found immediately and participants start laughing, vocalising, acting in a more animated way. Two women have a kind of face-off, whereas two others work together in stop-and-starts, where each pause or stop, evidently caused by the feeling of self-consciousness, makes them genuinely wait for the other to resolve the issue and restart. The resulting work is a beautiful example of organic action–reaction. After this experience, participants are more open to the previous focus, though perhaps the focus on physical awareness is to some extent forgotten.

22 December 2013. I return to the sense of physical awareness by using variation focused on the eyes. I also add the imaginative association: What if they are each in their invisible shells, with each step poking their heads out like tortoises? I ask participants to start with the eyes, and then the nose, the face and the extended neck to give themselves an opportunity to really find the details again. Perhaps they can even think of their skin as hard like the tortoise's to see how they feel the air? Is it difficult to slide out of the shell? Or is it smooth and easy? These questions lead to various results – some performers remember events and stories through the work and want to tell the rest, while others are suddenly blocked, finding it infantile trying to imitate a tortoise. Asked to focus just on the movement of the eyes, even the doubtful begin to gradually fill up the container with detailed, multifaceted images. The recurring physical action also becomes identifiable, palpable in the space. It is one of searching. In that space, doing the stepping exercise, I suddenly see women looking for something, and the most significant transformation of the container takes place.

I stand in neutral, balanced and still. I am loosely aware of a circle around me, like lace in the air or a shift in temperature. I poke my head out of it, followed by a foot. I let my whole body follow. I note how different it is where I have landed, how it feels, looks or smells different until I can no longer stay. I retreat, but once again I sense something out

there, to which I am drawn, and before I can hold back, I find my foot wandering in yet
another direction. I follow then pull back, and then again . . .

We build towards yet another aspect of the container that can be called the
theatrical or the performative. By creating awareness within as well as without,
the container invites its doer to notice impulses, dilate moments of decisions,
reversals and *sats*, and experience a theatricalised sense of occupying the world.
The steps do not ever go anywhere and the doer allows the experience of being
stuck – the seemingly unending repetition of the moment of not going – to
grow, fill up, resonate. The feelings attached are often annoyance, frustration,
anger, which seem at times to be directed at the exercise itself, and at others, to
the person leading it! It is possible to get help from the exercise itself to contain
these feelings. Perhaps this is also where the archetypal presence comes into play,
as the image of the shell around one's body implies. It is through experiencing
this containment within a confined space, out of which one is able to emerge
only temporarily, but from which one is compelled to continue to step out, ad
infinitum, that one meets the wandering tortoise.

2 February 2014. During the rehearsal phase, we repeat the exercise regularly.
One day, as I lead up to the final layer, I decide to add yet another element based
on a quote I remember noting from Luce Irigaray's *Elemental Passions*: 'Call
yourself. Give, yourself, names' (1992: 7). I recall reading something similar in
one of the drift journals and envision a sad, poignant image. So in search of a
scene, when I lead the Stepping container, I ask participants to add yet another
layer and to say their names with each step, picturing and calling the attention of themselves standing somewhere far or near, in front or behind. And
it makes perfect sense: the image has been there all along. The container is of
women calling themselves, quite literally, searching for themselves, and by the
same token re-owning their names by giving them to themselves. Paradoxically,
this is the element of the container that the majority of the participants find
the easiest. They are most relaxed and playful while playing with the action of
calling alongside the stepping and retracting. At times the voices echo the calls
of others – husbands, children, elders – and at others it is very clear that each
woman is herself calling herself, sometimes discreetly and shyly almost behind
others' backs, and at others freely and openly, as if calling out to play. Rather
differently from my premonition, we laugh a lot that day and the performative
incarnation of this moment makes the audience laugh as well. After an initial
ensemble song and dance sequence which serves to greet the audience, a performer is left behind. She confides in the audience, quoting from the journal:
'Years ago, I came to London imagining material riches. But in the meantime I
forgot to enrich my soul. And I got lost, disappeared. Now on a rainy autumn
morning in London, I am looking for the me I lost, longingly.'[4] At which point
she takes a step and calls out her name: 'Periiiihaaaan!' She repeats facing different directions and one by one, she is joined by the rest of the group, all calling
out their names, in this direction then that, until the room is filled with the
cacophonous yet alive voices of women shouting out their own names.

Final steps

A hare, a hound, a horse raced by –
so rapidly they seemed to fly.
The tortoise gasped, sat goggle-eyed –
'I'll never be that quick,' she sighed.
Buckley and Carle 2009

The repetitiveness of a container embodies the slow, continuous process of a laboratory. Other strategies fly ahead like hares, while working repeatedly with containers moves at the pace of a tortoise. Yet the example of the Stepping exercise demonstrates how unpredictably containers can develop and transform. While the initial instruction 'Take a step and retreat' remains, it echoes differently in each instance the container is embodied. Focusing on the experience contained allows the practitioner to hold the technical/ethical aspects lightly and respond to the lived event. It also permits the dialectic of techniques and ethics – the craft or the engagement with the primary material – to be transmitted within the exercise, often indirectly.

The hollowness of the container indicates the space for play. Each time a container is embodied, it activates the dynamic interplay of difference and repetition, allowing what is known and what is unknown to shift and change. While it is tempting to draw divisions between what is repeated and what is changed by attempting to observe quantifiable elements, the power of a container lies in its resistance to being contained. When describing or leading the work on a container, its elusiveness becomes apparent. Points of attention, ways in and out, and various layers coexist and operate not as parts of a machine but as leaves in the wind. For instance I have articulated how working on the eyes not only activates an awareness of their corporeality but also invites into the work emotion, sensation, feeling. Furthermore, it activates purposeful seeing, opening up a whole other layer of perceptions, the placement of one's attention, as well as imagination, memory and association. It is in this sense that I find containers most helpful in archetypalising or archetypally engaging with actions as they allow a literal experience of what might otherwise be seen symbolically, such as looking for oneself, thus providing an experience of specificity and the unknown.

Acting containers function by way of drawing contours around experiences; they shape the materiality of performance or acting in a way to render it repeatable. While exercises exercise certain faculties or skills and improvisations rely on free play within given sets of rules, containers (and viewing exercises or improvisations as containers) liberate the form from its own function and allow it to have a life of its own. This aspect of the container reconciles how performance can at once be a form of sustained inquiry, a repetition, as Kathleen Vaughan emphasises, 'a *re*-search, a re-cherche, a looking again *at* and *for* fundamental elements' (2009: 167), yet always have its eye on originality, difference. Kershaw articulates this paradox as 'boundless specificity' (Kershaw and

Nicholson 2011: 66). On the one hand the event of live performance – here, the embodiment of a container – is utterly bound by the surrounding temporal spatial details, therefore always one of a kind. On the other hand, a container exists as an entity in and of itself, apart from and beyond its ephemeral articulations. It crosses linguistic, geographic, cultural and generic boundaries, and may even appear in unexpected places. The knowledge within achieves boundless specificity as it is always at once infinitely situated in the experiences of the practitioners occupying it, and independently, as if it had its own life.

Notes

1 A note from my original walking notebook. 28 November 2010, Stamford Hill Walk.
2 During my walks I fell in love with the Lloyds Tower and found myself returning to it unintentionally. One day I set this instruction and followed, got close to and took photographs of the tower without being seen by it. 6 March 2011, Visiting 1: Lloyds Tower.
3 15 October 2008 and 22 October 2008. Two four-hour workshops for two groups of final-year students on the BA European Theatre Practices programme.
4 Shared Journal 2, 13 October 2013, Liverpool Street Station Walk.

References

Barba, Eugenio. 1997. "An Amulet Made of Memory: The Significance of Exercises in the Actor's Dramaturgy." *TDR* 41 (4): 127–132.
Barba, Eugenio. 2002. "Actor's Training (1959–1962)". In *Towards a Poor Theatre*. New York: Routledge.
Buckley, Richard and Eric Carle. 2009. *The Foolish Tortoise*. London: Simon and Schuster.
Cambray, Joseph and Linda Carter. 2004. *Analytical Psychology: Contemporary Perspectives in Jungian Analysis*. Hove: Brunner-Routledge.
Carnicke, Sharon Marie and Jean Benedetti. 1993. "From 'The Actor: Work on Oneself'." *TDR* 37 (1): 38–42.
Casement, Ann. 1998. *Post-Jungians Today: Key Papers in Contemporary Analytical Psychology*. London: Routledge.
Christoffersen, Erik Exe. 1993. *The Actor's Way*. London: Routledge.
Christofferson, Eric Exe. 2004. "Introduction to Peripeti and Serendipity." *Peripeti* 1 (2): 5–15.
Croyden, Margaret. 1974. "The Phenomenon of Jerzy Grotowski." In *The Contemporary Experimental Theatre: Lunatics, Lovers and Poets*, 135–168. New York: McGraw Hill.
Cull, Laura. 2009. *Deleuze and Performance*. Edinburgh: Edinburgh University Press.
Davis, Robert H. 2003. *Jung, Freud, Hillman: Three Depth Psychologies in Context*. Westport, CT: Praeger.
Debord, Guy. 2006. "Theory of the Dérive." In *Situationist International Anthology*, translated and edited by Ken Knabb, 62–66. Berkeley, CA: Bureau of Public Secrets.
Deleuze, Gilles. 1994. *Difference & Repetition*. London: Athlone.
Deleuze, Gilles. 1997. "One Less Manifesto." In *Mimesis, Masochism, & Mime: The Politics of Theatricality in Contemporary French Thought*, edited by Timothy Murray, 239–258. Ann Arbor, MI: University of Michigan Press.
Grotowski, Jerzy. 1997a. "Performer." In *The Grotowski Sourcebook*, edited by Richard Schechner and Lisa Wolford, 376–380. London: Routledge.

Grotowski, Jerzy. 1997b. "Tu es le fils de quell qu'un." In *The Grotowski Sourcebook*, edited by Richard Schechner and Lisa Wolford, 294–305. London: Routledge.

Hauke, Christopher. 2000. *Jung and the Postmodern: The Interpretation of Realities*. London: Routledge.

Heidegger, Martin. 1993. *Basic Writings*. New York: Harper Collins.

Hillman, James. 1977. "An Inquiry into Image." *Spring* (39): 62–88.

Hillman, James. 2008. *Animal Presences*. Putnam, CT: Spring.

Hunter, Lynette. 2009. "Valuing Performance/Practice as Academic Knowledge." In *Mapping Landscapes for Performance as Research: Scholarly Acts and Creative Cartographies*, edited by Shannon Rose Riley and Lynette Hunter, 199–205. London: Palgrave.

Irigaray, Luce. 1992. *Elemental Passions*. New York: Routledge.

Kapsali, Maria. 2010. "'I Don't Attack It, But It's Not for Actors': The Use of Yoga by Jerzy Grotowski." *Theatre, Dance and Performance Training* 1 (2): 185–198.

Kershaw, Baz. 2009. "Practice as Research Through Performance." In *Practice-led Research, Research-led Practice in the Creative Arts*, edited by Hazel Smith and Roger T. Dean, 104–125. Edinburgh: Edinburgh University Press.

Kershaw, Baz and Helen Nicholson. 2011. *Research Methods in Theatre and Performance*. Edinburgh: Edinburgh University Press.

Kumiega, Jennifer. 1985. *The Theatre of Grotowski*. London: Methuen.

Pitches, Jonathan, Simon Murray, Helen Poynor, Libby Worth, David Richmond and Jules Dorey Richmond. 2011. "Performer Training: Researching Practice in the Theatre Laboratory." In *Research Methods in Theatre and Performance*, edited by Baz Kershaw and Helen Nicholson, 137–162. Edinburgh: Edinburgh University Press.

Richards, Thomas. 1995. *At Work with Grotowski on Physical Actions*. London: Routledge.

Riley, Shannon Rose. 2009. "Lab/Studio." In *Mapping Landscapes for Performance as Research: Scholarly Acts and Creative Cartographies*, edited by Shannon Rose Riley and Lynette Hunter, 137–141. London: Palgrave.

Samuels, Andrew. 1985. *Jung and the Post-Jungians*. London: Routledge & Kegan Paul.

Saner, Göze. 2009. *From Tyrant to Clown and Back: An Actor's Practical Study of Archetype in Performance*. PhD Thesis, Royal Holloway, University of London.

Schino, Mirella. 2009. *Alchemists of the Stage: Theatre Laboratories in Europe*. Holstebro: Icarus.

Slowiak, James and Jairo Cuesta. 2007. *Jerzy Grotowski*. London: Routledge.

Spatz, Ben. 2015. *What a Body Can Do: Technique as Knowledge, Practice as Research*. Oxon: Routledge.

Stanislavski, Konstantin. 1993. *The Collected Works of Konstantin Stanislavsky*. Translated by Jean Benedetti. New York: Routledge.

Stanislavski, Konstantin. 2008. *An Actor's Work*. Translated by Jean Benedetti. Oxon: Routledge.

Stein, Murray and Raya A. Jones. 2010. *Cultures and Identities in Transition: Jungian Perspectives*. London: Routledge.

Tacey, David. 1998. "Twisting and Turning With James Hillman: From Anima to World Soul, from Academia to Pop." In *Post-Jungians Today: Key Papers in Contemporary Analytical Psychology*, edited by Ann Casement, 215–234. London: Routledge.

Vaughan, Kathleen. 2009. "*Mariposa*: The Story of New Work of Research/Creation, Taking Shape, Taking Flight." In *Practice-led Research, Research-led Practice in the Creative Arts*, edited by Hazel Smith and Roger T. Dean, 166–186. Edinburgh: Edinburgh.

Wangh, Stephen. 2000. *An Acrobat of the Heart*. New York: Vintage.

Watson, Ian. 2009. "An Actor Prepares: Performance as Research (PAR) in the Theatre." In *Mapping Landscapes for Performance as Research: Scholarly Acts and Creative Cartographies*, edited by Shannon Rose Riley and Lynette Hunter, 84–90. London: Palgrave.

Young-Eisendrath, Polly. 2004. *Subject to Change: Jung, Gender and Subjectivity in Psychoanalysis*. Hove: Brunner-Routledge.

Video and online sources

Erdoğan, Alev. *Göçmen Adımlar/Migrant Steps*. Documentary Film, 20 minutes. 2014. www.migrantsteps.com/tr/video.

Odin Teatret. *Calendar 2011*. Webpage. www.odinteatret.dk/arrangementer/2011/december/iben-arbejder-med-the-bridge-of-winds-paa-odin-teatret/ev•de•yol•da – at•home•on•the•road.aspx.

Odin Teatret Web TV. *Bridge of Winds 2015*. Online Video. 17 January 2015. http://livestream.com/OdinTeatretLiveStreaming/thebridgeofwinds.

Physical Training at Odin Teatret. Directed by Torgeir Wethal. 1972. Denmark: Odin Teatret Film. VHS.

Saner, Göze. *Göçmen Adımlar/Migrant Steps*. Video Documentation of Live Performance, 35 minutes. 7–9 March 2014. London: North London Community House. www.migrantsteps.com/tr/video.

Saner, Göze. *The Journey So Far*. Webpage. www.cafila-aeterna.com/the-journey-so-far.html.

Training at the "Teatr Laboratorium" in Wroclaw: Plastic and Physical Training. Directed by Torgeir Wethal. 1972. Denmark: Odin Teatret Film.

Vocal Training at Odin Teatret. Directed by Torgeir Wethal. 1972. Denmark: Odin Teatret Film.

Mad Lab – or why we can't do practice as research

Ben Spatz

> How is it possible to utter the word 'God' in a university seminar?
>
> Jonathan Boyarin (2008: 21)

This introduction/intervention responds to the title and underlying assumptions of the present volume rather than to its content.[1] Intended as a speculative polemic, it probes the boundaries of what is possible and what is desirable in PAR, highlighting some of the tendencies and assumptions that the concept of performance brings to research. As I see it, performance is both indispensable and limiting: an essential genealogy for the work discussed in this volume, but one that increasingly requires critical alternatives in order to continue pursuing its promise. In this piece I compare performance with practice as a basis for PAR, gesturing towards what may be an impossibly radical notion of experimentation in practice. I ask, without knowing the answer, where the epistemological and political boundaries of the PAR movement truly lie. While I do not attempt to analyse the specific contributions to this volume in these terms, I hope to pose a question that may be applied to these and other case studies – namely, whether research is unfolding through performance or through practice – and to show why that question matters.[2]

Genealogies of PAR

The distinction between 'performance as research' and 'practice as research' is usually glossed as a regional difference with little conceptual substance.[3] In this essay I reflect on the distinct lineages of performance and practice in contemporary thought, in order to show why it is necessary to think 'practice' and not just 'performance' as research; to demonstrate that the former is in a certain sense the more radical proposition; and to explore a few of its implications. My question is what would happen if PAR's implied reference to (theatrical) performance were allowed to expire, so that all that which may be called 'practice' became imaginable as research. In the wake of the practice turn in social and critical theory, we know that the concept of practice includes not only the performing, martial, and healing arts but also daily rituals of identification, enactments of kinship structure, religious calendars, domestic arrangements, sexual and professional relations, childrearing and education, repeated violences and micro-aggressions, and many other lived lineages. Here I challenge practitioner-researchers to question the assumed limits of 'practice' as an area of research and to face the ethical and political questions that arise from doing so – questions that are already of central concern to research in science and technology, but which are rarely deemed relevant to the apparently less dangerous fields of arts and humanities.

I will not attempt to develop a full genealogy of performance here, but merely mention a few books in which the concept of performance plays a central role and which have in turn contributed to the current circulation of that term: Schechner's *Performance Theory* (1988), Phelan's *Unmarked: The Politics of Performance* (1993), Carlson's *Performance: A Critical Introduction* (1996), McKenzie's *Perform or Else: From Discipline to Performance* (2001), Schneider's *Performing Remains: Art and War in Times of Theatrical Reenactment* (2011), and Taylor and Steuernagel's recent digital book *What Is Performance?* (2016). In an interview in the latter, Barbara Kirschenblatt-Gimblett is asked to name the main tenets of performance studies. 'The first tenet,' she replies,

> is to use performance as an organizing idea for thinking about almost anything. So I would start with that: performance as an organizing idea. That means that I can think about museums, everyday life, streets, cities, architecture, space, world's fairs, food. . . . Performance as an organizing idea is a very, very powerful concept.

Similarly, Richard Schechner has recently asserted that although performance studies (PS) is today almost always housed within theatre, dance, or communications departments, it is actually conceptually larger than any of these, because the 'broad spectrum' of performance is a more inclusive category.[4] For Schechner this suggests that, in the future, subjects like theatre and dance might well be housed within PS departments rather than the reverse. Yet one of the reasons why PS in its current incarnation has to be considered 'smaller' than theatre or dance (setting communications aside for now) is that the latter have well-developed practical wings while PS does not.

Theatre studies is taught alongside acting, directing, and theatrical production. Dance studies is taught alongside dance technique and choreography. Precisely because 'performance' is such a broad category, it is not clear what kind of artistic or embodied practice would go alongside PS other than some combination of theatre, dance, and visual and media arts. Although PS takes as its objects of study not only those artistic fields but also much wider areas of everyday life, cultural and religious practices, the performance of identity, and more, it is not clear how these 'broad spectrum' elements might be rendered within a situation of training and experimentation. What would it mean to create a university laboratory for practical experimentation in the performance of everyday life, or in the performance of cultural identity, or in the performance of religion? What problems might arise from attempting to implement such laboratories? Finally, is the concept of 'performance' strong enough to support experimentation in these areas? What does it mean to think about 'almost anything' in terms of performance, as Kirschenblatt-Gimblett suggests? What does this conceptual move accomplish, what kinds of practical and experimental work does it enable, and what does it prevent?

Let us begin from two senses of performance – two ways in which 'almost anything' can be analysed as performance – and consider how they are intertwined in the primary concerns of performance studies. As shorthand I will refer to these two meanings of performance as *representation* and *embodiment*, although I realize that those terms are no less contested than performance itself. By representation I mean the circulation of signs across one or more public spheres, those jointly imagined but culturally very real spaces in which communities and societies produce shared meaning through language, images, and other discursive forms (Warner 2002). By embodiment, on the other hand, I mean the centrality of the living organism in all that we might wish to discuss, even when we aim to displace the human and focus instead on technology or ecology, animals or plants.[5] In the core examples of performance, such as theatre and theatrical dance, representation and embodiment are tightly bound together in the singularity of an event that is both public and embodied. Performance, in this narrow sense, is what happens when embodiment enters a public sphere. At the intersection of representation and embodiment, we find the core tensions that have animated performance studies: efficacy and entertainment, liveness and mediation, autobiography and politics. However much the broad spectrum approach to performance exceeds these core examples, it always tends to return to them. The concept of performance is like a rubber band: it can be stretched quite far away from its central focus on *public embodiment*, but there is always a kind of centripetal pull or tendency returning it to this centre.

What if that centripetal pull were abandoned? What if the rubber band that pulls performance back towards theatre were allowed to snap? What if the junction of representation and embodiment were not accorded special priority, so that each of these could be explored independently of the other? It is easy to see what would happen on the representation side of the equation. Performance studies already pushes towards representation and away from embodiment when it studies films and television shows, musical soundtracks, advertising imagery, the Internet, and other forms of technology and media that circulate in today's cultural landscape of contested publics. Without its special allegiance to embodiment, PS merges with media studies, cultural studies, and literary studies. It is then just as easy to imagine what the 'practical' wing of such a field could include: from graphic design and music production to creative writing and journalism, there are plenty of crafts to choose from and many ways to negotiate the tensions between various artistic, commercial, and political aims. But let us consider the other side of the equation: embodiment. What would happen if performance studies were to move freely towards a concern with embodiment and embodied practice, abandoning the centripetal force that pulls it back towards representation and the idea of the public? Because the concern with public representation has been accorded so much priority in recent thinking, it is tempting to respond to this question by pointing out that no practice can avoid circulating in one or more relatively public spheres. Isn't the distinction between public and private itself an ideological myth, and the possibility of a purely private act merely an illusion? But this sidesteps the question, which is twofold: first, how far can the study of performance be stretched towards embodiment and away from representation? Second – more difficult – what kinds of practical experimentation does that stretching suggest?

I can take the most intimate, private-seeming, inward-directed practice and analyse it from the perspective of its implications as a representation circulating in a public sphere. (Isn't this very often what PS has done?) But if we can recognize that mediatized representations of embodiment circulate in public apart from any actual embodiment, then we must also recognize that embodied practice exceeds its public representation. This 'excess' has often been a focus of PS, but it has been figured as ephemeral rather than substantial and durable.[6] By treating performance as an artistic medium alongside literature, painting, and cinema, PS has continually reinscribed the containment of embodied practice within concerns about public representation. As a result, if we try to envision practical experimentation in embodied practice taking place outside any public sphere, it is difficult to know whether this should still be called performance. The concept of performance, despite its allegiance to embodiment, prevents us from fully grasping the potential of embodied experimentation. Although it stretches towards embodiment, the rubber band of performance always pulls embodiment back towards representation. In order to snap this rubber band, we have to shift from performance to practice. To think about something 'as' practice is to think about its embodied repetition rather than about its representation. In this way, practice provides a very different conceptual basis for experimentation than performance.

'Practice' in the context of 'practice as research' is often left undefined. We may think that by not defining practice we are leaving it radically open, but in fact this lack of a rigorously epistemological definition of practice compels us to fall back continuously upon mainstream, vernacular, and above all professional definitions and standards. Practice then seems to refer by default to something like 'professional' practice, which leads to a confusing tension since the professional application of knowledge is exactly what ought to be postponed by the invocation of research. If we want PAR to offer a substantive alternative to professional practice, then we need to base it on a more powerful definition of practice, one that draws upon the conceptual genealogy of that term to offer a different approach to rigour: not the rigour of professional application but the rigour of method.[7] What would happen if one were to establish a domain of practical experimentation that was founded on *practice* in this sense? What if, in other words, the theatrical reference point that prioritizes the public dimension of performance were removed so that practice itself became the sole reference point for an experimental field? We could think of this version of PAR as a kind of experimental philosophy, or as an extension of the impulse in performance art to postpone or abandon the audience. In either case the result is the same: all aspects of practice, regardless of whether they explicitly orient themselves towards a public sphere, become available for recognition as fundamentally epistemic and potentially experimental processes.

A genealogy of practice would likely begin from the work of Marx, Foucault, Certeau, Lefebvre, and Bourdieu, and then draw on more recent proposals by Saba Mahmood (2005), Nigel Thrift (2008), Elizabeth Shove et al. (2009), and other theorists of practice. The important question here is what might constitute the 'practical wing' for this field of practice studies. If performance studies begins from theatrical examples, then practice studies begins from everyday life. Yet it certainly includes many examples of everyday life that are in no sense mundane, such as life in a prison or a monastery, the lives of virtuosic athletes and performers, the lives of scientists, and the lives of indigenous peoples (insofar as ethnography has been richly informed by and contributed to the study of practice). The difference between performance and practice is therefore not aligned with a distinction between the liminal and the mundane. Rather, while performance continually pulls us back towards representation in the public sphere, practice does not. Practice studies is 'broad spectrum' PS without the latter's centripetal pull towards theatre. It includes fully technologized practices, from driving to particle physics, but it emphasizes embodied repetition rather than the circulation of representations across publics. There is in fact a rich legacy of *experimentation in practice* that looks quite different from the history of performing arts. Thinking for the moment only of established academic examples, we might include the 'first-person methodologies' of Francisco Varela (Varela and Shear 1999); the 'carnal sociology' of Loïc Wacquant (2006); the 'sensuous scholarship' of Paul Stoller (1997); the 'experimental anthropology' of Tim Ingold (2011); 'fieldwork in philosophy' as suggested by Paul Rabinow (2003); the ritual pedagogies surveyed by Catherine Bell (2007); critical martial arts studies (Bowman 2015); and embodied research in dance (Pakes 2010) and dance/movement therapy (Oerton 2012). Of course, the practices discussed by these theorists – social, cultural, economic, religious – do produce mediated publics as well as individuals and small groups. But there is no sense, in the literature on practice, of theatrical spectacle as a reference point.[8]

With these examples in mind, the difference between 'performance as research' and 'practice as research' can perhaps be linked to an ongoing tension in research between outcome and methodology. It is common to hear that performance as research has a natural affinity for the creation of public outcomes. Building on the association of performance with theatre, it may be assumed that PAR events (unlike experimental events in the sciences) will circulate relatively easily in public. Less often do we hear strictly methodological arguments on behalf of PAR, articulating its value purely in terms of knowledge produced. In the language of this volume's subtitle, the question is whether knowledge and methods necessarily generate impact through 'performance' or whether there might be some other ways. The importance of methodological arguments for PAR is that methodology is not immediately concerned with public representation. If we look at other fields of research, we see that methodology focuses precisely on the non-public dimension of research. We might even say that methodologies are specific alternatives to the idea of the public. Methodology, for better and for worse, pulls one away from the social implications of research and towards the emergent matter of inquiry. For this reason there can never be a methodology of performance, only various kinds of performance craft. Methodology cannot concern itself directly with the public sphere. It can, however, concern itself directly with practice, which can be both object and method of research. On these grounds, we might draw a conceptual distinction between performance studies, which can study 'almost anything' as performance, but only by relying upon relatively traditional methodologies, and practice as research, which suggests a field of experimentation as large as that of performance studies, but which treats practice as methodology rather than object of study. The implications of the latter are so wild that – as the somewhat whimsical title of my chapter suggests – it may not be desirable or even possible to implement. Without committing to the actual possibility or impossibility of practice as research in this sense, I will now consider some of these implications.

Duration, kinship, identity

The radical implications of conceiving practice as research are evident as soon as we think about duration. I recall André Gregory's somewhat sharp reply to Stephen Wangh's use of the name Grotowski in his book on actor training: 'There is something very important you somehow leave out of your book,' Gregory writes, 'namely the question of time' (Wangh 2000: 323). The question of time is one of the key factors that shapes and limits undergraduate education. This is not only because of its overall duration but also more fundamentally because of the limitations on how time can be structured in university life. How can we speak of 'practice' in the broad sense and then confine our research to the kind of temporal structures that academic institutions support? If we structure our practice around a standardized work week, do we not immediately foreclose many of the most powerful techniques of temporality, such as those related to sunrise and sunset, to the experience of staying awake overnight, and to the change of seasons? Ritual calendars are laid out by of the day, days of the week, seasons of the year, and sometimes longer cycles. How then could a university-based laboratory, with its rigorously seasonless time, undertake experimentation in practice? It is difficult enough to study a long-term phenomenon like kinship or identity using sociological methods that require tracking individuals across many years. How much more difficult would it be to explore such phenomena through longitudinal experimentation?

Duration is the opposite of a symbol because it cannot be detached from its materiality. Duration cannot circulate as a sign of itself because it always takes exactly as long as it means.[9] As an alternative, one might engage with kinship or identity by extracting and working with a mere slice of technique. This is surely more feasible, but if the goal is to intervene substantively in the practice of life – producing new forms of kinship, new identities, new lifeways – then surely more than a slice of technique will be needed. To work experimentally on kinship or identity is first of all a logistical problem: How can the methodological clocks of long-term experimental practice be aligned with the institutional clocks of the university? But it is also an ethical and even a spiritual problem. More than we realize, secularism is produced through a detachment from seasonality that prevents us from making full use of the hours of the day. Perhaps, then, it is not that contemporary academic institutionality just happens to block durational experiments. Rather, durational experimentation is explicitly proscribed in institutional contexts because it is enormously powerful. To experiment with duration is to risk destabilizing kinship, identity, and other fundamental building blocks of human ontology. It is not that university timetables happen to be incompatible with other approaches to temporality, but that they are intentionally designed to prevent alternatives from being realized. It is already risky enough to assert the validity of diverse lifeways from a sociological or anthropological perspective. Can we imagine going further, to instantiate such alternatives within a framework of university research?

Here again we find that the concept of performance, with its constant referral of practice back to the public sphere, works to provoke experimentation and at the same time to contain it in harmlessness. Performance makes space for durational acts that push the limits of contemporary practice, as in the work of Tehching Hsieh and Marina Abramovic. At the same time, defining these practitioners as *performance artists* distances their potentially world-breaking durations from the domain of practice and contains them within the more restricted domain of performance. By framing them as exceptional acts deserving of spectatorship, performance prevents us from imagining these kinds of durations as ones that could transform the everyday. The same ambiguous tendency of performance appears whenever publicly embodied acts provoke controversy, as in the famous 1990 case of the 'NEA Four' in the United States (Zeigler 1994). Artists push the envelope of what is socially allowable under the cover of artmaking. The fact that they are making works in the public sphere brings controversy but may also help to defuse it. Obviously those who were offended by the NEA Four would have had fewer grounds for public complaint if the acts had been purely private. But I wonder what kind of outcry might arise today if similar acts were funded as academic research and intended to produce not individual artworks but new embodied techniques for general dissemination. The performance acts of the NEA Four were provocative in the public sphere, but it was the growing movement of queer and feminist sexual politics – a field of practice rather than performance – that constituted the radical basis for those acts. To what extent did the defence of these acts consist of distancing them, as performance, from the transformation of everyday life? In many places one can now probably teach the work of the NEA Four from a historical, spectatorial perspective without too much controversy. Teaching practical classes based on their embodied techniques could be considerably more risky.[10]

There is some consensus within PS that the sexual, cultural, durational, and bodily transgressions of late twentieth-century performance art were beneficial, an important part of parallel feminist and queer social movements. Yet I suspect that the implicit reference to representation in the public sphere plays an important role here. Would Chris Burden shooting himself or Marina Abramovic carving a star in her abdomen be accorded the same historical assessment if these acts had not been undertaken within the frame of performance art but as research projects in an academic laboratory? When we teach our students that these radical acts were accomplished, do we also teach them how to use their bodies in these ways? I am not suggesting that we reevaluate these acts or that we ought to be teaching these techniques today. I am simply pointing to how performance can function as a container for radical embodied acts by framing them as isolated and exceptional. On inspection, it appears that performance can be used as a kind of 'cover' insofar as the performing artist is understood as not actually transgressing accepted norms of sexuality, religion, racial identity, or kinship structure but merely putting images of such transgression into the public sphere (where they may be debated and perhaps condemned). In this way the centripetal pull towards theatre protects the transgressive embodied act by referring it back to representation, decreasing its apparent reality and repeatability as practice. The question here is whether a context of research could serve to cultivate and protect radical acts in a different way, not by framing them as representations but by establishing their methodological rigour at the level of practice.

A few more recent examples can be found in Katherine Profeta's account of her long-term collaboration with dancemaker Ralph Lemon. This work is framed as a precedent for PAR: 'Performance was a laboratory for everything else: ontology, epistemology, anthropology, sociology, politics. I understood "performance as research" before that phrase took on its current cachet' (2015: xi). Notably, Profeta sets up a tension between the 'research' underpinning Lemon's *Trilogy* and the necessity of producing an artistic work within a fairly conventional theatrical situation. She describes her own 'gut feeling that the dialogues, tensions, and provisional solutions of our process, all of which I was attempting to archive in my notebook, were always going to be more interesting than any scene we might stage inside a proscenium frame' (205). Profeta proposes that by 'declaring that the larger process and all its many by-products were, collectively, the product', Lemon 'did much to shift the thinking, within the rehearsal room, among his presenters, and among his long-term audiences'. Nevertheless, she returns again and again to acknowledge the capture of this reframing by the institutional realities of theatrical production, wherein 'the economics support-ing all this process dictated that the largest number of people experiencing the work would be experiencing whatever part we put forward on the proscenium stage' (205).[11] At least for Profeta, it seems clear that some of the radical poten-tial of the embodied research was undercut by the need to return, via perfor-mance, to the field of public representation.

Can we imagine a context in which this return would not be economically necessary, a situation in which the potentially transformative discoveries made along the way could be supported on methodological grounds and made avail-able as practice rather than as research? Under such conditions, could experi-ments with interculturalism then be understood to produce new microcultures and new hybrid or composite identities rather than new artistic works?[12] This is perhaps primarily a question of power and economics, but it also depends upon the relationship between performance and practice. For Profeta and Lemon, the framework of theatrical performance enabled long-term research in practice. At least in a U.S. context, it remains unthinkable that universities could support long-term embodied research without such a goal. Indeed, without any real alternative to the production of artistic works, it may seem as if 'pure research' would indicate a kind of dwindling or reduction, with artists disappearing into an invisible private domain. But the domain of research is not private in the sense of being socially isolated or politically ineffective. Rather, research can be a site for the development and transmission of radical practices that are not shaped into or contained within an artistic work. Freed from the need to func-tion as representations of alternatives, research in practice could become a site for actual alternatives, for living research. This is a more, not less, radical propo-sition than can be sustained by the frame of performance. But it also presents certain problems.

I am currently working on a research project designed to test the possibility of developing a new embodied technique of Jewishness in a laboratory setting.[13] My claim is that, rather than working with Jewish songs in order to create a performance or an approach to performer training, I am experimenting directly with Jewishness itself. By singing particular songs, with particular people and in particular ways, I am attempting to produce new techniques of identity – perhaps even what Deleuze might call 'molecular' races (Saldanha 2006). At the moment this claim is largely conceptual, functioning at the level of language. However, I can already observe how a certain feeling of safety disappears as soon as I cut the rubber band that attaches my experimental practice to performance. After all, it is not uncommon to learn 'traditional' songs as part of actor training. When learned in this way, songs are treated like dramatic scripts, as embodied forms intended for public representation. The moment I sever the connection with public performance, the frame of the project shifts and the relationship to songs becomes at once more open and more risky. Why are we singing reli-gious songs, if not for performance? Are we crossing the ethically and politically significant boundary between secular and religious practice, between theatre and ritual? Perhaps the teaching of songs seems innocuous enough even when unframed as performance. What if I ask my research assistants to keep the sabbath, in order to discover what effect this ancient Jewish embodied technique might have on individuals not identified as Jewish?[14] There are too many questions arising from the project to investigate further here. I only want to underline how different these questions are once the goal of performance is removed. I suspect it would raise no eyebrows if I directed my team to observe the sabbath publicly, as performance art. Even in a university context, this act would be rendered safe through its relationship to performance. We would be performing the sabbath rather than practising it. Asking a researcher to keep sabbath as an experimental practice, with no public performance in mind, is a more thoroughly experimental and perhaps more culturally provocative idea.

Are we willing to go beyond the performance of kinship, identity, ritual, or any other powerful human territory, in order to engage them experimentally at the level of practice? Can we imagine alternative lifeways touching upon sexuality, religion, racialization, and economics being practised within an academic framework, not as performance but as research and justified not in terms of public representation but on methodological grounds? If not, I suggest, then we are not yet ready to undertake practice as research.

Epistemic futures

How far might the bounds of prevailing academic embodied technique be pushed by such a logic of practice as research? In an interview about the relevance of his social epistemology to artistic experimentation, Hans-Jörg Rheinberger describes research in this way:

> What I just called "exploratory activity" is something that situates itself in the space of *bricolage*, and this is a dangerous space. It is an unsecured space. . . . [I]t is not something that one would wish to impose on everyday life, or on society as a whole.
>
> (Rheinberger with Schwab 2013: 218)

Rheinberger's comment tacitly assumes that everyday life is experienced as relatively secure, so that experimental interruptions of the status quo are not worth the risk. This is a position of privilege. If one lives under conditions of insecurity or precarity, then perhaps the manifestation of 'exploratory activity' and 'dangerous' or 'unsecured' practices in the midst of everyday life is precisely desirable. If dominant techniques of kinship, identification, sexuality, or temporality are experienced as violent, then perhaps a logic of rigorous experimentation in everyday life is exactly what is needed.

My research in Jewish identity-as-technique aims to push academic institutionality towards increasingly radical experiments in practice. At the same time,

I acknowledge a certain conservatism in this approach. It is a methodological conservatism, stemming from my respect for the durational dimension of academia itself. In Europe and the United States, culturally dominant forms of art were thoroughly interrogated in the twentieth century along with much debate and controversy. The legacy of European 'high' art has now been through so many formalisms and deconstructions that little can surprise the jaded in these areas. As I argued above, the arts have been marked as a zone of experimentation in a way that both allows them to transgress and defuses the power of their transgression. Knowledge, in the sense of academic disciplinarity, has not yet undergone such radical experimentalization. Countercultural impulses have led to the establishment of critical fields like cultural studies, postcolonial studies, queer studies, and of course performance studies, but in most cases the traditional methods and forms of academic knowledge production remain in place. Because I too respect these forms, I am not calling here for something like a Dadaism of the sciences in which the frameworks of knowledge production would be smashed and replaced by entirely different forms. As tempting as such a proposition might be, my sense is that it would merely reproduce the same formalisms and transgressions that we have already seen, unless it were able to build upon – rather than dismissing – the history of academic disciplinarity. What I describe here is therefore not a chaos of postdisciplinarity but a purposeful and politically aware expansion of what counts as knowledge. Rather than getting rid of disciplinarity, I am asking what would happen if we treated fields of practice as disciplines and created formal spaces for experimental approaches to those practices we consider most fundamental.

The more rigorously methodological PAR is, the more powerful it becomes as a site for developing genuine alternatives to the world, effectively incarnating what Rheinberger and others have called 'machines for making the future'. The power of such machines resides in their detachment from existing social structures. But this means that there is no inherent link between experimental practice and any particular vision of politics or the future. Instead, links between the knowledge produced through experimental practice and the kinds of social and political worlds we want to live in will have to be built, step by step. This is already evident to anthropologists of science, who remind us how easy it is for laboratory researchers to forget that what they are making may in turn remake the world. There is no inherent 'ethics on the laboratory floor' (van der Burg and Swierstra 2013); such an ethics must be constructed. The same holds for the ethics and politics of experimental practice, which are quite different from those that apply to performance. The ethics and politics of experimental practice are above all institutional. They are not about manifesting singular radical acts in the public sphere but about radically transforming the structures of institutionality. They invite us not to ignore the power of spectacle and event but to locate and ground this power as much in their undercurrent flows of shared knowledge as in the circulation of their representations. They ask us to turn our focus away from what heightened moments represent and towards where they come from and what they accomplish at the level of practice. Most of all, they suggest that even the most basic and unquestioned practices that structure our shared worlds may be open to radical transformation through experimentation.

In its radical expansion of theatre studies, performance studies has remained bound to a conceptual model that is implicitly attached to the appearance of embodied practice in fields of public representation. Approaches to performance as research that build on this genealogy tend to incorporate tropes of performance – such as the ephemerality of the event, the presence of the performer, and the authority of the work – which simultaneously make cultural transgression possible and render it merely theatrical. It can seem then as if public representation is the more radical aspect of performance, with embodiment only a throwback to the bourgeois illusion of a private sphere. Yet I wonder how often public representation also functions as a safety valve to contain the vast potential of experimental practice. In this sense, the genealogy of practice points towards a methodological basis for a kind of practice as research that we have yet to attempt.

Exercise: 'slice of ritual'

Teach a prayer to a group of students or workshop participants in a language they do not understand. Try out different ways of vocalizing the prayer, such as: in unison and with solos; spoken, chanted, and sung; seated, standing, and kneeling. Once this has been done, distribute a printed copy of the song and its translation, pointing out any explicit references in the text to a particular god, nation, or religious community. Now lead the group through the same series of embodied techniques, taking note of any questions or concerns that arise.

Discuss the delicate boundaries that separate three possible framings of this moment of practice: (1) the exercise as harmless training or theatrical performance, merely the enactment of a script; (2) the exercise as genuine religious act, with specific and perhaps blasphemous consequences for the practitioners; (3) the exercise as an epistemic object of embodied research, with unknown emergent meaning and consequences. What is the nature of the prayer, and of this exercise, as structures of embodied practice that can be taught? What effects did the exercise have in this particular moment? How did the meaning of the prayer change once the words were translated? Which imagined publics became present during the exercise, in which moments?

Notes

1 This chapter was made possible by the University of Huddersfield and the Arts and Humanities Research Council (AHRC) Leadership Fellow project 'Judaica: An Embodied Laboratory for Song-Action' [grant reference AH/N006879/1]. For details see forthcoming publications and visit www.urbanresearchtheater.com.

2 I note with gratitude that Juan Manuel Aldape Muñoz's chapter engages explicitly with my proposals for 'practice as research' and 'embodied research' in Spatz (2015). I agree with Muñoz that 'performance' has a more explicitly politicized conceptual history and I recognize the danger that distancing PAR from performance could have the effect of depoliticizing it. Given recent developments in U.S. politics, this concerns me more than ever. My essay was written without knowledge of Muñoz's critique and I hope it will be clear that my intention here is not to depoliticize PAR but to point towards another possible politics, with different substance and temporality, that would be grounded in practice rather than performance. This is very much a question of which 'bodies and practices . . . make the university institution possible' (Muñoz, this volume) and of what the university can (be made to) do.

3 Previous PAR anthologies (Barrett and Bolt 2007; Allegue et al. 2009; Riley and Hunter 2009) have sometimes attempted to distinguish between practice as research, performance as research, practice-based research, artistic research, and the like on substantive grounds, but the field of usage is so varied that these definitions almost always return to geographic and historical contexts.

4 Plenary dialogue with William Sun at Performance Studies International #20 in Shanghai, 2014.

5 For an elaboration of embodiment as a paradigm for embodied research, see Spatz (2017).

6 The ephemerality/liveness/documentation debates in performance studies are summarized by Matthew Reason in the introduction to his book on documenting performance (2006: 8–27). Reason accurately characterizes the contradictions of a cultural situation in which embodied practice and documentary technologies are imagined to be merely different 'media of performance', one live and the other non-live (20). This leads to the bizarre idea that performance 'disappears' – as if that is unusual – and a tendency to forget the historical recentness of recording technologies.

7 Erin Manning, who has explored the analogous territory of 'research-creation' in Canada, has recently written 'Against Method' (2016: 26–45). Manning's criticism of method as a 'safeguard against the ineffable' is based on a more rigid understanding of the relationship between knowledge, research, and method than the one I have proposed. Following sociologists of science like Hans-Jörg Rheinberger, I see method as the crucial iterable sediment that brings forth the unknown, rather than as a rigidly formal structure of knowledge that blocks discovery.

8 Where theatre is explicitly referenced, as in the work of Erving Goffman, the primacy of public-oriented performance is reinforced and the possibility of experimentally oriented embodied practice falls away.

9 The apparent ephemerality of performance is an example of this, but it is not at all unique to performance. Conversely, when duration is treated symbolically – as in prison sentences, which attempt to map the severity of a crime onto the duration of an incarceration – then we are in the presence of a particular kind of violence.

10 In the United States there has been a major pedagogical movement to radicalize the teaching of introductory English composition. An analogous shift has not yet transformed the introductory pedagogy of acting, which is still most often designed as if to prepare students for professional theatres rather than to give them essential critical skills. We are only recently beginning to see political analyses of actor training (Margolis and Renaud 2010; Kapsali 2014) that lay groundwork for such future curricular transformations.

11 In her search for alternative models of production, Profeta briefly invokes the Workcenter of Jerzy Grotowski and Thomas Richards, pointing to the similarities between the projects undertaken by Lemon and Richards (Profeta 2015: 82). I have argued that the Workcenter is an important example of embodied practice as research (Spatz 2015: 132–147) for precisely the kinds of reasons that Profeta applies to Lemon's work.

12 Profeta recounts in some detail an early attempt by Lemon to have West African dancers perform trance movements from Maya Deren's documentary of Haitian ritual practice (72–77; and see 173–187). The exercise is blocked when many of the dancers refuse to follow this instruction on the grounds that possession is real, dangerous, and inappropriate within the frame of a theatrical project. This conversation would surely unfold quite differently – in ways that no one can predict – if the collaboration were framed as experimental practice rather than performance-making.

13 See note 1.

14 This idea brings a host of contradictions to the fore: if I pay researchers for the Saturday hours in which they do not work, then I return to the practice of resting to an academic frame and undermine its religious significance. This is no longer an authentic Sabbath, although it may be identical at the level of embodied technique. What is it then?

References

Allegue, Ludivine, Simon Jones, Baz Kershaw, and Angela Piccini, eds. (2009) *Practice-as-Research: In Performance and Screen*. New York: Palgrave Macmillan.

Barrett, Estelle, and Barbara Bolt, eds. (2007) *Practice as Research: Context, Method, Knowledge*. New York: I.B. Tauris.

Bell, Catherine (2007) *Teaching Ritual*. Oxford: Oxford University Press.

Bowman, Paul (2015) *Martial Arts Studies*. London: Rowman & Littlefield International.

Boyarin, Jonathan (2008) *Jewishness and the Human Dimension*. Oxford: Oxford University Press.

Carlson, Marvin (1996) *Performance: A Critical Introduction*. New York: Routledge.

Ingold, Tim (2011) *Being Alive: Essays on Movement, Knowledge and Description*. New York and London: Routledge.

Kapsali, Maria (2014) *Theatre, Dance and Performance Training* 5.2 (special issue on Training, Politics and Ideology).

Mahmood, Saba (2005) *Politics of Piety: The Islamic Revival and the Feminist Subject*. Princeton, NJ: Princeton University Press.

Manning, Erin (2016) *The Minor Gesture*. Durham, NC: Duke University Press.

Margolis, Ellen and Lissa Tyler Renaud (2010) *The Politics of American Actor Training*. New York: Routledge.

McKenzie, John (2001) *Perform or Else: From Discipline to Performance*. New York: Routledge.

Oerton, Sarah (2012) '"Touch Talk": The Problems and Paradoxes of Embodied Research'. *International Journal of Social Research Methodology* 7.4: 305–322.

Pakes, Anna (2010) 'Original Embodied Knowledge: The Epistemology of the New in Dance Practice as Research'. *Research in Dance Education* 4.2: 127–149.

Phelan, Peggy (1993) *Unmarked: The Politics of Performance*. New York: Routledge.

Profeta, Katherine (2015) *Dramaturgy in Motion: At Work on Dance and Movement Performance*. Madison, WI: University of Wisconsin Press.

Rabinow, Paul (2003) *Anthropos Today: Reflections on Modern Equipment*. Princeton, NJ: Princeton University Press.

Reason, Matthew (2006) *Documentation, Disappearance and the Representation of Live Performance*. Basingstoke: Palgrave Macmillan.

Rheinberger, Hans-Jörg with Michael Schwab (2013) 'Forming and Being Informed'. In *Experimental Systems: Future Knowledge in Artistic Research*, ed. Michael Schwab, Ghent: Orpheus Institute and Leuven University Press, pp. 199–220.

Riley, Shannon Rose and Lynette Hunter, eds. (2009) *Mapping Landscapes for Performance as Research: Scholarly Acts and Creative Cartographies.* Basingstoke: Palgrave Macmillan.

Saldanha, Arun (2006) 'Reontologising Race: The Machinic Geography of Phenotype'. *Environment and Planning D: Society and Space* 24: 9–24.

Schatzki, Theodore R., Karin Knorr Cetina, and Eike von Savigny, eds. (2001) *The Practice Turn in Contemporary Theory.* New York: Routledge.

Schechner, Richard (1988) *Performance Theory.* New York: Routledge.

Schneider, Rebecca (2011) *Performing Remains: Art and War in Times of Theatrical Reenactment.* New York: Routledge.

Shove, Elizabeth, Frank Trentmann, and Richard Wilk, eds. (2009) *Time, Consumption and Everyday Life: Practice, Materiality and Culture.* New York: Berg.

Spatz, Ben (2015) *What a Body Can Do: Technique as Knowledge, Practice as Research.* New York: Routledge.

——— (2017) 'Embodiment as First Affordance: Tinkering, Tuning, Tracking'. *Performance Philosophy* 2.2: 257–271.

Stoller, Paul (1997) *Sensuous Scholarship.* Philadelphia: University of Pennsylvania Press.

Taylor, Diana and Marcos Steuernagel (2016) *What Is Performance?* Hemi Press and Duke University Press. Online: <http://scalar.usc.edu/nehvectors/wips/index>.

Thrift, Nigel (2008) *Non-Representational Theory: Space, Politics, Affect.* New York: Routledge.

van der Burg, Simone and Tsjalling Swierstra (2013) *Ethics on the Laboratory Floor.* Basingstoke: Palgrave Macmillan.

Varela, Francisco J. and Jonathan Shear, eds. (1999) *The View From Within: First-Person Approaches to the Study of Consciousness.* Thorverton and Bowling Green: Imprint Academic/Journal of Consciousness Studies.

Wacquant, Loïc (2006) *Body & Soul: Notebooks of an Apprentice Boxer.* Oxford: Oxford University Press.

Wangh, Stephen (2000) *An Acrobat of the Heart: A Physical Approach to Acting Inspired by the Work of Jerzy Grotowski.* New York: Vintage Books.

Warner, Michael (2002) *Publics and Counterpublics.* New York: Zone Books.

Zeigler, Joseph Wesley (1994) *Arts in Crisis: The National Endowment for the Arts Versus America.* Chicago: A Cappella Books.

Chapter 10

PAR produces plethora, extended voices are plethoric, and why plethora matters

Yvon Bonenfant

Introduction

Between 2013 and 2015, I made a grand, vocal mess. I created this mess – or really, this series of messes – with audiences. Firstly, we developed a model for a performance for children aged 6–11 and tested it with audiences. Then, using our learning from that process, we enhanced, refined, and toured the performance, and developed both an interactive, sculptural installation and an iPad app from its principles. The nature of the mess in question had much in common with other kinds of performance as research or practice as research (PAR) processes and products. One of these commonalities was that it produced a plethora. Indeed, messes are, by definition, excessive, and if viewed positively, plethoric in and of themselves.

What exactly is a plethora? The *Oxford English Dictionary* (OED) traces the first documented usage of the term, in circa 1541, to have indicated an 'overabundance of one or more humours – especially blood', or an 'excessive fullness of blood vessels'. By 1835, the word was being used to signal, pejoratively, 'excessive supply' or 'overabundance' in any domain, not merely the medical. By the beginning of the twentieth century, it was being used in a more 'neutral or favourable sense' to signal 'a very large amount, quantity, or variety' (2006, accessed 20 November 2015).

A research project inflated by excessive blood – seeking to deliver oxygen, and seeking to whoosh rapidly through the tissues of the research project's body – seems an apt metaphor for the subjective nature of PAR and for the 'too much'-ness or, indeed, what is often perceived as the excess of material of different kinds that PAR processes and products can generate.

Any qualitative research that incorporates input from, investigates the qualities of, or explores the individual trajectories of human creative behaviour is likely to generate some sort of plethora. However, I assert that PAR projects do this in a way that is extra-excessive, and that the vocal qualities of this project make it a celebration of an even more exaggerated form of that plethora. In harmony with the title of this book, the project I talk about in this chapter wallows in a kind of piggish indulgence in, and even regales you with long lists that illustrate, what we might call data excess. There are both a very large *quantity* and a very large *variety* of types of information and research data feeding into and decanting from the project. Some of this information, for example, the embodied technical knowledge of the performers in a live performance, and the embodied experience of young audiences, is impossible to distil, refine, or simplify into a form that can communicate its outcomes verbally, without cheating it of its complexity – not just in artistic but also in research terms. This chapter asserts that that very impossibility has both a research value and a cultural value.

I ask for your patience. This chapter does not give you enough detail about the artworks themselves, or about the research processes that underpinned their development, for you to imagine what took place. Many of its assertions are incomplete. It does not attempt to distil scientifically construed, logical conclusions from the project's results. In the academic world, we are trained to be critically attuned generators and consumers of products we call 'research outcomes'. So, this chapter intends to illustrate the plethoric nature of the project in order to make an argument about how (else) we might 'read', or at least understand, the data excess of the sort typically generated by PAR. Through so doing, this chapter raises questions about how we construe 'rigour', and queries the logics of our processes of articulating what we learn from our research to our larger academic and creative communities.

In addition to this, the qualities of plethora interlaced throughout this project are metaphorically representative of the nature of vocality itself, and in particular of extended or extra-normal vocality. The vocalisation, once produced, shares this with research: it is not us, but it is of us; it is an emanation from the human bodymind which, once departed from us, takes on a life of its own. We decode the information embedded in vocality in ways that are complex, and that still are not fully understood, in part because that information is so plethoric in its complexity. Like decoding the research outcomes of PAR, we necessarily read voice incompletely while bathing in the complex stimuli it transmits. This opens up space for us, and indeed even requires us, to respond to both voice and PAR, on metaphorical, poetic, and sensory planes as well as intellectual ones. Viewed as the result of an artistic product, and as the medium of complex processes of intersubjective communication, both the voice and what I would consider to be 'quality PAR' are overflowing with . . . data.

Data

The OED defines data as "[r]elated items of (chiefly numerical) information considered collectively, typically obtained by scientific work and used for reference, analysis, or calculation" (2006, accessed 4 April 2016). If typical research projects are made up of the collection of information, followed by the making of meaning from analysis of that information, then the question of exactly what information we glean from art making in PAR arises. This question has been considered at length by theorists of PAR,[1] when discussing how and what to document in artistic process and product, and how best to distil conclusions from the analysis of such documentation. But is all documentation data? And is all the 'information' we generate and glean from our processes documentable? The ways we make meaning from our processes of research are not 'chiefly numerical': they tend to be qualitative in the most profound sense.

In 2014, in preparation for a grant-writing process for the UK's Arts and Humanities Research Council, I attended a workshop at Central Saint Martin's College of Art and Design, which addressed the question of 'data archives' in the creative arts. It would shortly become a condition of funding that any research supported by the UK's research councils would be required to develop a publicly accessible data archive, regardless of discipline of origin. The driver behind this process – like so many others in the academic world – was derived from challenges facing the world of quantitative data collection and analysis in the hard and social sciences. The government wanted publicly funded researchers to share raw data so that multiple analyses of data sets would be possible, and so that researchers could investigate, analyse, and critique each other's data sets. UK institutions were in a rush to invent systems to store, catalogue, and make accessible these archives, and to deal with all the attendant problems that archiving, and making publicly accessible, such data throws up. In the creative arts, the challenges were stark. What could our 'data' be? It certainly wasn't numerical. Some of it might be similar to the raw data used in some social sciences or other humanities fields: databases, interview transcripts, videos of interviews themselves, perhaps observational analyses of body language using specific protocols. However, in PAR, much of the data would necessarily be made up of what hard scientists might consider 'intangibles': rehearsal notes, sketches, drawings, mumblings into sound recording devices, fragments of scores, various forms of textual accounts, video fragments, and beyond this, embodied knowledge that cannot be documented using even the most encompassing digital means.

Exactly what would the expectations be from funding institutions vis-à-vis the content of these archives, then? How on earth would others be able to interpret raw 'data' in, say, a devising process for performance? How would users be able to navigate the contents of such archives in ways that made their contents useful to them? What exactly constitutes 'information' in our domain?

The UK's Visual Arts Data Service had been struggling with this question for some time, and the University of the Arts London had been grappling with the need to develop data archives for the wide range of projects across artistic disciplines. At an event I attended at UAL in 2014, Jonathan Rans of the UK's Digital Curation Centre[2] offered up a PowerPoint slide that cited the US government's and Leigh Garret's – of the KAPTUR[3] project – definitions of data.

Here's a science-centric definition: "[T]he recorded factual material commonly accepted in the scientific community as necessary to validate research findings" (United States Office of Budget Management 1999).

And another from the visual arts:

> Anything which is used or created to generate new knowledge and inter-
> pretations. Anything may be intersubjective or subjective; physical or emo-
> tional; persistent or ephemeral; personal or public; explicit or tacit; and is
> consciously or unconsciously referenced by the researcher at some point
> during the course of their research.[4]

In the same presentation, Rans then moves on to point out that 'digital data in
the Arts is as likely to be an outcome of the creative research process as an input
to a workflow' (Rans 2014).

While transcripts of further conversations were not kept at this event, to my
memory, the ensuing discussion about data related to PAR went something like
this: representatives of the research councils pointed out that the notion of data
in the arts is so open-ended that various regulatory bodies purposefully left
its constituent parts without absolute definition. Attendees were challenged to
develop and create archives that would demonstrate what data from our sector
might actually be. The artists present saw an opportunity: data archives could
actually be creative products, to be negotiated and explored in ways that take
advantage of, and work with, the wide range of information that might flow
into, out of, around, or through any given archive. In this context, data archives
might even be imagined as supplementary artworks, or as integral components
of the final artworks themselves. The opportunity to reimagine processes of
data negotiation in academic contexts was actually opened up, rather than shut
down, by this series of assertions. An agreement that data could even be . . .
unconscious, and still be of research value, was of particular surprise. And wonderful, impossible questions are then raised about how to document . . . unconscious, embodied experience . . . as 'data'.[5] I assert that the 'too-muchness' of
this data is an elemental part of what makes it 'artistic' in nature . . . an assertion
to which I'll later return.

When I use the term 'data', I thus use it in the spirit of the plethoric – even
utopian – sense suggested by Rans's citation of Garrett.

(Extra-normal) voice, data, and plethora

We are only at the beginning of exploring the human voice in a way that
focuses on its potential as a performative utterance, which transmits meaning
in and of itself, regardless of its textual content. Thus, when I use the term
'voice', I am wantonly separating the voice from speech, or the lexical content
of vocalisation, which, of course, has been examined as a performative since the
inception of performance studies. This permits an embodied deepening of the
discourse arising from the long history of examining voice as a *metaphor* for
agency. When we speak of 'voice' in the humanities, we usually use voice as a
lens through which we analyse whose speech gets listened to, as well as under

what conditions that speech gets paid attention to, and subsequently, engaged with or acted on. Beyond this metaphoric use, we can extend this concept into the embodied voice *underneath* these speech acts – the actual, literal, physical phenomenon of vocal sound production, vocal sound projection, and the relationship of these two bodies, relationships, and the construction of social agency. What's more, we can use the phenomenon of the embodied voice, and particularly embodied vocal identity, to query the nature of philosophical frameworks that underpin our methodological thinking across disciplines.

I am, of course, not alone in this interest. Almost all theatre and performance studies scholars will have read Barthes's (1991) seminal meditation on the "grain of the voice" as a foundational text. This meditation certainly raises and problematises the ineffable qualities of the voice, albeit in a masculinist and essentialist fashion.[6] The performance studies canon does not interest itself in the nature of the embodied voice beyond this concept. In the last decade, however, a number of explorations of the embodied voice have emerged, which, taken together, open up new kinds of discourses exploring what the voice is, what it does, and how it acts on the world. These currents problematise the voice in exciting ways.

Cavarero (2005) extends the anti-ocularcentric current in post-structuralist philosophy to assert that the profoundly individual nature of the embodied voice, and its resistance to easy description, identification, and categorisation – indeed, the fact that it is inextricable from the deeply subjective nature of its production and perception – challenges the bedrock of Western philosophy and its methodological underpinnings. Cavarero asserts that through de-vocalising logos, indeed, through removing live, vocalic discourse from the means through which we come to (scientific, research-derived) conclusions about the world around us, we adopt a masculinist perspective that removes breath, life, body, and subjectivity from linguistic exchange. Through so doing, that perspective reifies the authority of the written word, detached as it can be from bodies and from the messy, changeable plethora of inter-sensory engagements that bodies and their emanations both evoke and require of us (Cavarero 2005, 26–41).

Building on Cavarero's work, Thomaidis asserts the possibility of a voice-inclusive methodology for PAR within which PAR might engage with the 're-imagining [of] voicing as praxical and intimately connected to practice *and* knowledge production' (Thomaidis and Macpherson 2015, 12, italics added). He uses the term 'voicing', implying vocal doing, rather than the term 'voice', thus underscoring, as does Cavarero, the act of voicing's processual nature. Thomaidis argues that a focus on voicing within PAR might be used to reconfigure the dissemination of the results of PAR processes through reintroducing vocalisation beyond the ritual of the viva voce and even beyond the ritual of the recital-style vocal performance (be this performance musical or theatrical or both). Inspired by his reading of the work of Karikis (2005), he posits that audio recordings, live and recorded performances of artwork, and performative presentations which are voiced could all form a part of this enrichment of PAR with voiced qualities, alongside the use of writing techniques – such as the use of multiplicities of fonts, scores of various kinds, and the use of script-style writing, where assertions are delivered by different imagined characters (and thus by different implied voices). These kinds of techniques would introduce a sort of voice-derived, dynamic subjectivity into PAR processes. Thomaidis extends Nelson's (2006) notion of a triangular model of PAR, in which mixed-mode research, mixed-mode practices, and practices themselves interact to generate new knowledges, to assert that a vocal approach to PAR would involve the unfolding of a 'triangular continuum between logos-as-reason, logos-as-language, and [vocal] practice' (Thomaidis and Macpherson 2015, 18), in ways that would attempt to re-vocalise aspects of research discourse, rather than merely using the analysis and discourse as a means to 'make logical sense of' PAR. We begin to see here how the re-vocalisation of research processes might introduce notions like the creative plethoric into the discourse of research, for the layers of voicing inherent in such PAR work imply multiplicities of perspectives and of bodies that 'normal' research discourses might frame as lacking in rigour or clarity.

From outside the world of PAR, indeed, from a 'hard sciences' perspective, voice scientists Kreiman and Sidtis (2011) use both empirical data and the holes and gaps in this data to illustrate the ineffable nature of attempting to describe the qualities of voice that make any given voice individual. In other words, they illustrate just how challenging it still is to describe, or even analyse, the acoustic data contained in voices, which allow us to map those voices onto the recognition of individuals (Kreiman and Sidtis 2011, 1–24, 173–188), even though we are incredibly good at this, given the thousands of voices we encounter in our lifetimes (Kreiman and Sidtis 2011, 159–164). We perceive and respond to the individual qualities of human voices beyond and beneath the cues afforded to us by verbal/textual content extraordinarily well, yet still struggle to name and describe the qualities that make voices individual: these remain largely in the realm of the ineffable. Musicologist Grant Olwage (2004), in his meditation on the politics of the racialisation of timbre in colonial South Africa, draws from Cornelia Fales's work to assert how bad we are at describing and talking about timbre in the sung voice, even though it is a core means through which we identify vocal identity in both narrow (individual) and broad (ethno-cultural) senses. From disciplines as disparate as voice science and musicology, scholars illustrate the abundance of information contained in acts of voicing that we, as listeners, respond to but never, it seems, fully consciously decode. The voice is pregnant with subjectivities, which are to varying degrees unknowable, and we dance with those subjectivities in ways that are always, at least in part, operating on the register of the unconscious. In the spirit of Leigh Garrett's (2013) definition of research data in the visual arts, in PAR processes, these subjectivities could be likened to veritable ganglia of (vocalic) data.

Stephen Connor's assertion of the existence of the voca*lic* (italics mine) body (2000, 36–37) helps describe the dynamics of the embodied nature of the manifestation of these kinds of subjectivities. To simplify his model, the vibratory field which we emit becomes both metaphorically and really a body. This field is made up of vibrations that travel through matter as if they were materially occupying space. The molecules that are vibrating in this field are structured and stratified like complex and contradictory architectures – or at least, they are made up of many simultaneously superimposed, three-dimensional shapes, which we can feel with our ears and sometimes with other tissues. As these shapes move through space, they evoke metaphors of coming and going, of life and death, while they travel past and through us. These shapes, these vocalic bodies, 'touch', through interacting with other bodies on a plane of physical vibration – even many other bodies at a time. Eventually, they dissipate and dissolve, their energy transferred elsewhere, as the vibrations attenuate. While these vocalic bodies exist, they evoke real human fleshy bodies. When we hear them, we can only associate them with the appearance, or even somatic sensation of, another body, even if it is a fantasised one. These fields of vibration can be understood to be sensory manifestations of embodied data when activated within vocally focused PAR processes. Who hasn't had a crush on the imagined bodily being of a voice on the telephone? Who hasn't fallen at least a little bit in love with the vocalic body's data-field? That is to say, who hasn't had a little soft spot for some voice data?

My artistic practice wraps itself around these vocalic bodies, and the data they play with, and in particular, the extra-normal manifestations of these bodies and data. Our voices are extraordinarily disciplined in the Foucauldian sense: this is a reality which extra-normal vocalisers encounter regularly when developing their technical prowess. When was the last time you heard a cry of anguish in a work meeting, or a genuine, loose sob at a funeral? These noisy voices are shut up, so that these queered gestures, and the queered, bothersome vocalic bodies they evoke, don't mess with our plans, our supposed needs, our assumed desires, or our social mores.[7]

Though what is 'extra-normal' in vocalisation is always culturally relative, these voices are always intransigent within their cultural context. In other words, what is viewed as vocally unacceptable or even vocally taboo in one culture – for example ululation at funerals in the United Kingdom – is not necessarily so in another – for example ululation at village funerals in Tamil Nadu, India. However, we know that patriarchal and authoritarian cultural value systems all police gesture in various ways, be that gesture physical or vocal. So, voices that are gesturing in ways that are 'extra-normal' are always refusing to play by some aspects of the local rules. They are exciting, because vibration excites; they are dangerous, because they disturb the social order of *who* or, we might say, what *kinds* of vocalic bodies are allowed to voice and gesture *what*, and *when*. Above all, they confuse because they mix up cultural codes. Their corporeal identities are too fluid. These voices are wonderfully hysterical in the Freudian sense. They are hyper-subjective. They are hyper-fluctuating data. Yet, they are in us all.[8]

If one is interested in the extra-normal voice, one can't help but be interested, indeed passionately interested, in the voices of children, whose relatively vital access to unbridled vocal sound has been less tampered with than that of adults; or they have practised conforming their vocal gesture to social codes for less long, and their habitus is less, well, habituated. By this I mean a simple thing: kids scream and yell. They imitate animal sounds. They imitate the sounds of machines. They sing into play microphones and imitate the exaggerated vocal styles of people they see or hear on television or through digital means. They generally – though certainly not in all cases – have access to a kind of vocal play that exceeds that of adults. They are perhaps more attuned to other kinds of vocal realities than those most adults do practise being attuned to. They are creatures of both expressive fluidity and relational attachment, in raw ways adults tend to practise not doing, because we have a habit of mixing up *being inured* with *civilized maturation*. While we may feel there is good reason for doing so, schooling in particular plays a key role in rendering the voices of our children more 'reasonably behaved'. Standard schooling is a venue for vocal curtailment. Moments of heightened vocalisation in school environments are often channelled into forms of choral singing, which are balletic in their technical need to shape styles of voicing into a very particular aesthetic value system.

So, let us return to the mess, the PAR project we created. Given my views, and given my long practice of cultivating extra-normal sound-making in my own creative practice, could I make space for children to be encouraged to, welcomed to, and indeed deeply enticed to make extra-normal sounds of a variety of kinds in a celebratory atmosphere? Could we somehow transmit a message that it was not just okay but also exciting, desirable, and aesthetically interesting for them to make these sounds? What would have to happen in order for these driving impulses to be made manifest?

What we did: first process

In 2012, an ensemble I assembled worked with the venue *The Point* in Eastleigh, United Kingdom, to run a series of performance-workshops with children aged 5–10 in their Creation Space centre. Here I describe the aims of the project through a list in order to illustrate the various aspects of the plethora of PAR. My goals were to make a performance that responded to the following drivers:

- It would find ways of engaging its target audience in making extra-normal vocal sound.
- The making of that sound would be integral to the performance experience. It would create space for the celebration of that sound, for the revaluing of that sound through the heightened experience of the formal performance environment.
- It would use audiovisual technologies to engage children in mirroring processes.

- It would introduce children to the basics of the functional anatomy of vocalisation, and explore and embody aspects of voice and speech science within its dramaturgical framework. It would therefore have an educational component embedded within it.
- Dialogues with a team of voice and speech scientists would give input – we didn't know how – into the creative process.
- It would have high production values, and counter the tendency towards low-value performance work for child audiences.
- It would involve transdisciplinary adventure and experimentalism in the ways it knit together the aesthetic languages engaging with it: the theatrical, spatial, and visual; the musical; and even the aesthetic languages of its educational components. It would plunder disciplines wantonly in order to engage its audiences in ways that met its needs.

The creation of the work was a collective endeavour. The team included improvising performers who demonstrated an ability to command the attention of rooms full of children, and who also had a good base of vocal performance skill. They were auditioned and tested for their vocal endurance; their ability to invent sound; to access the widest possible range of vocal effects, and to be able to 'command' a room full of potentially rowdy children. The team further consisted of a digital artist to design and manage audiovisual interaction, a designer experienced in working with child audiences whose visual language was also highly evocative of the tactile register, a production manager, a creative producer, myself as artistic director, and a research scientist in psycholinguistics.

It would be safe to say that we worked in a sort of reflexive and dialectic maelstrom. We only had four total weeks together to try to develop these performance experiences. We began by running interactive workshops – some led by me, some by the performers – that were watched by the rest of the team. Production meetings, formal communication, tonnes of informal conversation, coaching, direction, discussions, arguments, especially between me and the original digital artist, and interactions with almost 300 children and 40 adults – parents, teachers, and arts professionals – resulted. We tried to determine what I cared about, what the performers cared about, what the artists cared about, and what the children cared about, and how to knit these things together into some kind of cohesive performance experience, which was also aesthetically intriguing. At times we had, working in the same physical space: children trying out ideas; a designer and production manager building, cutting, sewing, and painting structures to alternately co-generate, contain, and channel the work's intentions while workshops and rehearsals unrolled; a digital artist taking inspiration from the designer and the children to generate sound experiences, somatic interactions, and responsive environments; performers trying to straddle the strange role of being both performer and a sort of workshop facilitator; and a producer working with us to see if we could make this into something funders and venues would understand enough to book and tour. These studio intensives were broken up into one-week chunks, between which I could discuss emerging ideas and phenomena with scientists, educational advisers, and our venue partners, and analyse any feedback gathered so far. The ideas could ripen and options to realise the goals of the work would open up and be explored in an ideational space outside of the studio.

We finished this process by showing semi-finished test works for three days: two days to schools, and another day to families, including during a symposium to which arts professionals, educators, and programmers were invited; we used this for collecting the widest range of formal feedback possible.

It's worth noting that the foregoing process was funded and resourced through external grant applications, internal grant applications, one interview process, and numerous networking meetings, as these processes of resourcing and encounter inevitably affected the outcome of the project. They flowed into the web of our project data-stream. Encounters with funders, individuals, and other enablers of the work left an imprint of their value systems on the creative team's dialogues in ways both conscious and unconscious.

There was no way we could track in detail all of the aspects of the unfolding of this devising process. There were too many simultaneous processes and journeys of discovery taking place, and many of them were inextricably interdependent. The entire dramaturgical shape of the work – including the dramaturgy of the architectures it ended up inhabiting – evolved in tandem with its content. All artistic team members had deeply dialectic missions, because they had to engage with profoundly intersubjective processes of negotiation of the development of the form and content of the work, including the development of these in interaction with our test audiences, who provided most of the sonic content of the work. We had to devise strategies to elicit this content and use all of the tools at our disposal to render it aesthetically interesting in extra-normal terms.

What resulted was a performance split into two experiences, which we thought of as the 'speech room' and the 'squeak room'. The speech room, an oval-shaped, straight-walled space, animated by a sort of librarian-like character, took the children on a journey through ever-expanding phoneme play, sourcing phonetic components from unfamiliar languages, and uniting these with explorations of the functional anatomy of the vocal tract, to finish off with the children inventing a magic spell from 'nonsense' sounds. In the squeak room, a charismatic, inter-gendered, regal figure escorted the audience through a wide range of non-verbal sounds and wild gestures, culminating in a beat-box fiesta, followed by a voice-generated tornado storm in which their circular, tented room seemed to spin and fly into the air as buildings came crashing down. In both rooms, performers and digital environments worked together to respond to the children's sounds, giving them audiovisual feedback that either stimulated the making of or captured their sounds, or did both simultaneously.

The data resulting from the first phase of research and development

In the preceding paragraph, I gave you only the most cursory of descriptions of the live performance results. For the purposes of this chapter, rather than analyse these results themselves, I focus on attempting to enumerate and describe the raw research data that decanted from the process and product. The following list is not exhaustive.

Memories

Each contributing team member is, of course, a repository of memories of what happened, and a unique interpreter of why it happened, filtered through the lens of his or her subjectivity. The diversity of the team and relatively large numbers of test audience, given the low capacity of the performance (near 300 children), mean that intimate and proximal subjectivities come into dialogue around what took place, why, and how. Much of this data was vocal in nature, and stored in us as memories of sensation, corporeal transformation, and inter-subjective play.

Conversations, dialogues, and disputes

Not just an aspect of what is remembered about the process, I recorded a number of conversations with team members so that I could reflect on these conversations between intensive meetings. These included developing characters, action, and content for the sets and conversations with the whole team, the digital artist, the set designer, and the production manager. There were a number of arguments about our working process that took place, in particular with the digital artist, which had a key series of effects on decisions made during creative turning points in the process. In retrospect, the most useful conversations were often the most difficult and challenging ones, which forced some sort of honing process to take place.

Documents of evolving artistic instinct: notes, sketches, lists, scores, photos in progress made by me or other team members

I have collected sketches, fabric fragments and swatches, paint samples, and other process-based documentation from the designer; fragments of lighting gels which were discarded; photos of computer screens when the digital artist was playing and attempting to design works; poster-sized scores; scripts; and sound recordings of various directorial coaching sessions.

Photographic and video documentation

Various team members took photos of the evolving set. Due to the legal and ethical issues involved with photographing or taking video images of children in the UK – centred largely around children who have need of identity protection in the Internet age, due to complex situations around fostering, adoption, or being sheltered from adults dangerous to them – it is extraordinarily difficult to take action shots or video of workshops or performances with children. Although some video documentation was taken with parent and guardian permission, it was stored securely in encrypted locations and then destroyed after a week as an added security measure, with the exception of final documentation. That week gave me time, as artistic director, to review the work we had done from a slightly more distant perspective, and to compare what the documentation had 'remembered' to the corporeal and personal embodied memories I had internalized from being in the space. The similarities and the gaps between these kinds of memories helped me address what I felt was missing, 'working', or 'not working' about the process.

Sound recording documentation

The foregoing being said, in fully anonymised group sound recordings, wherein no single individual voice is identifiable (and particularly in situations like this where children are producing little in the way of lexical verbal material), it is relatively safe to get permission to store sound recording fragments from workshops and use these for reflection.

One full-length video recording

We also worked carefully with The Point and a partner school to take releasable, public domain video of one full run of the resulting R&D performance, largely for the purposes of developing a promotional trailer.

The set itself

The intricate set – made to be both portable and configurable in both one- and two-room formats, its marbled floor cloths and hanging silk draperies – with all of its initial flaws, was a character in and of itself, whose input into the shaping of the audience experience could be contemplated through spatial and structural analysis.

The programming and the technical kit

Our digital artist left behind intricate circuit diagrams of the audiovisual and audience-responsive content of the works, embedded within the MAX software working environment. The video and audio samples the children interacted with, and the technical infrastructure, also provided fodder for reflective legacy: seven projectors, nine microphones, two iMacs, two full audio interfaces, three motion capture devices, a remote-control wizard's wand . . .

Observations of children on the physical, verbal, vocal, and spatial planes

Performers, the larger creative team, the outreach staff at The Point, teachers, guests, and many others watched, listened to, and followed the activity of the children involved in our process in different ways. We collected their views both formally and informally throughout the process.

Observations by children

Inspired by experiments undertaken by Reason and analysed in his work *The Young Audience: Exploring and Enhancing Children's Experiences of Theatre* (2010), we collected more than 300 drawings and other forms of meandering through their impressions of and ideas about the performance experience by children. We asked them to draw what mattered to them about the experience – whether positive, negative, or both – or in some cases, what they 'most remembered about it'. Older children often accompanied their drawings with lists of words. We interpreted these metaphors in order to hone and shape the children's experience to my artistic and educational ends.

Verbal feedback from children

We had informal conversations with children around their drawings, giving us a way in to discussing their experience of the workshops and the works that didn't require direct, rational analysis of their experience.

Verbal and written feedback from teachers

We spoke with teachers after the experiences and elicited observations from them about how they thought both the children and they themselves experienced the work. In complement to this, we developed a written questionnaire for adults. Questionnaire design aimed to elicit their general impressions and then to measure their views of the children's experience against my aesthetic, educational, and vocal-political goals. These goals were not made explicit to all parties at all times, because the goals themselves evolved, transformed, and transmuted in relation to what we learned. What's more, we discarded some goals and transformed others when these were tested in light of 'real' experience with our audience.

Conversations with scientists

Our conversations with our advising scientists were curated by Professor Catherine Best, chair of Psycholinguistics at the University of Western Sydney. Because Best began her scientific pathway as a research psychologist of child development, and then integrated these interests with psycholinguistics, her unique knowledge of children's developmental engagements with the acts of phonation and play was of immense use to informing how we might entice children into our world. Verbal exchanges with Cathi, during which I plumbed her knowledge and creative impulses, were key to realising the work. While my engagement with Cathi was verbal, contact with her colleagues was usually by email, leaving a digital trail of documented exchange in its wake.

A library of scientific articles

Through curating our access to people, Cathi also curated access to bodies of knowledge. Scientific articles and magazine articles about work of colleagues associated with the Haskins Labs – including key understandings of vocal gesture as choreographic process – influenced the work, literally and metaphorically. A file of these articles remains. The journey through these areas of study was wide-ranging. It included examples of Best's own seminal work that developed and then further tested her key contribution to psycholinguistic study of infant language acquisition, the perceptual assimilation model (Best 1994; Best and McRoberts 2003). The Haskins Labs take a kind of whole-body approach to understanding the perception and production of language, and key scientists Michael Studdert-Kennedy's and Louis Goldstein's views on the 'gestural' and indeed choreographic nature of phonation (Studdert-Kennedy and Goldstein 2002; Goldstein and Rubin 2007) were exciting: through attempting to come to grips with their work, I could begin to think of phonation and vocalisation as dancing, and children phonating as a kind of dance improvisation. Their work, which also explores the gestural origins of phonation within the evolution of human language, opened up access to publications by Stephen Brown and his neuro-arts lab, some of whose body of work focuses on voice, music, and the evolution of vocal capacity in humans (Brown, Ngan, and Liotti 2008; Brown 2007).

Input from education specialists

Two education specialists – one from primary science education, and another in embodied education – came to see the work at different developmental stages and discussed it with us. They made recommendations about how we could better engage with and relate to the children.

Verbal feedback at showings

The whole team elicited informal verbal feedback during the final showings.

Written feedback

At the final showings, all adult witnesses and participants were asked to fill in evaluation questionnaires. These asked free-form, open-ended questions about the experience.

Ineffable embodied knowledges

An emerging 'technique' surged forth in the bodies of the performers, because being able to deliver the content of these experiences interactively, to time, in a semi-improvised format, was a significant challenge, and meeting that challenge meant developing idiosyncratic embodied skill syntheses of a very particular nature, a topic for an article in itself.

Administrative and mechanical data

Contracts with team members; statistics on budget, spend, time use, attendance, age ranges; producer contracts with venues and promoters; and production management, health and safety, and portability issues all emerged from the process.

Final reports articulating 'learning' in the language of the arts assessor

An extensive and detailed report detailing what I, and the team as a whole, claimed to have learned from the process of making the work was drafted in three versions, one for each key funder. These provided us with space to assess the work against its targets and goals, but also to describe unlooked-for discoveries that we felt we made, outside of the need for more academic contextualisation and analysis.

A next series of impulses and goals

The reports detailed earlier ended with a series of ideas for ways forward from this R&D process. These involved the following:

- Improving and refining the performance before embarking on a tour of UK venues.
- Using key practices and aesthetic, educational, and audience involvement strategies developed from the process to test performance experiences for both young adults with moderate learning disability and young adults with profound and multiple learning disabilities, exploring their potential with these underserved audiences.
- Developing an installation without performers from our discoveries about the vocal interests of our target age group, in order that they be given self-directed space to use 'digital mirroring' to explore, expand, and aesthetise their extra-normal voicing in their own time, enabling those who really enjoy the experience to dwell on and in it, and deepen their personal engagement with it.
- Developing an iPad app so the digital experience could also be explored at home in intimate and private spaces.

The second process and the data it generated

The live performance was named *Uluzuzulalia*: a hybridisation of 'ululate' and 'glossolalia'. It was improved, taking into account my and the teams' analysis and reaction to the foregoing interlocking rivulets of data flow. The teacher character was transformed; the set and digital effects largely reimagined, rendered more sensual. This small-capacity work – each showing could accommodate only a maximum of 34 children, and we could do only two showings per day – was toured to 11 UK venues, reaching around 1,000 audience members, over 29 days. In addition to the foregoing data, this tour generated:

- About 95 hours of anonymised audience sound recordings, which were analysed and curated into fragments of interest from sonic/vocal/aesthetic perspectives.
- Animations, further video documentation, and photo documentation of the set.
- Recorded verbal feedback from about 200 distinct audience voices.
- A website; education packs; and feedback from teachers, schools, venues, professional programmers, parents, and arts professionals.
- Six days of work with children with profound and multiple learning disabilities, resulting in about 23 hours of raw video documentation of work with them.
- Promotional material, reviews, and some social networking.

Some of the data derived from the live installation development process of the work *The Voice Trunk* included:

- Sketches, models, and photos of the build of the work in progress.
- Conversations with acoustic consultants to help sound insulate the work while leaving it open to airflow.
- Extensive photographs of the work in progress.
- Conversations with an animator.
- Sculptural modelling.
- Visual, annotated, and remembered work towards surface texture treatments for the installation.
- More programming, and wiring diagrams.
- Extensive records of engagement with the fabrication company, including group conversations; detailed and complex contracts; notes; emails; photos.
- Observations by, and informal conversations undertaken with, a team of five intervention workers who accompanied the work during its test phase at the Natural History Museum, London, of about 3,000 people, including numerous families and during one special late evening, slightly drunken adults.
- Intensive engagement with the staff of the Winchester Science Centre in the run up to and first weeks of showing the installation.
- Once installed and running at the Winchester Science Centre, four total weeks of direct observation of audiences using the installation, with some informal

interviews integrated into the observation. Observation was by the creative team but also by a research assistant using a carefully designed questionnaire.

- More education packs, designed specifically to be used by teachers who might visit the centre with classes of primary school-aged children, which linked the artwork to in-class creative and scientific activities that could be integrated into the national curriculum for England.
- Video and audio documentation of selected audience use where ethically cleared.
- Visitor statistics, education pack download numbers, website visit statistics.

The installation has now reached to date about 190,000 users, and will likely reach as many more before it is dismantled.

Some of the data derived from the app *Voice Bubbles* for iPad development and launch process included the following:

- Extensive records of email communication around the creative process.
- An intense, carefully negotiated contracting process.
- Documentation of several test phases of visual, tactile, and functional design.
- Crash data and crash testing.
- Download, user, and sales data from the iTunes store.
- Promotional material.
- Online discourse around the app: reviews, mentions, and so forth.
- Video documentation of use of the iPad app.
- Formal and informal conversations about the iPad app.
- Information derived from three intensive promotional campaigns around the app.

The iPad app has reached just under 5,000 downloads. Its ownership is being transferred to OKIDO children's media, who will upgrade some of its graphics, upgrade other aspects of it based on our learning, and relaunch it under its aegis, reaching a much wider audience over the next years.

Across the three strands of the project – the performance, the installation, and the app – supplementary data included the following:

- More than 83,000 words of grant applications to three separate funders to support the project.
- Documentation of a new series of conversations with three key scientists, two of whom were new on the project, all of which developed new and additional thematic material that underpinned the work: which we might summarize as explorations of voice as literal and metaphorical contact, of the use of digitally mediated voice-expanding mirrors across age groups, and of creating space for robust vocal gymnastics.
- A 3,200 item budgetary report, and near 60,000 words of final reporting to funders.
- A web hub, which served to collect and collate information about those interested in learning more about the work.

Making sense from plethora

Co-composed artistic experiences are, by necessity and by design, rife with sub-jectivities. I would not want to approach what can be learned from processes like these, in critically engaged, academic contexts, the way we approach even the most heuristic of social sciences methodologies, because a good part of the meaning that can be distilled from these subjectivities might well lie in letting them breathe as they are, or perhaps we might say, letting them take on indi-vidual voices of their own. Yet I think a reader – even a 'hard scientific' reader – would agree that there are things we might well learn from such processes and products, which are of import to a larger understanding of the functioning of the extra-normal vocal self in art, in culture, and perhaps even, in a small way, in the politics of our relationships with children, whose unusual voicings we might facilitate and celebrate, rather than curtail. And so the question arises: what is the relevance of this kind of project?

To my mind, Patricia Leavy (2009) makes the clearest and most succinct and compelling case for when artistic approaches to research might be of particular value to the larger world of formally construed academic research. To be sure, Leavy makes this argument within a model she calls arts-based research, within educational research rather than practice-as- or performance-as-research. In her American context, the relationship between practising art-making and the generation of social import is often inextricably interlinked in the academic mind.

In any case, Leavy asserts that art's capacity to engage the emotional and sensual register (2009, 13) means that it can evoke meaning (2009, 14) rather than merely directly delineate and prescribe the contours of that meaning for readers, witnesses, and immersed participants. It is clear that while this research project emerged from a web of intertwining goals, there is no way that any one dominant set of internal experiences could emerge from it for any of its inter-actors, or even that those experiences could be expressed exclusively in words, rather than through engaging with processes of making metaphor. She also asserts that arts-based research practices use metaphor as a 'poetic form of data representation' (Leavy 2009, 13) and through so doing can open up space for 'giving voice to subjugated perspectives' (ibid.). The subjugated perspectives at play in this project are made up of impulses to generate literal, embodied, extra-normal voicings. Her perspective opens up the subjective experience of the audience member, and the ineffable qualities of their voices, to multiple readings. These multiple readings make space for the plethoric nature of the data embodied in these audience experiences and reactions to be given space and time to breathe. Indeed, this makes space for the reader – the 'academic analyst' of the situation, so to speak – to interpret the inexpressibly idiosyncratic through both straightforward verbal articula-tion and poetic interpretation. It also makes space for us to 'hear' voiced engagements and responses to the work, in both real and imagined, evoked ways.

Leavy's view is that arts-based research 'promotes dialogue', through 'connecting people on emotional and spiritual levels' (2009, 14). Through accessing the 'subjugated voices', the methods 'continue problematizing dominant ideologies' (Leavy 2009, 14), through providing people with 'tools (such as passion)' (ibid.) in order to do so, and as such, serve as 'postmodern attempts at subversion' (ibid.). If you could hear the audio samples we've collected from this project, reader, it would be difficult to deny that audiences had a strong tendency to experience passionate engagement with the live performance, in particular, and that the majority of users of the installation and iPad app also show tendencies towards passionate expression and engagement, even if fleeting, if we can believe the observations we've made of users. The conjoining of this passion to strategies that evoke non-normative voicing is precisely a part of what this work intends to celebrate and reify with audiences, in a countercultural framework. To what *extent* it succeeds in doing this, and the import of such, is of course fodder for further, detailed analysis, which takes account of the combination of ambiguities, subjectivities, and even empirical measurements of numbers of audience who engage in such a way. And to what extent this develops new, cooperative forms of audience-generated, sophisticated sonic aesthetics of the extended voice remains to be evaluated and analysed within frameworks of both academic and professional-artistic rigour.

Most importantly and most pertinently, however, Leavy claims that a 'key strength of arts-based practices' is to 'get at multiple meanings' (2009, 15). In direct contrast to the classical, positivist scientific method, the projects I have described here cannot and should not be reduced to a singular set of positivist assertions in response to hypotheses. They cannot directly answer research questions, though they certainly can explore them, and through so doing, 'access the multiple viewpoints made imperceptible by traditional research methods', leading to the potential 'opening up of . . . discourse' (Leavy 2009, 15). Layers and layers of contrasting types of data can be plundered, juxtaposed, rearranged, viewed at new angles, listened to, touched, and otherwise sensed and cognitively processed in order to suggest new sets of assertions and observations about how we did what we did and to what extent this project succeeds and fails in its aims. The only way to articulate these assertions and observations is through mixed modes of presentation and re-presentation, using artistic strategies to address multiple modalities of address to the mind and body. This requires both artistic and intellectual skill. As such, this chapter sits alongside the following foreseen outputs of this project:

• A library of audio documentation.
• Still photographs of the works.
• Three 'how they work' video essays that bring the witness inside a summary of the results of the artistic processes.
• Two technical video essays that demonstrate how we made technical choices and what these choices were.

- Interview transcriptions with team members.
- An archive, curated from the documentation listed earlier, which illustrates turning points in the process of making the works, which were derived from then-ongoing creative discoveries.
- Databases that sum up audience feedback; samples of children's drawings; word clouds.

The foregoing will be deposited in the university research data repository. Further writing – a book chapter and four journal articles – is in the course of being developed from the foregoing data, and right now, the topics of these writings include the following:

- The articulation of the notion of 'vocal-somatic dramaturgies', relating these to the choices we made in each of the artworks regarding the depth of encounter of audience experience, built on Synne Behrndt's (2014) notion of the 'dramaturgy which facilitates encounter' as it collides with interiorized, somatic, kinaesthetic sensation of vocal sound production.
- An aesthetic analysis of the sonic, spatial, visual, and general dramaturgical-structural nature of the resulting artworks, evaluating the level to which they achieved innovation within the artistic contexts of extra-normal voice and alternative artworks for children.
- An articulation and analysis of the method we seem to have developed for converting conversations with voice and speech scientists and aspects of their bodies of work and their opinions into artistic metaphor.
- A comparison and contrast of the power dynamics involved in using the artworks to reach child audiences and elicit non-normative voicing, comparing and contrasting strategies used, and the effectiveness and appropriateness thereof, across the three different works.
- An exploration of what it seems to have meant to work with this age group of child audiences: for them, and for us as artists; and an elucidation of the mechanics and challenges of such work, when introducing deeply unfamiliar artistic concepts to them.

In addition to this, a number of further ideas for projects have already decanted from this work. Other writings and ideas may well also decant from the material. The foregoing sets of formally construed research outputs distil pertinent moments and meanings from the seeming chaos of our research process and articulate them for, and to, a wider academic audience. They find ways to make some of the multiple meanings that have emerged from the work more explicit.

After I write these, it will be important to sing their meanings back into contactful and passionate, relative ambiguity in performance-lecture form, or to find other means of re-vocalising the content of the work and the experiences that have decanted from it, in order to reinvigorate them with voiced idiosyncrasy.

Engaging audiences, and impact in the British context

Leavy also suggests that arts-based representational strategies bring academic scholarship to a wider audience (2009, 14). However, some art made in academic contexts doesn't leave those contexts, and not all art represents the results of research processes. With this project, however, I have been taken by surprise, for my works have reached larger numbers than I expected, surpassing six digits; and although, as articulations of research process and product, they are incomplete, they are at least partially embodiments of academically construed research, albeit in a challenging format to decode, from a traditional academic perspective.

Academics not located in the UK, or new to the country, might not be aware of the extent to which higher education has become an overt tool of state instrumentalism here. Of the many ways institutions are audited by the state, every UK institution that wants to be considered research-active must participate in a national exercise currently called the Research Excellence Framework. That exercise essentially makes all relevant researchers submit their four 'best' 'outputs' – by best, I mean 'likely to please a national jury of your peers' and by outputs I mean research commoditised as industrial production. Your subject area and institution do not get any money for research if you do not participate in this exercise; and the way you score is linked to funds eventually granted from central government for research over a six-year cycle. Essentially, institutions compete for money in a cleverly designed national hamster cage.

However, REF 2014, the most recent of these exercises, suddenly placed value on a measurement of research quality the government has decided to call 'impact'. The factor of impact is very distinctly defined, and somewhat confusingly, the definitions can be slightly different depending on which government agency is talking. However, 'public engagement' is seen to be a form of impact – that is to say, public engagement with either the processes or products of rigorous, high-quality research, in ways that are at least, to some extent, transformative.

This has meant that while some institutions devalued PAR outputs because they were seen to be a risk – to the impression of individual or departmental rigour – this revaluing of one aspect of impact, audience engagement, has meant a resurgence of interest in the creative outputs of PAR which engage large audiences. Indeed, to the extent that it reaches audiences, PAR has become re-valued at many institutions, because it might now have an actual value in terms of institutional and departmental reward.

Beyond the potential for PAR to take on some sort of market value – and in that sense, in some cases, become more valued than more traditional forms of qualitative research – this is probably a time in which we should take advantage of the shifting sands to advocate for what PAR can do for other research domains. If it's true that one of the particular strengths of arts-based research and PAR is to 'get at multiple meanings' (as per Leavy 2009, 15), then the whole of academia needs PAR-style thinking right now. The information flow we are exposed to increases exponentially. The data streams we encounter on a daily basis become increasingly complex and make more and more demands on us. We hurtle towards a situation of data and stimulus excess, and need to find ways to experience that excess as plethora rather than as pejorative or negative excess. When fear grows of future terrorist strikes or of the complexities climate change might throw up for us, we need artistic approaches to navigating the data that surround us. We need to be able to look at big pictures of data, to listen to, touch, feel, and even be immersed in the confusing effervescence of drives, goals, and activities which surround us, and still find a way to take focused and constructive action in their midst. This can help us distil meaning from our encounters with these big pictures: for their complexities cannot be reduced, only navigated, the way we navigate artistic data. We also need to engage with others on a highly inter-subjective level in order to solve these problems, and to hear the voices and bodies speak, underneath the lexical content of the languages used – which complicates the data environment further. We need to re-vocalise dialogue so that we can solve problems in ways that include the navigation of subjectivities.

As business schools integrate ever more curricular content which applies 'design thinking' to business and managerial problems, we might also ask our fellow academics, as well as businesses and governments, to value artistic thinking and artistic methodologies beyond the mere 'public engagement' qualities they might represent. They need our tolerance for ambiguity, our ability to engage with metaphor and representation, our ability to stimulate discourse about the ineffable. They need our voices, and they need us to enter the realm of extra-normal embodiment, as a way out of the trap of oversimplification of social, political, and ecological dynamics. Indeed, they need to apply our definition of data to the complex pictures they are looking at. They can also refuse to de-vocalise their processes of meaning making. They can re-vocalise them and navigate their plethoric subjectivities.

We can offer to other disciplines a talent for the reconstruction of excess as plethora. We can perhaps redefine the very notion of data, extending Garrett's (2013) qualities of artistic data into other fields, while re-vocalising strategies for argument, discourse, and making meaning.

We can make metaphor and meaning from plethoric celebration.

Notes

1 See, for example, Piccini and Rye's (2009) seminal meditation on the nature and role of documentation in PAR; Nelson's (2013) consolidation of his highly influential model of PAR within which documentation is nested integrally; the approach to integrating documentation into an 'exposition' model of publication about PAR by key thinkers in the artistic research movement (Schwab and Borgdorff 2014); and examples of practice (e.g., Ledger, Ellis, and Wright 2011).

2 The Digital Curation Centre is run as a joint venture by the Universities of Edinburgh, Glasgow, and Bath, to develop models for best practice in data development, archiving, and management across the UK's university sector. For more information, see www.dcc.ac.uk/about-us/.

3 The KAPTUR project was a time-limited initiative to investigate and develop models of best practice for data archiving and management in the visual arts sector, managed by the UK's Visual Arts Data Service. For more information, see www.vads.ac.uk/kaptur/about.html.

4 Leigh Garrett, KAPTUR project: see http://kaptur.wordpress.com/2013/01/23/what-is-visual-arts-research-data-revisited/ (Rans 2014; accessed 4 April 2016).

5 Some first experiments with, and examples of, the creation of data archives that might respond to these sorts of challenges include the Siobhan Davies *Replay* archive, created by Professor Sarah Whatley of Coventry University and the artist herself (visit www.siobhan-daviesreplay.com/ and browse). As part of the development of this archive, guest 'artists', 'curators' and 'researchers' were asked to browse and explore the archive and create meaningful thematic collections. Though these are no longer available on the Replay site, you can log in and explore how this worked, and indeed, even try the functionality yourself, by following the instructions at: www.siobhandaviesreplay.com/help_faqs#scrapbook/. It's worth noting that this archive's development was funded by the UK's Arts and Humanities Research Council itself. While Davies's output was not understood to be made up of formal academic research outcomes, it provided an interesting test case for exploring how data archives might be shaped in performance practices.

6 This is not a mainstream view of Barthes. For more detail underpinning this assertion, see Bonenfant (2010).

7 Both Connor in his recent monograph *Beyond Words* (2014) and sound theorist Labelle (2014) have attempted to explore the a-textual or a-verbal qualities or components of vocalisation in extended meditative explorations. In my view, both are unsatisfactory with regards to exploring the politics of the extra-normal voice, in the sense that the former construes and devalues the a-verbal sound as 'noise'; the latter dissects the verbal and works from a treatment of the a-verbal sound as abstract sound phenomenon. However, both signal an upswell in interest in non-normative vocal sound in exciting ways.

8 There is a canon of sorts of extended voice artists who have worked within post-Artaudian theatre, intercultural theatre, experimental music, post-1950s classically derived art music, live/performance art, and in hybrid forms. On a spectrum from the musical to the theatrical – and involving widely varied degrees of technical mediation of the voice – we might name key figures, such as Cathy Berberian, Diamanda Galas, Jaap Blonk, Joan LaBarbara, Pamela Z, Mikhail Karikis, Laurie Anderson, the Roy Hart Theatre, the Gardzienice tradition, and the intercultural theatre experiments of Barba/Odin Teatret. The penetration of non-Western, oppressed, subcultural, and gender-challenging vocal textures into pop music in successive waves since the invention of sound recording could also be charted, but such an analysis is beyond the scope of this article.

References

Barthes, Roland. 1991. *The grain of the voice.* Berkeley, CA: University of California Press.

Behrndt, Synne. 2014. "Dramaturgy and the facilitation of encounters." *Forum Modernes Theater* 44:130–141.

Best, Catherine. 1994. "The emergence of native language phonological influences in infants: the perceptual assimilation model." In *The development of speech perception: the transition from speech sounds to spoken words,* edited by Judith C. Goodman and Howard C. Nussbaum, 167–224. Cambridge, MA: MIT Press.

Best, Catherine, and Gerald McRoberts. 2003. "Infant perception of non-native consonant contrasts that adults assimilate in different ways." *Language and Speech* 46 (2/3):183–216.

Bonenfant, Yvon. 2010. "Queer listening to queer vocal timbres." *Performance Research* 15 (3):74–80. doi:10.1080/13528165.2010.527210.

Brown, Steven. 2007. "Contageous heterophony: a new theory about the origins of music." *Musicae Scientiae* XI (1):3–26.

Brown, Steven, Elton Ngan, and Mario Liotti. 2008. "A Larynx area in the human motor cortex." *Cerebral Cortex* 18:837–845.

Cavarero, Adriana. 2005. *For more than one voice: toward a philosophy of vocal expression.* Stanford, CA: Stanford University Press.

Connor, Steven. 2000. *Dumbstruck: a cultural history of ventriloquism.* Oxford: Oxford University Press.

Connor, Steven. 2014. *Beyond words: sobs, hums, stutters and other vocalizations.* London: Reaktion.

Garrett, Leigh. 2013. "What is visual arts research data? (revisited)," https://kaptur.wordpress.com/2013/01/23/what-is-visual-arts-research-data-revisited/, accessed 4 April 2016.

Goldstein, Louis, and Philip Rubin. 2007. "Speech: dances of the vocal tract." *Odyssey Magazine* 14–15.

Karikis, Mikhail. 2005. *The Acoustics of the Self.* PhD Thesis, London: UCL.

Kreiman, Jody, and Diana Sidtis. 2011. *Foundations of voice studies: an interdisciplinary approach to voice production and perception.* Malden, MA: Wiley-Blackwell.

Labelle, Brandon. 2014. *Lexicon of the mouth.* London: Bloomsbury.

Leavy, Patricia. 2009. *Method meets art.* New York: The Guildford Press.

Ledger, Adam K., Simon K. Ellis, and Fiona Wright. 2011. "The question of documentation: Creative strategies in performance research." In *Research methods in theatre and performance*, edited by Baz Kershaw and Helen Nicholson, 162–185. Edinburgh: Edinburgh University Press.

Nelson, Robin. 2006. "Modes of PaR knowledge and their place in the academy," accessed 12 April 2017. www.westminster.ac.uk/_data/assets/pdf_file/0011/74594/RobinNelson.pdf

Nelson, Robin. 2013. *Practice as research in the arts: principles, protocols, pedagogies, resistances.* Basingstoke: Palgrave Macmillan.

Olwage, Grant. 2004. "The class and colour of tone: an essay on the social history of vocal timbre." *Ethnomusicology Forum* 13 (2):203–226.

Oxford English Dictionary. 2006. www.oed.com, accessed 4 April 2016.

Piccini, Angela, and Caroline Rye. 2009. "Of fevered archives and the quest for total documentation." In *Practice-as-research in performance and screen*, edited by Ludivine Allegue Fuschini, Baz Kershaw, Simon Jones and Angela Piccini, 34–49. Basingstoke: Palgrave.

Rans, Jonathan. 2014. "UAL slides Jonathan Rans, DCC," accessed 12 April 2017. ualresearchdata.myblog.arts.ac.uk/files/2014/07/UAL-slides-rans.pptx.

Reason, Matthew. 2010. *The young audience: exploring and enhancing children's experiences of theatre.* Stoke-on-Trent: Trentham.

Schwab, Michael, and Henk Borgdorff, eds. 2014. *The exposition of artistic research: publishing art in academia.* Leiden: Leiden University Press.

Studdert-Kennedy, Michael, and Louis Goldstein. 2002. "Launching language: the gestural origin of discreet infinity." In *Language evolution*, edited by Morton Christiansen and Simon Kirby, 235–254. Oxford: Oxford University Press.

Thomaidis, Konstantinos. 2015. "The re-vocalisation of logos?: thinking, doing and disseminating voice." In *Voice studies: critical approaches to process, performance and experience,* edited by
Konstantinos Thomaidis and Ben Macpherson, 10–21. Abingdon/New York: Routledge.
United States Office of Budget Management. 1999. "Circular A-110 revised 11/19/93 as
further amended 9/30/99," accessed 4 February 2016.

Chapter 11

Choreographic practice-as-research

Visualizing conceptual structures in contemporary dance

Stephan Jürgens and Carla Fernandes

Introduction

This essay consists of two interrelated parts. Part 1 distinguishes specific contemporary choreographic processes by critically reviewing the state-of-the-art literature and discusses how adequate practice-as-research methods can be designed. Looking at what we call the development cycle and the iteration cycle in the production of a new stage work, we differentiate those stages in the choreographic process that can be best investigated through PAR methods. Subsequently, we examine the role of video annotation and of recent digital media technologies that support the visualization of choreographic thinking and practice. We argue that these media practices can contribute much to recent developments in performance documentation and can be employed as analytical lenses for critical reflection on artistic practice.

Part 2 of this essay presents a case study on the choreographic process in selected solo works by João Fiadeiro. Since Fiadeiro can arguably be best described as a conceptual artist, we had to develop an adequate specific research design to investigate his particular *modus operandi*. Our research methods included: artistic collaboration on a new version of his solo work *I Was Here*; annotation of the video documentation of this work; and the development of a novel form of visualizing the conceptual structures in Fiadeiro's work. As a result, we have produced an animated infographic film, which complements this essay and is discussed in Part 2. We conclude by looking at the impact that our study design and outcomes have produced in scientific and artistic communities beyond our own.

Part 1: how choreographic practice-as-research can produce new embodied knowledge and new formats of public presentation

Many authors have tackled the complex question of which (artistic) practices constitute research in the context of PAR theory. However, the kind of knowledge created in each artistic field varies greatly. Coming from the field of contemporary dance and choreography, we intend in this essay to have a closer look at which specific practices, and which stages of the artistic process, in the area we are referring to can indeed constitute research in a PAR context.

In fact, the term "contemporary dance" describes a wide range of very divergent choreographic practices and presentation formats. Friederike Lampert in her important book on dance improvisation (2007) and Gabriele Klein have provided thorough surveys of the main choreographic practices in Western artistic stage dance. Gabriele Klein examines contemporary choreographic practices in an introductory essay to *Choreographischer Baukasten* (2015), a resource book for choreographers, dancers, and everyone else involved in theatre and performance, with a focus on choreographic processes and productions. Looking at contemporary dance and choreography in the twentieth and twenty-first centuries, Klein presents the reader with a succinct survey of the main stage dance forms and related choreographic practices – namely expressionist dance, modern dance, postmodern dance, contact improvisation, (neoclassical) ballet, Tanztheater, and more recently, self-reflexive postmodern dance and concept dance.

In particular, concept dance declares the self-reflexivity of the medium of dance as aesthetic object. The performed act of dancing and the execution of movement are replaced in concept dance by onstage reflections on choreographic practice. Hence the dancing body is no longer the sole medium of contemporary choreography and choreography is no longer understood only as the organization of the movements of human bodies in space and time. Instead, contemporary choreography is conceived as a "collection and organization of heterogeneous materials, as an intermedial arrangement of bodies, spoken language, texts, images, light, sound and objects" (Klein 2015: 43). In the words of choreographer Jérôme Bel, "choreography today introduces the shift from dance towards that which surrounds dance, the life of dancers, the audiences, the history of dance, the role of the author, dance as culture and inter-culture, the rules of dance and choreography" (Bel in Klein 2015: 46).

According to Klein, concept dance has initiated a process that conceives choreographic practice as research practice, research practice as a collaborative form, and collaborative form often as critical sociocultural praxis. However, choreographic practice as research is not limited to artistic research, such as the enquiry into appropriate themes and materials for a new production. Choreographic practice as research rather produces new embodied knowledge in the form of specific techniques, new methods for the generation and composition of movement material, and new models for collaboration.

Furthermore, self-reflexive choreographic practice and choreographic practice as research have produced concomitant formats of public presentation. For example, the presentation of the artistic creative process onstage in the (hybrid) form of lecture-demonstration is a clear example of a novel performance format that has recently entered mainstream theatre programs. Another experimental format that has been widely implemented is real-time composition as live performance, which allows simultaneous presentation of the content and the presentation of the artistic methods and techniques onstage, which in turn may encourage certain forms of active participation from audiences. The choreographic work of João Fiadeiro, which we discuss in the second part of this essay, can be best situated and contextualized in that area of contemporary artistic practice as conceptual and self-reflexive postmodern dance.

Combining theory-generating practice and artwork exegesis

In the following section, we synthesize dance theory with PAR theory and discuss how adequate practice-as-research methods in the field of contemporary choreography can be designed.

Klein and her collaborators' *Choreographischer Baukasten* exemplify Barbara Bolt's notion of "material thinking" and "materializing practices", which produce new knowledge that "emerge[s] in the involvement with materials, methods, tools and ideas of practice" (2007: 31). In Bolt's contribution to the collection *Practice as Research: Approaches to Creative Arts Enquiry* she contends "that it is art as a mode of revealing and as a material productivity, not just the artwork that constitutes creative arts research" (2007: 34). For Bolt, "through the vehicle of the exegesis, practice becomes theory generating" (2007: 33)[1], which plays a critical and complementary role. Brad Haseman elaborates on exegesis in his contribution to the same essay collection:

> However, if we take an alternative understanding of exegesis "that it is, at root, a leading or guiding out of a complexity" (dictionary.com: 2003) then we have a more open and rich field of possibilities for practice-led researchers to complete their contribution to knowledge.
>
> (2007: 156)

Reading Haseman with Bolt, it seems that an understanding of artwork exegesis as a critical, complementary, and theory-generating practice directed towards "leading out of the complexity" of the multilayered material thinking of the artistic work represents a methodological key for PAR projects on all levels of academic endeavour. However, the crucial question here is whether the artwork exegesis is for the most part based on the actual materializing practices in the studio and on the stage, or predominantly based on documents (usually simple video recordings) that supposedly 'preserve' and represent these practices.

We propose that material thinking as the logic of practice can be better preserved and complemented by a form of exegesis that is not interpretative or representative of the artistic process and work, but adopts a Sullivanian "create to inquire" art-based research approach (2006: 28).[2] In Piccini and Rye's words,

> Only art can inquire about the truths that art produces. In other words, documentation can neither properly comment on nor reveal and disseminate

the research dimensions of art, as demanded by the peer review and assessment structures outlined above. Again, it is important to be clear about the difference between the use of recording technologies to produce art in proximity of practice-as-research and the use of recording technologies in the impossible task of documenting practice-as-research.

(2009: 42)

In relation to our field of inquiry, this passage is remarkable for two reasons: (1) from this perspective the knowledge produced by contemporary choreography can be articulated only through the methods, techniques, and performance of contemporary choreography; and (2) since the task of documenting choreography-as-research is (virtually) impossible, dissemination of the research dimensions of contemporary choreography will be more successful by employing recording technologies to produce art in proximity of choreography-as-research. Piccini and Rye's observations resonate with discussions of performance documentation systems we have witnessed for decades in the field of contemporary dance, and for that matter in the entire field of performing arts and live art.

"The Body as Archive": reinventing dance performance documentation

From our point of view this discussion took a different direction, away from the focus on the supposedly ephemeral nature of dance, when André Lepecki published his exceptional study *Exhausting Dance: Performance and the Politics of Movement* (2006). Through Lepecki's insightful analysis of the major transformations in contemporary dance since the 1990s, it became evident that dance performance documentation had to reinvent itself to accompany the radical changes in artistic practice and research. In a subsequent article, "The Body as Archive: Will to Re-Enact and the Afterlives of Dances" (2010), Lepecki advances the concept of "the body as archive". This view proposes that dance knowledge is tied to individuals, to bodies themselves, thus suggesting that performance is documentation in itself. Artistic skills can then hardly be archived if not by direct and affective transmission from bodies to bodies. A similar view is shared by the team working on the future Pina Bausch archive,[3] where the challenge is one of attempting to build a "living archive (. . .) inspiring visitors to engage in creative work themselves".[4] According to the Pina Bausch Foundation, Bausch had long collected items with the aim of ensuring that her work would be kept alive and seen on stage in the future.

In this chapter we assume that documentation presupposes the description *and* reflection of working processes: looking at how and where "performative networks" (Klein 2015: 47) originate, whether during rehearsals or unexpectedly on stage for instance, and what materials are generated as a result. In performative processes, something new always emerges. It is precisely here that we see the "translation" of performances as an empirical research project, because the praxis of translating creative processes provokes us to understand the boundaries between aesthetic practice and discourse. The several possible discourses that emerge around a work of art are not meant to be interpretations, but must rather be understood as "translations of the untranslatable" (32). They will always miss something, leave something out, and add something else, but they will never be identical to the original aesthetic processes under analysis. They should work as entrance doors, as *complementary* contributions, rather than as re-presentations. The same applies to new media technologies and other modalities, such as documentaries or infographic visualizations, that attempt to translate choreographic concepts or processes: they try to express the latter through various solutions, but in its essence the problem remains – that is the solutions remain merely different ways of approaching the problem.

Fresh perspectives on the complex interrelations between choreographic practices, documentation, and dissemination of research

Based on the notion of "body as archive" we will look at more recent approaches to how embodied knowledge can be accessed and researched, appropriately presented and documented, and how research can be disseminated in a form that allows for academic appreciation as much as for practical experimentation.

The question "What can a body do?" serves as a starting point for a theory of embodied knowledge, or "epistemology of practice", recently proposed by Ben Spatz (2015). He argues that technique is knowledge that structures practice and, accordingly, that if technique is knowledge, then practice can be research. Spatz writes, "As a field of knowledge, technique is constituted by the dynamic interplay of *training* and *research*, where the latter refers to the development of new techniques through processes of investigation and exploration" (Spatz 2015: 60–61). Spatz's "epistemology of practice" resonates with methodologies of academic and artistic research in dance composition and choreography which are predominantly based on codified movement languages and styles, offer training in a particular system, and use specific sets of compositional principles, techniques, and methods. For Spatz, training in a specific technique enables the researcher of embodied knowledge to evaluate more objectively whether his or her findings only represent personal discoveries and growth or whether the results of the research are significant for a larger community. In the latter case the community will recognize important discoveries, which may lead to the evolution of existing techniques or innovation and the development of new techniques.

However, when we investigate concept dance, real-time composition, or generative performance systems (as is the case of our case study on João Fiadeiro), we are looking at a different set of practices, methods, and techniques. Hansen and House ask,

> How can we archive and pass on dance works that are not set in repeatable ways, but generated systematically on stage? Performance-generating systems are best described as a semi-closed form of instant composition in dance

and theatre: a dramaturgy of pre-identified tasks, rules and sources within the boundaries of which performers interact on stage. These performer-interactions are neither pre-determined nor arbitrary; they self-organize around shifting components that attract certain kinds of behaviour over time. They also tend to involve cognitive challenges that initiate and accelerate a process of learning how to perceive differently while performing.

(Hansen and House, 2015: 65)

Drawing on Thelen and Smith's version of dynamical systems theory (DTS), Hansen and House propose a novel conceptual lens to identify the key components of performance-generating systems, which aids archival work as much as it provides tools for the re-embodiment of the work in each application. They suggest the following:

The archival traces left in, for example, a dancer's embodied memory are of a practice within the system instead of the spatial, temporal and relational markers of set movement known from more conventional approaches. (. . .) Performance systems cannot be remounted by re-enacting captured movement; it is by re-engaging generating principles that the works may be performed anew.

(Hansen and House 2015: 65)

Hansen and House link the process of "re-engaging generating principles" of a performance system to Lepecki's "will to archive" – namely "a capacity to identify in a past work still non-exhausted creative fields" (2015: 65).

João Fiadeiro's real-time composition method and his dramaturgic *modus operandi* certainly can be described as a 'performance-generating system'. In our case study we show in detail what key components generate\ performance in each instance and how Fiadeiro explores Lepecki's "non-exhausted creative fields" in a past work based on a methodology he has developed over more than two decades. At the heart of Fiadeiro's method is what he calls "being affected", a state of being intrigued, moved, or disturbed by something. The relation with that which affects Fiadeiro constitutes the creative field to which Lepecki refers and which is explored within a given performance-generating system.

In the following we also link these ideas to those of Derek McCormack, who has recently presented a seminal book introducing the concept of "affective spaces", which can be researched using a methodology he calls "experimenting experience".

McCormack asks,

How to explore and make sense of how bodies and spaces co-produce one another through practices, gestures, movements and events?
    . . . I argue that making sense of this generative relation – that is, learning to think through and within the spaces produced for and by moving

bodies – demands particular attention to the affective qualities of these spaces combined with a commitment to experimenting with different ways of becoming attuned to these qualities. Affective qualities are those heterogeneous matters of the sensible world we often try to capture through terms such as emotion, mood, and feeling. As part of the "affective turn" across the social sciences, these qualities of everyday life have been explored in a range of interesting and important ways.

(McCormack 2014: 2–3)

For McCormack, affective spaces are relational, processual, and nonrepresentational. If, as he claims, moving bodies participate in the generation of affective spaces, these affective spaces in turn cannot exist without the moving bodies. In other words, the affective qualities of the rehearsal work at the studio or of a live performance are essential qualities in choreography and cannot possibly be perceived and captured through video recordings alone. This observation clearly resonates with Piccini and Rye's first affirmation earlier.

Drawing on William James and John Dewey, McCormack proposes "experimenting experience" as an appropriate empirical method to research affective spaces:

When I use experimented in this book it is not, therefore, to reintroduce some experimental distance, but to draw a conjunctive and transitional relation between the process of thinking and the process of experience.

To learn to be affected by affective spacetimes is not, then, to strip away the experience of these spacetimes, but to make more of this experience through experimentation with techniques, concepts, and materials.

(McCormack 2014: 9)

Klein's *Choreographischer Baukasten* is both consistent with the ideas advanced by the theorists set forth earlier and a concrete example for 'experimenting experience'. The materials contained in this choreographic resource book (theoretical introductory essay, interviews with established choreographers on specific aspects of choreographic practice, two sets of exercise books and cards) were extracted and developed from choreographic practice. Choreographic principles, techniques, and methods can be used to initiate artistic and research processes, as much as they can be simultaneously employed to reflect upon ongoing and concluded practice.

Similarly, William Forsythe's well-known CD-ROM *Improvisation Technologies: A Tool for the Analytical Dance Eye* (1997) consists of 60 video chapters in which he demonstrates key principles of his motional language at the time. A layer of motion graphics on top of the video recordings helps to visualize the respective principles more thoroughly. The user can navigate back and forth between the video lessons and annotated example excerpts of filmed improvisations by four of Forsythe's dancers. As the title indicates, all principles can be tried out in dance improvisation practice. Alternatively, the principles can be employed as analytical lenses when watching Forsythe's choreography (and eventually that of others as well).

Publications such as the *Choreographischer Baukasten* and *Improvisation Technologies* do not simply shift the focus from the art product to artistic and research processes in the studio but also instigate the reader/user to "re-engage generating principles". They represent a very different approach to the dissemination of the research dimension, in which *choreographic thinking and practice are made visible and simultaneously re-enactable, presented to be experienced in practice.*

Making choreographic thinking and practice visible

Coming back to Piccini and Rye's "use of recording technologies to produce art in proximity of practice-as-research", we now need to take a closer look at what it might mean "to produce art" in proximity to choreography. As we have described elsewhere in more detail (Fernandes and Jürgens 2013), the choreographic process can be broken down into "development cycles" and subsequent "iteration cycles", both of which comprise different stages at which different techniques, methods, and strategies for collaboration come into play. The iteration cycle differentiates three phases: (1) the public performance of a piece; (2) the documentation of the work (including rehearsals and performances); and (3) the restaging, or re-creation of a piece. Conventionally, the focus of research dissemination – even in the case of many PAR research projects – is the final product, the artistic artwork presented to the public in combination with its analysis and interpretation.[5] In other words, the tendency is to consider only information and materials that are accessible to the public (that have been published in some way), so no direct contact with the artist is requisite for the research project.

However, *most of the choreographic practice-as-research is carried out in the studio, during the production phase.* The development cycle describes four production phases: (1) developing the artistic concept based on research and preparatory training; (2) creating material; (3) designing strategies for interaction; and (4) developing micro- and macro-structures of the performance. In most cases artistic choreographic production during this first cycle is not open to the public and rarely documented with publication in mind. Hence it is not surprising that very few academics know more in depth about contemporary choreographic thinking and practices. We argue that, particularly in the development cycle, there is a wealth of artistic knowledge production to be discovered and research design needs to be rigorously developed in proximity to the specific techniques, methods, and processes employed in each of these phases.

During the past two decades we have seen an increasing number of publications that have provided some access to the development cycle of choreographic work.[6] Two tendencies can be highlighted, which for us constitute promising developments towards a deeper understanding of choreographic practice:

firstly the shift from the use of notational languages to the use of annotation techniques;[7] and secondly the application of recent digital media techniques to visualize motional data and compositional structures.

In Part 2 of this article we go on to describe our approach to combining video annotation with data visualization in our study on João Fiadeiro's work. We made use of these media practices to produce four short animated infographic films – which in itself is a novel format of performance documentation – and also employed these visualization techniques as an analytical lens for critical reflection upon Fiadeiro's choreographic *modus operandi*.

Part 2: a case study in researching and visualizing compositional structures and dramaturgical strategies in the solo work of choreographer João Fiadeiro

Motivation to work with João Fiadeiro

João Fiadeiro belongs to a generation of choreographers that emerged in the late 1980s and which, following the movement of American and French "postmodern dance" and Belgian *Nouvelle Danse* movements, has given rise to the *Nova Dança Portuguesa [New Portuguese Dance]*. Much of his training was received between Lisbon, New York, and Berlin, after having been a dancer at the Dance Company of Lisbon (1986–88) and the Gulbenkian Ballet (1989–90). In 1990, he founded the Company RE.AL, which, in addition to the creation and touring of their own shows – regularly presented in Europe, the United States, Canada, Australia, and South America – has accompanied and represented emerging artists and has also welcomed and presented transdisciplinary artists in the framework of the LAB/Projects in Motion.

In the framework of our research project BlackBox,[8] Carla Fernandes invited Fiadeiro to be the first long-breadth case study out of the three cases planned for the five-year project. Fiadeiro welcomed this invitation enthusiastically, as he had previously collaborated with scientists and scholars from the domains of neuroscience, sociology, economics, and anthropology and found those interchanges extremely productive.

Fernandes's main motivation was to analyze Fiadeiro's compositional processes, starting from the concepts he had both developed in theory and applied during 25 years in workshops and theatre stages all over the world. The aim was to "translate" the concepts and processes underlying his performative work in order to arrive at new forms of visualizations that would hopefully contribute to a deeper understanding of his creative universe.

Fiadeiro is a rather particular contemporary choreographer, one who can even be considered a conceptual artist if we take into account that the well-defined concepts and ideas involved in most of his pieces take precedence over traditional aesthetic and material concerns. He has developed his working method over more than two decades and has called it "Composition in Real Time". This method was initially designed to support his choreographic and dramaturgical work, but it has gradually evolved into a tool and theoretical platform to think about decision-making, representation, and collaboration. The latter aspect was one of the main reasons for us to invite him for collaboration. For a project where the performing arts are being analyzed as a rich *corpus* of data allowing us to learn more about human behaviour, collaborative decision, creativity, and the complexity of the mind, Fiadeiro seemed to be an ideal case study.

Fiadeiro's compositions start from reflections about situations, objects, photos, films, and so forth, which have deeply "affected" (in the sense of having an impact on) him, but then emerge almost naturally by letting the events assume their own life, by observing them carefully and by taking decisions collaboratively, according to what exists ("o que há", in Fiadeiro's terms) around the dancers and in their own actions. Moreover, when Fiadeiro talks about his methodology and intentions, his discourse is thoroughly articulated, although always in process from session to session, in (e)motion according to each day's environment and never obvious or crystallized.

The SOLOS | ENACTMENTS performance series presented in November 2014 in Lisbon, Portugal

After six years of absence from the stage, during which Fiadeiro dedicated himself to investigating, systematizing, and developing his Composition in Real Time method, he initiated a new choreographic cycle. For his first re-appearance he chose to present his audience with an "updated topographic map of concerns".[9] In other words, Fiadeiro selected three solo works from different decades for the SOLOS | ENACTMENTS performance series, reworked two pieces (*I Am Sitting in a Different Room From the One You Are in Now*, 1997; and *Este corpo que me ocupa* [This body that occupies me], 2008) and presented the third (*I Was Here*, 2014) in the hybrid format of a lecture-performance in which he shares his artistic research and choreographic *modus operandi* with the audience.

For us as researchers interested in the initial stages of Fiadeiro's creative process, it was a rare opportunity and great privilege to witness and accompany this beginning of a new choreographic cycle, particularly because Fiadeiro started this new phase presenting his audience with a reflection upon his entire career. One of the authors of this essay, Stephan Jürgens, was invited by Fiadeiro to collaborate as a video designer on a new version of *I Was Here* (one of the solo pieces). This collaboration represented a unique opportunity to research Fiadeiro's artistic *modus operandi* from a PAR perspective, and helped us to develop a novel research method, which we will describe in detail in the course of this essay.

The lecture-performance *I Was Here* (2014) revisits the signature piece *I Am Here*, and provides an in-depth insight into Fiadeiro's creative process and artistic methodology. *I Am Here* (2003, premiere at the Centre George Pompidou, Paris) is a solo piece inspired by the work of the well-known visual artist Helena Almeida and several personal encounters with her during Fiadeiro's creative process. Visual artist and architect Walter Lauterer created the scenography-sculpture for the piece, which serves as the conceptual and physical environment that allows Fiadeiro to translate specific images and situations in Almeida's work into his own medium and to test the limits of his dramaturgic ideas.

What affected Fiadeiro? Choreography, neurophysiology, and the psychology of perception

In *I Was Here* (2014) Fiadeiro sits motionless at a square table made of dark wood. He quietly looks above a laptop computer in front of him into the audience, or maybe into the far distance. A headlight is mounted on a metal structure behind and illuminates him diagonally, casting a long black shadow on the floor. Suddenly the light changes: cold fluorescent light from four neon tubes hung centre stage illuminate the scene. Apart from the alteration in the lighting, absolutely nothing has changed. Fiadeiro continues to sit motionless in front of his laptop, the shadow continues exactly the same – and it may be right in this moment that the audience realizes that this is an impossibility: an impossible shadow, because a shadow cannot be identical when cast from two different light sources mounted in different places and angles. So this cannot be a shadow. What else might it be?

At this point Fiadeiro breaks his silence, looks calmly at the people in the audience, smiles, and starts in a relaxed manner to talk to them. Every night he varies to some extent what he says, in accord with the contact he has established with the audience. "More than half of this conference-performance has already passed. Precisely in the moment of entering this room, when you came from the outside, from the different worlds you have inhabited, all of you have arrived here. You came through this door over there, distracted, looking for your seat, you have briefly looked at the stage over here, at this area here, recognized, okay, João is sitting over there at a table, a headlight, a shadow . . . hold on – a shadow? This shadow, that's not possible, this cannot be a shadow. This is theatre . . . (laughs)." A different night in a different place before a different audience he begins,

> This silence that I have offered you existed to give you time, or, better: to give your brain the time it needs to assimilate and process what just has happened. And what has just happened is an impossibility. In other words: this shadow shouldn't actually be there.

These first minutes of the conference-performance *I Was Here* (2014) are not simply a cognitive exercise. Fiadeiro invites his audience to experience for themselves what for him has been a decisive discovery in the creative process of one of his most important stage works, *I Am Here* (2003). Subsequently he projects

Figure 11.1 Video still *I Was Here* (2015, Caldas de Rainha version).

images and video documents of the rehearsals and performances to share with the audience how *I Am Here* was made. Intrigued by the work of Portuguese artist Helena Almeida, and inspired by personal encounters with her, Fiadeiro created a new stage work that can be best described as "concept dance", but also understood as transmedial live art. The opening scene of the conference-performance *I Was Here* allows the audience to live through a personal experience of a significant shift in perception that Fiadeiro himself experienced when he had a conversation with Almeida about a particular photograph of hers.

The photograph shows Almeida from behind, stepping away from the observer (see left image projected in figure 11.1). On the floor one sees a black figure that seems to be a shadow of Almeida at first glance, but doesn't have a head or hands. During their conversation Fiadeiro mentions how he was intrigued by the "shadow" and Almeida corrects him, saying that the dark grey pigment on the floor is not a shadow, but for her represents a dress. . . . The experience of forming an image in his mind, which in parts ignores details of the photograph, motivated Fiadeiro to research into the field of neurophysiology and the psychology of perception.

Dramaturgical strategies: performance mode
and conference mode

Fiadeiro employs two dramaturgical strategies in the conference-performance *I Was Here* to transmit his choreographic *modus operandi* in the making of *I Am Here*: firstly, he provides the opportunity for the audience to experience the beginning scene of *I Am Here* first-hand by performing it for them. Secondly, he shows how he had developed that scene and provides detailed information about the creation process of *I Am Here*, which becomes the material for the conference-performance *I Was Here*. In other words, Fiadeiro is both present as a performer/author and a researcher/lecturer who illuminates his own artistic process from a first-person perspective. This sounds more complicated than it is in the audience's experience of the conference-performance, because Fiadeiro uses the conventions of stage dance in a theatre to clearly distinguish those scenes in which he re-enacts excerpts from *I Am Here* from those in which he acts as the researcher/lecturer. In other words, he employs a "performance mode" and a "conference mode". When in performance mode, his presence on stage is that of a dancer inviting the audience to perceive with all their senses what he is doing. The conventional separation between audience and performers on stage exists and is felt. In conference mode this separation does not exist, and Fiadeiro talks directly to the audience about his artistic process.

After Fiadeiro has shown (in conference mode) how he translated Almeida's photograph of the shadow/dress into choreography, he switches into performance mode again. That photograph is the first in a series of seven (which he projects for the audience). On each successive image the dress made of dark grey pigment appears increasingly deformed. However, there is no hint as to what has happened from one moment to the next, or what could have caused the deformation. Fiadeiro translates this missing information, this missing space-time between the photographs, as six moments of total darkness onstage. During these moments he dances invisibly to the eye of the audience. These

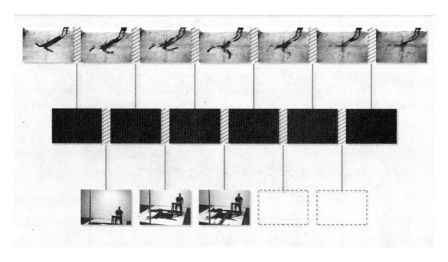

Figure 11.2 Video still from our infographic film about *I Was Here*. Film by Stephan Jürgens; copyright BlackBox project.

dances in the dark are interrupted by short moments in which the stage is brightly illuminated and the spectator can see how Fiadeiro's dance has likewise transformed the pigment on the floor. Gradually a large-scale drawing emerges (see Figure 11.2, images on the bottom).

The diagram image shown here visualizes the conceptual reasoning behind the dance-in-the-dark scene. It emerged during the rehearsal for the Caldas version of *I Was Here* (March 2015), in which Jürgens collaborated with Fiadeiro. Given the scope and purpose of this chapter, we will not discuss the remaining scenes in this much detail, but instead shift our focus to the effects that Fiadeiro's invitation to collaborate had on our research design and findings.

An invitation to research through artistic collaboration

Fiadeiro's invitation to collaborate on his re-enactment of *I Was Here* was spontaneous, during an interview with him in March 2015. I (Jürgens) had asked him for a meeting because I wanted to discuss my research project about his *SOLOS | Enactments* performance cycle.[10] I had prepared a questionnaire, but towards the end of the conversation João told me that he had a suggestion for me. In his opinion I could best research his work through practice, so he invited me to cooperate on a new version of *I Was Here*. His idea was to rework the conference-performance and to develop a format that would be portable and could be quickly and easily adapted to the circumstances of each performance venue. He invited me to develop the video design for the piece based on my experience in theatre interaction design.

This invitation was particularly interesting because it was preceded by a conversation about performance documentation. I had asked João how he documented his pieces and whether he made use of some sort of score. He responded,

> No, there is no score. There is no video either. There is what I have called fields, or landscapes, which in essence are questions, which are areas that the piece approaches and which need some kind of translation, some kind of materialization or execution, which are translations of the field. And what I have to do is to recover this field, I have to clarify.[11]

When I asked Fiadeiro how he preserved such a field or landscape, whether he used his body as "living archive", he explained as follows:

> Yes, (. . .) it's like going back to a place where you have lived twenty years ago, and when you enter the apartment, its architecture helps you to remember. (. . .) It's enough to reconstruct the method and I remember that body, the quality of that particular body.[12]

This moment in the interview with Fiadeiro reconfirmed for us that it is crucial to experience the *modus operandi* of a specific artistic practice before endeavouring to analyze that same practice with any type of discourse predetermined by academic theories. Constraining empirical research by pre-established terminologies or discourses would limit the mutual discovery process that can then lead to more generative practice-based theories.

I developed the video design for *I Was Here* using the software Isadora[13] in rehearsals for a performance at Escola Superior de Arte e Design, an art and design college at Caldas da Rainha in the north of Lisbon. The Isadora document, which I programmed, provides Fiadeiro during live performance with total control over each element of the video projection in every scene. It is a tool that can be compared to a sophisticated PowerPoint presentation. At the same time, the Isadora document helped me to set down and describe the structure and content of the piece in great detail. In other words, the Isadora document functions like a performative score in that it generates live performance (for Fiadeiro) and generates documentation (for Fiadeiro and for us). For our research, the Isadora document serves as a transmedial score – a document in which the different strands of a performance are coordinated and the dramaturgical structure of the work is put on record.[14]

Research method 1: video annotation

Using a camcorder, I recorded the performance from a dedicated seat in the audience. The entire stage could be captured from this viewpoint and I also could zoom in to focus on details. Afterwards I imported the video recording into the annotation software ELAN, which makes it possible to mark the exact time at which Fiadeiro transitions from one scene to another on a dedicated annotation track, or "tier".[15] I also added a number of text annotations on an additional tier. On a further track I annotated the names which Fiadeiro himself had given the scenes; on another track I labelled the scenes in the performance and conference mode categories; and on yet another track I grouped the scenes thematically in five categories: perception, affection, translation, discarded material, and collaborations.

Research method 2: visualizing the scene structure and compositional aspects graphically

The ELAN software allows one to export annotations in various formats. In this case it was particularly important to get a complete list of all the scenes of *I Was Here*, including the corresponding time code to calculate the exact duration of each scene. With this information I could, for example, visualize how much time Fiadeiro spent respectively in performance mode and in conference mode. Especially in comparison with other performances of *I Was Here*, this information is very revealing, as we will show in the next section.

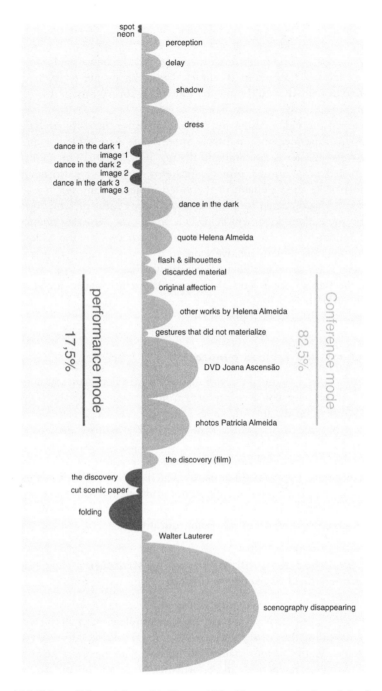

Figure 11.3 Video still from infographic film on *I Was Here* – organization of the five thematic areas. Film by Stephan Jürgens; copyright BlackBox project.

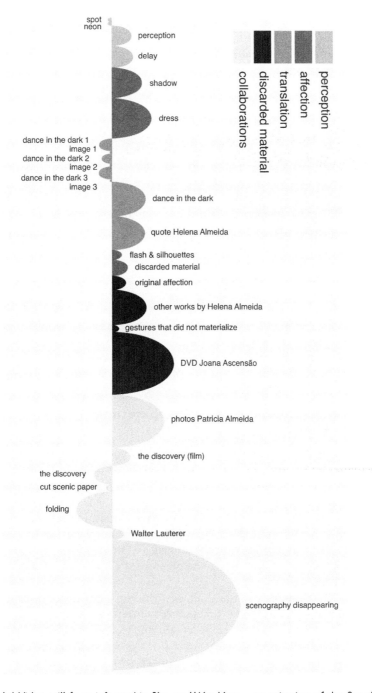

Figure 11.4 Video still from infographic film on *I Was Here* – organization of the five thematic areas. Film by Stephan Jürgens; copyright BlackBox project.

Following the annotation work in ELAN, I used the vector drawing program Affinity Designer[16] to visualize the scene list and duration of scenes in the form of a stream graph diagram (figure 11.3).

An identical scenic structure was then used to visualize graphically how Fiadeiro organized and developed the five different topics in *I Was Here*. Each section is colour-coded[17] and gradations between two colours indicate transitions between two topics in a single scene or that the contents in a scene belong to more than one thematic area. Again, the graphic (in figure 11.4) is of particular interest for comparisons between different iterations of *I Was Here*.

Which infographic techniques one uses depends on what precisely is to be visualized. In order to contemplate and analyze Fiadeiro's compositional strategies, we have used a flow chart for the dance in the dark example (as shown in figure 11.2) and a timeline-based stream graph to display the scenic structure of *I Was Here* (as shown in figures 11.3 and 11.4). In our study we have particularly focused on the structural aspects of Fiadeiro's dramaturgy in order to answer two very complex questions through this analysis:

1   How does Fiadeiro create different *affective spacetimes*[18] in *I Was Here*? When, where, and how do they evolve from one state to the next?
2   How can we understand the important concept of "accumulative writing" and represent it so that it becomes accessible to interested parties who do not have the opportunity to see the same stage work by Fiadeiro in different places?

Creating and modulating affective spacetimes *in* I Was Here

By virtue of the graphic visualization we can draw some interesting conclusions regarding the first question. If we examine the graph in figure 11.3 more closely, we recognize that Fiadeiro spends significantly less time in performance mode than he is spending in conference mode. In the Lisbon version he communicates just 17.5% of the time in performance mode. During the greater part of the time spent onstage (82.5%) he creates an atmosphere that is reminiscent of a personal conversation with the audience – although Fiadeiro rarely poses a direct question, or answers a question from the audience, so that an actual dialogue could start.

As a result of this dramaturgical strategy (shifting between performance mode and conference mode several times), an intimacy between the artist and his audience develops: Fiadeiro literally reveals "the secrets" of his artistic process, of which there is little or no publicly available documentation. The short scenes in performance mode here function as enhancers of intimacy: each time Fiadeiro changes from performance mode to conference mode (three times in total), he gives up the distance, usually created by the performer on stage, to move on to a more conversational level of communication with his audience. Through first-hand contact with Fiadeiro, the audience is increasingly engaged with the performance process and as a result can witness the scenes in performance mode with a sense of appreciation of what is happening on stage.

Fiadeiro employs an additional strategy to reduce the distance usually created in the proscenium theatre: the original scenic design of *I Am Here* is presented in *I Was Here* in a smaller-scale version. In performance mode this mock-up version is fully functional and used to present selected excerpts of *I Am Here*. In conference mode the metal structure frames the video projection of the images showing rehearsals and performances of *I Am Here*. This duplication of the main scenic elements of *I Am Here* (the physical presence of the mock-up version and the projection of the original scenic design) supports the breakdown of the distance between performer and audience and facilitates the involvement of the spectators.

Interestingly, the ratio of 17.5% performance mode to 82.5% conference mode reveals nothing about the perceived intensities in the respective mode, and just as little about the subjective experience of duration of the scenes. In performance mode *affective spacetimes* are constructed with high dramatic intensity and the information is communicated in a different language – namely the language of the artistic stage dance. Here, the kinaesthetic dimension is activated and perceived, in which all the senses are stimulated, and the concentration focuses on what is happening on stage in real time. In conference mode this kinaesthetic dimension takes second place to verbal language, which is often accompanied by visual information.

However, the projected images only mediate other *affective spacetimes* (for instance, the rehearsals and other performances of *I Am Here*). It is Fiadeiro's presence on stage, in the real-time dimension of the performance, that creates the link to these other *affective spacetimes* (recorded situations) and allows them to "come to life" again.[19] In other words, the documents from his personal archive gain a different status through their utilization in the real-time context on stage: they become the material for the real-time composition[20] that unfolds in front of the audience. For example, when Fiadeiro projects the video recording of the rehearsal, during which he and his collaborators discovered that dancing on the pigment had produced a drawing of several square meters, the audience can – in McCormack's words – "experiment the experience" for themselves. That is to say, Fiadeiro's presence on stage is comparable to that of a host who invites the audience to enter the door of his studio and witness an intense moment of discovery.[21]

A second example of such an intermedial real-time situation[22] is the scene in which Fiadeiro shows an excerpt of Joana Ascenção's documentary film about Helena Almeida's artistic process and work. The audience witnesses a recorded conversation between Fiadeiro (who was ten years younger then) and Almeida. Again, it is Fiadeiro's presence on stage that allows the audience to experience a different, more affectionate relation with the presented material than the kind one usually experiences watching the DVD at home or in a gallery or museum space. The situation in *I Was Here* is reminiscent of an evening spent with friends during which someone presents a slide show of holiday pictures, accompanied by stories that spice up and complement the visual material.

By presenting selected documents from his personal archives and from published media in the performative framing of a theatre stage, Fiadeiro can modulate the emerging intensities of the *affective spacetimes* in real time. In other words, through being attentive and open to the subtleties of the audience's immediate and ongoing reception of his work, Fiadeiro can work with his dramaturgical material, composing it in real time. In every performance of *I Was Here* he uses this close connection with his audience to re-enact his documents again. He is constantly "experimenting experience".

Re-enactments and the concept of "accumulative writing"

The process of variation and evolution from one presentation of the work to the next, which we have described earlier, is a good example of the choreographic working method that Fiadeiro has called "accumulative writing". This term contains two important concepts: accumulation and writing (as in dramaturgical writing).

"Accumulative" denotes the unfolding creative process during the development cycle of a work as much as it stands for the continual evolution of the work across several iteration cycles. Experience working with the choreographic materials of the piece is accumulated during rehearsals, in performances, or through conversations with other people. For Fiadeiro it is the total amount of experiences that constitutes an artwork as a whole. Consequently, a section of *I Was Here* is dedicated to sharing those experiences with the audience that were discarded and did not enter the final version of the piece. In this section, Fiadeiro discusses in detail how he explored several works by Helena Almeida that affected him and why he came to the conclusion that a particular experience could not enter the piece.

In the subsequent section of *I Was Here* Fiadeiro talks about his collaborations with other artists during the creation process of *I Am Here*. Among other examples, he shows a series of photographs by Portuguese photographer Patrícia Almeida and excerpts from the documentary film mentioned earlier, and discusses different stages of the development of the scenic design by Walter Lauterer. Fiadeiro has a very expansive view of what an artwork is: all experiences together, realized by him and his collaborators, constitute the artwork, which consequently is much more than the stage performance that the audience sees.

"Writing" – the second important concept in the term "accumulative writing" – stands for the dramaturgical dimension of the choreographic process. In this dimension, choreographic elements and materials are organized in a way that the piece, on the one hand, has a coherent structure and clear recognizable identity and, on the other hand, provides enough flexibility to include the unique characteristics and affective qualities in each performance venue.

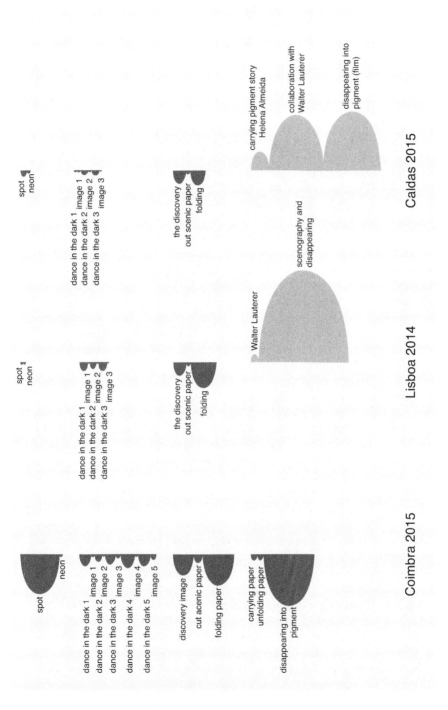

Figure 11.5 Video still from infographic film on *I Was Here* – comparison between scenic structure of three versions. Film by Stephan Jürgens; copyright BlackBox project.

Particularly interesting is the visualization of the scenic structure of the Coimbra version (figure 11.5) of *I Was Here*. In Coimbra, under the identical title *I Was Here*, Fiadeiro presented a 20-minute performance piece which included all scenes in performance mode from the original Lisbon version. However, the entire part in conference mode was left out. Instead, Fiadeiro presented the large drawing that emerges during the dance-in-the-dark scenes as an independent artwork in a gallery space during a few weeks following the performance, and entitled the work *I Am Not Here*.

As the visualizations of the scenic structures of the different versions of *I Was Here* clearly show, the Coimbra version corresponds dramaturgically to the Lisbon and Caldas versions, if we compare the scenes in performance mode to each other. The "accumulative writing" technique is evidently producing coherent dramaturgical structures and performances; but how exactly does Fiadeiro achieve this coherence between the different versions?

Fiadeiro has recently described his choreographic method as being comprised of four stages[23]: (1) affection, (2) formulation, (3) dispositif,[24] and (4) dramaturgy. In the first phase Fiadeiro identifies what affects him, moves him, or disquiets him. The second phase is dedicated to the formulation of that which affects him and to defining the thematic areas of a piece. At the third stage Fiadeiro develops a method, or generative system, which produces the choreographic materials and elements for the piece. The last stage, as described earlier, organizes these materials and elements in the context of the specific circumstances of each performance venue.

For Fiadeiro, the remembering body-as-archive can identify, even after a decade or two, what constituted his original affection. Subsequently he can actualize the original affection through sensing and examining what is still relevant for him today.[25] Hence, the third stage is crucial: here the body-as-archive is provided with a method, a generative system, that can produce new variations of the choreographic materials and elements, which will always emerge from and be coherent with the original affection.

Research outcomes . . .

Subsequently, in carrying out our case study on João Fiadeiro's solo work, the PAR context – and Jürgens's artistic collaboration with Fiadeiro – informed performance theory and allowed us to develop a distinct approach to performance documentation.

In this case, the artistic collaboration as research on the solo *I Was Here* produced a transmedial score (the Isadora document), which allowed us to analyze the coordination of the different strands of the performance and the dramaturgical structure of the work.[26] Developing a transmedial score for a real-time composition represented an important methodological step, as we subsequently could devise an annotation scheme to annotate the video documentation of the performances of *I Was Here*. In other words, the artistic collaboration with

Fiadeiro informed our thinking as researchers and allowed us to devise a novel method for the analysis of Fiadeiro's performance-generating systems.

The annotation data was visualized infographically, so that two essential aspects of Fiadeiro's choreographic *modus operandi* could become visible: (1) Fiadeiro's techniques for the modulation of *affective spacetimes*, and (2) the inner workings of the re-enactment process, designated as "accumulative writing", which we have visualized and compared from version to version of Fiadeiro's work. This knowledge about the choreographic *modus operandi* in João Fiadeiro's solo work constitutes our second kind of research outcome.

... and research impact

As of the time this essay is written, our animated infographic films have raised considerable interest in scientific and artistic communities outside of our areas of expertise. During an art and technology think-tank event at the Champalimaud Foundation in Lisbon in October 2015, Fernandes presented excerpts from the films before a heterogenous audience of scientists, artists, and producers. The feedback was very positive and led to further discussions about our approach and contributions to visualizing and promoting academic knowledge presentation. On another occasion, Jürgens was invited to present the animated infographic films at *Monstra* 2016, an international animated film festival in Lisbon. In the context of a symposium on the relations between animated film and other art forms, Jürgens, Fernandes, and the art director of the films, Francisco Henriques, discussed the (artistic) use of animated infographics for the purpose of the dissemination of academic discovery and knowledge. Again our work was received with keen interest, and artists from the fields of video game design and artistic software development have approached us to discuss common interests and possible future projects.

The feedback from these scientific and artistic communities showed that there exists an important current tendency in employing digital media practices, which can be described as a shift from the documentation-oriented approach towards a media-practice-as-research approach. The latter not only may represent a more adequate method for PAR projects but also could benefit collaborating programmers and digital artists for whom these novel visualization tools simultaneously trigger ideas regarding possible aesthetic, methodological, and technological advances in their respective areas. We see a high potential in the research design and approach described in this essay for further case studies in the field of contemporary dance and beyond.

Acknowledgements

This work was supported by the ERC (European Research Council) under the project "BlackBox: A Collaborative Platform to Document Performance Composition: From Conceptual Structures in the Backstage to Customizable Visualizations in the Front-End" (Grant Agreement ref. 336200). We extend our acknowledge-ments to João Fiadeiro and the dancers who have participated in this case study, as well as to the team at Re.Al for their technical support and collaboration.

Notes

1 Several PAR theorists use the term "exegesis" outside of its original meaning as the explanation and interpretation of a religious scripture, to signify the "critical explanation or interpretation of a text" (*Oxford Dictionary of English*) in general. While we don't use the term ourselves, we recognize the importance of the discussion in PAR theory referred to earlier, and suggest the use of "artwork exegesis" instead.

2 Sullivan discusses four kinds of research acts to arrive at his "create to inquire" approach, which can be employed to create art forms "from which critical options can be more clearly assessed and addressed."

3 Cf. Wagenbach, M. and Pina Bausch Foundation (Eds.). 2014. *Inheriting Dance: An Invitation From Pina*. Bielefeld: Transcript Verlag.

4 Bausch, S. in Wagenbach, M. and Pina Bausch Foundation (Eds.). 2014. p. 177.

5 See critique in Piccini and Rye (2009); Gale and Featherstone (2011).

6 Anne Teresa de Keersmaeker (*A Choreographer's Score*, Book/4DVD, 2012); Emio Greco / PC *Double Skin/Double Mind* Interactive Installation and interactive DVD/DVD-ROM and Book (*Capturing) Intention*; Rosemary Lee (*The Suchness of Heni and Eddie* DVD, 2005); Siobhan Jeyasingh (Animating Architecture: *Foliage Chorus* DVD); William Forsythe (*Synchronous Objects* website, 2010, and *Motionbank* online score), Deborah Haye (*Under The Sky,* a *Motionbank* online score), among numerous other examples.

7 See Blades, H. (2015), "Affective Traces in Virtual Spaces" and the whole *Performance Research* special issue in which it appears: *On An/Notations*, 20.6.

8 As an ERC-funded Arts&Cognition project, BlackBox aims at the analysis of the invited artists' unique conceptual structures and compositional methods, by crossing the empirical insights of contemporary creators with research theories from multimodal communication (human interaction, gesture studies, cognitive linguistics), performance studies, and computer vision. For more info: http://blackbox.fcsh.unl.pt. This chapter has been supported by the ERC-funded BlackBox: Grant Agreement ref. 336200.

9 Fiadeiro uses this expression in the program notes.

10 In this section the first-person singular is used when Stephan Jürgens's direct collaboration with Fiadeiro is described.

11 Transcription of recorded interview session with Fiadeiro, 10 March 2015.

12 Ibid.

13 Isadora is a well-known interactive media presentation tool that allows one to creatively utilize, operate, and interact with all kinds of digital media in real time. See http://troikatronix.com/isadora/about/.

14 See also: Jürgens, S. (2013). Transmedia Choreography: Integrating Multimodal Video Annotation in the Creative Process of a Social Robotics Performance Piece. *BST – Body, Space & Technology Journal*, Brunel University, UK, 12.1. Available from: http://people.brunel.ac.uk/bst/vol1201.

15 The ELAN software is a professional tool for the creation of complex annotations on video and audio resources, developed by the Max Planck Institute for Psycholinguistics. Annotations can be added on stacked tracks (called "tiers"), similar to the tracks in a conventional video editing program. For more information see: https://tla.mpi.nl/tools/tla-tools/elan/.

16 Affinity Designer is a recent vector drawing program, comparable to the industry standard *Adobe Illustrator*.

17 Figures 11.2–11.5 are video stills taken from our infographic film on *I Was Here*, available at https://vimeo.com/149282563.
18 We are using McCormack's terminology here.
19 It is beyond the scope of this essay to discuss connections with media theory here. However, our perspective resonates with authors such as Auslander, Dinkla, Dixon, Grau, and others.
20 For more information on João Fiadeiro's real-time composition method see our article "Moving From an Artist-Led Practice Into Self-Emerging Educational Approaches", *Performance Research* Volume 21, Number 6: 'On Radical Education'.
21 For an in-depth discussion of this approach see our article: Jürgens, S., Henriques, F. and Fernandes, C. (2016), "Re-Constructing the Choreographic Studio of João Fiadeiro Through Animated Infographic Films", *PARtake: The Journal of Performance as Research*, 1.1.
22 See Chapple and Kattenbelt's edited book on intermediality in theatre.
23 During 2015 rehearsals for his latest production. Please see our documentary film on Fiadeiro's stage work *O que fazer daqui para trás (What to Do With What Remains*, 2015), which introduces these stages of Fiadeiro's creative process. Available from http://blackbox. fcsh.unl.pt/joao-fiadeiro-what-to-do-with-what-remains.html.
24 This is "dispositivo" in Portuguese.
25 This is exactly the process that Lepecki describes earlier.
26 See also: Jürgens, S. (2013). "Transmedia Choreography: Integrating Multimodal Video Annotation in the Creative Process of a Social Robotics Performance Piece". *BST – Body, Space & Technology Journal*, Brunel University, UK, 12.1. Available from http://people. brunel.ac.uk/bst/vol1201/.

References

Blades, H. 2015. Affective traces in virtual spaces, *Performance Research*, 20.6, 26–34.
Bolt, B. 2007. The magic is in handling. In: Barrett, E. and Bolt, B. (eds.). *Practice as Research – Approaches to Creative Arts Enquiry*. London: I.B. Tauris.
Fernandes, C. and Jürgens, S. 2013. Video annotation in the TKB project: Linguistics meets choreography meets technology. *International Journal of Performance Arts & Digital Media*, 9.1, 113–132.
Fernandes, C. and Jürgens, S. 2016. Moving from an artist-led practice into self-emerging educational approaches, *Performance Research*, 21.6, 71–77.
Forsythe, W. 1997. *Improvisation Technologies: A Tool for the Analytical Dance Eye* [CD-ROM and booklet]. Ostfildern: Hatje Cantz Verlag.
Gale, M.S. and Featherstone, A. 2011. The imperative of the archive: Creative archive research. In: Kershaw, B. and Nicholson, H. (eds.). 2011. *Research Methods in Theatre and Performance*. Edinburgh: Edinburgh University Press.
Hansen, P. and House, C. 2015. Scoring the generating principles of performance systems, *Performance Research*, 20.6, 65–73.
Haseman, B. 2007. Rupture and recognition: Identifying the performative research paradigm. In: Barrett, E. and Bolt, B. (eds.). *Practice as Research – Approaches to Creative Arts Enquiry*. London: I.B. Tauris.
Jürgens, S. 2013. Transmedia choreography: Integrating multimodal video annotation in the creative process of a social robotics performance piece, *BST – Body, Space & Technology Journal*, Brunel University, UK, 12.1. Available from: http://people.brunel.ac.uk/bst/vol1201/

Jürgens, S., Henriques, F. and Fernandes, C. 2016. Re-constructing the choreographic studio of João Fiadeiro through animated infographic films, *PARtake: The Journal of Performance as Research*, 1.1. Available from: scholar.colorado.edu/partake/vol1/iss1/3/

Klein, G. (ed.). 2015. *Choreographischer Baukasten. Das Buch*. Bielefeld: Transcript Verlag.

Lampert, F. 2007. *Tanzimprovisation*. Bielefeld: Transcript Verlag.

Lepecki, A. 2006. *Exhausting Dance – Performance and the Politics of Movement*. London and New York: Routledge.

Lepecki, A. 2010. The body as archive: Will to re-enact and the afterlives of dances, *Dance Research Journal*, 42.2, 28–48.

McCormack, D. P. 2014. *Refrains for Moving Bodies: Experience and Experiment in Affective Spaces*. Durham, NC: Duke University Press Books.

Piccini, A. and Rye, C. 2009. Of fevered archives and the quest for total documentation. In: L. Allegue, S. Jones, B. Kershaw and A. Piccini (eds.). *Practice-as-Research in Performance and Screen*. London and New York: Palgrave McMillan.

Spatz, B. 2015. *What a Body Can Do – Technique as Knowledge, Practice as Research*. London and New York: Routledge.

Sullivan, G. 2006. Research acts in art practice, *Studies in Art Education*, 48.1, 19–35.

Wagenbach, M. and Pina Bausch Foundation (eds.). 2014. *Inheriting Dance: An Invitation From Pina*. Bielefeld: Transcript Verlag.

Chapter 12

The city (as) place
Performative remappings of urban space through artistic research

Shana MacDonald

This essay examines the potential value of artistic research within the urban environment by outlining three public art projects I have worked on over the last decade. These projects include two collaborative public art installations, *Collect My Junk* (2005) and *Dear Ruth* (2009), and my current artistic research project, *Mobile Art Studio* (2014-). The three projects share a commitment to performatively remapping urban space via site-specific, intermedial installations. The work investigates the interanimating layers of history, culture and matter that make up the spaces we live in. Each project employs phenomenological and performative inquiries into the relations between spaces and the objects and architectural structures contained within them. Drawing on methods of dwelling, collecting and remediation, each project aims to address the complex, varied and at times invisible histories of our city landscapes. The public art component of the projects fosters discussions with the audience around how our lived experience of spaces inflects our sense of self, our migrations and mobilities, our encounters with development and gentrification, and our civic responsibilities to one another and to the environment.

I trace a course across these three works, showing my purposeful move from implicit research questions in the earlier works towards an explicit practice-based research agenda in the current project. This trajectory reveals both the potential and limitations of various methods I have explored. It also speaks to where my work fits within the terminology currently used to discuss work at the intersection of creative and scholarly research practices. Under the broad continuum of artistic research, I situate my work as practice-as-research, or as it is termed within Canadian social science and humanities discourse, research-creation. I am an interdisciplinary artist-scholar working between communication studies, performance studies, film and media studies and visual culture. As such, research-creation is apt as it is the term most commonly used across the majority of these fields within the Canadian context.[1]

In defining research-creation, Kim Sawchuk and Owen Chapman outline four types of research that fall under its purview: "research-for-creation," "research-from-creation," "creative presentations of research," and "creation-as-research."[2] I find the distinctions productive for mapping the shifts across different types of research creation approaches within my own trajectory. While earlier projects employed "research-for-creation" and were concerned with "research-from-creation" after the fact, the more recent work is more consciously "creation-as-research." Sawchuk and Chapman define this latter term as "projects where creation is required in order for research to emerge," or a "gathering and revealing through creation" whereby researchers are "seeking to extract knowledge from the process."[3] I am interested in the ways that "creation-as-research" echoes Brad Haseman's concept of performative research wherein "practice is the principle research activity." These performative research practices produce aesthetic forms that iteratively situate themselves as research through both the doing of the research and its presentation.[4] The centrality of practice as the starting point in both "creation-as-research" and performative research holds resonance for my work as it is in the doing – the "gathering and revealing" – that the hidden and tacit knowledge of a given research project is able to emerge. Haseman's linking of performative research to methods of reflexivity, narrative inquiry and participant observation speaks to the methods I have developed around dwelling and collecting as initial forms of auditing leading to self-reflexive inquiry and the aesthetic remediation of data for and with the public audience.[5] These methods emerged organically from experiments undertaken throughout the creative process in each project. As such, I frame the trajectory of my work as building concretely towards forms of performative research that hold a model of "creation-as-research" as central to their frame.

Abandoned objects: dwelling (on) and collecting invisible narratives of the city

Collect My Junk (2005), the earliest piece in my artistic-research trajectory, was commissioned for Alley Jaunt, an annual Toronto art festival where residents surrounding Trinity Bellwoods Park invited artists to transform their alley garages into microgalleries. For the project I collaborated with Angela Joosse on a projection installation that mapped the areas surrounding the park through the garbage discarded within them. The final project was a series of three-dimensional, sculptured screens suspended within a garage that played a stop-motion animation of the familiar park landscapes being transformed into fantastical garbage-filled renderings of the same space. These animated screens were open to the public over the course of a weekend. The use of abandoned objects that were repurposed through the installation was visually fitting for the garage with its own array of discarded and underused objects.

This was where my interest in dwelling and collecting originated, two methods that have become central in subsequent works. Dwelling as method in *Collect My Junk* came out of the work Joosse and I were doing with the research collective L.O.T.: Experiments in Urban Research. The collective sought new urban research methods for exploring the dialectical relationship between different iterations of space as outlined by Henri Lefebvre and Michel de Certeau.

The research question at the core of this work was how to access and convey this layered nature of space. Dwelling was a method arrived at by chance as we decided to visit the spaces we were researching in order to better understand how to engage, represent and circulate the narratives they contain that are not readily articulated. From these initial impulses to be in the space we noticed the odd ephemera of junk that were scattered across them. This became the point of inspiration for the final project and led to the second method of collecting that I will discuss in more detail ahead.

Taking seriously embodied forms of engagement with space as layered and multidimensional, *Collect My Junk* underscored the importance of dwelling as a form of aesthetic research. Dwelling is an embodied act that we do on a regular basis. In *Collect My Junk* the common definition of dwelling as a place to live in was transformed into a formal approach that recognized public space as intimately *lived-in* places. By dwelling in the research space over time, we became better attuned to the idiosyncrasies and intimate details that make up the site. Dwelling in the Trinity Bellwoods area highlighted as well a personal desire to aesthetically remap city sites that may be overlooked or taken for granted by their public users. Dwelling as an artistic research method underscored the specificities of space that are overwritten by dominant perceptions and uses of it. The practice not only reveals insights for the aesthetic shape a project may take but also equally foregrounds the gaps in knowledge, the undervalued narratives of the space that would ultimately frame the research component of future projects. Further, as an embodied practice it encouraged us to reconceive of the space in highly personal terms, foregrounding the value of lived experience and quotidian practices in envisioning the final iteration of the project for public engagement and exhibition.

Lefebvre's framing of the mutually constitutive relationship between spaces, objects, embodied subjects and the constantly shifting psycho-geographies of cities greatly influenced the creative process in *Collect My Junk*. Lefebvre argues in *The Production of Space* that we must shift away from studying *"things in space"* to consider the different practices which produce space, including its built structures, symbolic and discursive articulations, and live flows of bodies and social practices. Lefebvre termed these the conceived, perceived and lived production of spaces respectively and emphasized the "dialectical relationship" between them.[6] Dwelling offers the potential to take note of these layers of lived, conceived and perceived space. It illustrates how "spatial practice is lived directly before it is conceptualized," thus placing greater attention on the "unconscious level of lived experience," which is often less visible in our dominant renderings of space.[7] Emphasizing the lived experiences of space challenges the neoliberal overwriting of place as designed solely for consumption. The critique against capitalism's reinscription of lived space as a site to reproduce itself is as important now as it was for Lefebvre. Dwelling offers a counterpoint to this by consciously reinhabiting spaces through embodied practices. When Michel de Certeau argues that dominant formations of space are "redistributed" by the *practices* of its residents who "consume" the space, he makes an important assertion around social practices as "enunciative procedures."[8] These procedures ensure that "urban space becomes not only the object of a knowledge, but *the place of a recognition*."[9] This transformation of city space from object of knowledge made legible by institutional mappings to a place of recognition via the enunciative practices of residents speaks directly to the method of dwelling applied to each of my projects. By expanding our sense of space we situate the potential of citizen-based action to counter the capitalist flattening of cities and imagine them differently.

From the initial phase of dwelling in my work on *Collect My Junk*, a second, related research method emerged: that of collecting. Practices of collecting have taken different forms in the three projects, including the collecting of trash, abandoned objects, life stories, photographic evidence and public perspectives. In the first two projects the practice of collecting informed the specific intentions of the final installation. The method draws on discussions of new materialism and specifically Jane Bennett's call to "bear witness to the vital materialities that flow through and around us."[10] Bennett's interest in how "found objects . . . can become vibrant things with a certain effectivity of their own"[11] echoes the approach Joosse and I took in both *Collect My Junk* and *Dear Ruth*.

In a 2011 public lecture "Powers of the Hoard: Artistry and Agency in a World of Vibrant Matter," Bennett discusses an experience of encountering "trash in a gutter" near her house and her desire to take seriously the call from these things, asking, what if these things can hail us?[12] She notes that artists[13] are well suited to the task of translating the enunciative call of things, or "to make whatever communications are already at work between vibrant bodies more audible, more detectable, more sensible."[14] The artistic method of collecting is a useful means of investigating the material vibrancy of urban space. My interest in uncovering the invisible or hidden narratives anchored in material objects, abandoned structures, pathways and cityscapes relates to Bennett's interest in exploring the "positive dimension of thing power," which can "draw us near to them and provoke our deep attachments."[15] This method of collecting opens artists, researchers and the public towards a more inclusive political ecology of urban space that importantly recognizes the ways we are hailed by and attached to the material layers of our environment.

Collect My Junk responded most explicitly to the call of things as we were drawn to the garbage we encountered while dwelling in popular Toronto spaces. Here the practice of collecting trash provoked a series of productive questions and reflexive inquiries. While collecting and documenting the garbage, we often wondered why this or that object was left behind, and inquired as to the significance it served before it was discarded. What did this trash reveal about the space, and how did it cause us to see the space differently? We wondered if the trash changed in each location, and if this could become the basis for understanding the spaces. We began to speculate about the narratives of the object's lives, owners and their separations – the kite in the tree, the baseball in

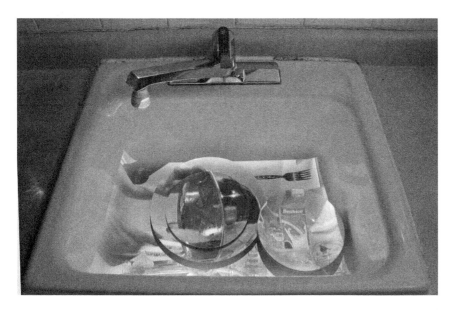

Figure 12.1 Dear Ruth (2009).

Source: Angela Joosse.

a bush. Were these purposeful separations or were they objects that represented loss? The experiences of collecting informed our decision to then remap the spaces with their trash in order to convey to audiences the wonder the objects had evoked in us. In the final installation we presented this altered perspective of space as reimagined through its junk to the viewer via sculptural projections within the garage exhibition space.

To create the sculptural projections out of discarded objects we placed Plexiglas sheets within the spaces we had collected from and attached the objects that 'called to us' the most from what we had collected. We recorded the process of creating these sculptures in stop-motion. This documentation showed the sculptures of junk as mirroring the cityscape behind the Plexiglas. In the final installation we turned the Plexiglas sculpture into a screen by spray-painting it white. On this highly textured screen we projected the stop-motion sculpting process so that audiences watched familiar city spaces transform incrementally from a realist image to one made entirely of trash. This shift in attention from the received notion of a lived space to its "junk" narratives spoke to our interest in forms of defamiliarization that have carried forward into the other two projects. For instance, in Fig 12.1 above, a similar type of projection was constructed by layering everyday objects in the sink of an abandoned house in our subsequent project *Dear Ruth*. However, *Collect My Junk* was where we originally developed an explicit interest in found objects and the underwritten narratives of urban space. This process encouraged a phenomenological relationship with these spaces and their objects, pushing us, and our audiences, beyond our immediate perceptions. The artistic approach in *Collect My Junk* foregrounded and clarified critical questions and practices we would further develop in our collaboration *Dear Ruth*. While *Collect My Junk* was well received by audiences, I felt the forms of knowledge arrived at while producing the work were not adequately served by their final dissemination. The process in this earliest project lacked a necessary reflexivity that did not allow for a full exploration of the potential dialogues that could be encouraged by our creative remediations of the space. These shortcomings were addressed in detail in *Dear Ruth* four years later.

Nostalgia, performative inquiry and the remediation of intimate, personal archives

Dear Ruth was one of eighteen works commissioned by curators Janine Marchessault and Michael Prokopow for the *Leona Drive Project* (*LDP*). The larger project focused on the impact of development initiatives in the Toronto suburb of Willowdale. The *LDP* was a site-specific exhibition occupying a cul-de-sac of vacant bungalows slated for demolition in North Toronto. The six houses, taken over by *LDP* artists during the fall of 2009, were left in disrepair by developers for over five years prior to the exhibit and subsequently turned into million-dollar townhomes six months after the exhibit.

LDP spoke directly to this transformation, opening a space for community dialogues about the shifting neighborhood landscape. *Dear Ruth* provided a microlens on these issues. It was housed in the kitchen of 9 Leona Drive and it addressed the erasure of daily rituals through an aesthetic remapping of household objects across cupboards and appliances. The objects were found in three boxes that were left in the basement of the house. They belonged to Ruth Gillespie, a long-time resident of 9 Leona Drive. These items became central to our aesthetic and conceptual inquiries at various stages of production. We placed the objects throughout the kitchen and encouraged viewers to re-enact daily gestures, such as opening cupboards, peering into a sink or looking through an oven window. We constructed the kitchen as a liminal space where viewers could traverse between Ruth's past and their present, and between her private domestic sphere and the public sphere of the exhibition. The installation produced a "living archive" that underscored the tensions between embodied practices and the archive,[16] transforming the kitchen into a site of remembrance. We positioned *Dear Ruth* as a counterpoint to a more 'official' archive presented on the outside of the house, which included projections of zoning maps and historical photographs. If the exterior mapping documented a broad economic and geographic history of the area, the kitchen asserted an intimate record of quotidian practices as equally important historical artifacts.

The process of dwelling informed our decision to conduct regular visits to Leona Drive and Ruth's home during the two months prior to the installation.

In these visits we were drawn to the kitchen early on. While it was not as well preserved as other rooms in the house, it held an aesthetic quality that we found compelling and comforting. It was intelligible in a way the other spaces of the house were not, mostly because it was not completely emptied of the traces of Ruth's everyday life. The cupboards, appliances and lush greenery crawling over the windows gave it a sense of aliveness that we craved in the midst of the surrounding decay. We felt the need to dwell in the kitchen by working in the space and formally trying to "bring it back to life" for the exhibit. The sense of loss tied to Ruth's absence from the house and the abandonment of her objects echoed a larger sense of abandonment that the area's redevelopment signified as a whole. Through dwelling we were able to translate the theme of absence into a metafocus of the overall work. This greatly informed how the public viewed the project as well.

In *Dear Ruth* the call of thingness emerged again through our experience of dwelling. While sifting through the house, a colleague found a series of boxes that were going to be thrown out because they were deemed by others to hold no archival value. We asked for the boxes and found they contained the contents of Ruth's life from age nine to her death. They included an assortment of recipes, a 1945 high school yearbook, two autograph books dating from 1936–1945, photographs, magazines, cards from her husband, letters, tax returns and knitting patterns. We questioned why Ruth's possessions were left behind, particularly as some had been kept safe since her childhood. If these objects had a lifelong value for Ruth, why were they rotting in a basement? Through this process items that would have been demolished alongside the house categorically shifted from abandoned junk to artists' materials and archival objects. The materials evoked intense reactions from Joosse and myself, and we decided this was the means by which we could reanimate the house. By selecting objects with a certain vibrancy we sought to provide a testament to the lives lived in abandoned or empty spaces.

While reflecting upon the large amount of material objects of Ruth's life Joosse and I began to note our embodied responses working with these objects in her abandoned home. As stated earlier, from early in the project, Joosse and I wanted to make explicit the link between official histories of development and the material realities of women's lived experiences in the suburbs. When we encountered Ruth's personal objects we found an important site for engaging these contradictions, but we equally questioned the ethics of aestheticizing personal archives, and especially our relationship as artists (and viewers) to these materials, spaces and memories. We became increasingly uncomfortable being in possession of Ruth's personal effects and the weight of our ethical responsibilities to Ruth's privacy. We were aware that we could never fully represent Ruth's lived history through our fragmented access to her life. This prompted us to develop a formal approach that performatively reimagined the banality of everyday life and its objects more broadly. We decided to foreground the tension between Ruth's daily objects and the aesthetic interpretations we were

Figure 12.2 Dear Ruth (2009).

Source: Angela Joosse.

imposing on them. As figure 12.2 demonstrates, this tension is evident in our visual re-inhabiting of Ruth's lived kitchen space. We framed the installation as a restaging of Ruth's objects and situated our own creative process via a series of performative reconstructions by turning the cupboards into lightboxes strewn with rephotographed iterations of her ephemera.

In aestheticizing Ruth's everyday domestic ritual, we publicly recognized how our representations were splintered through the idiosyncratic array of objects and our fictionalized story of Ruth's life. We used various media to magnify, distort and frame our reperformed daily rituals as practices of display. We turned the drawers into archive boxes, the oven into a projection space, the sink into a sculptural screen, and the cupboards into textured light boxes. We rephotographed many of the objects and displayed the images as mediated artifacts. The tensions between bodies, histories, abandoned spaces and objects were further emphasized by our address of the audience. The drawers just to the right of the oven contained a replica[17] of the autograph books pinned onto display boards and enclosed by Plexiglas covers. The archival drawers produced a discordance with the sensory experience of the oven projection and represented the more static forms of display used in museums.

In one specific instance we stacked white plates and bowls in the sink as a sculptural screen. We projected images into the sink from a small projector concealed in a birdcage hanging in the window above. The images projected into the sink show Joosse and myself remaking several recipes that Ruth highlighted through handwritten notes in her recipe books as "good." This reiteration of her lived experience was formally marked as incomplete through the projector's displacement of the performance onto the visually fragmented curves and lines of the stacked dishes. Corresponding images of the recipes were in the light box cupboards to the right of the sink. These images were presented on photographic slides, back lit by a web of LED lights, tangled in a collage of cobwebbed materials (yarn, fabric, lace) and distorted by convex plastic covering the front of the cupboards. These light boxes magnified objects repeated throughout the kitchen, and distorted them in order to question the veracity of visual documents as historical artifacts. These formal collisions highlighted the tensions between the embodied ephemerality of daily rituals and the preserving function of archives. Through these juxtapositions we explored different aesthetic ways of rendering explicit the less visible histories, memories and identities found within both public and private space.[18]

This practice of reflexive self-inquiry and performative remediation in relation to the materials gathered in the dwelling and collecting phases is a significant component of my work. This approach draws on a central tenet of performance studies "to open the space between analysis and action, and to pull the pin on the binary opposition between theory and practice."[19] It functions as a pause between analysis and action where I try to situate my embodied experiences as an index of whatever investments I may hold. The application of this critical lens helps to envision a final project that is attentive to my own biases and ethical commitments to the space and its community. Particularly relevant to this practice is a desire to bring to the fore subjective, tacit forms of knowledge that "reflect new social and other realities either marginalized or not yet recognized in established social practice and discourses."[20] This push towards reflexivity echoes Dwight Conquergood's support of a research practice that embraces a "performance paradigm," which "insists upon immediacy, involvement, and intimacy as modes of understanding."[21] In my own work this approach helps account for the powerful forms of immediacy experienced through the acts of dwelling and collecting when interpreting and re-expressing data. It requires me to check my involvement within the sites of research and how it informs my approaches to further researching and disseminating information about that space. As Conquergood suggests, the potential here is found in the "move from cultural *invention* to *intervention*" where performance and, I would argue, performative forms of inquiry excel "in the liminal, contested, and re-creative space between deconstruction and reconstruction, crisis and redress, the breaking down and the building up of the workshop-rehearsal space."[22] The practice of reflexivity I am describing is a form of performance-as-method or performative research built on breaking down unexamined subject positions, investments and power dynamics within communities in order to provoke important points of crisis and ideally new forms of awareness. While Conquergood locates these practices in the workshop-rehearsal space, I position them in the particular spaces I investigate and in the liminal space of the public urban art installations.

Taking a performative approach to reanimating Ruth's space with her belongings became a productive and critical gesture of placemaking as both cocreated and cross-temporal, revealing once again the layered nature of space. Incorporating this reflexivity and performativity as part of our research method integrated questions about our personal investments as artist-researchers into our process.

For Della Pollock this reflexivity creates an important shift from objective research to subject-centered narratives. While speaking of oral history research practices, her methodological frame can be extended to researching the narratives of urban space. Pollock suggests researchers "investigate the performative nature of the subject" by asking, *"Who speaks? What difference does speaking make? To what extent is the much-heralded agency of the speaker conditioned by prior speech acts? To whom does her story belong? Whose interests does it serve?"*[23] The methods of dwelling and collecting extend this by asking, what speaks? Both methods are concerned with how spaces and material culture communicate to and with their inhabitants within the official and nonofficial structures of city space. These questions are also central for the process of creating visual narratives that address the power dynamics within city space – who can speak here? How are their stories conditioned by the structures and limitations of the space? This reflexive awareness further asks what is constrained by the researcher's subject positions both inside and outside of the space. It also importantly investigates who is best served by the final installation. Pollock's definition of oral histories as *"reflexive, rehearsed*, and *renewed* narrative performances whose meanings . . . are *emergent* and *contingent"* is useful as it points to the role of researcher as "performative co-witness."[24] I am drawn to this approach as it speaks directly to my own sense that "creation-as-research" projects must attend to the specificities of place and participant subjectivities in order to construct a viable research frame for productive public dissemination. If these subjective investments and perspectives are not indexed then it closes the artist-researcher off from valuable conversations with the audience. This is what increasingly marks the projects as research-creation. Built into their frame is the intention for an overt dialogue with the public as both a further process of data collection and an outcome of earlier research conducted.

Dear Ruth highlighted a need to performatively frame my, at times nostalgic, interpretations of Ruth's everyday space. Our use of remediation in *Dear Ruth* acknowledged the idiosyncratic responses we held about the exhibition space. By referencing our subjective relatedness to the space we invited equally affective responses from an audience. Acknowledging that this was not Ruth's stuff but rather our performative imagining of it cautioned viewers against any easy projections onto the past lives of the space. These practices of performative re-enactment drew upon Pollock's view of (oral) history as a "(shifting and transformative) mode of making meaning" which "gains an additional political valence in the performance of retelling."[25] *Dear Ruth* (and to different degrees the other two research projects) tests the transformative potential of narrativizing lost, invisible, undervalued histories through performative and mediated retellings.

One specific research task I have set for future projects is to document the affective materiality of cityscapes in order to move from "the endorsement of ethical principles to the actual practice of ethical behaviors."[26] *Mobile Art Studio* directly questions whether artistic research into the city can encourage more ethical relationships between self and space. For Bennett such research must undertake "a cultivated, patient, sensory attentiveness to nonhuman forces operating outside and inside the human body" in order to decenter the primacy of human subjects as masters acting upon their passive environment.[27] This decentering of human subjects as the masters of space is precisely what is at stake in artistic research attentive to the materialities of cities as it provides both "a vigilant critique of existing institutions but also positive, even utopian alternatives."[28] It is crucial for any urban art intervention to engage city spaces as sites with a multiplicity of meanings and histories. Equally crucial is the need to locate these layers of signification in both the social structures and material objects of the space. This provides an expanded sense of space that leaves researchers better attuned to both its promises and constraints. I would argue this is a necessary point of analysis for artistic research interested in encouraging critical forms of placemaking. This practice seeks to provide a break in researcher and audience perceptions, revealing the forms of power that go unexamined in everyday life.[29] By defamiliarizing our lived experience of space through creative interventions we can try to examine the power structures that devalue or silence these experiences, asserting them instead as important aspects of urban discourse. For example, by inventing a narrative or fiction of Ruth and her home, we animated what was lost and tried to bring the importance of that loss to public discourse. Our intention here was to produce an alternative trajectory to what can be seen and said, and felt and acknowledged. The abandoned space of her kitchen was remapped as a site of remembering and critical inquiry into what is lost within both official archives and the rampant forms of redevelopment that were overturning older histories and materialities for the promise of the new.

Tactical engagements: participatory art and the remapping of urban space

An imperative at the center of my artistic research is to make meaningful connections between our experiences of city space. The outcome of the site-specific installations that have marked the culmination of *Dear Ruth* and *Collect My Junk* encouraged the viewing public towards embodied, phenomenological experiences of each site in order to question the tensions of presence and absence, the marked and the invisible. In this way my work shares a set of concerns with a range of recent research-creation work in Canada. There has been a significant emergence of labs, artistic-research collaborations and site-specific media-based research across the country over the last decade. This includes research-creation labs and exhibitions, such as *The Visible City Project* (2005–2014), *Mobile Media Lab* (2006), *Maraya Project* (2007–2011), *Land | Slides: Possible Futures* (2013), *The Situated Cinema* (2015), and *Meeting in the Middle: Stations of Migration and Memory Between Art & Film* (2014–2017).[30] In addition, scholarship and creative work by Natalie Loveless, Kathleen Irwin and Julie Nagam, and Chris Salter resonate with the range of research-creation questions I am interested in exploring further.[31] Nagam's work in particular (*singing our bones home* [2013], *Where White Pines Lay Over the Water* [2011]) reflects an overlapping set of aesthetic concerns and research commitments around the layered histories of place, which perhaps derives from the time we both spent working with the *L.O.T* collective during 2008–2010. Nagam's installation *singing our bones home* was a part of *Land | Slides: Possible Futures* (2013), the follow-up show to the *Leona Drive Project* by curator Janine Marchessault.[32] The work projects ghostly figures haunting uninhabited landscapes on the inside and outside of a wigwam projection structure. Nagam constructed the domed screen from willow saplings, fabric and branches. Viewers sitting on cedar branches inside the wigwam activate sounds of honor songs that sing bodies displaced from occupied burial grounds to a place of rest in a variety of Indigenous languages. Situated inside an agricultural shed, the projection installation performatively indexes the overwriting of Indigenous burial lands by the permanent structures of settler culture. While my work differs in focus, themes and output from Nagam's and others mentioned earlier, the overlap among our projects is that they are developed by artists-researchers committed to intermedial explorations of public space within the Canadian context.

My most recent project, *Mobile Art Studio*, directly investigates the relationship among research-creation, public engagement and urban space. It questions whether creative research practices can promote deeper community experiences of the city as a lived space. The initial stages (2014–17) were funded by two University of Waterloo research grants. I worked with graduate students, devising a set of research questions around the concepts and creative practices associated with placemaking, dwelling, collecting and remediation. These questions directed the compilation of a database of texts and artist-researchers that stood in the place of a more traditional literature review. The database offered an idiosyncratic, flexible and highly visual working document to guide the project. This research continued more recently to include a mapping of various research-creation projects focused on forms of placemaking within Canada and internationally.

In constructing the frame for the *Mobile Art Studio*, I considered both the successes and limitations of *Dear Ruth* and *Collect My Junk*. Points of dissatisfaction at the end of *Collect My Junk* and *Dear Ruth* prompted further critical reflection on questions of frame, research goals and the role of the public in the research process. The first limitation I address in *Mobile Art Studio* is one of shifting from solely producing a public art installation to devising an explicit research-creation project. In *Collect My Junk* and *Dear Ruth* I was commissioned as an artist to create pieces for larger exhibitions. In both cases I was a graduate student with close research ties to the themes of the exhibitions; however, any overlap between my artistic and academic work was implied at this point and never operated as a central condition of the work. Together *Collect My Junk*, *Dear Ruth* and *Mobile Art Studio* chart a move away from my earlier solo practice in experimental film and towards collaborating on public art installations as an artist-researcher. One of the central dissatisfactions that drove me away from my film practice was the limited engagement with audiences that the work offered. This led me to seek out more public, noninstitutional settings for my work and pushed me into intermedial, sculptural and performative relationships to the moving image. However, even within my public projection installations, I still felt the potential for audience engagement was limited. For instance, in *Dear Ruth* and *Collect My Junk* the alternative mapping of the city of Toronto was based on artistic collaborations with Angela Joosse, often in conjunction with curators of the broader exhibitions they were housed within. Here the public was invited in as an audience only. What left me dissatisfied in each case was that the expectations for dissemination did not extend past the timeline of the exhibition or the viewing experience of the art. My attempts to discursively frame the experience of these shows later on fell short, I believe in part because I had not built this as an intention of the work early on. Rather than being commissioned or curated into an existing exhibition, *Mobile Art Studio* began as a research-creation project. With *Mobile Art Studio* there is a direct intention to recognize the work *as* research and to explore the ways in which research questions and aesthetic processes can advance simultaneously in mutually informing ways.

I addressed these points of dissatisfaction by testing the methods used early on in the *Mobile Art Studio* project during a workshop on artistic research run by Bruce Barton (University of Calgary) and Natalia Esling (University of Toronto) in 2015.[33] My experience within the workshop confirmed my interest in including greater public participation in the overall project.[34] Within a one-hour time frame collaborators Kimber Sider (University of Guelph), Natalie Doonan (Concordia University) and myself engaged a group of approximately fifteen participants in a set of placemaking exercises. Our focus was to determine the potential utility derived from the exercises for our disciplinarily diverse group of participants. We gave participants instructions to engage the spaces around them, seeking major and minor voices that emerge through observing their surroundings at the University of Ottawa campus. We asked them to document these themes by any means, providing them with creative materials, including construction paper, oil pastels, a Polaroid camera and envelopes. After a period of dwelling and collecting we had participants return to the workshop space and in two groups discuss their experiences and documentation. In the group I facilitated with Sider we invited participants to explain their experiences and then collectively create a collage of their visual documentation. A set of common themes emerged within the groups' different individual stories. These themes included the tension between the body and the built environment, the way built structures constrained movements, as well as an interest in how nature functioned as site of play and spontaneity. Many had collected ephemera like rocks, bark, leaves and the sound of wind as counterpoints to the concrete stairs, halls and façade of the interior workshop space. This gesture towards a greater bodily connection to the space as place was key for many participants. When we asked participants to articulate the utility of the exercise they noted that it activated sensory memories, displaced the dominant experience of the architecture, and encouraged an expanded perception of the space, giving it more depth than one ordinarily encounters. The workshop was the first time I had explicitly examined the utility and potential outcomes of dwelling, collecting, reflexive inquiry and remediation. Central to this was inviting the participation of workshop attendees and encouraging a dialogue on their experiences working with the method in this somewhat abridged form. By setting out a small-scale workable version of our existing research practices, Sider, Doonan and myself set ourselves the specific challenge to determine what, if any, desired outcomes would be articulated by the participants through engaging in the workshop exercise. The success of the workshop and the insights it provided suggest that this is a constructive format for future artistic research. While earlier iterations of my artistic research practices may not have framed these goals so explicitly, the *Mobile Art Studio* project keeps them at the forefront with each new project, eliciting a participatory model that encourages the public to articulate through a variety of visual and audio media their understandings of the spaces they live in. This invitation to include a broader group of researchers may be one means by which meaningful and collective placemaking can occur in city space. Rather than relying solely on the experiences and perspectives of the artist researcher, it is the gestures and practices of the community that can reveal additional tensions, marginalized narratives and elided power structures of space. The result of these works is the development of an urban art practice that is participatory, process-oriented, situated in public space and focused on urbanization "as the dramatic concentration of everyday inequality."[35] Tying these various projects together, my trajectory reveals that the results of each project have greatly informed the subsequent ones. The progression of this narrative offers a case for how artistic research processes can provide knowledge suited for traditional academic contexts, while also gesturing towards new forms of collaboration between academic research and the broader public.

In *Mobile Art Studio* while creating new installations and art events I encourage a larger practice of collaboration by inviting students and the public to share their stories, perspectives and experiences of Kitchener-Waterloo in order to better represent a diverse sense of the area. This is where the shift from artist to artist researcher is most clear, as I have become both a creative player and a facilitator for other sources of creative input. The shift from artist to researcher also allows me to set out a different set of goals for dissemination that are not commonly associated with art exhibitions.

In the summer of 2015, I applied the method of dwelling in the context of Kitchener-Waterloo through a collaboration with artist Aislinn Thomas. As the initial research for the formation of the *Mobile Art Studio* we wanted to research any gaps, tensions or idiosyncrasies of that lived environment. This dwelling revealed an active engagement by the community with the region's series of festivals that were scheduled across the summer and into the fall and winter. Many of the events hosted by the two cities worked in conjunction with community groups, the two universities (University of Waterloo and Wilfrid Laurier University) and the region's vibrant tech sector (which includes Google Canada, Communitech, RIM/Blackberry, Christie Digital). These well-established events offer a range of opportunities for the public to participate in the civic life of the city. Observing this constellation of events led to the idea for a mobile art studio that would iteratively establish itself as a fixture of this local urban practice of public gatherings in order to gather insights on the issues and concerns of residents that could be further addressed through performative research projects. The durational and public frame of the project seeks to develop an ongoing narrative of the city from the residents as an intentional way of expanding and revealing existing perceived notions of the area.

The projects within *Mobile Art Studio* function as ad hoc, "pop-up" mobile art events in conjunction with various festivals throughout the year. The intention is for the pop-up format to performatively "make space" for creativity as both a complement and a challenge to the institutionalized activities of the festivals. As a research project, it invites public participants to articulate some aspect of their lived experience of the city via the artist materials and creative prompts provided. Participants and audiences of each project are encouraged to share their creations more broadly via a site-specific hashtag that will document the work for the larger *Mobile Art Studio* archive. Between 2014 and 2016 an early prototype of this project has included a yearly pop-up show on the University of Waterloo campus, where undergraduate students reflect on their experience of university life in various contexts.[36]

The artist materials, aesthetic form and creative prompts that are offered at each iteration of the project are specific to the context itself. For example, during the 2016 *Night\Shift* (Kitchener's all-night art event), the *Mobile Art Studio* produced a time-based performance installation *Reconstruction* (2016). The project invited city residents to help remake the King St. corridor, a central transit passage between Kitchener and Waterloo that was under construction for over a year as the region built a light rapid transit system. We set up a "construction zone" and had participants creatively rebuild the city by tracing photographic images of twenty-four well-known city blocks that were projected by overhead projectors onto 4x4 blank white screens on 6-foot-tall wooden frames. The performance installation created an interactive sculpture of this corridor that was built up (traced, retraced and graffitied on) over a four-hour period. In

Reconstruction, the space was set up by myself and a group of student volunteers who both facilitated the process and also engaged in a highly structured, timed performance script that unfolded throughout the installation. We each assumed roles as "architects" responsible for assembling the overhead transparency images of building for each new block, "builders" responsible for tracing the buildings being projected onto the building, "graffiti artists" responsible for amending the traced buildings once they were moved away from the projector by adding details, commentary and narratives to the drawn spaces, and finally a "labor crew" and "foreman" who maintained the smooth transition of the city block screens from each point in the process. If and when audiences entered the construction site, the workers at each station invited their participation and would step away from their work, only offering supplies and minimal instructions to audiences so they could engage in the rebuilding. The scripted nature of the installation unfolded a performance that constructed a sculpture made over a four-hour time period. It functioned in a sense as a choreographed event that was integral to meeting the final goal of fully reconstructing the twenty-four blocks between the core points of the cities of Kitchener and Waterloo. At the end of the performance, this central section of the city had been reconstructed across the twenty-four screens so that you could walk along as you would the actual city street.

As figure 12.3 shows, participants started by faithfully retracing the photographic projections but then began intervening into the spaces traced on the

Figure 12.3 Reconstruction (2016).

Source: Sidra Hasan.

screens by renaming certain blocks, adding drawn figures and caricatures, new buildings, different configurations of well-known buildings and commentary about the city on the screens. At the end of fifteen-minute intervals the "foreman" (a student performer) would yell out a "shift change" and construction crew workers flipped some screens away from the projectors, so they were now in the hands of graffiti artists with colorful markers, and moved other screens away from the projectors and graffiti artists to build the new "roadway." The student presence as "workers" on the "construction site" made a huge difference with audience, and the scripted performance we were tasked with as a crew provided a direction and fluid momentum to the installation that enabled an easy entry point for audiences. Participant relationships to the space and their own level of interaction notably shifted when we finished our portion of the installation after three hours and left the space, keeping it open to further audience engagement for an additional hour.

The aim of *Reconstruction* was to gather a cross-section of narratives around people's reactions to the city's disruption of their sense of place during this moment of redevelopment. Setting up a flexible space for the public to creatively express their lived experience of this time period encouraged an alternative means of dialogue between residents on the municipal activities that directly impact their lives. *Reconstruction* also created an archive of this fleeting moment in time. The photos taken of sections of the city that were then traced by residents recorded a series of city blocks, routes and dug-up throughways that have already shifted into new formations. Three weeks after the installation many of these sections of the roadway were reopened to pedestrian and auto traffic. The twenty-four screens that remain, as well as their documentation online across various media platforms, reveal an archive of a specific moment in time that may otherwise become forgotten in the flow of everyday life, despite existing as a real site of disruption for the duration of the construction project.

As this example of *Reconstruction* shows, *Mobile Art Studio* functions specifically as performative research, or "creation-as-research." *Reconstruction* performatively frames itself as an event within the existing and institutionally sanctioned space of *Night\Shift Placehacking Festival*, an annual all-night art festival in Kitchener.[37] Its doing – making space for public creative expression – inscribed research-creation priorities within both the frame of the festival and more specifically the exterior spaces of Kitchener City Hall, within which it was centrally located. This reflexive framing calls audiences to critically consider their affective responses to the city's promotion of festivals and art events and the potential for city spaces to engage citizens as a site of meaning making more broadly.

To this end, participants were encouraged to share their "reconstructions" with other *Night\Shift* attendees as well as with virtual audiences by uploading documentation of the performance and their work to social media via the hashtag #ReconstructKW.[38] In this way, the project performatively enacts a playful dialogue between older, material forms of media (overhead projectors, tracing, sharpies, paper) and more contemporary digital mobile practices. Like my previous projects, *Reconstruction* interrogates the historically layered nature of space by inviting both erased and new narratives of the city at a moment of transformation. What I am left with as a researcher after the event is an archive of twenty-four large screens filled with these stories and many other sorts of interventions and articulations by city residents. Going forward, I see great potential in treating these as the collected materials of the research project and will now work in collaboration with students and local artists to inquire into how we may make further meaning of these inscriptions in a way that remediates and reflects back to the public their perspectives through future pop-up events. Relying on a similar methodological trajectory that was used in *Collect My Junk* and *Dear Ruth*, I am optimistic that the processes of dwelling, collecting and remediation can provide insight and new research questions around the value of public art in local city contexts.

Artistic research as thick urbanism

My research works with a definition of cities as "living entities deeply connected to and fabricated through collective memories, social relations, and built structures expressed in material culture."[39] This emphasis on the living city as a web of socialities, histories and materialities is an anchor for all three projects. One outcome I hope for in future projects developed through the *Mobile Art Studio* is the production of alternative maps of collective urban life. While much has been written on how public art functions as a form of social engagement (Bishop 2012, Jackson 2011, Kester 2004), I specifically utilize forms of public art as an artistic research process that foregrounds interdisciplinarity, site-specificity and intermediality. I am committed to a reflexive, collaborative and provisional research-creation practice geared towards building civic engagement and providing an expanded view of urban life that is sensitive to the local context. In "Walking in the City" Michel de Certeau argues against the dominant conceptualization of cities from an objective, distanced, aerial view, which mimics the forms of legibility offered by "official" maps. He counters this with an alternative way of knowing the city through the everyday movements and gestures of the lived body traversing and reinterpreting the city on the ground.[40] Certeau's writing is echoed within contemporary urban art practices, such as flashmobs, mass street actions like Critical Mass, knitbombing, and *derive* apps that encourage alternative routes for walking in urban space. Particularly suggestive for my work is Certeau's situating of practices of everyday life as "actions that reconstruct the space proposed by the environment" beyond those institutionally sanctioned by city councils, urban design and ideological biases.[41] More recently Saara Liinamaa's call for an urban art practice that is participatory, process-oriented, situated in public space and focused on urbanization "as the dramatic concentration of everyday inequality" has been equally suggestive for my work.[42] For Liinamaa this aesthetic frame ensures urban artists retain a critical ambivalence that does not celebrate the city but rather focuses on "the city as the concentration of myriad inequalities."[43] Seeing the city as locus of inequality is a key element of dissemination in my work. Examining the invisible histories told by junk and abandoned personal effects in *Collect My Junk* and *Dear Ruth*, Joosse and I made critical interventions into what is lost or undervalued in dominant constructions of city space. Audience responses to *Dear Ruth* reflected our goals to convey a critical sense of loss within redevelopment. One reviewer noted how the exhibition's interventions into abandoned bungalows "explore the deep territory of this suburban landscape, the one we're led to believe (at least by popular mythology) has no worthwhile stories and isn't interesting."[44] After touring the entire exhibit the reviewer stated,

> Every one of these near-identical bungalows suddenly seemed filled to the rafters with stories of so many Ruths who dreamed quiet dreams and lived quiet lives but weren't boring and did matter. Nothing seems to happen in the suburbs because the stories haven't been told as much, and the Leona Drive Project started to tell some of them.[45]

The fact that viewers responded to the personal nature of the exhibition, acknowledging the importance of untold histories of suburban development, signals a successful point of knowledge dissemination for both our project and the exhibition overall. Significantly, the houses were still demolished and replaced shortly after *LDP*. Under the immanent context of development, the exhibition illustrated the tensions between private experience and the institutional structuring of lived space. Viewers were presented with this tension, as they were placed into a role of familiarity when opening the cupboards of the kitchen space, only to be confronted with the preserved and distorted artifacts of a woman's life on display. Through their tour of Ruth's kitchen audiences bore witness to both the passage of time and the profound sense of loss and absence this passage entails. From this intimate experience a larger set of conclusions around the tensions and affective consequences of redevelopment – namely, an overwriting of place – were accessed by a large public audience.

All the examples of artistic research I have outlined in this essay explore what Liinamaa calls the practice of thick urbanism. With this term Liinamaa reformulates the ethnographic practice of thick description for urban art practices. She situates it as a process of "immersion into the environment" which importantly acknowledges "the complexity of forms of communication between participants" and comes to terms with "the fullness and partiality of the documentation and representation of ideas, actors and issues."[46] The points of dwelling, collecting, reflexivity and remediation I have outlined recognize the complexities and limitations of representing the multiple players of the city in urban art. For me thick urbanism provides an important guiding principle for the artist researcher of urban space as it recognizes the city as a "multidimensional and active agent within its representation."[47] The artistic research program I am invested in aims to convey this vision of the city in dialogue with its residents and the audiences through the visual remappings created by public art installations. The intention is that any such mapping encourages further iterations and reconceptualizations of the space to occur spontaneously and independently beyond the piece. By trying to turn space into a recognizable form of place, the research hopes participants and viewers recognize both the potentials and consequences of their own forms of daily placemaking. Thick urbanism as a research model values lived experience as a productive practice, recognizes material histories as a counterpoint to spatialized power dynamics, and engages the public in creative acts of reimagining that may offer greater agency over their experience of city space. It is these three interrelated benefits of the research that underscore both the need and possibilities of conducting artistic research within urban space. As my examples from *Collect My Junk, Dear Ruth* and *Mobile Art Studio* have shown, practices of dwelling, collecting, reflexive inquiry and remediation provide certain insights and agencies within cities that cannot be accounted for by more traditional forms of scholarly research.

Notes

1 It is also the term used to identify practice-based research projects when applying to government academic funding agencies, like the Social Science and Humanities Council (SSHRC), in Canada.
2 Owen Chapman and Kim Sawchuk, "Research-Creation: Intervention, Analysis and 'Family Resemblances'," *Canadian Journal of Communication* 37 (2012): 7.
3 Chapman and Sawchuk, "Research-Creation," 19.
4 Brad Haseman, "A Manifesto for Performative Research," *Media International Australia* 118 (2006): 7.
5 Hasemen, "A Manifesto," 9.
6 Henri Lefebvre, *The Production of Space*, trans. Donald Nicholson-Smith (New York: Wiley-Blackwell, 1992), 37–39.
7 Lefebvre, *Production of Space*, 34.
8 Michel de Certeau, *The Practice of Everyday Life: Living and Cooking*, Volume 2 (Minneapolis: University of Minnesota Press, 1998), 13. Certeau argues cities are "poeticized" by the subject: "the subject has refabricated it for his or her own use . . . (and) imposes his or her own law on the external order of the city."
9 Michel de Certeau, *Practice*, 13.
10 Jane Bennett, *Vibrant Matter: A Political Ecology of Things* (Durham, NC: Duke UP, 2010), x.
11 Bennett, *Vibrant Matter*, xvi.
12 Jane Bennett, "Powers of the Hoard: Artistry and Agency in a World of Vibrant Matter," Public Lecture at The New School, September 27, 2011. Date accessed: May 21, 2015. www.youtube.com/watch?v=q607Ni23QjA.
13 Alongside hoarders, who are her subject of inquiry.
14 Bennett, "Powers of the Hoard."
15 Bennett, "Powers of the Hoard."
16 See Diana Taylor, *The Archive and the Repertoire: Performing Cultural Memory in the Americas* (Durham: Duke UP, 2003), 16–33.
17 We also refused to disassemble any of Ruth's personal items for the show and instead created replicas of the many objects we put on display.

18 The growing connection we felt to the figure of Ruth is best reflected in the shifting title of the piece. We began by naming the piece *Attention to Detail* but over the course of the installation we changed the name to *Dear Ruth*, which reflected how our relationship to Ruth developed through our encounters with the fragmented story her objects told. The title became a way of addressing her intimately.

19 Dwight Conquergood, "Performance Studies: Interventions and Radical Research," *TDR: The Drama Review* 46, no. 2 (2002): 145.

20 Estelle Barrett and Barbara Bolt, eds., *Carnal Knowledge: Towards a 'New Materialism' through the Arts* (London: I.B. Tarus, 2013), 4.

21 Dwight Conquergood, "Beyond the Text: Toward a Performative Cultural Politics," in *Cultural Struggles: Performance, Ethnography, Praxis*, ed. E. Patrick Johnson (Ann Arbor: U Michigan Press, 2013), 47.

22 Conquergood, "Beyond the Text," 57.

23 Della Pollock, "Oral History," in *Mapping Landscapes for Performance as Research*, eds. Shannon Riley and Lynette Hunter (New York: Palgrave Macmillan, 2009), 145. Emphasis in original.

24 Pollock, "Oral History," 146.

25 Ibid., 147.

26 Bennett, *Vibrant Matter*, xi.

27 Ibid., xiv.

28 Ibid., xv.

29 Ibid., 41.

30 See *Visible City Project + Archive* (Janine Marchessault, 2005–2014), http://visiblecity. ca; *Mobile Media Lab* (Kim Sawchuck, Owen Chapman, Barbara Crow, Michael Longford, 2006-), http://mobilemedialab.ca; *Maraya Project* (Glen Lowry, M. Simon Levin, Henry Tsang, 2007–2009), http://marayaprojects.com; *Land | Slides: Possible Futures* (Janine Marchessault, 2013), www.landslide-possiblefutures.com; *Meeting in the Middle: Stations of Migration and Memory Between Art & Film* (Christine Ramsay and Elizabeth Matheson, 2014–2017), https://meetinthemiddle.squarespace.com; *The Situated Cinema* (Sol Nagler, Melanie Wilmink, 2015), www.cinemaofruins.com/documents/ SituatedCinema_program_final_web.pdf.

31 See Natalie Loveless, http://loveless.ca; Kathleen Irwin, www.uregina.ca/mediaart performance/faculty-staff/faculty/f-irwin-kathleen.html; Julie Nagam, http://abtec. org/iif/iif_team/julie-nagam/; Chris Salter, http://chrissalter.com.

32 For an extended discussion of the work and an overview of the *Land | Slides* exhibition please see my article "On Resonance in Contemporary Site-Specific Projection Art," *Performance Research* 19, no. 6 (2014): 64–70.

33 "Articulating Artistic Research 3.0: Ideas of Knowledge," at the annual Canadian Association of Theatre Research (CATR) conference at the University of Ottawa, May 30–June 2, 2015.

34 The workshop "Articulating Artistic Research 3.0," led by Bruce Barton (University of Calgary) and Natalia Esling (University of Toronto), was part of the annual meeting of the Canadian Association of Theatre Research (CATR) during the national SSHRC Congress, Ottawa, June 1, 2015.

35 Saara Liinamaa, "Contemporary Art's 'Urban Question' and Practices of Experimentation," *Third Text* 28, no. 6 (2014): 534, 536.

36 For a student-generated documentation of the 2015 event please see www.youtube.com/ watch?v=W9ilU3M10A4.

37 See http://nightshiftwr.ca.

38 Documentation of *Mobile Art Studio* events can be followed on www.instagram.com/ mobileartstudio/ and https://twitter.com/mobileartkw.

39 Michael Darroch and Janine Marchessault, eds., *Cartographies of Place: Navigating the Urban* (Montreal: McGill-Queens UP, 2014), 3.

40 Michel de Certeau, *The Practice of Everyday Life*, 3rd ed., trans. Steven F. Rendall (Berkeley: California UP, 2011), 91–111.

41 Michel de Certeau, *The Practice of Everyday Life: Living and Cooking*, Volume 2, trans. Pierre Mayol (Minneapolis: U of Minnesota P, 1998), 11.

42 Saara Liinamaa, "Contemporary Art's 'Urban Question' and Practices of Experimentation," *Third Text* 28, no. 6 (2014): 534, 536.

43 Ibid., 531.

44 Shawn Micallef, "Psychogeography: Bungalow's Last Stand," *Eye Weekly*, October 21, 2009, 8.

45 Shawn Micallef, *Stroll: Psychogeographic Walking Tours of Toronto* (Toronto: Coach House Books, 2011), 208.

46 Liinamaa, "Urban Question," 540.

47 Ibid., 534.

Chapter 13

Resonance in the steps of Rubicon

Monica Sand

Prologue: moving backwards

On a warm and sunny day in May 2014, a group of about ten people line up beside each other, an arm's length distance on the grassy slope, and start to slowly walk backwards, every step an attempt to bridge time through space. In front of the Humanities library in Gothenburg, Sweden, students and other citizens regularly stretch their bodies in the sun in the open green area close to the 'water lily pond'. With a quick glance over their shoulders, while trying to keep the distance and rhythm, the people in line avoid walking into small kids playing, people sun bathing, and students reading or chatting on the ground. When reaching the large chestnut tree covered with big green leaves and clusters of white flowers, each individual finds his or her own way of experiencing it – its stable uprising trunk and crispy smell, the soft wind in the leaves, points of sunlight vibrating in the shadows. Even if the walk resembled a public art performance, it actually enacted a desire to literally walk back in time – in the steps of Rubicon.

In June 1988 the dance performance group Rubicon performed on that same slope, dressed in yellow rain gear, despite the sunny day. Rubicon was established ten years earlier by a group of female choreographers and dancers.[1] Lacking a permanent stage and influenced by international art movements, they claimed a stage for performing arts in the public spaces in the city centre of Gothenburg, Sweden's second largest city, located near the sea on the west coast. During 1986–1989, through their project *The City Dancers*, Rubicon became visible to a larger audience outside the institutional dance scene.

Rubicon performed a new dynamic and powerful relation to public space with a varying number of dancers, both female and male, nearly always in their yellow rain gear. At that time this outfit was used mainly by outdoor workers, a dress they kept as a sign in any weather. The urban setting – stairs, benches, and bridges – was transformed into temporary stages. While approaching the citizens in the street, *Rubicon* performed the deep social dependency between art and the public, and claimed public space to contest the given rules. With their spatial and discursive *passages* between art institutions and the street, between fine art and dance, between dance performers and outdoor labour, their choice of places and movements was political in its implicit critique of art as something foreign to and absent from daily life. Simultaneously, those performances in public space generated something foreign to ordinary routines through difference and repetition. Despite their provoking attempt to break the boundaries between fine art and daily life, and their contribution to an advanced spatial re-interpretation of what a dance performance in collaboration with artists, composers, and musicians could be, Rubicon remains almost invisible in the written art history, in Sweden as well as in Gothenburg.

It is not lack of documentation, though, that has left Rubicon nearly invisible in art history; the problem is rather that social life and performance, like female choreographers outside the Swedish capital, are often left out of the written history. Another problem is well known to everyone trying to get a grip on ongoing life or an art performance; documentation never captures and stores the 'real' thing and tends to assume a life of its own as well, creating – in a mixture of visual material, texts, and rumours – mythology rather than knowledge. The sensation of rain, the tactile exchange with surfaces, the smell or taste that evokes memories are rather stored and transformed in and through bodies, in space and time.

The complexity of representing, documenting, and archiving dance and art performances makes them in many ways critical as heritage; first of all the 'archive' is not a neutral collection of objects or documents. It stages a field of power relations (Bacon 2013, 89), a space in which visual objects and vision as a source of knowledge are shaped. In a logocentric construction of human experiences, dance, as well as daily routines in the continuing ordinary life, become nearly invisible, not only due to their complex character but also because the relation of bodies in space seldom counts as a source of knowledge in itself. Thus any archive determines what can be brought into existence or not, in historical terms (Schneider 2012). Anyhow, regardless of the form of documentation, it is impossible to grasp the *poetic* rhythms and resonances of movements and activities of human life or of a city in a single moment, and to find a proper way of storing that moment over time.

A lived and living archive

In the spring of 2013, in collaboration with Marsha Meskimmon, professor in art theory at Loughborough University, UK, and me, Monica Sand, artist and researcher at the Swedish Centre for Architecture and Design, Stockholm, as visiting researchers, Astrid von Rosen, art historian and former dancer, initiated a collaborative research project entitled *Dance as Critical Heritage* (DACH). The collaboration was organized within Critical Heritage Studies at the Department of Cultural Sciences at the University of Gothenburg. With the intention to explore dance as 'critical heritage', we used Rubicon with *The City Dancers* project as a case study for 2013–2015.

As an artist and researcher my interest in the DACH collaboration grows from the understanding that the city establishes a living, lived, and dispersed 'archive'; (re)activated, (re)acted, and (re)searched daily through and with the human body. Hence if the city is to be understood as an archive, in order to produce knowledge, an activation of history has to *take place* in the present (Schultz 2013).

Every day citizens and visitors relate to the city and to each other by repeating, (re)producing, and (re)performing social beliefs in a cultural rhythmic structure. A *routine* (French *route* – road, path) establishes spatial and temporal rhythmic sequences related to the body, the house, and the working sphere. *Rituals* (Latin *ritualis, ritus* – holy use) often work through symbolic actions in public space, with the function to strengthen collective agreement on basic values (Bell 2009). Human experience, performed and expressed in daily routines and social rituals, acts out history in a corporeal, spatial, and temporal sense through imitation and transformation. Hence the archive of the city is (re)acted every day in gestures and social situations within the transversal and transforming relations between 'bodies and cities' (Grosz 1995, 108). With each step history is re-activated in a corporeal rhythmic encounter between feet and surface, past and present, fiction and facts, experiences and knowledge that change and transform expressions and impressions of the city. 'One step after another, one foot moving into the future and one in the past' with the body caught in the present, history takes place in the here and now (Cardiff and Schaub 2005, 75).

My question '*Where* is the history of *The City Dancers* to be found?' emphasizes place, the different places in the city where Rubicon performed. What kind of places did *they* choose? And if places are one key to their history: What kind of processes will support the re-activation of disappeared and complex urban art actions? Is it possible to walk in Rubicon's footsteps and what would it mean to do that? Those questions immediately locate the exploration in the current urban situation; public space has transformed since Rubicon performed. In what sense is it possible to influence the contemporary city through art interventions? What does it mean in terms of historical strata? At a disciplinary level: how do we interpret the archive/history at the intersections of art, artistic research, and heritage studies?

How do we approach past art practice and keep it alive? With one foot in contemporary art and the other in artistic research, I had for a long time 'walked in the steps' of art history. This experience of *walking* as a human capacity, its impact on urban art history, its metaphorical character paired with the knowledge that Rubicon dedicated several months to 'learning to walk' before they took the crucial step out into public space, made me propose walking as an explorative method from the beginning of the collaborative process.

What does it mean to walk in the steps of Rubicon? With an ethical awareness of the serious friction between different memories, in this phase the aim is neither to find the true story of nor to try to repeat, re-enact, or represent the choreographic work by Rubicon. The intention is rather to map out an unknown terrain of subtle relations while exploring the artistic potential of public space through various (re)actions: reactions to the transformation of the city, to bodies in space re-acting, and to the re-actions of urban historical art. With that question we enter the archive of the city, in which memories, stories, conflicts, and power have been preserved, selected, organized, and mapped. The urban archive could easily be interpreted as the material and visual construction of buildings, streets, and squares. In this project, though, we are rather searching for the elusive, transient, disappearing patterns and dimensions of past urban artistic practices in the present. Urban archives differ from other archives because they are activated every day, unconsciously, in individual routines and social rituals. To extract knowledge, however, the researchers need to *walk through* the material in a conscious and methodical way.

Performing re-search

The interpretation of the city as an archive, described in this chapter, made it possible to literally walk through it in a resonance between the past and the present. This was one among several methods used in our collaboration. To approach the poetic complexity of dance and performance as a critical heritage we have found it necessary to stage another kind of research process with a combination of practices, artistic research methods, gender perspectives, and archival theories and methods (von Rosen, Sand, and Meskimmon 2017). Our approach came from the awareness that engaging with the city as an archive could not possibly be a solitary procedure, as often is the case with research in a common archive. Thus different kinds of processes have been developed and collectively performed within the collaboration with our different professions and interests as the starting point. Von Rosen explored Rubicon's history in close collaboration with the practitioners, undertook interviews, and explored the archives through, among other methods, 'dancing with images' (von Rosen 2014). Based in feminist corporeal-materialist aesthetics Meskimmon (2017) discussed remembering processes taking place through artistic practice. Film producer Linda Sternö constructed a living collective archive by filming throughout the process. Dancer and choreographer Marika Hedemyr invited us to a public re-visit of one place where Rubicon performed.[2] An interesting rhythm between actively guiding each other and taking part has made this explorative collaboration extremely fruitful.

Together those explorations of dance as critical heritage and the new perspectives on *where* and *how* the archive can be approached in an urban context have influenced an interesting process of documentation as part of our collaboration. Participants, audience members, and professionals have been recording sound and video footage and producing 'space-writing', images, texts, poems, and sketches, with the intention to create an archive of the research process itself, free for everyone in the group to (re)use in various ways. Thus the first report from the process includes images, texts of various kinds, and video sequences (Meskimmon et al. 2014), while the second report takes the form of a memory collage with collectively produced video and sound, as well as historical archival images (Sand 2015).

The title *Walk in the Steps of Rubicon* was meant to be an engaging invitation to artists and researchers alike to rethink heritage and the archive, and establish walking as a literal and figurative, site-specific, and linguistic method. With its intriguing position in-between body, space, time, and language, walking proposed another way of re-activating public space. This process has served several purposes besides helping to explore the places where Rubicon performed. Most importantly it offered a space in-between the original performance by Rubicon and the present, in which contemporary researchers could move, pose questions, and explore ideas. Thus it was bringing the research group together by building common experiences *in situ*, developing methods of re-acting urban history in the present, and re-activating the artistic potential of today's diminishing public space. For walking to be useful as a research method it has to be transformed from its common course into an explorative process, and we must – in line with *Rubicon* – re-turn to walking as a basic human corporeal grammar within a cultural paradigm of walking forward.

The insistence on the prefix *re-* (Latin 'again') marks that something either is repeated, comes back, or is made anew, re-constructed and re-interpreted. It seems that there is important knowledge to be gained through re-turning, but also re-inventing through re-activations and re-actions. *Walk in the Steps of Rubicon* undertook to *perform* re-search as a literal, corporeal, and spatial rhythmic collective process of re-actions by *re*-turning to the places once used by Rubicon. Organised in a combination of two-day symposia with seminars, explorations, and presentations of different methods and theories, the research process stressed the 'space-time of bodies' (Grosz 1995, 84). Through re-turning to urban art history *in situ*, the aim was to respond to and resonate with the past in the present, re-act within the contemporary urban situation, record different perspectives, and re-present remembering as a collective process (Meskimmon et al. 2014).

Re-search – to search and search again – cannot be abstracted to methods, theories, and concepts. Rather a spatial rhythm of difference and repetition engages the body of the researcher in performing re-search as an achievement and enactment in front of an audience (Berner 2008). Here *body* is understood in its full complexity (as not possible to define entirely), beyond the notion of the individual entity, immersed in and in relation to society as a living archive of movements and relations, both a source of and producer of knowledge. Dancers performing in front of an audience work in line with how their practice is usually defined, while researchers seldom, or never, are defined by how they move their bodies in space and time.[3] However, knowledge production in any research organises the professional bodies in space only partly for functional reasons; researchers, too, *embody* ideological and social values while performing their skills. Performance defined as situated human action organises bodies in space and produces both a 'position as a subject' and '*a perspective* on the world' (Grosz 1995, 89).

Writing space into body

Not only citizens store and transmit knowledge in and through the body by routines and rituals. Even a dance performance is the result of repetitive processes of rehearsing, re-interpretation, re-playing, re-activating corporeal memory, and re-using movements. Rubicon started off their career as *The City Dancers* by dedicating several months to re-learning how to walk – or rather to un-learn the corporeal grammar of walking learned through and in society. Rather than simply walking forward, walking became a rhythmic process of taking in information through the feet step by step. How do the feet meet the ground? What kind of sensorial information is transmitted? How does gravitation influence the rhythmic movements? How do bodies occupy space? Small steps through the basic grammar of walking prepared the dancers for the larger uncertain step into the city and public space. This method transformed the well-known, quite unconscious walking procedure into something strange, unfamiliar, and difficult, filled with political meaning and social impact. The attempt to 'start from the beginning' re-produced nomadic walking and the experiences of gravitation by the baby walking and falling. Gun Lund, one of the founders and choreographers of Rubicon, underlines the complexity of the process: 'it is extremely difficult to walk', a logical conclusion after this period.[4] Through the walking process they had to re-invent and re-install another corporeal memory, another 'archive' of movement, a strategy opposed to the common interpretation of walking as a natural, neutral, liberated, and healthy act, possible to be performed everywhere by everybody.

Rather, experimenting with walking strategies we soon realised that an adaptation to the flow of the city is almost a social and cultural must. Breaking or deviating from 'natural' walking rhythms defines bodies as being out of or in place (Cresswell 1996). Due to the recent popularisation of walking to meet health ideals and its use as a developing method in various fields of art and research, the question is whether an interpretation of walking as 'natural' makes this desire to walk nearly impossible to critically explore. The naturalisation of walking, by simplifying its potential meaning and political impact, is maybe the very reason why 'it is extremely difficult to walk'.

Götaplatsen, one of Rubicon's chosen locations, constitutes a cultural square with the Art Museum at the end of the once prestigious Avenue. This stretches a line through the centre, with the Gothenburg City Theatre and the main library to the left, the concert hall and the art hall to the right. In the centre of the square, the god of the sea, *Poseidon*, a seven-meter-high sculpture by the famous Swedish artist Carl Milles, stands in the fountain. In 1996 the entrance of the Gothenburg Art Museum was moved to the first level of the stairway. Rubicon performed here in November 1986 when the public was still forced to enter through the heavy door at the very top of the impressive stairway, divided in a left and a right section connected further up. On those stairs Rubicon for the first time made themselves visible through their yellow rain gear. In a playful dance they occupied the stairway, which normally constituted the passage, or barrier, towards art's higher values. Defining themselves as 'the city nomads', Rubicon reacted to and acted upon the very fundamental idea of art as a visual, nearly eternal, object, confined in the institution, by bringing art out to the passers-by. With every step the preset conditions dissolved and the closed powerful building opened up towards the street; the stairway became a stage composed of a variety of movements, and of rhythmical drum sounds mingled with traffic noise, so that the perception of a dance performance was publicly changed.

At the end of October 2013 the two-day symposium *Dance as Critical Heritage: Archives, Action, Access* staged the beginning of the collaboration, with an invitation for everyone to contribute. About 35 artists, researchers as well as former dancers, producers, and two of the choreographers from Rubicon, attended the symposium, together with some who saw Rubicon live, others who had heard about the events, and others who neither had heard of Rubicon nor had been in Gothenburg before, but had had their own experiences of urban art interventions. On the second day in heavy rain, thunderstorms, and hard wind, we returned to the stairs in front of the Art Museum (figure 13.1).

The stairway showed its capacity to create a passage that altered the perception of the place, producing a corporeal awareness of distance, the body becoming heavier by gravitation, and the transformation of scale between the human body and the building. On the way towards the old and distant entrance the body turned heavier and the steps slower. While on the top, turning towards the Avenue, scale and perspective changed in a powerful way; the city lay at our feet with the powerful visual overview with its tempting impact: we were able to follow the rhythmical order of the city, its patterns and re-occurring sequences from above, while not forced to confront its reality. While we were sitting in the stairway with our eyes closed the sonic environment changed; background noise came closer. Between the columns, close to the historical entrance, a wall of sound made by our voices created a resonance between history and the

Figure 13.1 The staircase in front of the Gothenburg Art Museum.[5]

Figure 13.2 Vasagatan, Gothenburg.[6]

surrounding traffic. Questions appeared: Do we hear the resonance of history? How to communicate through time? What do the stairs remember (Arlander 2014)? Walking on the stone made slippery by the rain which poured down on our faces and bodies, with frozen feet in rubber boots, a sudden smell of the 'city in rain' appeared. This unpredictable reality, outside the weatherproof archive and laboratory, might scare some researchers. In this case the rain is important not only because it cannot be avoided; Rubicon performed in this climate and with a perceptive awareness of it.

Our subtle and sensitive explorations of Götaplatsen present us with different and additional corporeal and perceptive ways of acquiring knowledge about the city through the body, combining the strengths of the overview of the urban choreography as seen from a distance with the intense experience of living it in the streets (Lefebvre 2004). The temptation to connect a certain spatial perspective to a consciously analytical and distant overview and the corporeal subjective experience to the streets is a simplification of human experience. Knowledge emerges in and through the body in a rhythmic interaction between direct perception and adaptation, analysis, and written after-constructions (Sand 2008, 294ff.). Like Rubicon, but with different aims and methods, we form, perform, and formulate a vibrating resonating system of writing the body into space and space into the body. The Canadian artist Janet Cardiff described her public sound walks as follows: 'it's like writing in three dimensions. Spoken lines have to feel right in sequences as well as location and the pacing of the lines has to be right with the footsteps' (Cardiff and Schaub 2005, 35). Those three dimensions – language, locations, and the walking body – organise this re-search process (figure 13.2).

Resonance between the past and the present

The human body is constructed for walking long distances every day, and it is one of the metaphors most present in language, even if, unfortunately, 'walking in the steps of' seldom gets the researcher out of the chair.[7] Rebecca Solnit (2002, 4) is not alone, however, in her analysis that the 'rhythm of walking generates a kind of rhythm of thinking.' Still there is a certain fear in academia of letting the body into the core of the research, not only as a topic but also as the most important tool for 'knowing the world through the body and the body through the world' (Solnit 2002, 29).

Experiences of walking established a turning point in the Western notion of art in the twentieth century when artists literally walked out from the galleries into the streets with new strategies of inhabiting the city (O´Rourke 2013; Sand 2008). In opposition to the modern urban development that formed an image of the rational citizen, the dadaists, surrealists, and situationists brought forth walking processes characterised by the casual, by confusion and playfulness. Every period of 'art walking' in history developed according to social and political questions. In contemporary society for example, the logic of the dérive (drifting) with its desire to lose control is the very basis of a consumption culture, and has lost some of its critical potential. Consequently the rationality of the common map, with its seemingly neutral overview, which leaves out human life and culture, is questioned and explored as a tool of power and control. A variety of mapping strategies have been generated to such an extent that walking and mapping to this day have come to presuppose each other. Instead of a neutralised overview many of those maps produce a dynamic and complex resonance between the moving body and the experiences along the route – between history and the present, perception and place, movement and new technology (O'Rourke 2013).

In this collaboration we enter into *dialogue with urban art history* and public space through walking. Every step in a city is in fact an encounter between the past and the present; memories and associations emerge through the contact between feet and surface, matter and language, in the sonic ambience created, in history becoming present through bodily routines and rituals. With each step, space is set in motion and thus more or less unconsciously contributes to an open-ended, time-based spatial dialogue, within the wider frame of *resonance*. Resonance refers to the Latin *re-sonare*, re-sounding, sounding again, in an ongoing interaction between bodies, time, and space. Together I and my colleague Ricardo Atienza, architect and sound artist, have developed *resonance* as an experimental site-specific method, developed through artistic practice and research, in close collaboration with sound artists, dancers, musicians, architects, urban planners, and researchers from different fields. As an artistic research method we understand resonance beyond its sonic terms, by using the phenomenon as an active response to and a corporeal and sensorial dialogue with public space. The body is in itself a resonating rhythmic system of 'respirations, pulses, circulations, assimilations [. . .] durations' that vibrate through and with space (Lefebvre 2004, 5). Resonance is to be understood as the wider methodological frame within which walking and other urban interventions take place, and from which various theories are developed.

Vibration in a system and between different systems makes the phenomenon of resonance not only problematic in architecture but also dangerous. The mythology tells us that the Italian opera singer Enrico Caruso could shatter a glass only with the help of the vibration of his voice. The truth is that a bridge that starts to vibrate can break, and that is why the Millennium Bridge across the river Thames had to close after just two days, due to the unexpected vibrations when people were walking on it. Often, resonance phenomena have been used as tools for speaking loudly in public, like church bells, cannon shots, and different warning signals. Churches and courtrooms have historically supported powerful voices with their resonance (Augoyard and Torgue 2006, 99ff.). Neutralisation of public space makes resonance a dangerous tool as it creates an active and critical response to the way we inhabit and act in public that draws us out of the seemingly neutral position of an individual consumer. Far from a distanced research approach or a reflective after-construction, resonance makes the artist/researcher vibrate with and in the situation. *Resonance* creates a practical, sensorial, and corporeal method within the complex situation itself and functions as both a description of urban life and as a practical tool for responding by influencing our common ground (Sand and Atienza 2012). We act and re-act together. Too much or too little resonance will break the construction – it could be a metaphor of a society.

Resonance in action

In an extreme worldwide commercialisation of cities, public space has decreased and art itself has been reduced to amusement, to such an extent that public art performances often have become just another way of promoting 'the creative city' (Zukin 2011; Sassen 2006). Consumption and gentrification have made it nearly impossible to perform in the way Rubicon did; people acting in a group are more likely to advertise a phone company than perform art.[8] Maybe a critical art performance is possible only the other way round. Rubicon performed with the aim of reaching a new audience. We were there to be observed by the passers-by while performing in public, with the main aim of learning to know the place, and making sense of its historical, political, and social impact through our sonic and corporeal responses to it. That is why we have to prepare our perceptions and senses to step in-between the present and the past, and thus perform, without aiming at an audience, a corporeal connection to and dependency of historical urban actions, in the present – in terms of *response-ability*. How and with what means are we able to respond to the challenges public space poses us beyond the neo-liberal individualistic paradigm?

In contrast to Rubicon, who (re)learned to walk in the dancer's exercise room, we have developed our walking strategies *in situ*. As a preparation for the second 'walkshop' in the seminar *Resonance as a Research Method*, the group of artists, researchers, and students was told to close their eyes and stand silent for a couple of minutes outside in front of the glass entrance of the university building. By closing our eyes, we open other ways of recognising space and our corporeal relation to it. It is part of a preparation process that requires time, the time it takes to change perceptions; usually we *look* around in a new place or building, heavily culturally influenced by visual perspectives and aesthetic constructions. Our capacity for understanding a building, a place, or a room just by listening and through other senses than vision is surprisingly high. It is a developed 'survival' skill – in a dense forest, in the desert, on the savannah, on the sea, and of course in the city, even if we seldom pay attention to the sonic influences on our sense of direction and sense of home.

Dimensions, scales, and distances emerge through the senses; sounds of moving leaves, birds singing, traffic noise, various smells pass by in the wind, the sun warms the skin cooled by the shadow, gravitation puts the feet heavily on earth. Start walking, blindfolded, and the passage from the outside to the inside is easily perceived, the feet sense every change in the surface, the rhythm slows down, the sensation is that walls, as well as people passing, come closer. Slowly the body becomes prepared to enter into a conscious spatial dialogue that integrates body, space, and time. Space is more than a point of view – it surrounds, includes, and vibrates with and between the bodies. This transformation from vision to other senses/sensations is not only a change of perception. It changes the spatial perspective of the researcher, who becomes a body immersed in space, in its dimensions and ambience. With every breath, heartbeat, step, and vocal expression the researcher stages a rhythmic vibrant communication between body and space.

Entering into another relation with the space, our bodies become vibrating spatial tools by walking around, and sonically trying out different materials in rhythmic movements in dialogue with the others. By touching, moving, and making surfaces and movements resonate together, resonance becomes more than a sonic method; it is an attitude, a corporeal dialogue with, in, and through space, in connection with the things happening around.

The day after this introduction, the participants divided in three groups, prepared a re-activation of each of one of three public places used by Rubicon: the area near the humanities library mentioned in the prologue, Trädgårdsföreningen, a central park along the moat at the end of the Avenue in the city centre, and the bridge and the canal along Södra Hamngatan. In line with the preparations the day before, the intention was to start a dialogue with the actual place, by moving, exploring, and re-acting together. This time the weather was sunny and, in contrast to the first rainy and stormy 'walkshop', the city was now filled with people relaxing and enjoying outdoor city life. Besides the line of people walking backwards, the different places influenced a sensitive awareness and response to structures and spatial organisation in playful tasks: trees supporting the body, improvised walks with closed eyes through stairs with running water, play on the public sculpture, wind passing into the open mouths. This kind of close relation to and response-ability to a place is possible almost only in a group, in a collective that performs their connection to the place and to each other.

An infrastructure of performance as heritage

What kinds of places did Rubicon choose? How do they relate to each other? How are they used today, and with what means is it possible to activate their artistic potential? Although five of the places showed a seasonal correspondence with Rubicon's performances, the intention was never to just map out a chronological structure or the seasonal relations or to pinpoint the places on a map. Through the process the city was activated as a historical archive within the present social and cultural rhythms, and an *infrastructure* of places, once performed by Rubicon, was created through our moving bodies. The combination of *infra* (= under) and *structura* (= structure) is most often referred to as the underlying technical and physical structures of a society, such as the railroads, roads, bridges, electrical grids, the water supply, and telecommunication. The French anthropologist Marc Augé (2002), however, defines another infrastructure within the metro of Paris; he locates his childhood, student period, and adult life in connection to different stations, so that the metro map becomes a map of his own lifespan. By commuting daily, he travels from one place to another and thus re-connects his life story in relation to the present and to the historical past of France (the metro stations are often named after political conflicts and powers). Within the metro infrastructure with its predefined lines, the individual story resonates with the history of society and with the social classes as a daily reality, thus producing another infrastructure re-activated through the body.

While re-turning to the places once performed by Rubicon we enter the archive of the city with its constructions of buildings, streets, and squares, searching for the rhythmic patterns of daily life and urban artistic practice. *In situ* we approach the specific urban art history of Rubicon through a set of creative, time-based, corporeal, site-specific processes, along with studies of archival material; we aim towards an integrated urban art history. The critical heritage of *The City Dancers* performed by Rubicon can be recognised and researched within the public places where they performed, forming an infrastructure of artistic urban practice to be re-activated. This kind of underlying structure is not defined by its given rails or roads; it is built on the spatial relation between the past and the present, re-activated in the body, re-presenting the poetics of bodies in space through history.

Epilogue: moving through

As very often happens, it has been raining in Gothenburg for a couple of days, and it still rains. The absence of daylight makes the day as grey as the muddy ground. Visible in their glowing rain gear with grey reflecting stripes, the dancers are far from objects to the viewers, dressed as they are, prepared for hard physical dirty work in any weather, like the park workers from whom they borrowed the clothes. They are subjects and actors, moving, running, and leaving traces with their bodies on the ground, followed by an uncertain group. Is this meant to be an audience, neither able to hide in the darkness in front of a stage nor able to find the very best position to see the dancers' formations? Where to go? Where to look? The rain increases and various umbrellas amplify the sound. The performers whisper: follow us! But what does it mean? Are we supposed to run and play with them? Just give in and follow the stream of consciousness in site-specific movements? Forward and backward, in line, out of rhythm, beside or behind, guided by a hand on the shoulder, and then lost again. Audience and dancers collectively take part in a mobile remembering process, walking through, beside, and with it. Spreading, running, and trying to find points of view, we form, inform, and formulate a memory, although the perspectives dissolve as in a dream. The underlying structure of dependency, of history as performed and formulated in and through bodies in space, forms a new societal member – an infrastructure of *re-members*.

Notes

1 They were Eva Ingemarsson, Gun Lund, Gunilla Witt, and a fourth member, Gunnel Johansson, who left the group before *The City Dancers* project.
2 *Rubicon Re-visited in Haga kyrkoplan* (Pilot), 24 October 2015, the experience described in the epilogue.
3 In earlier research, I have used the idea that professionals embody their practice by performing in time and space, comparing dance performances with physicists acting physics at the international particle laboratory CERN (Sand 2008, 224ff.).
4 From a private discussion with Gun Lund in her studio *3 våningen*, Gothenborg, Jan. 31, 2014.
5. Left image: Rubicon performance, November 22, 1986. Photographer: Elisabeth Ohlson Wallin. Right Image: Walkshop, October 29, 2013. Photographer Linda Sternö, responsible for the collectively produced video and photos in the project.
6. Left image: Walkshop, October 29, 2013. Responsible photographer Linda Sternö Right image: Rubicon performance, November 18, 1989 Photographer: Lars Persson
7 The candidate thesis *Move Your Ass and the Mind Will Follow* by Elisabeth Jonsved (2009) at the University College of Arts, Crafts, and Design explores literally what the title suggests.
8 In advertising a phone company the stairway in front of the Gothenburg Art Museum was lit up. A young couple danced a waltz inside a heart of candles placed on the ground with music in loudspeakers – the woman beautifully dressed in a thin armless dress, the man in a dark costume, none of it giving any protection from the rainy and cold evening, 23 October 2015.

References

Arlander, Annette. 2014. 'Vad minns träden? – What Do the Trees Remember?'. In *Dance as Critical Heritage: Archives, Access, Action. Symposium Report 1. Beginnings*, edited by Meskimmon, Marsha, von Rosen, Astrid, Sand, Monica, 86–89. Critical Heritage Studies (CHS). Gothenburg: University of Gothenburg Press.
Augé, Marc. 2002 [1986]. *In the metro*. Minneapolis, MN: University of Minnesota Press.
Augoyard, Jean-François and Torgue, Henry. 2006. *Sonic Experience: A Guide to Everyday Sounds*. Montreal: McGill-Queen's University Press.

Bacon, Julie Louise. 2013. 'Unstable Archives: Languages and Myths of the Visible'. In *Performing Archives, Archives of Performance*, edited by Borggren, Gunhild and Gade, Rune, 73–91. Copenhagen: Museum Tusculanum Press, University of Copenhagen.

Bell, Catherine. 2009. *Ritual Theory, Ritual Practice*. Oxford: Oxford University Press.

Berner, Bodil. 2008. 'Working Knowledge as Performance: On the Practical Understanding of Machines'. *Work, Employment and Society*, 22(2): 319–336.

Cardiff, Janet and Schaub, Mirjam. 2005. *The Walk Book*. Köln: Walther König Verlag.

Cresswell, Tim. 1996. *In Place/Out of Place: Geography, Ideology, and Transgression*. Minneapolis, MN: University of Minnesota Press.

Grosz, Elizabeth. 1995. *Space, Time, and Perversion: Essays on the Politics of Bodies*. New York: Routledge.

Jonsved, Elisabet. 2009. *Move Your Ass and Your Mind Will Follow: samtidskonstens pedagogiska potential genom en undersökande metod*. BA thesis. Stockholm: Konstfack.

Lefebvre, Henri. 2004. *Rhythmanalysis: Space, Time and Everyday life*. London: Continuum.

Meskimmon, Marsha. (forthcoming) 2017. 'Art Matters: Feminist Corporeal-Materialist Aesthetics'. In *The Companion to Feminist Art Practice and Theory*, edited by Robinson, Hilary and Buszek, Maria Elena. Oxford: Blackwell.

Meskimmon, Marsha, von Rosen, Astrid, Sand, Monica (eds.). 2014. *Dance as Critical Heritage: Archives, Access, Action. Symposium Report 1. Beginnings*. Critical Heritage Studies (CHS). Gothenburg: University of Gothenburg Press.

O'Rourke, Karen. 2013. *Walking and Mapping: Artists as Cartographers*. Cambridge, MA: MIT Press.

Sand, Monica. 2008. *Konsten att gunga. Experiment som aktiverar mellanrum*. Doctoral dissertation. Stockholm: Axl books.

Sand, Monica (ed.). 2015. *A Vibrating Research. Memory Collage. Report II*: https://vimeo.com/144635774 (accessed 10.12.2016).

Sand, Monica and Atienza, Ricardo. 2012. 'Playing the Space: Resonance, Improvisations and Variations of Urban Ambiences'. In *Ambiances in Action/Ambiances en acte(s) – International Congress on Ambiances*, edited by Thibaud, Jean-Paul and Siret, Daniel, 153–158. Montreal, Canada: International Ambiances Network.

Sassen, Saskia. 2006. 'Public Interventions: The Shifting Meaning of the Urban Condition'. *Hybrid Space*, Open No 11. http://archivepublic.wordpress.com/texts/saskia-sassen/ (accessed 10.10.2016).

Schneider, Rebecca. 2012. 'Performance Remains'. In *Perform, Repeat, Record: Live Art in History*, edited by Jones, Amelia and Heathfield, Adrian, 147–150. London: Intellect.

Schultz, Laura Luise. 2013. 'The Archive is Here and Now: Reframing Political Events as Theatre'. In *Performing Archives, Archives of Performance*, edited by Borggren, Gunhild and Gade, Rune, 199–219. Copenhagen: Museum Tusculanum Press, University of Copenhagen.

Solnit, Rebecca. 2002. *Wanderlust: A History of Walking*. London: Verso.

von Rosen, Astrid. 2014. 'Dansa med bilder. Att artikulera kroppens kunskap i livsberättelser om dans'. In *Personligt talat. Biografiska perspektiv i humaniora*, edited by Sjöberg, Maria. Göteborg: Makadam.

von Rosen, Astrid, Sand, Monica, Meskimmon, Marsha. (forthcoming) 2017. 'Transversal Dances Across Time and Space: Feminist Strategies for a Critical Heritage Studies'. In *Gender and Heritage*, edited by Grahn, Wera and Wilson, Ross J. London: Routledge.

Zukin, Sharon. 2011. *Naked City: Death and Life of Authentic Urban Places*. Oxford: Oxford University Press.

Chapter 14

Violence and performance research methods

Direct-action, "die-ins," and allyship in a Black Lives Matter era[1]

Juan Manuel Aldape Muñoz

During the 2014 and 2015 "Black Lives Matter" (BLM) demonstrations in the United States, pro-Black and Black demonstrators used the particular tactic "die-ins" as performative acts in support of the BLM movement to honor the deaths of Black and Brown people killed at the hands of state police. BLM is a network of social justice and civil rights activists, workers, and concerned citizens working to undo the violent legacy of racial injustice in the United States. This die-in was organized in Berkeley, California, in the fall of 2014, as part of other nonviolent, direct-action strategies after the acquittal of the White police officer who killed the Black teenager Michael Brown. The four minutes of silence in Berkeley had the objective of showing solidarity with other demonstrations occurring simultaneously in streets across the United States in a spate of documented violence and murders caused by police forces and vigilantes in such states as Missouri, Florida, California, and Utah. These nonviolent, direct actions present an opportunity for pro-Black allies and members of the Black community to represent death as a gesture to sympathize with the deaths of Sandra Bland, Michael Brown, Oscar Grant, and Trayvon Martin, among many other Black citizens.

The interval between the start of silence and the continuation of the demonstrations reveals uneasy cultural fissures in a country with a long history of policing Black and Brown bodies. In the presence of constant violence and death carried out by police forces, citizens in democratic societies have limited avenues for democratic participation to demand justice when excessive force is used by police who are supposed to protect and serve the community. The gap between just participation and the unfulfilled needs pressures communities that are seeking justice to adopt nonlegislative actions. Performance practice is one such expression of these demands and the BLM demonstrations reveal more than an assessment of the social situation in the United States. The demonstrations call for social, civic, and judicial change at the institutional, relational, and conscious level.

I began participating in the die-ins and documenting these reflections in 2014 during the month-long demonstrations in Berkeley and Oakland, California. Since that time, the discussion about the BLM movement has shifted in significant ways. First, pro-Black lives allies debate the use of BLM direct-actions. Some allies equate the actions with violent actions because in some cases these demonstrations shut down public transportation or lead to arson. Second, community-recorded videos continue to surface online on platforms such as Facebook Live or YouTube Live. These videos capture police inter-action with citizens and the use of deadly force when the police stop Black citizens or when Black citizens call the police for help but end up being killed and arrested by the very police they called for. Third, President Donald Trump bolstered alt-right, pro-White sentiments throughout his campaign. By using the phrase "law and order" throughout his bid for the White House in response to the BLM demonstrations, he hailed the BLM demonstrations and the offshoot direct-action protests as methods of political participation that are violent and chaotic. Fourth, even though the BLM movement was created by Black citizens who are concerned about Black trans men and women, these dimensions of the movement are often left out of the larger narrative.

As a formerly undocumented, working-class, brown-skinned Latino male from Mexico residing in the United States, who has been the victim of racial and violent attacks by authorities, vigilantes, and passers-by, I identify with the urgent call for a reevaluation of the militarization of police and border forces, the purging of a systemic culture of violence against Black, Brown, and Indigenous lives, and an end to the United States' systemic consolidation of white supremacy in the judicial, executive, and legislative branches of govern-ment. What is at stake in my alignment with a pro-Black consciousness as a non-Black participant, and how do these alignments operate in an anti-Black system? How do the performance and practice of empathy function in the die-ins? What happens to allies when we conceptualize Black lives that matter in a context that privileges social justice along gendered lines? I am concerned with the privilege that allies of the BLM movement possess in desiring to show solidarity in a violent context that operates across a matrix of racial, gendered, and class divisions.[2]

To examine the foregoing stated concerns, I find it necessary to look to per-formance as research methodologies and frameworks to apprehend the change that happens through direct and self-critical participation in nonviolent actions in pro-Black demonstrations. It is not enough to observe the demonstrations through a performance studies frame because these questions developed for me as a consequence of participating in the demonstrations. Moreover, it is not enough to focus on a performance analysis framework because the issue at hand for me is not focused on a participant/observer paradigm. As I will argue later in detail, I choose performance as research because it offers an approach that might transfer the contours and affect of the BLM movement into an academic setting.

In this essay, I reflect upon my experience of participating as an ally in the BLM movement to argue that when we look to and participate in the political demonstrations of the BLM movement as a performance as research methodology we can assess, document, and disseminate an epistemic strategy of disembodied knowledge that is rooted in a de-colonial and feminists of color strategy. In what follows, I examine and assess my experience in the 2014 demonstration in Berkeley, California, my involvement in the graduate research working group "Social Death: Race, Risk, and Representation," and the 2016 BLM demonstrations in Minneapolis, Minnesota. I consider how participating in pro-Black lives demonstrations fashions an anti-Black embodied experience and the consequences of this realization for performance as research. I offer to the reader the use of "accompliceship" rather that allied strategies. At the center of this complex and shifting phenomena, I ground my experience as an ally of the pro-Black lives consciousness and use performance as research as a process to dismantle the lingering effects of the colonial enterprise against Black and Brown bodies in the United States that moves in and out of the academic setting and shapes knowledge production.

I recognize that speaking from the trenches of an unresolved social conflict might appear to offer a limited perspective.[3] Yet I underscore the generative possibility of a paradigm that supposes an incomplete picture of social justice from a mobile, disjunctive position. This essay is structured in four "one-minute" sections and examines the disembodied manner in which performances of death reveal the ambivalent predicament for non-Black allies – such as myself – that erase part of the Black experience. However, such performances also expose a political practice where accomplices can create the conditions to make social justice claims that are attuned to the color, gender, and race of the accomplice in an anti-Black landscape. I invite the reader to sit-in with me for four minutes in this struggle for liberation.

Minute one: "bursting of the self" for/as/in a social justice methodology

A proposal to examine the methodologies of performance as research with issues of the Black Lives Matter movement might appear at first as an odd advancement. This connection appears disjointed because the former is perceived to deal with questions of methods, knowledge, and dissemination, often in a university setting, and the latter is conceived as a social protest movement concerned with, and dedicated to, unveiling and undoing the systemic and state-sanctioned destruction of Black and Brown lives in the United States through nonviolent direct-action. I see in common in these processes, concerns, and practices a commitment to undoing the violent institutionalization of social-historical conditions that privilege White, upper-class, Westernized, capitalizable, neoliberal, heterosexual knowledge forms that require the labor, management, disenfranchisement, and oppression of working class, queer, trans, Black, and Brown bodies, as well as "other" forms of knowledge. This claim appears too bold for the argument at hand, but let me be clear when I say that if we are to take seriously the task of reimagining and advocating for alternative forms of knowledge research and production, such as performance as research and embodied research, we must contend with the enduring effects of the colonization of Black and Brown bodies in the development and management of knowledge production.

Third-world feminist Chela Sandoval argues that research examination from within the university can be a fraught project from the beginning precisely because the parameters of the investigation require a particular logic of assessment, documentation, and dissemination that works within "academic apartheid." To decode and transcode the theoretical, methodological, and practical tools that continue the regimes of ideological domination, Sandoval combines third-world feminist theory, method, and criticism. Her objective is to apprehend social movements that can be deployed against dominant ideologies to create new forms of resistance that do not, themselves, become ideologies that oppress across lines of gender, sex, class, culture, and nation: "The methodology of the oppressed is that interfacing: it demands the recovery of meaning through movement called for by Fanon: the bursting of the self into social categories for the sake of their reapportionment and conversion" (2000: 129). Social categories, such as education and power, can undergo change when the oppressed burst the self to decolonize with care and love. For Sandoval, "The methodology of the oppressed is a set of processes, procedures, and technologies for decolonizing the imagination" (68). Sandoval invites us to consider the tools of documentation, assessment, and dissemination in the academic setting because domination works across intersecting modes of oppression even as performance researchers develop alternative methods. She calls for intellectual ground in the academy that recognizes new forms of theory and methods and focuses on a grammar of oppositional consciousness that values mutation and an ethical commitment to justice (129).

My choice of performance as research as a framework, rather than "practice as research" or "embodied research," is based on Sandoval's challenging task of assessing how colonization of the imagination occurs through performance research. Performance as research (PAR), a designation more common in the United States, is not easy to discuss. Disagreement over its name, its efficacy, and even its existence is frequent and animated. Some performance studies programs disregard it completely while others triumphantly declare it as a bastion of hope for the humanities in a mostly neoliberal research setting. Still, even the programs in the United States that value the PAR process or processed-based research do not provide robust methodologies to frame dissertation-length research projects. The University of California, Davis, offers some hope on this front. Researchers' discussions about PAR are further complicated by attempts to identify the varying strands in the UK and continental Europe, and to distinguish between practice as research and performance as research. I perpetuate the confusion by not elaborating on the discussions about PAR across other oceans, be they Baltic, Indian, or Pacific.

The intent here is to position PAR in political discussions crucial to the current academic and social settings in the United States. I focus on performance as research in an effort to maintain the animacy of the term "performance" and to underscore the epistemological stakes at hand. In *Research Methods in Theatre and Performance* (2011), Baz Kershaw and Helen Nicholson offer an illuminating account of PAR researchers and situate the intersecting topographies of interdisciplinary thought. The volume spans from Maggie Gale and Ann Featherstone's bifurcating and reflexive process in looking at the archive, through the unpredictable deconstruction of the workshop in Jonathan Pitches and Simon Murray's training, to Jennifer Parker-Starbuck and Roberta Mock's body-centered interpretation on the ephemeral. From a macrolevel perspective, the edited collection captures the array of reflexivity, unpredictability, and ephemerality that dwells in PAR strategies. Though Kershaw and Nicholson situate PAR's possible antidiscipline character within the larger epistemological debates, they limit PAR's contributions to the understanding of research to academic settings. Kershaw and Nicholson inquire about the metaforces that researchers enact to destabilize the interplay between epistemologies and ontologies, but they do not address the metapolitical forces at play in the process of researching.

More recently, Ben Spatz makes an illustrious case for choosing to adopt practice as research alongside embodied practice. In *What a Body Can Do* (2015), Spatz examines the history and concept of "technique" outside the confines of theatre, in spaces and practices such as gender and yoga, to conclude that embodied knowledge can generate knowledge. He evaluates the lessons that researchers and practitioners can learn by adopting the lens of technique to theorize a connection between embodied knowledge, embodied research, and academia. According to Spatz, the university can benefit from including "embodied technique [. . .] as a major branch or division of human knowledge, alongside the sciences and humanities, and that universities could legitimately design and support major research projects in this field" (219). His call to incorporate embodied technique in the university is an effort to thwart the neoliberal university's focus on information and product development within the growing instrumentalization of education and research. This research follows in line with Kershaw's earlier emphasis that "the most crucial effect of performance practice as research is to *dis-locate* knowledge" (Kershaw 2009, 105). For Spatz, the current structural crisis of the university is an opportunity to imagine anew radical methods to transform the epistemic landscape of a system undergoing systemic changes.

My concern with such a proposal on embodied knowledge is that we perpetuate pedagogies that privilege particular social forms of embodied knowledge by choosing to make a case for practice on the basis of a social epistemology framework. To remove the term "performance" from the title and to emphasize practice is to do away with the animate and political possibilities of a shapeshifting word and process. I focus on "performance" because I want to continue to propagate an animate and decentralized understanding of research that deals with the politics of epistemology. In this way, I evoke Mel Chen to honor the animate possibilities of language, where terms such as "queer" and, in our case, "performance" animate power structures. In using performance as research, I see the "alchemical magic of language" (Chen 23). If we make the claim that we want to induct performance into a research framework in the socially crafted understanding of knowledge by erasing the term "performance" from the conversation at hand, we risk subsuming performance into a Westernized epistemic field of knowledge production that functions through erasure. De-colonial theorist Ramon Grosfoguel (2013) argues that epistemic racism/sexism undergirds the foundation of the Westernized university. In particular, this racist/sexist foundation functions through the destruction of other knowledge forms that developed through the genocide/epistemicide during the long sixteenth century, from 1492 to the mid-1600s. According to Grosfoguel, Descartes's philopolitical proposal "Cogito ergo sum" is the development of "epistemicides" achieved through the extermination of Indigenous people and the enslavement of Africans. *Cogito ergo sum* is possible only after the process of *ego extermino*, "I exterminate, therefore I am." Thus, we must contend with the social-historical conditions that bind "I think" with "I conquer" and "I exterminate" in our efforts to examine the possibilities of embodied research.

What is more, I choose to adopt PAR as opposed to performance studies analysis for two main reasons. First, my concern with the Black Lives Matter movement grows out of a desire to unveil and undo the violence perpetuated against me as a Brown, undocumented body who was hailed at the age of fourteen by a vigilante in our apartment complex with the shout "put your hands up" and a gun pointed to my back. A neighbor had called the apartment's private security firm because I looked suspicious and was, apparently, carrying what appeared to be a gun. This encounter stays with me in all of my interactions in the public sphere and is an affective frame in which I perceive the ever-shifting policing and surveillance of Black and immigrant communities. Second, my choice to use a methodology of performance as research in the social justice movement aims to investigate the questions of knowledge moving inside, outside, within, and through the university. By bringing the BLM movement to the concerns of performance as research, I confront the ethical questions connected to the very idea that bodies and practices of exclusion make the university institution possible. When we consider the sociohistorical dimensions of exclusion and colonization through the process of epistemicide/genocide, we lay bare the privilege that is granted to us as advocates of performance and performance as research within the academia, a knowledge production institution founded on the genocide and continued exclusions of people of color, and trans, queer, and Indigenous communities. The task must become for us to examine, assess, and understand the exclusion and privilege that work alongside each other in performance as research practices.

For me, it is not enough to retreat to the university performance spaces to ask these questions of performance as research. This approach is tenable and provides particular parameters for those of us interested in academia, but I see this approach as one concerned with legitimizing a White/Westernized understanding of performance as research at universities in countries that colonize, such as the United Kingdom and the United States. While her topic is not directly performance as research, artist-scholar Marta Savigliano astutely remarks that the university "colonizes" the researcher and the subject matter being investigated. For those of us concerned with PAR, the type of academic justice and liberty we seek with this research orientation can manifest as a version of colonization that masquerades as liberatory politics. Instead, Savigliano offers a call to self-examine the manner in which education and research in the Westernized world can be a site for resistance against the violence of academia.

In what follows, I take up Sandoval's framework of a "methodology of the oppressed" to demonstrate how the Black Lives Matter movement can function as a site for pro-Black allies to traffic in new forms of theory and methods that value an oppositional consciousness. By participating in the BLM movement, the parameters for marking off the documentation, assessment, and dissemination of knowledge generated in the experience of the "die-ins" and other BLM-related events burst across spaces and require a reappraisal of the very idea of these boundaries. Mutant methodologies cannot be wholly constituted because the value does not come from one's participation in one or two events. The value arrives when one bursts oneself and makes oneself available to the scenarios of police brutality to fight epistemicide/genocide in the academy and on the street.

Minute two: surrogacy in the space of violence

Demonstrators have been walking angrily around varying parts of Berkeley, California for over an hour on the evening of December 6, 2014, intersecting through the streets of Bancroft and Telegraph. Before coming to the cross-streets of Shattuck and Allston, hundreds of bodies shout in an indignant tenor and ignite the darkness with sonic distortions against an unperformed justice and the unfair treatment of Black people in the United States. Among the splintering corteges crisscrossing streets, some groups demand, "No justice, no peace, no racist police," while others chant "Black lives matter." Still, others invoke their counterparts by shouting, "Shut it down for Michael Brown." Police in military fatigues surround the protestors and control the traffic ahead in an effort to kettle the moving direct-actions. City and media helicopters hover above with sharp spotlights surveilling the people's movement. The moment arrives when one leader calls for the "die-in" and four minutes of silence. Each minute represents an hour that the body of Ferguson, Missouri teenager Michael Brown was left on the street on August 9, 2014, after being shot by White police officer Darren Wilson.

A multiplicity of actions unfolds in the silent grandeur of the four minutes in Berkeley. While some protesting bodies sit on the black asphalt with their backs fully erect, their eyes peering up and their bodies silhouetted by the darkened street lamps that are chromatically accented by the turning red and blue police lights, some reflect with their eyes closed and their faces turned straight up at the black sky. One protestor rests completely on her back while still being able to take an inverted photograph of the others on the ground. Others look puzzled as they watch the multitude of bodies. Simultaneously, demonstrators withdraw their vociferousness, lying down with the demonstration placards that state "We are all Ferguson" on the ground to cover their bodies. The four minutes of dying-in on the gritty asphalt on Shattuck and Allston reveal the tectonic cultural overlaps – a situation that might be best categorized under what Arjun Appadurai (1996) identifies as disjunctures – in American subjective practices defined by Blackness and non-Blackness.

Figure 14.1 captures the demonstrators taking various positions during the die-in. In that moment I consider a litany of doubts and questions: How are these living bodies relating to the dead? Is this gesture sympathy or empathy? Whose death and whose destruction was/is at stake? Is it the spectacle of death without violence, but with an already assumed, normative violence on Black lives that attracts us? Whose death is on the stage of the street? How do the dies-ins participate in the spectacle of "black-death"? This discharge of questions situates the urgency of the deadly performance.

Joseph Roach's framework is useful to analyze these questions because it crystalizes the dynamic and fraught relationship between memory, performance, and substitution happening in the die-in. In *Cities of the Dead* (1996), Roach

Figure 14.1 "Street Death" (2014). Berkeley community members perform a four-minute die-in to remember the Black and Brown bodies killed by the police.

Source: Juan Manuel Aldape Muñoz.

argues that in the act of performance, on the one hand, that which is absent is presented, and, on the other hand, that which is present stands in for something and erases or forgets. He argues, "Memory is a process that depends crucially on forgetting" (2). Performance's phenomenological function instantiates directional forces, or, as Diana Taylor maintains, "Histories and trajectories become visible though performance" (2003, 271). For Roach, surrogation is the process by which culture represents and reproduces itself. When something or someone dies or is lost, a community's attempt to substitute that which is now gone is a process that continues, fails, makes errors, and at times creates a deficit (2). Performance "stands in for an elusive entity that is not but that it must vainly aspire both to embody and to replace" (Roach 3). Performance operates in contrapuntal fashion because while something is being remembered and (re)presented, something is being forgotten. What is more, a performance's ability to represent something which is not present, to create a memory, provides the possibility to create new worlds and unspoken pasts (Dillon 2014, 19).

Looking at the four minutes of silence from the perspective of surrogation, it is possible to observe that the demonstrators embodying the actual lives of Black bodies killed by police forces are selectively presenting the vacancy of the materiality of the dead Black bodies that are not present. The materiality of the demonstrators' expressive movement and their breathing bodies become the surrogates for un-breathing, murdered bodies that become socially and affectively visible to White-subjectivity and legal space only after their death. The demonstrators, by exclaiming "Black lives matter," and subsequently representing dead bodies, bring forth the past moments of Michael Brown's and others' deaths. The performative gesture cuts through time and space, a genealogic transmission connects the black asphalt of Missouri to the black asphalt of California, recreating an ongoing cultural struggle to remember dead Black bodies. Collapsing the uniqueness of each death makes it possible to witness a cultural problem: "Same story every time, being Black is not a crime." Through this narrative phrase, demonstrators make the statement that Blackness does not equal criminality, while also acknowledging a systemic narrative that perpetuates the exclusion of the Black community across time and space in the United States.

The predicament of remembering a Black death through the spectacle of protest vis-à-vis die-ins is that the privileged position and the non-Blackness of the everyday lives of non-Black subjects performing the die-ins are forgotten. As Roach succinctly summarizes, "The fit cannot be exact" (2). Performance, as Diana Taylor argues (2003, 275), reveals the social power relations at hand, and, in this case, the substitution that occurs in the performance erases the bodies that were actually killed, like those of Sandra Bland and Trayvon Martin, and brings breath to Eric Gardner – something that he lost.[4] Speaking about the uniqueness of Michael Brown or any one individual dead body detaches the experience from the larger systemic violence pressing upon Black communities every day.

Conversely, this bodily displacement results in the instantiation of what Harvey Young calls the abstraction of the Black experience, that which he terms "phenomenal blackness." Young contends, "As an instantiation of a concept (blackness), the black body does not describe the actual appearance of any real person or group of people" (Young 2010, 7). A Black body is an abstraction and imagined figure that shadows and doubles the "flesh-and-blood body" that is the target of a racial system (Young 7). Thus, the non-Black surrogate bodies for Black bodies during the demonstrations in Berkeley carry a tinge of temporal and spatial erasure that collapses the uniqueness of the individual bodies that die at the hands of the police. More worrisome, this temporal and spatial erasure evacuates the gendered dynamics that affect Black citizens because a Black female experience becomes background to a Black male experience. A slippage occurs between the materiality of the everyday gendered, classed, and raced Blackness and an abstracted Black body. The demonstrators performing a dead Black body restore the loss of the deceased and instantiate a forgetting that Black experiences are subject to constitution from the outside.

Saidiya Hartman argues that the specticality of violence perpetuates the techniques of Black subjectivation from the outside. For this reason, Hartman refused to recount in detail the violent stories that Frederick Douglass, a nineteenth-century African-American writer and abolitionist, saw as the formation of his Blackness. Refusing to recount Douglass's concerns of the "terrible spectacle" in Aunt Hester's beating, Hartman disavows the explicit violent moments that demonstrate the ease with which the ravaged Black body is reiterated and remembered through the routine of violence. She maintains, "The oft-repeated or restored character of these accounts and our distance from them are signaled by the theatrical language usually resorted to in describing these instances" (3). To repeat and retell the accounts of violence at a distance reiterates the powers of slave domination and violence imposed through the optic of specticality, wherein the Black body is subjectivated. Instead, Hartman argues for an analysis of subjectivitation where the familiar dimensions of the slave experience, such as practices of enjoyment, property, and paternalism, are defamiliarized to show the extent to which violence and terror are maintained. Focusing on the quotidian in slavery, she reveals how the Black subject is subjugated and constituted in scenes of subjection, in the mundane and in performance practices that were heretofore considered autonomous and processes of individuation. The practice of everyday slavery is more constituted than assumed and forms of resistant tactics are small moments of gestural assaults on domination.

Accepting Hartman's focus on the "terror of the mundane," rather than the "exploit of the shocking spectacle," we can see how violence occurs in the quotidian and that emancipation is a complex endeavor that moves inside of/outside of/through private and individual actions. Yet the persistent adoption of the die-ins by both Blacks and non-Blacks, as joint performance calls to social justice, reveals the ambivalent fashion in which violence can be corporeally reproduced and memorialized without the exploit of the spectacle violence.

Where Hartman defined the violent spectacle as that which is phenomenologically resonant through visibility and written description, I am compelled by the manner in which the die-ins serve as an embodied and affective violent remembering as silent representations outside the terms of spectacular seeing and reading. A Black community member's effort to "die" alongside non-Blacks in the die-ins reveals the minor and small acts of resistance, this despite the non-Black community member's reproduction of the dominant relationships.

I want to extend Hartman's thinking to the extent that an allied peaceful, silent, and non-gruesome representation of death, violence, and suffering perpetuates social death and violence of Black lives. Building on Diana Taylor's (1997) astute contributions on percepticide – "the self-blinding of the general public" – I argue that the die-ins usurp the spectacle of violence and death to provide a way to see the state violence and policing apparatus. The protestors who take the picture while dying-in or holding the sign "We are all Ferguson" force witnesses of the demonstration to look in, and alongside, rather than away from the systemic confinements that operate against Black communities. "Being Ferguson" and capturing the "deaths" of the bodies protesting reveal the subterranean politics of Black resistance and provide a frame to highlight the micro spaces of violent complicity when allies support Black acts of resistance.

Hartman clearly indicates that at stake when we talk about the scenes of violence is the way in which we participate in the scenes of subjection. She notes, "At issue here is the precariousness of empathy and the uncertain line between witness and spectator" (4). If the non-Black demonstrator chooses and is able to represent death, is he/she not in a position to enact an assumed agency and secured relation that perpetuate the domination of the Black body? Surely, a body does not choose to die, but is instead made dead through excessive force by police officers and departments that preemptively see the Black body as threatening. Thus, the scene of someone who is non-Black putting on display "death" and uttering the declarative statement "Black lives matter" perpetuates a small act of violent empathy where relations of domination reside.

Consequently, I arrive at the dilemma: if "silence is violence" and "White Silence = White Consent," as some demonstrators vociferously express throughout the demonstrations and hold forth on signs during the die-ins and current demonstrations, how can a non-Black ally resist a violent U.S. democratic system that excludes Black communities without being the surrogate for the abstracted Black body? An alternative for pro-Black lives is to shout "All lives matter." Hartman argues that in imagining the suffering of the Black captive the White witness "becomes a proxy and the other's pain is acknowledged to the degree that it can be imagined, yet by virtue of this substitution the object of identification threatens to disappear" (19). Succinctly, non-Black subjects can die only for an imagined, mythic, and abstracted Black body; their experience is outside the horizon of an embodied experience of Blackness.

Between Joseph Roach's performance evaluations on surrogation and Saidiya Hartman's ideas of empathy and spectacle, we can see the stakes at hand when a non-Black ally participates in the die-ins. Where protestors acknowledge a kindred desire to be allies, finding satiation by their empathetic identification, their acts of performing the die-ins furnish the double-edged nature of social justice. A non-Black ally's performative concern towards the Black body is a relation of substituting an imagined Black pain with a privilege over Blackness – one afforded by the ability to possess and embody the Black body, given the acceptance of its fungibility, and a willingness to accept it as a place that is disembodied and available for substitution by non-Black protestors' desires and feelings.

Minute three: sitting in disembodied research

Throughout this examination, I have grappled with the slippage between ally and perpetrator and an unresolved anxiety about my place in the Black Lives Matter movement. On one hand, my inaction performs in perpetuity a violence against Blackness; conversely, I acknowledge my participation is unable to embody the Black experience. My fleshiness is not Sandra Bland's fleshiness. When my fleshiness attempts to give presence to her death, it erases her lived experience. If the die-ins surface the experience of the dead Black body and not the experience of Blackness, is it doubly performing two deaths? Is one death that of the material body that is physically shot at the hands of police while the second death is the performance of the die-ins, where the representation of a social exclusion is fleshed out and other bodies replace the materiality of social Blackness? If we lie down with these deadly thoughts, I think we can begin to ascertain the contours of a disembodied performance research.

Despite recent efforts from performance/practice as research scholars to call for the value of embodied research, BLM direct-actions provide the generative potential of disembodied awareness that is part of an oppositional consciousness. Figure 14.2 captures the hundreds of Black Lives Matter demonstrators gathered on July 7, 2016, outside of the governor's mansion in Saint Paul, Minnesota. The crowd rallied on the footsteps of Mark Dayton's office in response to the murder of Philando Castile, a Black man pulled over in his car and killed by the Latino police officer Jeronimo Yanez in a suburb of Saint Paul. As news of Castile's death started to spread on the night of July 6, the Black Lives Matter chapter in Minneapolis relayed information through social media platforms like Twitter to gather the following morning in front of the gubernatorial incumbent's residence.

Thinking about disembodied research is not so much a dismissal of the generative potential of embodied research practices or a rebuke of the possibility of a complete subjectivity. Rather, I focus on disembodied research as a result of participating in the Black Lives Matter demonstrations in Minnesota and the "Social Death" working group at University of California, Berkeley, in the spring of 2015. Jamaal Batts and Britanny Meché organized a "Social Death" UC Berkeley reading group after initial ideas developed during *The Rover*, a performance as research series initiated between Natalia Duong and myself that

Figure 14.2 "Black Lives Matter in Minnesota" (2016). Community members gather in front of the Minnesota governor's residence.

Source: Juan Manuel Aldape Muñoz

gives graduate students across disciplines an opportunity to facilitate a movement-led workshop in their area of research. During the session on March 8, 2015, Joshua Williams and Gowri Vijayakumar facilitated a movement workshop where participants responded to the textual staging of the deaths of thirteen Black people. Williams and Vijayakumar used archives from 1955 to 2014 that depicted the deaths of Black people killed at the hands of police and armed vigilantes – including Oscar Grant, Emmett Till, and Eleanor Bumpurs. They incorporated coroner's reports, courtroom testimonies, and newspaper articles into the workshop to examine the representations of Black bodies in relation to democracy, legal records, and state violence.

The questions and feelings that I experienced during the workshop and the working group led me to focus on Castile's death because I wanted to examine questions about disembodiment and state violence, but I wanted to be outside of the university setting. On July 6, 2016, Officer Yanez stopped Castile for a simple traffic violation, a broken taillight. Yanez fired his gun within seconds after Castile informed the officer he was carrying a permitted weapon. Castile possessed a permit to carry a gun, but the police responded with deadly force. Castile's partner, Diamond Reynolds, began recording the incident seconds after Castile was shot. On November 16, 2016, Ramsey County Attorney John Choi charged Yanez with second-degree manslaughter.

My response to Castile's death is angry and unresolved, much like other cultural workers at that time who were trying to recover from the death of Alton Sterling, a Black man killed on July 5, 2016, at the hands of two Baton Rouge, Louisiana, officers after the police were called to investigate the suspicious behavior of a person selling CDs in front of a convenience store. I present at length the social media entry I uploaded online while I sat on site next to where the officer shot Castile:

> I mourn for #Philandocastile and I am angry. I woke up this morning trying to fuel the sorrow and anger I felt over the death of Alton Sterling into actions. Instead, I read on my Twitter feed about Philando Castile's killing. This killing happened late last night! The killing happened about thirty minutes from where I'm staying. Now, I sit here, where he was killed. Philando had a conceal-and-carry permit. He told the officer that he had a gun in his possession. He reached for his wallet and not the gun. Still, the police murdered him. Philando was murdered! He told the officer that he had a conceal-and-carry and he was shot four times.

After hearing about Castile's shooting, I drive thirty minutes to Falcon Heights to be with Castile in thought and presence, giving witness to the aftermath of the situation. However, I cannot reconcile the disastrous conditions of the violence that often feels so far away from non–Black subjects. I might think about Castile's touch and body, but, as noted earlier, there are limits to this type of onto-political thinking because colonization is webbed in a hierarchy of power where bodies are separated along racial, gendered, and class social constructs.

I arrive at the intersection and see the local and national news networks waiting to interview mourners and passers-by. As I sit on the grass, a White woman walks up to me with a bag in hand. She pulls out one bottle of water after another, offering a drink to the mourners and protestors. The woman and the supporters do not speak to each other as the water is received. After distributing four bottles, she sits on the grass and looks at the flowers resting on the location where Castile was shot. The woman's gesture stands out not only because she is handing out water but also because she distributes the bottles and proceeds to sit in silence to wait as other supporters arrive at the scene and I sit to document her experience on social media. Figure 14.3 captures the angle from where the White woman and I sit next to each other as we look at the flowers dispersed on the sidewalk and the street.

When the White woman gestures with the water bottle, she animates a conviviality of care and concern for the people present *in situ*. The gesture indicates her concern with the well-being of the supporters who are present and who mourn and contemplate Castile's death. The water bottle enacts a transversality of allyship that underscores the liveliness of the people present while gesturing to the disembodied dimensions of the situation. As she passes out water I wait with my phone in hand to document her actions and the actions of the police. By 'disembodied dimensions' I mean to suggest that the water bottles animate the bodies that are present – and in doing so highlight the bodies' separation from the dead bodies. The materiality of the water bottle and the phone mediate two concurrent and transversal indexes. Through the bottle the woman's care and concern become present in the situation. The phone makes material my awareness that the social media world is waiting to visibilize and disseminate any violent interactions of the situation that might arise when police arrive to tell the mourners to stay off the street. The phone and the water enact and animate the social-political possibilities of resistance to the police's past and potential brutality.

In a recent article on the role of political responsibility around violence and death, Iván Ramos argues that in the face of absolute violence in a space such as Mexico, griefability for political action might be possible if we shift the focus of relating to the dead and the disappeared away from a requirement that the subject be known. In examining the work of Mexican artist Teresa Margolles, who uses the blood from crime scenes for her installations, Ramos sees a political potential in valuing the material remains of the dead. Ramos writes,

> Her work reveals the need for forms of grievability beyond subjecthood, an attachment to vulnerability beyond bodies. It is this visceral sorrow that attaches itself to our bodies where we can find a contestation that dares us to reimagine a we.
>
> (312)

Ramos is interested in challenging the prevailing view that in order to grieve for the anonymous dead and the disappeared it is necessary to know their names and biographies. He lingers in the aftermath of the violent scene to explore the vulnerability of the human body. A political project exists in emphasizing the material remains of the violent moment. It implicates the audience's experience in the art installation and a way to conceptualize the relationship between the dead and the living, which often feel so divided. Ramos's words on the dead and their aftermaths challenge social justice workers and artists concerned about social justice to confront these disembodied aspects.

Can Castile's death and the protests that erupted after it offer a similar site for analysis? Throughout the grieving next to Castile's death site, the White woman and I cannot know Castile in that moment. We know partial truths about his story, his death, and the lives of those who have disappeared. The scenario fills the street with unrecognizable bodies and names, yet we know their lives by what they leave behind and I relate to the woman through the water bottle.

These moments invite us to linger with the anonymous dead bodies through their material remains and through the material objects that we exchange as we grieve and address our anger together.

I agree with Ramos in that we are provided with the opportunity to grieve for the anonymous through their material remains. However, the death of Black citizens at the hands of the police complicates the ally's relationship to the anonymous subject because we are not presented with materials of the crime scene. The materials of the crime scene are ushered off to the coroner's office as evidence. Our allyship experiences are the sticky dimensions that become animated through the material remains in a relationship that is disembodied because Castile's body is not present. We are left with the material remains either in the form of flowers in make-shift shrines such as those captured in figure 14.3 or in coroner's reports that are made public after a jury reaches a verdict. Still, within these sticky dimensions, I see a way to consider Ramos's proposal for how we might find a way of "mourning those who remain unknown to us." By being present at the demonstrations and emphasizing the inability to feel the remains

Figure 14.3 "Castile Flowers" (2016). Community members brought flowers to the site where Officer Jeronimo Yanez killed Philando Castile.

Source: Juan Manuel Aldape Muñoz.

of Castile we become complicit in consumer culture and are confronted with the need for a way to mourn the life of Castile through his remains.

While I sit in front of the flowers that are being left for Castile, I think about his wallet. In a recorded video, Castile's partner Diamond Reynolds narrates how the police officer pulls up to Castile's car and asks for proof of identification. Castile reaches for his wallet and informs the officer that he has a gun and is permitted to have one. The officer, feeling threatened, shoots Castile. Seconds later, Reynolds begins broadcasting the incident live via Facebook. As I contemplate Reynolds' actions and Castile's wallet, I write the following: "Anti-black media will accuse Philando of reaching for his wallet. 'He should have complied with the law and listened to the officer's words,' they will say. He was and he did! Can't we see the problem! The officer should have listened to Philando's words. The officer was not listening to Philando. Are we listening?" In the encounter, Castile's words misfire. Though Castile is protected by constitutional rights and privileges as a citizen of the United States, his words cannot perform in the Austinian sense and the officer shoots him. The officer's implicit bias distorts Castile's performative utterances and his action of reaching for the wallet to provide proof of his legal privilege to carry a gun. His words are not allowed to perform in legal discourse because the police officer considers them outside the performative spectrum of White constitutionality. By contrast, as I document in figure 14.4, Saint Paul police officers show up to the site where Castile was shot and they prevent the crowds from being on the streets by placing barricades to redirect the oncoming traffic. At the moment of the encounter with Castile, Yanez feels that Castile's body, speech, wallet, and gestures are both ineligible and legible because they impose an immediate threat. Yet, after Yanez kills Castile, Castile's death and the subsequent shrine that results from his death make White social space legible and administrable because it enters White constitutional civil space when White allies show up to the shrine to claim the value of Castile's body.

In a similar way, Kayla Moore's and Jacqueline Craig's respective words are not allowed to perform. Berkeley police strangled and killed Moore, a Black trans woman living in Berkeley, California. On February 12, 2013, Moore's friends called the police because they were concerned about her schizophrenic behavior. The officers responded to the call, but wrongfully arrested Moore, confusing her for a suspect in the police's warrant database. As this essay goes to publication, no officers involved in her death have been charged and, almost four years later, on January 13, 2017, Moore's family appeared in a San Francisco appeals court to challenge a judge's initial ruling to dismiss part of the civil lawsuit that focuses on the officers' excessive force and wrongful arrest. On December 21, 2016, Jacqueline Craig, a Fort Worth, Texas, resident, called the police to report a White neighbor who assaulted her seven-year-old son after the child threw raisins on the ground. In a video recorded by Craig's daughter, a White male officer brutally arrests Craig after arriving on the scene and questioning Craig's ability to raise her child. The officer asks Craig, "Why don't you teach your son not to litter?" The officer throws Craig and her daughter on the ground, arrests them, and presses charges. Craig's and Moore's words are not allowed to perform because the police question the ability of the words to represent, create, and act the reality of Craig's and Moore's lives.

Castile's, Craig's, and Moore's respective encounters with the police, the officers' implicit bias, the ally's gesture to offer water, and my presence at Castile's site expose two aspects that are important to our understanding of performance as research. First, in these encounters we observe the limits to J.L. Austin's model of the *performative*. All three citizens enact their constitutional rights. In Castile's case, he exercises the "right to bear arms," but he is shot nonetheless. The misfire of his words is made even more evident in the fact that the National Rifle Association, the United States' largest advocate for "the right to bear arms," does not issue a statement in support of Castile's rights and to denounce the police's actions. Second, by focusing on the material objects of these deadly and brutal encounters, we are implicated in the material, consumer culture that drives and contributes to the escalation of police enforcement to keep White communities

Figure 14.4 "Falcon Heights Triptych" (2016). The police manage the crowds on the site where Philando Castile was killed.

Source: Juan Manuel Aldape Muñoz.

"safe." This is the most poignant stance; to sit-with the dead invites us to dwell in the aftermath of their life precisely because we mourn their death through the material remains that they leave behind, the evidence that is used to unjustly convict them, the water we need to survive as allies, and the phones we need to disseminate the systemic and implicit bias against Black and Brown lives. These material encounters pose the challenging task of taking seriously Castile's life and its circulation through the merchandise we consume, need, and use when we attend as allies. We make ourselves affectively available to the lives of Craig, Moore, and Castile *in situ*, through an intimacy with the materiality of things in the direct-action.

If all of these thoughts are leading to a point, it is this: the Black Lives Matter demonstrations, the circulation of videos that capture brutal and deadly encounters, and our allied desire to perform pro-Black justice operate within a network of disembodied terrains where objects mediate a transitivity of care and intimacy that is understood alongside racialized Black, Brown, and trans bodies. This terrain is disembodied in the sense that non-White bodies are considered outside of White subjectivity and that non-White grammar is not allowed to perform within constitutionally protected social space. It is a terrain where racialized bodies are not considered whole and deserving of concern even when they say they can't breathe.

Minute four: deadly endings and raisins for the privileged researcher

I get up from the four minutes of silence, my lungs expand, and I begin to walk with an ambivalent consciousness and with the acceptance that "Black lives matter." Black lives can act and gesture towards an acceptable social context in the struggle for liberation in the United States' violent democracy. Moving forward, the question for me becomes, "How do bodies survive?" rather than, "What can bodies do?" By focusing on the methods and processes of survivalship in a violent context, we can attune to the modes of assessing, documenting, and disseminating knowledge of social justice that moves inside and outside our desire to relate as allies in an anti-Black landscape. As a Brown male, I seek a small-scale assault so that my regimes of social death and praxis imposed on Black lives stand not only as a practice that can witness suffering and a desire for the materiality of suffering for self-reflection but also as a disembodied everyday consciousness. My entry into this desire is found by participating in the Black Lives Matter die-ins, sit-ins, and demonstrations because they provide a direct and critical involvement to expose the challenges to embodiment thinking and to the abundance of privilege in knowledge production.

In an early draft of this chapter in July 2015, I end with a gesture towards Baltimore, Maryland, and the protests in the aftermath of Freddie Gray's death on April 19, 2015. I look with humility to Fanon for the reminder that indeed this dilemma is a colossal task. Fanon contends that one way forward is to "confess that [European masses] have often rallied behind the position of our common masters on colonial issues" (Fanon 2007, 62). I confess, albeit in a U.S. context, the task of (r)allying is at the expense of others' positions, wherein resting on the ground suggests rallying behind anti-Black quotidian performances due to the entrenched regimes of violence and scenes of subjection of the imagined Black body. The die-in performance is a violence itself that repeats systemic displays of/on dead Black bodies. What is more, this violence abounds in material objects, such as wallets, raisins, and CDs, that are connected to racialized bodies and become avenues for the continued control and discipline of Black and Brown bodies and their movement. What recourses for justice exist in a social landscape where a raisin on the ground becomes the justification for the violence against unarmed mothers and their children?

For the oppressed, methods have to be varied. In the preface of the documentary *Concerning Violence* (2014), Gayatri Spivak contextualizes Frantz Fanon's call for violence. Fanon, Spivak argues, insists on a dialectical relationship between violence and nonviolence because there is no other response, there is no other practice. Spivak declares that Fanon's social rally in *The Wretched of the Earth* (1961) is a teaching text where the reader is witness to how "[t]hose lives count as nothing compared to the lives of the colonizers." Though Spivak tempers Fanon's calls for liberatory, decolonial politics by observing that both colonized and colonizers are united in gender violence, she underscores the importance of violence against violence on the road to liberation. This approach is one of many strategies available as a methodology for the oppressed. Our goal is to continue shape-shifting the strategies of liberation in a violent context where raisins and wallets become *á raison d'une action*. For this reason, projects such as "Copwatch" provide avenues to hold the police accountable in their encounters with citizens. Copwatch is a self-organizing community project started in Berkeley, California, in the late 1990s, now based across the United States, dedicated to training and encouraging community volunteers to observe and record police interactions in case of any police misconduct. Though the project started before the advent of cell phones, the 2011 case *Glik v. Cunniffe* became the first court ruling that constitutionally protects a citizen's right to record a public official, which encouraged more community members to volunteer for the organization. Copwatch and BLM demonstrations are recent manifestations of the persistent development in the anticolonial movement, and they offer opportunities for pro-Black allies to take direct-action in the call to justice.

I reach a complex and unsettling understanding of performance as research because the demonstrations are a desire for social change through embodied knowledge. However, an analysis of the die-in performances of 2014 in Berkeley, California, and a moment of silence in 2016 in the aftermath of Philando Castile's death in Minnesota reveals that these embodied actions are at best partial. They are, in and of themselves, partial in that participating in the demonstrations is about recognizing that the victims' physical bodies are not present and that our physical bodies participate in a necro-political sphere that all too easily justifies deadly force on Black bodies. The ally body and the absent Black body connect through the resonances of objects, and we fortify that relationship by showing up to watch and disseminate the violent knowledge that is used in an interaction with the police.

Admittedly, the discussion here about die-ins, BLM's sit-ins, video surveillance, and these processes' relationship to performance as research mutated and did not seem clear at all times. This apparent bifurcation is sinuous and the two modes of anticolonial resistance refuse to constitute each other. As such, when we look to performance as research as a methodology of the oppressed, we must engage this movement through a problematically personal and physically disembodied entry point into research practice, one focused on analyzing, understanding, and giving account to the injustices that we perpetuate as researchers both inside and outside the White, Westernized university.

Notes

1 The original scope of this analysis included Mexico within its frame. However, I felt it appropriate to focus on one country. The analytic frame for the observation of the United States is the same, and asks the same questions. A comparative approach felt beyond the limits of this chapter, given the concurrent social development as the chapter was being written. I wish to thank the members of the Performance as Research Working Group that met in 2014 and 2015 during the yearly gathering for the International Federation for Theatre Research. Your feedback helped me narrow the scope of this study.

2 On July 13, 2013, George Zimmerman was acquitted of all charges in the murder of 17-year-old Trayvon Martin. Florida state "Stand Your Ground" law protected him from any conviction.

3 I want to note that protests are unfolding as I write this chapter. The tragedy in the death of Baltimore resident Freddie Gray at the hands of police once again ignited riots, rebellion, and looting. In this instance, similar to what occurred in Ferguson, the National Guard was called in, and a curfew was imposed.

4 Eric Gardner died at the hands of New York Police on July 17, 2014, as a consequence of there being a chokehold on his neck while police tried to restrain him for supposedly selling cigarettes on the sidewalk. Video footage shot by passers-by exists of him pleading, "I can't breathe."

References and further readings

Anderson, Patrick. 2010. *So Much Wasted: Hunger, Performance, and the Morbidity of Resistance.* Durham, NC: Duke University Press.

Anderson, Patrick, and Jisha Menon. 2011. *Violence Performed.* London: Palgrave Macmillan.

Appadurai, Arjun. 1996. *Modernity at Large.* Minneapolis, MN: University of Minnesota Press.

——— 2002. "Deep Democracy: Urban Governmentality and the Horizon of Politics." *Public Culture* 14(1): 21–47.

Austin, J.L. 2007. "How to Do Things with Words." In *The Performance Studies Reader.* Edited by Henry Bial. New York and London: Routledge.

Benjamin, Walter. 2005. *Walter Benjamin: Selected Writings: Part 1 1927–1930.* Cambridge, MA: Harvard University Press.

Butler, Judith. 2004. "Performative Acts and Gender Constitution." In *The Performance Studies Reader*, 187–99. Edited by Henry Bial. New York and London: Routledge.

Cacho, Lisa Marie. 2012. *Social Death: Racialized Rightlessness and the Criminalization of the Unprotected.* New York: New York University Press.

Chen, Mel Y. 2012. *Animacies: Biopolitics, Racial Mattering, and Queer Affect.* Durham NC: Duke University Press.

Dillon, Elizabeth Maddock. 2014. *New World Drama: The Performative Commons in the Atlantic World.* Durham, NC: Duke University Press.

Fanon, Frantz. 2007. *The Wretched of the Earth.* New York: Grove Press.

Grosfoguel, Ramon. 2013. "The Structure of Knowledge in Westernized Universities: Epistemic Racism/Sexism and the Four Genocides/Epistemicides of the Long 16th Century." *Human Architecture* 1: 73–90. Print.

Hartman, Saidiya V. 1997. *Scenes of Subjection: Terror, Slavery, and Self-Making in Nineteenth-Century America.* Oxford: Oxford University Press.

Holland, Sharon Patricia. 2002. *Raising the Dead: Readings of Death and (Black) Subjectivity.* Durham. NC: Duke University Press.

Kershaw, Baz. 2009. "Practice as Research Through Performance." In *Practice-led Research, Research-led Practice in Creative Arts*, 105–123. Edited by Hazel Smith. Edinburgh: Edinburgh University Press.

Kershaw, Baz and Helen Nicholson. 2011. *Research Methods in Theatre and Performance.* Edinburgh: Edinburgh University Press.

Moten, Fred. 2009. "The Case of Blackness." *Criticism* 50(2): 177–218.

Musser, Amber Jamilla. 2014. *Sensational Flesh: Race, Power, and Masochism.* New York: New York University Press.

Noland, Carrie. 2009. *Agency and Embodiment: Performing Gestures/Producing Culture.* Cambridge, MA: Harvard University Press.

Patterson, Orlando. 1982. *Slavery and Social Death.* Cambridge, MA: Harvard University Press.

Ramos, Iván A. 2016. "The Viscosity of Grief: Teresa Margolles at the Scene of the Crime." *Women & Performance: A Journal of Feminist Theory* 25(3): 298–314. Web.

Ritskes, Eric. 2015. "The Fleshy Excess of Black Life: Mike Brown, Eric Garner and Tamir Rice." *The Black Scholar* 43(4): 124–31.

Roach, Joseph. 1996. *Cities of the Dead: Circum-Atlantic Performance.* New York: Columbia University Press.

Sandoval, Chela. 2000. *Methodology of the Oppressed.* Minneapolis, MN: University of Minnesota.

Spatz, Ben. 2015. *What a Body Can Do.* London: Routledge.

Spivak, Gayatri Chakravorty. 2014. "Preface to Concerning Violence: Nine Scenes from the Anti-Imperialistic Self-Defense. *Film Quarterly* 68(1): 61–62.

Taylor, Diana. 2003. *The Archive and the Repertoire: Performing Cultural Memory in the Americas.* Durham, NC: Duke University Press.

——— 1997. *Disappearing Acts: Spectacles of Gender and Nationalism in Argentina's 'Dirty War.'* Durham, NC: Duke University Press

Weheliye, Alexander G. 2014. *Habeas Viscus: Racializing Assemblages, Biopolitics, and Black Feminist Theories of the Human.* Durham, NC: Duke University Press.

Young, Harvey. 2010. *Embodying Black Experience: Stillness, Critical Memory, and the Black Body.* Ann Arbor, MI: University of Michigan Press.

Multiple futures of performance as research?

Annette Arlander

The future of performance as research is linked to its past; following the thinking of Karen Barad, among others, the past and the future are continually reworked and negotiated. And things change fast these days. A few years ago, at the meeting of the performance as research (PAR) working group at a conference in Osaka, Japan, I tried to look at some earlier influences on the development of PAR in order to understand the developments then under way. I will return to them later in this text, which is based on some previous publications (Arlander 2011, 2014, 2016). My aim is to discuss two developmental trends within the field – performative research and artistic research – but first a few words on terminology.

One of the issues that influence the future of performance as research is how we understand the meaning of the term; is it something specific, distinguishable from research designated by other related terms, like practice as research, practice-led research, practice-based research, arts-based research, creative arts research, artistic research and so on? Or is the name "performance as research" exchangeable, allowing an interchangeability among its many designations – one option within this broad field in development? Even more pertinent is our relationship to the word "performance". Associations related to the term, like "public performance", "peak performance", "performing properly", "performativity" or even "performance art", influence our understanding of what can be done within the realm. Although performance has been understood in a broad sense as a "doing", there is a tendency to hark back to the colloquial uses of the word associating to performing arts and theatre, and the idea of "showing doing". People accustomed to what could be called an "audience-oriented-ontology" feel comfortable with the term "performance as research", especially in the US, as exemplified by the new PARtake journal of performance as research (see www.partakejournal.org). In the UK the term "practice as research" is mostly preferred. Often the acronym PaR is used, because it blurs any distinction between the two. Practice as research could be criticized for separating theory and practice, and for not distinguishing between artistic practices and other practices; theorizing is a practice, too. The latter criticism goes for performance as well; all research is performed in some manner. The problem with the word "performance" is that researchers working within theatre often understand performance as the result, not as the action or process. In some sense performance as research is too narrow as a term, linked to performance as the topic investigated. In another sense performance as research is too general and needs to be specified – for instance by the particular doing in question – in order to be useful, as in acting as research, choreography as research, writing, singing or painting as research.

The term "as" in performance as research could be criticized for indicating that something is not research, but only presented as if it were research. While we can study something that "is" performance, we can also study almost anything "as" performance, even a map can be analysed as (if it were) a performance, an active entity (Schechner 2006, 38). In a similar manner we could consider any artistic process as (if it were) a research process. A clear distinction between a thing that "is" something and a thing considered "as" something is hard to maintain. This "is/as performance" distinction has been criticized as an ontology-epistemology binary and "a form of modernist behavioural humanism" (Kershaw and Nicholson 2011, 4), and debated in performance philosophy (Cull, 2014). We could understand research as performative in the same ways that documentation is performative and actually produces what it is supposed to document; documenting an action as performance art constitutes it as performance art (Auslander 2006, 7). Documenting or exposing an artistic project as a research project probably constitutes the project as research. Another way of looking at it accepts that sometimes an artistic practice is research (in whatever way we want to define research); sometimes an artistic practice can be exposed (presented, documented, staged, translated) as research; and sometimes research could be presented in a more artistic, sensuous or experiential way. These perspectives produce widely diverging ideas of what performance as research could be used for. A key issue is whether we want to see performance as research as a methodology or as a field.

One future development of performance as research, a continuation of previous developments, is a methodological understanding of PAR. PAR is increasingly used as one methodology among others within humanities and social sciences, although most frequently in theatre and performance studies. If we understand PAR as a mode of "investigating by doing", like learning by doing, it can be developed as one research tool, either as part of the qualitative paradigm, or even as a separate performative paradigm, as Brad Haseman (2006) has suggested. Emphasizing the methodological aspect of PAR foregrounds performance or doing as a method in producing research material or data, or as a method in sharing research results, or any combination of these. This methodological approach is what PAR mostly has come to mean.

Another future development for performance as research is to coevolve with the contested field of artistic research, with its roots in the contemporary art world and the legacy of conceptual and critical art, and all the challenges that entails. PAR can be linked to developments within the arts, including artists entering academia, research entering art institutions, and a growing interest in practitioner knowledge within the study of arts. Although the contributors to this volume do not necessarily see themselves as engaged in artistic research, but rather in performance as research or practice as research or embodied research, most of them are practicing artists. Clearly the interests and needs of artists entering the world of scholarly practices differ from those of scholars exploring physical or practical research methods or artistic modes of presenting research results, based on their previous experiences and skills.

Performative research?

Should performance as research be understood as part of the performative turn? Does it have any relationship to the performative research paradigm? The first version of this text was presented for the meeting in Osaka in 2011 of the performance as research working group of the IFTR, founded by Baz Kershaw and Jacqueline Martin in 2004 and at the time led by Mark Fleishman and Anna Birch. The publications quoted are all fairly recent; the history of performance as research remains to be written and other layers should be included to complement the ones mentioned here.

The performative turn in social sciences and humanities is characterized by Tracy C. Davis in her introduction to *Cambridge Companion to Performance Studies* (2008) as a recent phase in the development of cultural studies, since the 1970s, after "the 'linguistic turn' (emphasizing language's role in perception), the 'cultural turn' (tracking the everyday meanings of culture, and culture's formative effect on identities)," and the most recent of them, "the 'performative turn' (acknowledging how individual behaviour derives from collective, even unconscious, influences and is manifested as observable behaviour, both overt and quotidian, individual and collective)" (Davis 2008, 1). A turn implies that our attention has been reoriented and broadened, in this case to consider the implications of bodies and embodied being, and to emphasize the importance of practices. Davis refers to performance, like culture, "as the corporeal knowhow of practice, as the organizing ethos of practice and as the experienced import of practice" (Biernacki 1999, 77, quoted in Davis 2008, 3), forming layers that are easily overlapping in a particular study. In that book Baz Kershaw (2008, 23–45) develops the focus on practice as research. The performative turn, as a focus on action and process or as an interest in production through repeated performances rather than representations or structures, has probably had a stronger impact in other areas than the study of performing arts. The emergence of the field of performance studies could be seen as an example of the performative turn.

In another overview of developments in performance studies, *Contesting Performance – Global Sites of Research* (2010), the editors Jon McKenzie, C.J.W.-L. Wee and Heike Roms use the term "performance research" rather than performance studies to emphasize local and regional approaches while investigating the globalization of performance studies. They argue, paradoxically reaffirming what they criticize, that the institutionalization of performance studies has been perceived as centred in the US, although there is also a profound decentring taking place. "Performance studies is no longer only about the West – specifically the United States – studying the 'Rest'" (McKenzie et al. 2010, 2) – despite the nested structure with NYU (New York University) PS at the centre, nested within the larger formation of US/North American PS, within the complex of US/UK PS, and that in turn within the vastest realm of the PS empire, the "Anglophone PS" (McKenzie et al. 2010, 6–9). Thus they want "to stress the 'situatedness' of local sites of research" and "the dense particularity of specific places and times" where "the variety and subtlety of contemporary performance research emerges" (McKenzie et al. 2010, 11–12).

Interestingly the writers also underscore the importance of performance practice as a challenge to institutionalized understandings of performance. They maintain that artists actually do the kind of productive and critical thinking about performance that is associated with critics and academic writing and suggest that we may grasp genuinely distinct approaches to performance through embodied, particular performance experience (McKenzie et al. 2010, 12). Heike Roms points out as one distinctive characteristic of performance research in the UK "its attention to artistic practice, whether manifest as a renewed focus on the materiality of theatre or as the expansion of creative modes of investigation" (McKenzie et al. 2010, 13). What

> may appear at first as a reversal of performance studies' focus from an extended consideration of cultural practices back to a narrow notion of performance as aesthetic production in fact presents a profound re-evaluation of the nature of practice itself and the study of it.
>
> (Ibid.)

In the German and continental European context, the future of performance research depends on the development of hybrid formats between research on performance and performance as research that challenge the dichotomy between theory and practice, Sybille Peters contends. She points to the possibility of a broader understanding of research, no longer as the privilege of science, theory and art, which could instead "help organize and make visible the collective research that is undertaken by everybody, every day, making use of a wide range of procedures and integrating all forms of knowledge" (McKenzie et al. 2010, 17). However, she also voices the concern that "performance" might come to simply mean "output" in the time of increased economic pressures on the university. These connections between the academic field of performance studies and actual aesthetic practices have been relevant for the development of performance as research.

Performance as research can also be located within the general field of practice as research. The theory-practice divide and the valorization of textual over embodied knowledge within academia have long been criticized, but the valuing of practice has not always meant emphasizing the importance of artistic practice. Dwight Conquergood presented one eloquent plea for balance in "Performance Studies, Interventions and Radical Research" (2004). Researchers turn to practitioners for knowledge (e.g., Aston 2007), but when artists start to carry out research on their own terms, complications tend to arise. In the introduction to *Mapping Landscapes for Performance as Research* (Riley and Hunter 2009), Lynette Hunter and Shannon Rose Riley point out that modern arts and humanities have structured a gap between practice and analysis while the sciences have long understood the value of practice-based research. "Perhaps the most singular contribution to the developing areas of practice as research (PaR) and performance as research (PAR) is the claim that creative production can constitute intellectual inquiry" (Riley and Hunter 2009, xv). They emphasize that PaR in the UK and performance as research in the US are not exactly the same, though what exactly is the difference is not very clear. They mention the influence of performance studies in the US, the inclusion of performative methods in ethnography and social anthropology, and the importance of experimental theatre for the development of performance as research (Riley and Hunter 2009, xvi–xvii).

In the introduction to the anthology *Practice as Research, Approaches to Creative Arts Enquiry* (Barrett and Bolt 2010), Estelle Barrett claims that the emergence of practice-led research has highlighted the relevance of theoretical and philosophical paradigms for contemporary arts practitioners and proposes "that artistic practice be viewed as the production of knowledge or philosophy in action" (Barrett in Barrett and Bolt 2010, 1). For her, "practice-led research is a new species of research, generative enquiry that draws on subjective, interdisciplinary and emergent methodologies that have the potential to extend the frontiers of research" (ibid.). She maintains that the personally situated, interdisciplinary, diverse and emergent approaches of creative arts research often contradict what is expected of research, although its very potential "lies in this capacity to generate personally situated knowledge and new ways of modelling and externalising such knowledge while at the same time, revealing philosophical, social and cultural contexts for the critical intervention and application of knowledge outcomes" (Barrett in Barrett and Bolt 2010, 2).

Barrett points out how situated learning or enquiry demonstrates the unity between problem, context and solution and how personal interest and experience often motivate the research process (Barrett in Barrett and Bolt 2010, 5). Reflexive questioning is crucial since the researcher's relationship to the object of study is of central concern; "both the researcher and her/his methods are submitted to the same questions that are asked of the object of enquiry" (Barrett in Barrett and Bolt 2010, 6). Furthermore, "just as the material basis of artistic research results in approaches that are necessarily emergent, the subjective and personally situated aspect of artistic research . . . results in research that is ultimately interdisciplinary" (Barrett in Barrett and Bolt 2010, 7). In the same anthology Brad Haseman suggests that practice-led research should be understood as a strategy within an entirely new research paradigm, performative research (Haseman in Barrett and Bolt 2010, 148).

In "A Manifesto for Performative Research" (2006) Brad Haseman points to a performative research paradigm as a development of, though distinguishable from, qualitative research. He "examines the dynamics of and significance of practice-led research and argues for it to be understood as a research strategy within an entirely new research paradigm – Performative Research" (Haseman 2006, 1). Taking the title from J.L. Austin's speech act theory, "performative research stands as an alternative to the qualitative and quantitative paradigms by insisting on different approaches to designing, conducting and reporting research" (ibid.). Haseman notes that there has been a radical push to lead research through practice under various names and opts for the term "practice-led research". He distinguishes two typical characteristics: (1) the research is not so much problem-based but rather led by "an enthusiasm of practice" and (2) the research outputs and claims to knowing are made through the symbolic language of the practice. "The 'practice' in 'practice-led research' is primary – it is not an optional extra; it is the necessary precondition of engagement in performative research" (ibid.). Haseman refers to Lincoln and Denzin (2003), who are welcoming "a performance turn" in qualitative research, but he maintains that "performative research represents something larger than the 'performance turn' (which for many is a form of emancipatory action through embodied and enacted storytelling) . . . [it] represents a move which holds that practice is the principal research activity" (Haseman 2006, 7). Questions, problems and challenges are formed by the needs of practice; the research strategy is carried out through practice and the methods used are familiar to practitioners.

Haseman presents a schematic model where performative research is juxtaposed with quantitative and qualitative research: while quantitative research is based on the scientific method and qualitative research is based on multiple methods, performative research is practice-led. While quantitative research functions and presents its results with numbers, figures and charts, qualitative research uses data and presents results that are non-numerical or verbal. Performative research is expressed in a non-numerical way and often uses symbolic data, other than words in a discursive text, including forms of material practices, moving and still images, sounds and music, live action and digital code (Haseman 2006, 6). According to him, symbolic data work performatively; not only do they describe the research, as so-called constative utterances do, but also, like performative utterances, the research does something in the world. "It not only expresses the research, but in that expression becomes the research itself. The context, as Austin makes clear, is crucial to this" (Haseman 2006, 6). Haseman considers performative research to be the appropriate research paradigm for all forms of artistic practice, and predicts that it will be used in creative and cultural industries as well "in an environment preoccupied with innovation and commercialisation" (Haseman 2006, 9). Haseman's claim for a distinct paradigm, rather than an expanded set of methodologies within qualitative research, is relevant as a possible development for performance as research. It seems, however, that this discussion has remained mainly within the qualitative research environment.

Patricia Leavy (2009), who writes in the tradition of qualitative research, propagates arts-based methods for research in social sciences. She has presented a schema rather similar to Haseman's, without mentioning him, and upholds arts-based research as the third mode, though more as an expansion of the qualitative paradigm (Leavy 2009, 256). She links quantitative research to numbers, measurement, tabulating, value-neutrality, reliability, validity, proof and the disciplinary, while associating traditional qualitative research with words, meaning, writing, process, interpretation, persuasiveness, the value-laden and the interdisciplinary. For arts-based research she lists characteristics like stories, images, sounds, scenes, the sensory, evocation, (re)presenting, political, consciousness raising, emancipation, authenticity, truthfulness, to compel and the transdisciplinary (ibid.). From Leavy's description we nevertheless understand that artistic methods are to be used mainly in the presentation and dissemination of the research results, to increase their performative power, although she does not use the term. Leavy's schema is interesting as an example of the discussion within qualitative research concerning the use of artistic methods to enhance the scope of available tools in social sciences. The term "arts-based", developed within educational research (see Barone and Eisner 2012) is fairly widely used and its roots in educational research are not always known. Despite the literal meaning of the word, arts-based research need not be based on art. Rather art can stand in service of the research, a tool to increase the outreach or impact in sharing the results.

A third way of categorizing research methodologies with relevance for the development of performance as research, presented by Hazel Smith and Roger T. Dean in *Practice-led Research, Research-led Practice* (2009), includes qualitative, quantitative and conceptual research. Rather than a schema of types they provide an elaborate cyclic and rhizomatic model of the research process. They see the main difference between qualitative and quantitative approaches in the possible degree of separation between the researcher and the researched material. They emphasize the specific character of conceptual research, which has "more to do with argument, analysis and the application of theoretical ideas", as well as the emphasis on reading and textual analysis and its importance in the humanities. For them "qualitative, quantitative and conceptual research are all approaches to research which creative practitioners will benefit from knowing about and engaging with" since the combination of creative practice and research can result in distinctive methodological approaches (Smith and Dean 2009, 4–5). In a way relevant for many artist-researchers they emphasize the cyclic nature of the relationship of practice-led research and research-led practice. Other discussions with a focus on performance both in a narrow and a broad sense have been influential (Allegue et al. 2009; Freeman 2010; Kershaw and Nicholson 2011). Related discussions within visual arts have influenced the field (Hannula et al. 2005; Borgdorff 2006, 2012; Macleod and Holridge 2006; Elkins 2009; Biggs and Karlsson 2011) and more recent contributions (Nelson 2013; Barrett and Bolt 2014) discuss methodology involving all the arts.

Besides these general trends in performance studies, the performative turn in social sciences, and the emerging performative research paradigm, a claim has been made for a performative turn in the arts, a transformation of the art-work into a shared event. Theatre historian Erika Fischer-Lichte argues in *The Transformative Power of Performance: A New Aesthetics* (in English in 2008) that a performative turn has characterized the creative arts from the 1960s until today. As a result of this turn the relationship between the observer and the observed, the artist and the audience has been reconfigured and changed into a dynamic and transformative event. There is no longer a difference between the artwork and its production; the audience becomes part of the work. The performative turn has transformed the artwork into an event (Fischer-Lichte 2008, 28). "Instead of creating works of art, artists increasingly produce events, which involve not just themselves but also the observers, listeners and specta-tors." She maintains that the conditions for the production and reception of art have changed. "The pivotal point of these processes is no longer the work of art, detached from and independent of its creator and recipient. [–] Instead we are dealing with an event, set in motion and terminated by the actions of all the subjects involved – artists and spectators." Moreover, "artistic performance opens up the possibility for all participants to experience a metamorphosis" (Fischer-Lichte 2008, 22–23).

Barbara Bolt compared the ideas of Haseman and Fischer-Lichte in "A Per-formative Paradigm for the Creative Arts?" (2008), noting that the notions of performance and performativity are often conflated and mixed. According to her we have to distinguish between performativity and "performative" in the sense of something "resembling or related to performance". If we seriously want to speak of a performative research paradigm alongside qualitative and quantitative research we need to return to the conceptual distinction made by philosopher J.L. Austin between constative and performative utterances and to Judith Butler's notion of performativity. She distinguishes between per-formance, which requires a subject, and performativity, which challenges the whole notion of the subject. Whereas performance can be understood as the conscious and intentional act by a subject or subjects, as in a dance or theatre performance, or even a painting, performativity must be understood as an itera-tive and citational practice, which produces that which it names. Thus perfor-mativity is all but singular; it is based on convention and repetition. Bolt argues that Butler's theory of performativity can be extended to concern art. There is no artist who would precede the continuous practice of art. The artist is born through practice, although the practices of art often hide the conventions they repeat. As Butler has shown, iteration is by nature productive. "Repetition is never repetition of the same. It is always repetition of difference" (Bolt 2008, 6).

The performative turn in the aesthetic sense used by Fisher-Lichte and the performative research paradigm proposed by Haseman are two very different things, she insists (Bolt 2008, 4).

Bolt posits a bold contrast between "science as research" and "art as research" based on their understanding of truth. Science as research could be compared with constative utterances; it is describing and modelling the world. Art as research, by contrast, is making things happen in the world. On a methodological level the first is repetition of the same, whereas the latter is repetition with a difference, in a Butlerian sense. And concerning interpretation the first is based on truth as correspondence whereas the latter is based on "truth" as power and effect, like the performative (Bolt 2008, 9). The performative can be felicitous or infelicitous rather than true or false. Bolt emphasizes that if we accept that a performative act does not describe anything but actually does something in the world, we must try to ascertain what that action (or research project) has accomplished. For Bolt "the work of art is not just the artwork/performance or the event, but is also the effect of the work in the material, affective and discursive domains". Consequently the main task for the creative arts researcher is "recognizing and mapping the transformations that have occurred" (ibid.).

How to evaluate these discursive, material or affective effects or consequences remains open. And we can ask how does this differ from or what does it add to the traditional approaches of reception research? One dimension is of course the experience of the performer. The challenge of trying to articulate the tacit knowledge involved in the making remains. Admittedly a focus on effects ameliorates the risk of solipsism in artistic research, as Bolt has later pointed out (Bolt in Barrett and Bolt 2014, 23–24). From the point of view of the artist and author, however, there are still mainly two indicators of effect: one's own experience and the feedback from viewers or participants. An interesting dimension is added through other effects and side effects, like a possible heap of waste that the work or its production process creates.

In a recent text, Bolt (2016) has returned to the topic, partly in response to Dorothea von Hantelmann's (2014) discussion around the performative power of art and the experiential dimension. Referring to Butler, Bolt elaborates on her earlier argument concerning transgression versus convention in art, explaining "how 'the new' emerges through iterative practice, rather than the singular act" (Bolt 2016, 136). She maintains that the performative paradigm needs to be carefully characterized and not confused with the term "performative arts" increasingly used today and argues that "Austin's notions of the illocutionary [the function an utterance performs] and the perlocutionary [the effect an utterance achieves on its hearers or readers] provide . . . a way of addressing the success or failure of our performative productions" (Bolt 2016, 139). According to Bolt "procedures in creative arts, like science, are based around repetition and iterability" with the distinction that the "performative paradigm would operate according to repetition *with* difference" (Bolt 2016, 139). She further reminds us that "the artwork must stand eloquently in its own way and if it doesn't it fails", but this does not exclude the fact that "through mapping what research does, artistic researchers are able to demonstrate not only how art can be understood as research, but also how its inventions can be articulated" (Bolt 2016, 142).

Between these two discussions of performative research (Bolt 2008, 2016) the term "artistic research" has gained ground in the Anglo-Saxon world as well. The idea of a performative research paradigm has not been as widely discussed as one would expect, perhaps due to difficulties in distinguishing the various meanings of the performative, performativity and performance and their associations to performing arts. This problem concerns performance as research as well, though is rarely discussed by researchers who use some form of performance as topic, method or mode of presentation in their research.

Performance as research is/as artistic research?

What distinguishes artistic research as it is mostly understood from performance as research is a stronger link to the art world and the claim that artistic research is a field or a discipline (perhaps an anti-discipline?), an area for knowledge creation, rather than a specific methodology. Although artistic research is still contested and many prefer to use other related terms in order to avoid the controversial tone of the term in English (with meanings like artificial, gay and camp), the debates around artistic research have continued long enough for us to acknowledge that something like that can be said to exist. Artistic research is undertaken by artists, and researching artists can adopt different methodologies. Different disciplines, however, tend to define themselves either through their research object or through their specific methods. Should not artistic research do the same? Every discipline produces knowledge via its own methods: "If we for instance apply the methods of cultural studies to art education research, we get cultural studies as an outcome. . . . There is no such thing as a neutral research method" (Varto 2009, 159). The same could be expected of artistic research. Although there is a general consensus that performance as research is not restricted to investigating performance, but is applicable to a broad range of topics, there is actually much overlap between method and topic within PAR.

Is it possible to talk about common methods for areas as diverse as music, theatre, visual art, literature, dance, film and architecture? Should we not have various methods based on the specific traditions of each art form? Perhaps we should limit our look to the traditions within each artistic discipline, as is often done within music, architecture or design, domains not necessarily actively engaged in the debates around artistic research on a general level. Or should we look for common denominators for all the arts? An artistic researcher within, say, choreographic practice, has sometimes more in common with dance scholars than with artists in other fields. Various art forms have such differing approaches to artistic practice, tradition, the position of the artist and the status of the artwork that any unified understanding of what constitutes artistic research is hardly achievable. There are such a variety of disciplines already within scholarship related to art (history of art, history of music, film studies, theatre research, aesthetics and so on); how could artistic research be a field less diverse? Add to that the variety of topics explored and investigated by artists, and we have a domain as large as life, or so it seems, and equally diverse. There is not one form of artistic research but many, partly because artistic research has evolved from different streams both culturally and institutionally.

The many trends contributing to a culture slowly accepting artistic research include the recognition of the value of tacit knowledge, practical knowledge or so-called Mode 2 knowledge and thus also of the artists' knowledge. In contrast to traditional scientific Mode 1 knowledge, Mode 2 knowledge refers to knowledge production that is context-driven and problem-focused, often in multidisciplinary teams working for short periods on real-world problems (Gibbons et al. 1994). Another stream mentioned earlier is the performative, bodily and lately the material turn in social sciences, which followed the linguistic turn of structuralism and post-structuralism, and has emphasized knowledge embedded in oral and material practices. A third is the work undertaken within feminist and postcolonial thought in order to reveal the biased nature of so-called objective and universal knowledge production. Current debates around artistic research tend to overlook and forget the work done already in the 1970s by feminist theorists like Sandra Harding, Donna Haraway and others, who developed so-called standpoint epistemologies and the idea of situated knowledge, as Pilvi Porkola has pointed out (Porkola 2014, 42–46). Estelle Barrett has recently taken up this legacy (Barrett 2014, 7–9). As a thread running alongside these trends is the critique of global capitalism and its instrumental approach to the resources of the planet, and to other beings sharing them with humans. Thus emancipatory and political struggles on one hand and epistemological debates on the other have created a ground for old dichotomies like art and science or theory and practice to crumble, at least momentarily and locally. Add to this perhaps the main requirement for the development of artistic research – that is changes within the arts, with conceptual art as one important starting point, together with socially engaged art practices that challenge the traditional role of the artist. The heavy emphasis on theory in art education since the 1990s and the attempt at synchronizing the third cycle in higher arts education in Europe, criticized as the academization of art, are other factors.

Artistic research is diversifying not only according to various methodological approaches, or by following artistic disciplines and their traditions, but also according to affinities with various traditional forms of research. Today interdisciplinarity, integration of knowledge across academic disciplines, is increasingly sought, to complement the ever-narrowing disciplinary expertise, and the possibility of a meeting ground or a (relatively) free space for various disciplines to interact offered by artistic research is needed more than ever. Transdisciplinarity, too, the production of knowledge with parties beyond the academy (Frodeman 2014, 3) and thereby the practising artist's point of view, is increasingly valued today. We could also claim, however, that we are moving towards a post-disciplinary condition of art and of knowledge production.

Interdisciplinarity seems to be linked with artistic research in at least two ways. Artistic research provides the site for interdisciplinary (and transdisciplinary) encounters. Various types of artistic research have developed through interdisciplinary entwinements, like art and critical theory, art and aesthetics, art and pedagogy, or art and anthropology, as exemplified in contributions to this volume. Interdisciplinarity becomes evident when creating multidisciplinary publications like the book at hand; how can we understand each other without unnecessary simplifications?

The first aspect, artistic research as an interdisciplinary (or multidisciplinary) meeting place, is a result of the eclecticism, which used to be considered the weakness of artistic research – artists simply picking up a mixture of incongruent thoughts and concepts and then combining them at will – and which can be considered a major asset today. When disciplinary knowledge production remains within the bounds of each limited domain, digging deeper and deeper into predictable knowledge sources, artistic research can provide a site for unexpected clashes and combinations, within the realm of art, thus creating new possibilities for understanding.

The second aspect includes the various types of artistic research created in interdisciplinary entanglement with supporting disciplines: artistic research utilizing the tools of art history, contextualizing the practice within previous discussions and works by artists, or artistic research using ethnographic methods and sociological or anthropological approaches. Artistic research which has developed in parallel with research in arts education could be called pedagogically inclined artistic research, and research devoted to questioning the conditions of the art form related to philosophical concepts could be described as philosophically inclined artistic research. Other types, depending on the collaborating parties, include technologically focused research or art-science collaborations. Even combining theoretical and practical work could be thought of as interdisciplinary. Some of these differing approaches can be found among the chapters of this book as well.

Creative problems tend to be transdisciplinary – that is involving real-world problems. Many researching artists are exploring various phenomena in the world. Although many would disagree with the conflation of art and problem solving, much artistic research is engaged with agents outside academia. This concerns not only so-called applied arts, or collaborations with institutions or NGOs. Many contemporary artists take pride in involving various communities in their work, although they might be showing the results mainly for art audiences. Artistic research is transdisciplinary simply by involving the art world and collaborators beyond academia.

Is artistic research to be understood as an area of its own, an in-between area between art and academia, the art world and the university, as for instance Biggs and Karlsson have asserted? They propose a:

shift of perspective that allows certain activities to become meaningful in the context of arts research, even though those activities may not have been meaningful in either the context of academic research *per se* or the context of professional arts practice *per se*.

(Biggs and Karlsson 2011, 409)

They understand arts research "as a distinct and separate field from the existing fields of arts practice and academic research" (Biggs and Karlsson 2011, 413), and maintain that art researchers should be professionals in art research, not in traditional academic research nor in professional arts practice, but in this "third professional category that is as yet undefined" (Biggs and Karlsson 2011, 423).

A slightly different way of looking at the hybridization of art practice and academic practice is to understand it as boundary work, as proposed by Henk Borgdorff (2012). Much advanced academic research today could be called post-disciplinary or transdisciplinary, he notes. "Artistic research is better understood as something that represents this border-violation rather than being a discipline alongside other art-related disciplines" (Borgdorff 2012, 177). Artistic research has two contexts, the academic environment and the art world, and is thus an example of contemporary academic research, which no longer takes place within the university alone. In the blurring of art and other life domains "artistic research is also transdisciplinary research, because it stretches out to the wider community, making it a good example of what people call Mode 2 knowledge production" (Borgdorff 2012, 179). Borgdorff distinguishes artistic research from other Mode 2 forms of knowledge production using two primary points: the fact that "artistic research takes place *in and through* the making of art . . . [and] the outcome of artistic research, which, partly at least, is art" (Borgdorff 2012, 182). Artistic research is "creating, a free space that is also in opposition to the demands of the market, to the creative industries, to the daily strains of production – a free space for 'material thinking', to use the term from Paul Carter" (Borgdorff 2012, 183). In performing artistic research we can influence what counts as art; "not only our understanding of what academia is might change in the future, but also our understanding of what art is" (ibid.). The presumed boundaries are under debate.

In the introduction to *Material Inventions – Applying Creative Arts Research* (2014) Estelle Barrett mentions her previous claim concerning "the intrinsically interdisciplinary dimension of this mode of research that is derived from its material and social *relationality*" (Barrett 2014, 3). She understands creative arts research as a successor science following Haraway, which means that

it articulates the notion of ethical or embodied forms of observation – ways of looking and being accountable for knowledge claims that do not deny the agency of the objects of research – in particular human participants; it is a mode that replaces traditional notions of objectivity with the idea of situated knowledge and partial objectivity; finally it asserts the potential of situated and partial knowledge for forging webs of connections – identifying for whom, how and where else knowledge can be put to use.

(Barrett 2014, 9)

And with whom it is created, I would like to add. Within contemporary art, critical questioning is the basis for art's self-understanding. Art can be understood as "a creative and intellectual endeavour that involves artists and other arts practitioners in a reflexive process where the nature and function of art is questioned and challenged through the production of new art" (Baker et al. 2006). This sounds very much like the traditional self-correcting scientific ideal. Not everyone in the performing arts would probably agree with this since, despite experimentation and questioning being valued, performing arts are more audience-oriented in their approach. Furthermore, research that entails an attempt to articulate and theorize an ongoing practice, based on acquired and thus usually more or less unconscious skills, has a different emphasis and uses different methods compared with research that attempts to develop a new type of art work or design product, and explain the route to that result. We could perhaps say that artistic research can be practice-oriented, when the practice of art is more important than an individual artwork, or product-oriented, when the main goal for the research is the creation of an art work. Furthermore the research process can be forward-looking, striving to create something new, or rooted in reflection, trying to understand and articulate what one has already done, or any mixture between them. These distinctions concern performance as research as well. For the critically minded, artistic research provides a space for questioning and criticizing the ingrained conventions of the art world. For the more conservatively inclined, artistic research offers an opportunity to formulate and document tacit knowledge and to articulate methods within an existing tradition. Moreover, much artistic research appears to find contact points with philosophical study, although it inevitably also has an empirical dimension. The aspect of experimentation and play with alternatives, artistic research as a speculative practice, imagining and trying out possible futures, is more and more needed within society at large.

The future of performance as research?

Imagining, envisioning and rehearsing futures are tasks suited for artist researchers as well as or even better than analysing, criticizing and recreating the past. Performance as research, like artistic research, could be understood as a speculative practice engaged in both. Rather than try to predict possible paths for performance as research, converging or diverging with performative research and artistic research or other emerging forms of inquiry, I will end with some questions concerning the future of performance as research. They were posed under the title "Multiple Futures of PAR?" in a call for presentations for the meeting of the performance as research working group in 2017. At the moment of writing this, they are awaiting responses:

1   What are the multidisciplinary, interdisciplinary or transdisciplinary poten-
     tialities of PAR? What can PAR contribute to the "transdisciplinarization"
     of knowledge beyond the academy?
2   What kind of futures can be imagined concerning the various trajectories
     of PAR based on specific geographical and methodological legacies? How
     are these reflected in the pedagogy or institutionalization of PAR?
3   What kinds of writing about, in or on PAR are emerging from the meet-
     ing of practice and research within and outside the academy? What (other)
     forms of hybridisation of artistic practice and research can be imagined in
     the future?
4   What can PAR offer to the sustainability of research practice both within
     academia and in the wider societies we live in? What sustainable forms of
     PAR are evolving at local and global levels and how does this reflect on
     wider social, ecological, geographical and even geological issues we face in
     working together across disciplines, methods and cultures?

References

Allegue, Ludivine, Simon Jones, Baz Kershaw, Angela Piccini (eds.). 2009. *Practice-as-Research in Performance and Screen.* Basingstoke: Palgrave Macmillan.
Arlander, Annette. 2011. "Characteristics of Visual and Performing Arts." In Michael Biggs and Henrik Karlsson (eds.). *The Routledge Companion to Research in the Arts.* London and New York: Routledge, pp. 315–332.
Arlander, Annette. 2014. "Om metoder i konstnärlig forskning/On methods of artistic research." In Torbjörn Lind (ed.). *Metod – Process – Redovisning Konstnärlig Forksning Årsbok 2014/Method – Process – Reporting Artistic Research Yearbook 2014.* Stockholm: Vetenskaps-rådet/Swedish Research Council 2014, pp. 13–25/26–39. https://publikationer.vr.se/wp-content/uploads/2014/08/– rsbok-KF-2014-pdf-hela-boken.pdf
Arlander, Annette. 2016. "Artistic Research And/as Interdisciplinarity – Investigação em Arte e/como Interdisciplinaridade." In Catarina Almeida and Andre Alves (eds.). *Artistic Research Does #1.* NEA/12ADS Porto: Research Group in Arts Education/Research Institute in Art, Design, Society; FBAUP Faculty of Fine Arts University of Porto, pp. 1–27.
Aston, Elaine. 2007. "Knowing Differently: Practice as Research and the Women's Writing for Performance Project." *Nordic Theatre Studies,* 19, pp. 9–17.
Auslander, Philip. September 2006. "The Performativity of Performance Documentation." *Performing Arts Journal,* 28(3), pp. 1–10.
Baker, Bob and Paula Crabtree, Tamiko O-Brien, Simon Saiz Ruiz. 2006. "Tuning template for Fine Art Higher Education in Europe." Second draft. Art, Engagement & Education, ELIA (European League of Institutes of the Arts) conference, Gent, Belgium 25,–28.10.2006.
Barone, Tom and Elliot W. Eisner. 2012. *Arts Based Research.* Thousand Oaks, CA: SAGE.
Barrett, Estelle 2010. "Introduction." In Estelle Barrett and Barbara Bolt (eds.). *Practice as Research – Approaches to Creative Arts Enquiry.* London: I.B. Tauris, pp. 1–13.
Barrett, Estelle. 2014. "Introduction: Extending the Field: Invention, Application and Inno-vation in Creative Arts Enquiry." In Estelle Barrett and Barbara Bolt (eds.). *Material Inven-tions: Applying Creative Arts Research.* London: I.B. Tauris, pp. 1–21.
Barrett, Estelle and Barbara Bolt (eds.). 2010. *Practice as Research – Approaches to Creative Arts Enquiry.* London: I.B. Tauris.

Barrett, Estelle and Barbara Bolt (eds.). 2014. *Material Inventions: Applying Creative Arts Research*. London: I.B. Tauris.

Biernacki, Richard. 1999. "Method and Metaphor After the New Cultural History." In Victoria E. Bonnell and Lynn Hunt (eds.). *Beyond the Cultural Turn: New Directions in the Study of Society and Culture*. Berkeley, CA: University of California Press.

Biggs, Michael and Henrik Karlsson. 2011. "Evaluating Quality in Artistic Research." In Michael Biggs and Henrik Karlsson (eds.). *The Routledge Companion to Research in the Arts*. London and New York: Routledge, pp. 405–424.

Bolt, Barbara. 2008. "A Performative Paradigm for the Creative Arts?" *Working Papers in Art and Design*. Volume 5.

Bolt, Barbara. 2014. "Beyond Solipsism in Artistic Research: The Artwork and The Work of Art." In Estelle Barrett and Barbara Bolt (eds.). *Material Inventions: Applying Creative Arts Research*. London: I.B. Tauris, pp. 22–37.

Bolt, Barbara. 2016. "Artistic Research: A Performative Paradigm?" *PARSE Journal*, 3, pp. 129–142.

Borgdorff, Henk. 2006. *The Debate on Research in the Arts*. Sensuous Knowledge: Series Focus on Artistic Research and Development 2/06. Bergen, Norway: Kunsthögskolen i Bergen.

Borgdorff, Henk. 2012. *The Conflict of the Faculties: Perspectives on Artistic Research and Academia*. Leiden: Leiden University Press.

Conquergood, Dwight. 2004. "Performance Studies, Interventions and Radical Research." In Bial (ed.). *The Performance Studies Reader*. London and New York: Routledge.

Cull, Laura. 2014. "Performance Philosophy – Staging a New Field." In Laura Cull and Alica Lagay (eds.). *Encounters in Performance Philosophy*. Basingstoke: Palgrave Macmillan, pp. 15–38.

Davis, Tracy C. 2008. "Introduction: The Pirouette, Detour, Revolution, Deflection, Deviation, Tack and Yaw of the Performative Turn." In Tracy C. Davis (ed.). *Cambridge Companion to Performance Studies*. Cambridge: Cambridge University Press, pp. 1–8.

Elkins, James (ed.). 2009. *Artists with PhDs – On the New Doctoral Degree in Studio Art*. Washington, DC: New Academia Publishing.

Fischer-Lichte, Erika. 2008. *Transformative Power of Performance: A New Aesthetics*. London and New York: Routledge.

Freeman, John. 2010. *Blood, Sweat and Theory – Research Through Practice in Performance*. Faringdon: Libri Publishing.

Frodeman, Robert. 2014. *Sustainable Knowledge: A Theory of Interdisciplinarity*. Basingstoke: Palgrave Macmillan.

Gibbons, Michael, Camille Limoges, Helga Nowotny, Simon Schwartzman, Peter Scott and Martin Trow. 1994. *The New Production of Knowledge: The Dynamics of Science and Research in Contemporary Societies*. Thousand Oaks, CA: SAGE.

Hannula, Mika, Juha Suoranta and Tere Vadén. 2005. *Artistic Research – Theories, Methods and Practices*. Helsinki, Finland and Gothenburg, Sweden: Academy of Fine Arts, University of Gothenburg.

Haseman, Brad. 2006. "A Manifesto for Performative Research." *Media International Australia Incorporating Culture and Policy: Quarterly Journal of Media Research and Resources*, 118, pp. 98–106.

Haseman, Brad. 2010. "Rupture and Recognition. Identifying the Performative Research Paradigm." In Estelle Barrett and Barbara Bolt (eds.). *Practice as Research – Approaches to Creative Arts Enquiry*. London: I.B. Tauris, pp. 147–157.

Kershaw, Baz. 2008. "Performance as research: live events and documents." In Tracy C. Davis (ed.). *Cambridge Companion to Performance Studies.* Cambridge: Cambridge University Press, pp. 23–45.

Kershaw, Baz and Helen Nicholson (eds.). 2011. *Research Methods in Theatre and Performance.* Edinburgh: Edinburgh University Press.

Leavy, Patricia. 2009. *Method Meets Art – Arts-Based Research Practice.* New York: The Guilford Press.

Lincoln, Yvonna S. and Denzin, Norman K. (eds.) 2003. *Turning Points in Qualitative Research: Tying Knots in a Handkerchief.* Walnut Creek, CA: Altamira Press.

Macleod, Katy and Lin Holridge (eds.). 2006. *Thinking Through Art – Reflections on Art as Research.* London and New York: Routledge.

Mckenzie, Jon, Heike Roms and C. J. Wan-Ling Wee (eds.). 2010. *Contesting Performance – Globals Sites of Research.* Basingstoke: Palgrave Macmillan.

Nelson, Robin (ed.). 2013. *Practice as Research in the Arts – Principles, Protocols, Pedagogies, Resistances.* Basingstoke, UK: Palgrave Macmillan.

PARtake Journal of Performance as Research. www.partakejournal.org

Peters, Sibylle. 2010. "The Performance Research. A Report from Germany." In Jon Mckenzie, Heike Roms and C. J. Wan-Ling Wee (eds.). *Contesting Performance – Globals Sites of Research.* Basingstoke: Palgrave Macmillan, pp. 153–167.

Porkola, Pilvi. 2014. *Esitys Tutkimuksena: Näkökulmia poliittiseen, dokumentaariseen ja henkilökohtaiseen esitystaiteessa.* [Performance as Research] Acta Scenica 40. Helsinki: University of the Arts Helsinki, Theatre Academy.

Riley, Shannon Rose and Lynette Hunter (eds.). 2009. *Mapping Landscapes for Performance as Research – Scholarly Acts and Creative Cartographies.* Basingstoke, UK: Palgrave Macmillan.

Schechner, Richard. 2006. *Performance Studies – An Introduction,* 2nd ed. London and New York: Routledge.

Smith, Hazel and Roger T. Dean (eds.). 2009. *Practice-led Research, Research-led Practice in the Creative Arts.* Edinburgh: Edinburgh University Press.

Varto, Juha. 2009. *Basics of Artistic Research: Ontological, Epistemological and Historical Justifications.* University of Art and Design, Helsinki Publication B 94. Helsinki: Gummerus.

von Hantelmann, Dorothea. 2014. *The Experiential Turn.* Living Collections Catalogue. Walker Art Centre. https://walkerart.org/collections/publications/performativity/experiential-turn/ (Accessed 24 October 2017).

Index

Page numbers in *italics* indicate a figure or photograph.

UNIVERSITY OF WINCHESTER
LIBRARY